# MARY IN THE CHURCH TODAY

Official Catholic Teachings
on the Mother of God

From the Second Vatican Council,
Pope Paul VI, Pope John Paul II and
the Catechism of the Catholic Church

**Written and compiled by
Father Bill McCarthy, MSA
and James Tibbetts, S.T.L.**

## St. Andrew's Productions
6111 Steubenville Pike
McKees Rocks, PA  15136

# DEDICATION

To Sister Mary Bernadette Sheldon, CSJ, Co-director of *My Father's House*, who images Mary our Mother so beautifully.

**Copyright © 2000 St. Andrew's Productions**
*All Rights Reserved*

**ISBN: 1-891903-22-5**

Published by:

**St. Andrew's Productions**
6111 Steubenville Pike
McKees Rocks, PA  15136

Toll-Free:    (888) 654-6279
Phone:        (412) 787-9735
Fax:          (412) 787-5204

Internet:     www.SaintAndrew.com

**My Father's House Retreat Center**
P.O. Box 22, North Moodus Road
Moodus, CT  06469

Phone:        (860) 873-1581
              (860) 873-1906
Fax:          (860) 873-2357

Internet:     www.MyFathersHouse.com

**PRINTED IN THE UNITED STATES OF AMERICA**

# JOHN PAUL II SPEAKS

\* \* \* \* \* \* \* \* \* \*

What can I wish for you but that you will always listen to these words of Mary, the Mother of Christ: "Do whatever he tells you". And may you accept these words with your hearts, because they were uttered from the heart. From the heart of a Mother. And that you will fulfill them: "God has chosen you... calling you to this, with our Gospel for possession of the glory of our Lord, Jesus Christ."

*Insegnamenti*, January 20, 1980

\* \* \* \* \* \* \* \* \* \*

And in the moments of weariness raise your eyes to Mary, the Virgin who, forgetting herself, set out with haste for the hills to reach her elderly cousin Elizabeth who was in need of help and assistance. Let her be the inspiration of your daily dedication to duty; let her suggest to you the right words and opportune gestures at the bedside of the sick; let her comfort you in misunderstandings and failures, hoping you always keep a smile on your face and a hope in your heart.

Address, Rome, June 18, 1979

\* \* \* \* \* \* \* \* \* \*

Was it not for our encouragement that God chose to come to us through the Immaculate Virgin, conceived without sin? From the first moment of her existence she was never under the power of sin, while we are called to be cleansed of sin by opening our heart to the merciful Redeemer whom she brought into this world. There is no better way to approach her Son than through her.

Address, Nagasaki, February 26, 1981

\* \* \* \* \* \* \* \* \* \*

\* \* \* \* \* \* \* \* \*

To succeed in your intention, entrust yourselves to the Blessed Virgin Mary always, but especially in moments of difficulty and darkness. From Mary we learn to surrender to God's will in all things. From Mary we learn to trust even when all hope seems gone. From Mary we learn to love Christ, her son and the Son of God. Learn from her to be always faithful, to trust that God's Word to you will be fulfilled, and that nothing is impossible with God.

Address, Washington, D.C., October 6, 1979

\* \* \* \* \* \* \* \* \*

In creating the human race "male and female," God gives man and woman an equal personal dignity, endowing them with the inalienable rights and responsibilities proper to the human person. God then manifests the dignity of women in the highest form possible, by assuming human flesh from the Virgin Mary, whom the Church honors as the Mother of God, calling her the new Eve and presenting her as the model of redeemed woman.

*Familiaris Consortio*, 22

\* \* \* \* \* \* \* \* \*

As the Church contemplates Mary's motherhood, she discovers the meaning of her own motherhood and the way in which she is called to express it. At the same time, the Church's experience of motherhood leads to a most profound understanding of Mary's experience as the incomparable model of how life should be welcomed and cared for.

*Evangelium Vitae*, 102

\* \* \* \* \* \* \* \* \*

# TABLE OF CONTENTS

# ACKNOWLEDGMENTS

I obviously want to thank the Council Fathers for the beautiful treatment of Mary at the Second Vatican Council and Pope Paul VI, not only for his devotion to Mary but for his encyclical on Mary's place in the liturgy. Above all, I want to thank Pope John Paul II for his overwhelming contribution in the field of Mariology. In regard to Mary, it can be truly said, "No one ever spoke as this man did."

I want to thank James Tibbetts, a true Mariologist and a faithful personal friend for his contributions in Chapters 1 and 2.

I want to thank Fr. J. Michael Miller, C.S.B. for his reflections on *Redemptoris Mater* and Father Bertrand Buby, SM for his reflections on Mary in the new Catechism.

I am especially grateful to Dr. Mark Miravalle for showing us that belief in Mary as co-redemptrix, mediatrix and helper is already the ordinary teaching of the Church, as can be easily seen in appendix 1.

I want to thank Sister Bernadette Sheldon, Blanche, Dolores, Lauren, Lea, and Nancy for exemplifying true Marian spirituality here at My Father's House.

I want to thank all the tremendous women of grace who touched my life, including my mother and my three sisters, MaryAnn, Alice and Kathleen.

And last, but certainly not least, I am deeply indebted to Brenda Lazar who has helped compile, organize and type every word of this manuscript. Without her assistance, it truly would have been impossible.

May all of us continue to look to Mary as our mother, model, mediatrix, intercessor and faithful friend, knowing that it was never known that anyone who fled to her protection or sought her aid was left unresponded to.

# ABBREVIATIONS – BOOKS OF THE BIBLE

Acts - Acts of the Apostles
Am - Amos
Bar - Baruch
1 Chr - 1 Chronicles
2 Chr - 2 Chronicles
Col - Colossians
1 Cor - 1 Corinthians
2 Cor - 2 Corinthians
Dn - Daniel
Dt - Deuteronomy
Eccl - Ecclesiastes
Eph - Ephesians
Est - Esther
Ex - Exodus
Ez - Ezekiel
Ezr - Ezra
Gal - Galatians
Gn - Genesis
Hb - Habakkuk
Heb - Hebrews
Hg - Haggai
Hos - Hosea
Is - Isaiah
Jas - James
Jb - Job
Jdt - Judith
Jer - Jeremiah
Jl - Joel
Jgs - Judges
Jn - John
1 Jn - 1 John
2 Jn - 2 John
3 Jn - 3 John
Jon - Jonah
Jos - Joshua
Jude - Jude
1 Kgs - 1 Kings

2 Kgs - 2 Kings
Lam - Lamentations
Lk - Luke
Lv - Leviticus
Mal - Malachi
1 Mc - 1 Maccabees
2 Mc - 2 Maccabees
Mi - Micah
Mk - Mark
Mt - Matthew
Na - Nahum
Neh - Nehemiah
Nm - Numbers
Ob - Obadiah
1 Pt - 1 Peter
2 Pt - 2 Peter
Phil - Philippians
Phlm - Philemon
Prv - Proverbs
Ps - Psalms
Rom - Romans
Ru - Ruth
Rv - Revelation
Song - Song of Songs
Sir - Sirach
1 Sm - 1 Samuel
2 Sm - 2 Samuel
Tb - Tobit
1 Thes - 1 Thessalonians
2 Thes - 2 Thessalonians
Ti - Titus
1 Tm - 1 Timothy
2 Tm - 2 Timothy
Wis - Wisdom
Zec - Zechariah
Zep - Zephaniah

# OTHER ABBREVIATIONS

| | |
|---|---|
| *AAS* | *Acta Apostolicae Sedis*, Rome, 1909— |
| *CCC* | *Catechism of the Catholic Church* |
| *CCL* | *Corpus Christianorum, Series Latina*, Turnhout, 1953— |
| *CPG* | *Solemn Profession of Faith*: Credo of the People of God |
| *CSEL* | *Corpus Scriptorum Ecclesiasticorum Latinorum*, Vienna, 1866— |
| *CSCO* | *Corpur Scriptorum Christianorum Orientalium*, Paris-Louvain, 1903— |
| *CT* | *Catechesi tradendae* |
| *DS* | Denziger-Schonmetzer. Henry Denziger and Adolf Schonmetzer, eds*., Ehchiridion Symbolorum, Definitionum et Declarationum de Rebus Fidei et Morum*, 33rd ed. Freiburg im Breisgau, 1964. |
| *GS* | *Gaudium et Spes* |
| *PG* | *Patrologia Graeca*. J.P. Migne, ed. Paris, 1857-1866. 162 volumes. |
| *LG* | *Lumen Gentium* |
| *LH* | Liturgy of the Hours |
| *MC* | *Marialis Cultus* |
| *MD* | *Mulieris dignitatem* |
| *PL* | Patrologia Latina. J.P. Migne, ed. Paris 1844-1864. 221 volumes. |
| *SCh* | *Sources Chretiennes*, Paris, 1941— |

## Fr. Bill McCarthy with Pope John Paul II, Rome, 1995

Fr. Bill is co-director and co-founder of My Father's House, a spiritual retreat center in Moodus, Connecticuit. Ordained in Rome, he is a Scripture scholar and is a member of the Holy Apostles Community in Cromwell. Fr. Bill devotes his time to giving retreats, counseling, spiritual direction, and teaching, as well as giving to parish missions and addressing conferences in Connecticuit and throughout the country.

# PREFACE

The theme of this book can be summed up in one sentence. The Catholic Church officially recognizes the all-pervading place of Mary in the work of redemption and therefore encourages us to give her a corresponding place in our spiritual life. This is an important book because it is about the Catholic Church's recent reflection on the second most important person in the Church, Mary our mother. By far, the most important place will always and forever be given to Jesus, her Son, the sole mediator between God and man and the sole Redeemer of the world. The place of authentic Mariology is always servant to and points to true Christology. The role of Mary is always to encourage us to do whatever He (Jesus) tells us. The Church's understanding, reverence and teaching on Mary have developed from Marian foreshadowings in the Old Testament, through the New Testament, through the fathers, through medieval Marian writers until now. Since the Second Vatican Council, there has been an explosion of official Marian teaching. Section 8 of the Constitution on the Church emphasized the role of Mary as model, mother, and member of the Church. It presented a truly balanced theology, not one of excess or defect. It is the fullest, most comprehensive and authoritative synthesis of Mary ever compiled by a Church council. The full text of Section 8 is presented here in chapter 3.

## New Developments In Mariology

Since Vatican II Mariology has developed impressively. Pope Paul VI published an apostolic exhortation on the role of Mary and the liturgy, the full text of which comprises chapter 4. Pope John Paul II wrote an entire encyclical on Mary, mother of the Redeemer. The full text is in chapter 5. Pope John Paul II approved of the writing of the new Catechism of the Catholic Church which, in each of the four sections, was imbued with teachings and insights on the role of Mary as model, mother, and member of the Church. Most impressively, however, from September 6, 1995 to November 12, 1997, he gave the most extensive official catechesis on Mary that the Catholic world has ever seen. These 70 addresses are presented in chapter 7 in their entirety. In addition, this Pope is so dedicated to Mary that he mentions her in virtually every discourse, encyclical and apostolic constitution. I have reproduced many of these in chapter 8.

## Sources

The Mariology contained in all these official writings, as you will see, does not flow from apocryphal or visionary writings but only from authentic sources: first and most importantly, from the Scriptures, both the Old Testament and New Testament; second, from the fathers of the Church, the giants of the Church who first received their faith from the apostles and passed it on to us; third, from the Church's official and perennial teaching on Mary as found primarily in ecumenical councils but also in the official preaching and proclamations of her saints and scholars; fourth, through art, music, sculpture, and poetry; and finally through ecumenical outreach. Mary's presence in the Church is at her core. Mary is seen here as the model and mirror for all Catholic belief and practice. She is thus the touchstone of orthodoxy.

## What God Does In Mary

What God does in Mary he wishes to do in us. Where she has gone, we must follow. She is the first disciple who becomes the paradigm of all disciples. Like her, you and I are called to be full of grace and will become so at least after purgatory. Like her, we must bear Jesus within us so that we, too, can say, "I live now, not I but Christ lives within me." Like her, we are called to bring Jesus to a darkened world as its light. Like her, as St. Paul reminds us, we shall reign with Christ in Heaven. Like her we, the sons and daughters of God, should praise the Father in the spirit of her Son forever.

# Rich Tradition Of Marian Teaching

In the rich tradition of the one true Church founded by Christ (cf. Mt 16:18 ff.) four divinely revealed doctrines concerning Mary have been declared as being revealed by the Holy Spirit, first within the Scriptures and then through the constant inspiration given to the people of God. These Marian doctrines have gradually been brought to light by the living Church which Christ founded to be "the pillar and standard of truth" (1 Tim 3:16).

## Mother Of God

The first Marian doctrine to be officially proclaimed is that Mary was the mother of God. The Council of Ephesus in 431 proclaimed that truly Mary was "Theotokos", mother of God. This doctrine has been ratified by subsequent councils, including Vatican II: "The Virgin Mary, who at the message of the angel received the word of God in her heart and in her body, and gave Life to the world, is acknowledged and honored as being truly the mother of God and of the Redeemer" (Vatican II, Constitution on the Church, #53).

## Always A Virgin

The Lateran Council in 649 defined the second Marian doctrine, the perpetual virginity of Mary and since then the Catholic faithful have held that Mary was a virgin before, during and after the birth of Jesus.

## Immaculate Conception

In 1854, Pope Pius IX declared that Mary, from the first moment of her conception, by a unique gift of grace, in view of the merits of her Son, was preserved from original sin, thus confirming centuries of Christian belief that she who would be at total enmity with Satan (Gn 3:15) was indeed, "full of grace"(Lk 1:28).

# Her Assumption

In our lifetime, Pope Pius XII, in 1950, declared that Mary was assumed body and soul into the glory of Heaven (cf. Rv 12:1-2). This woman, who intimately shared in the victory of Christ over the serpent (Gn 3:15) was not allowed to suffer the effects of sin and death that came from the evil one and his seed, with whom she was given complete and total enmity by the father.

# Further Developments

The second Vatican council reminds us, "Taken up in Heaven, she did not lay aside the saving office but by her manifold intercession continues to bring us the gifts of eternal salvation. Therefore, the Blessed Virgin is invoked in the Church under the titles of advocate, helper, benefactress and mediatrix (*LG*, n. 62). "Thus the daughter of Adam, Mary, consenting to the word of God, became the mother of Jesus, committing herself wholeheartedly and impeded by no sin to God's saving will, she devoted herself totally, as the handmaid of the Lord, to the person and work of her Son, under and with him serving the work of redemption...." (*LG*, n. 56). Mary's intimate cooperation with the Redeemer began at the annunciation, where she freely participated in the work of salvation through faith and obedience (cf. Lk 1:28). But the cooperation of the mother of the Redeemer in the work of redemption did not cease with her "fiat" to the angel. "The blessed virgin advanced in her pilgrimage of faith and faithfully persevered, in union with her Son, unto the cross, where she stood, in keeping with the divine plan, enduring with her only-begotten Son the intensity of his suffering, associated herself with his sacrifice in her mother's heart, and lovingly consenting to the emmolation of this victim which was born of her" (*LG*, n. 58). These profound words of the Second Vatican Council describe the spiritual sufferings and intimate cooperation Mary experienced with her Son at the foot of the cross (cf. Jn 19:26) in perfect maternal obedience. It is in light of Mary's unique and intimate cooperation with her Son, both at the incarnation (cf. Lk 1:28) and at Calvary (cf. Jn 19:26) that caused John Paul II to say, "Mary's role as co-redemptrix did not cease with the glorification of her Son" (Papal address at the Sanctuary of Our Lady of Alborada in Guayaquil, 31 Jan, 1985). It should be mentioned strongly that the prefix "co" here does not mean equal but comes from the Latin word "cum" which means "with". This title of co-redemptrix applied to the Mother of Jesus never places Mary on a level of equality with Jesus Christ, the divine Lord of all in the saving process of humanity's redemption. Rather, it denotes Mary's singular and unique sharing with her Son in the saving work of our redemption. The mother of Jesus participated in this redemptive work as St. Paul reminds us, that we also should make up what is lacking in the cross of Christ. We too should work with Mary and Jesus for the salvation of the world, for Christ has chosen to work in and through his mystical body of which Mary is at one and the same time both its preeminent member and also mother.

# INTRODUCTION

Since the Second Vatican Council (1962-1965) there has been an impressive development of the theology of Mary. Besides the six official documents presented in this book, there are also new frontiers of Mariology opened up by theologians. Studies in Luke, Matthew and John have enriched many of the Marian themes (cf. Letter from the Congregation for Catholic Education, Marian Studies, #39, pp. 204 - 211). A more balanced and realistic development has taken place concerning the four official Marian dogmas. A more critical study of the historical circumstances of these dogmas continues, together with a critical Biblical exegetical perspective on the Marian text used in the formulation of these dogmas.

## Balanced Devotion

In the area of piety and devotion to Mary, both historical and cultural studies have led to a balanced teaching about true devotion to Mary. Since 1967, six International Marian Congresses have taken place under the aegis of the Pontifical International Marian Academy in Rome. Ecumenical studies have produced numerous books and articles on Mary. Pope John Paul II has emphasized, "How profoundly the Catholic Church, the Orthodox Church, as well as the ancient churches of the East feel united by love and praise of the Theotokos." Demetrius I, the ecumenical patriarch states, "Our two sister Churches have maintained throughout the centuries an unextinguished flame of devotion to the most venerated person of the holy mother of God" (Letter from the Congregation of Catholic Education, Marian Studies #39, p 211, #14). He added, "The subject of Mariology should occupy a central position in the theological dialog between our Churches... for the full establishment of our ecclesial communion." The reformation churches are also part of this dialog. Several churches have invited Catholic scholars to present ideas about Mary from the Scriptures. Studies of Mary as a woman of faith and as a disciple of the Lord have also appeared in Protestant circles. There have also been Jewish presentations about Mary in the Jewish-Christian dialog, especially in Rome and in Dayton, Ohio where the International Marian Research Institute contains the largest library of Marian books, perhaps in the world. Mary as the daughter of Zion is an especially rich title that is being developed between Jews and Christians. Mary's own Jewishness helps many Christians to see Judaism as the foundational source for their own beliefs in Jesus, the Jewish Messiah. The conciliar documents and papal statements of Paul VI and John Paul II suggest several working principles which assist both the faithful and scholars in seeing Mary always in the history of salvation in her relationship to the super-eminence of her Son Jesus Christ and a primary model of what the Church is called to be in modern society. These principles and guidelines have been followed carefully in the two great centers of Marian studies, the International Marian Research Institute at the University of Dayton in Ohio (already mentioned) and the Pontifical "Marianum" Faculty of Theology in Rome. Since the study of the Sacred Scriptures must be the soul of Mariology (letter from the Vatican Congregation for Catholic Education, Mar 25, 1988) this official synthesis should provide a convenient source for all Catholics and Protestants alike striving to ascertain the exact place of Mary in the work of salvation and in the lives of the faithful. This would fulfill the direction and vision given by the Second Vatican Council in its decrees on divine revelation and on the Church. The Bible testifies to a living tradition which venerates the mother of the Lord and hence offers the believer a basis for an authentic devotion to Mary unencumbered by exaggerations in the direction of either too much or too little. Mary is a reality and a given of divine revelation and her maternal presence is always operative in the life of the Church. May this work help to appreciate her role ever more deeply.

Holy Mary, mother of God, pray for us as we search to follow you in the ways of your Son to the fulfillment of the plan of the eternal Father, whose daughter you are. May Jesus your Son, who gave you to us as our mother be born more fully in our hearts with your intercession. And may the Holy Spirit, whose spouse you are, lead us like you into all holiness, wisdom and grace so that we, like your Son under your direction, may grow in wisdom, age and grace before God and men (Lk 2:52).

Jesus came to give us everything – a share in his own divine life, his Gospel, his love, his very body and blood. There is one gift that he reserved to the very end and that was the wonderful gift of his mother. May we within the Church he founded come ever more fully to appreciate that the mother of Jesus is the mother of Jesus in us.

# -Chapter 1-

# VATICAN II'S DEVELOPMENTAL SHIFT IN MARIAN THEOLOGY
### by James Tibbetts, S.T.L[1]

I t is safe to say that theology in the Catholic Church operates on two distinct levels. The first level of theology could be referred to as "professional piety" and is an historical critical level of scientific and theological inquiry and investigation from the Magisterium of the Church. This involves the normal course of scholarly research and publications in professional journals and Vatican documents. All the official Church teachings, doctrines and dogmas, as well as the sacraments, liturgical norms and practices, are involved on this level of a critical scholarly approach of the Magisterium.

The second level of theology is usually referred to as the "popular piety" level. Popular piety encompasses all the popular devotions, prayers and practices of each culture. The various popular Marian prayers, songs, devotion cards and sayings, Marian pictures, statues and icons are all part of this popular piety level. Even public and private apparitions would fall into this category. Different cultures and continents tend to emphasize different popular piety devotions, practices and apparitions, such as in the Americas, where Our Lady of Guadalupe is emphasized.

The Documents of Vatican II, the Catechism of the Catholic Church, the formal writings of the Popes would all be on the level of professional piety with historical critical scholarship. The Vatican II Council was a time of well known transitions in Church teachings and practices and many changes took place. One change was in the area of Marian theology. On the professional level there was a developmental shift in Marian theology. This shift on the professional level influenced the popular piety level over the course of time.

This is important to understand because some of the literature, devotions and movements out today on the Virgin Mary are still in the pre-Vatican II mind-set and formulation. This is OK since it is part of the Catholic Tradition, but the Church moves on. The Church needs to continue to seek a modern post-Vatican II approach, which is the approach the Holy Spirit is leading the Church today and the approach Pope John Paul II is emphasizing for Mary the mother of Jesus. The following points will emphasize and help explain the reasons for this developmental shift in Mariology, the study of the Blessed Virgin Mary.

1. "A shift has taken place from a privilege-centered to a sharing-oriented consideration of Mary, in association to Christ (Christocentric) and in relation to the Church (ecclesiotypical). In contrast to pre-Council decades, there have been few recent studies on such themes as principles of Mariology or Marian mediation, but many positive investigations, especially into Biblical sources. The Mary-Church analogy has attracted serious notice."[2]

Yet even though a shift has occurred Pope Paul VI did not hesitate to call Mary's prerogatives privileges. By the angel's message Mary's "exalted privileges were revealed."[3] She is "the privileged one" whom we cannot extol too much,[4] and her privileges come from Jesus.[5] Especially because of her divine motherhood is she privileged: she is "the most elect mother" and simply "the incomparable one."[6] Because of her immaculate conception she is "the unique woman, in whom human nature appears in its original beauty."[7] She is privileged also because of her virginity.[8] With the intention of interpreting the Vatican Council, the Pope said, "The Council multiplies its teaching precisely in regard to Mary's privileged position and unique function relative to the mystery of Christ."[9] After finishing his thoughts on Mary's privileges he appropriately closes, "Mary herself, I believe, indicated that her privileges must always be kept in focus in our cult to her when she chanted, '...all generations will call me blessed: for he who is mighty has done great things for me...' (Lk 1:48-49)."[10]

2. A second view on this shift indicates that with Vatican II

there is a development in how to deal with Marian dogmas. Trying to find an adequate theory of doctrinal development is difficult. "Indeed, since Vatican II the problem has taken an unexpected turn. Prior to the Council, the problem was to construct a theory broad and supple enough to account for all the things which the Church had, in fact, dogmatized. Today the problem is to find a theory stringent enough to provide a rational basis for evaluating the tendencies being proclaimed as developments."[11] The shift here is from content (taking into account the dogmas) to process (a rational basis for evaluating). This also appears to be what is occurring in the transition from Marian principles to Marian Scriptural theology. The Marian principles in theology are content and in some ways dogmatic, while the Marian Scriptural theology emphasizes process and a rational basis for understanding and acceptance.

3. An important paper delivered at the 1972 Mariological Society of America conference was Rev. Theodore Koehler's "Mary's Spiritual Maternity After the Second Vatican Council." He did not indicate any specific decline in interest in Mary's spiritual maternity but did indicate that there was an evolution. "To understand this double approach to the Marian doctrine [Christotypical and ecclesiotypical], let us keep in mind that Vatican II took place during a time of well-known evolution in Marian theology."[12] He opens his paper citing Cardinal Suenens who had asked Karl Rahner how he would explain the evident decline in Marian devotion. The German theologian responded, "Today too many Christians, no matter what religious affiliation they may have, try to make their Christian faith into an ideology and abstraction and abstracts certainly do not need a mother."[13] Koehler went on to write: "That answer indicates a present danger: to transform Christ into a pure idea and abstraction; and, consequently, the mother of Christ, as a pure idea, doesn't interest us anymore. On the other hand, with Karl Rahner, we also have to say that the Marian piety must rediscover in Mary a mother. That points out the actual importance of the doctrine of Mary's spiritual maternity after Vatican II."[14]

Fr. Koehler, founder of the International Marian Research

Institute, points out that there are two conciliar indications in the
doctrine of *Lumen Gentium*: first, in the doctrine in which our
relation to Mary is designated by the title, Mother;[15] second, for
our devotion, the Church's piety towards Mary is indicated by the
use of "filial",[16] as is summarized in various texts.[17] But the Council
did not intend to propose a complete Marian doctrine. These two
approaches can be defined as Christotypical and ecclesiotypical.
"Mary is mother of Christ and mystically the mother of Jesus'
brothers. These are two aspects of one sole maternity which retains
more and more the attention of the present theology."[18]

In a concluding comment Koehler notes the ongoing of
evolution in Marian theology. "The traditional titles, 'Mary ever-
Virgin', 'all holy', 'Theotokos', 'Mother of Life', 'Mother of the
Living', 'Mediatrix', 'Mother of Mercy', 'Our Mother', and 'Mother
of the Church', all manifest an evolution: all say that Mary is mother
of Christ and therefore related to us; and the Church sought out
these expressions, the titles, and the Biblical references, which
could express our relations with Mary. The terminology of Mary's
messianic maternity developed into doctrine. Today we will know
the meaning of our filial relations to Mary by taking into account
what the natural sciences concerning man know about maternity.
The Marian theology must face the complexity of the analogy
between God, Mary and human motherhood."[9]

4. Fr. Neumann notes the following change in Mariological
method from the Council: "I refer to the two conceptions of method
in Marian theology that met each other at the opening of Vatican
II. Philips repeatedly cites Father Carlo Balic's [founder and
president of International Marian Academy] opinion that the
difference between the first and final draft of Chapter 8 of *Lumen
Gentium* is summed up in this difference of method."[20]

"Proponents of the earlier draft followed a method with its
point of departure in the papal magisterium, where Mary had
figured with increasing frequency; they proceeded by way of exact
speculative analysis of the concepts and principles involved,
sought probative texts in Scripture and tradition, were preoccupied
with constructing a solid doctrinal system, and expressed warm
concern throughout for Mary's 'privileges', building on previous

positions endorsed by the magisterium.

"Advocates of the other method began with the earliest Scriptural and patristic sources of Marian doctrine, proceeded more by way of positive study, traced the evolution of the history of salvation and Mary's role in it, followed the subsequent development of Marian doctrine and devotion, and generally avoided polemic encounters, though not espousing any false irenicism....[T]he shift towards the second method has been for the whole of Mariology the occasion more of a silent growth so far, rather than of any strides of renewal that catch public attention."[21]

The clash between the Bishops at Vatican II over the Document on the Virgin Mary was analyzed and there was no division, in terms of basic doctrine. "Disagreement came over the matter of the appropriate language, thought patterns, formulas, and titles with which to express the insights agreed upon. Both Karl Rahner and René Laurentin, who were present as 'periti', [experts at Vatican II] have analyzed the clash as due to differences in national cultural characteristics, with the Mediterranean temperament stressing Mary's prerogatives in exuberant and affective terms, while the Northern temperament took a more critical and rational approach."[22] "In addition, Rahner noted a differing methodological approach, as those more enthusiastic for Marian privileges drew heavily on papal teaching as a source, while those who wished a more tempered approach engaged in the return to Scriptural and patristic sources."[23]

5. After Vatican II there has developed an anti-doctrinal bias in theology today which handicaps Mariologists who have been most accustomed to discourse on the doctrinal level. "The shift of interest in our day has moved from doctrine to ethics, from orthodoxy to orthopraxies.... One cause of the relative disinterest in Mariology today remains the deafness with which any doctrinal presentation is greeted."[24]

6. Canon Gerard Philips gives an appropriate conclusion, "Mariology stands before a future profoundly different from its past, perhaps less brilliant on the surface, but more productive within. Its rejuvenation is a fact; it has been purified and deepened, not

impoverished. Similarly, though so much more demanding, the intensification of our devotion is more precious than the extension and multiplication of pious practices."[25]

As the literature has indicated, there is a development away from dogmatic and doctrinal interest and towards ethical and social interest in the theological world today. Lay people and scholars are more interested in theological applications to practical questions about: war, crime, violence, abortion, sexuality, divorce, social ethics and other contemporary problems. Even though these are broad statements, the doctrinal interests of the 40's, 50's and 60's gave way to pastoral, ecumenical and liturgical interests of the 70's, 80's and 90's. The literature also indicates that there has been a shift from a privilege-centered to a sharing-oriented Mariology after Vatican II and a need for less abstraction in religion and more integration into society.

7. Vatican II was not the only reason for this shift in emphasis. Other theological problems affecting Mariology have also been a catalyst for the shift in Mariology. The Mariology of the future would seem to focus more on; 1) Biblical Mariology; 2) Theology of the Holy Spirit; 3) Christian Anthropology; 4) Hierarchy of Truths and Ecumenism; 5) Mariology within Theology; and 6) Mariology and the Involvement of the Faithful.

To give a concluding comment, "Since we share this problem of dogmatic development, we must collaborate. This is not to ask the exegete to engage in 'eisegesis', rather than exegesis, but this is to ask him to be alert to 'leads', 'possibilities' within the Scriptures that may be the setting-out points, or points of departure, for the subsequently defined dogma."[26] Carroll gives as an example Cardinal Newman's comparison of an underground river that eventually comes to the surface. "All along, the river supplies moisture to the plant life above it, so it is ever a vivifying force, but it becomes visible only when it reaches the surface. Similarly, in the course of time the implicit tributaries of the river of revealed truth eventually, in God's good time, become explicit and receive names."[27]

8. These two levels of theology in the Catholic Church, the level of the scholarly critical approach and the popular piety level,

are not mutually exclusive or independent of each other. In addition, these levels are not necessarily one above the other, even though scholarly literature does usually prevail over popular piety literature. There is a great deal of truth and accuracy in popular piety practices and devotions. In fact, sometimes these are closer to "the Way, the Truth and the Life" of Christ then the scholarly approach. Pope Paul VI explains to us the "Way of Truth" and the "Way of Beauty" in which we can recognize the scholastic critical approach and the popular piety approach to the faith.

In the opening address of Pope Paul VI to the International Mariological and Marian Congresses (May 16, 1975), he stated, "What is our contribution? We wish to offer an answer to a question that is very important both for pastoral action and for doctrine. In what new and suitable manner is Mary to be brought to the attention of the Christian people so that they will be stirred to renewed zeal in their devotion to her?

"In answering this question, two ways lie open to us. One is the 'Way of Truth'. By this we mean the path of Biblical, historical, and theological study of Mary's proper place in the mystery of Christ and the Church. This path, traversed by learned men in the past, is the one you are following and it is very profitable for Mariology. But there is another way, one that is open to all, even the less learned. We shall call it the 'Way of Beauty'. It is opened to us by the mysterious but wonderfully beautiful doctrine of Mary's relation to the Holy Spirit, which the Marian Congress will be studying.

"Mary is 'entirely beautiful' and 'a spotless mirror.' She is also the supreme model of perfection which artists of every age have tried to capture in their work. She is the 'woman clothed with the sun,' (Rv 12:1) in whom all the purest rays of human beauty converge with those rays of heavenly beauty which are of a higher order but which we can nevertheless perceive."[28]

Pope Paul VI sums up the purpose of Marian scholarship and devotion in a two-fold orientation, the "Way of Truth" and the "Way of Beauty". Perhaps in the world today some scholars are more drawn to the intellectual "Way of Truth" while others more drawn to the affective "Way of Beauty" in Scripture interpretation. Both are necessary for the growth of the Church and to have a healthy understanding and appreciation of Our Lady.

* * * * * * * * * *

## Endnotes

[1]      This chapter is edited from "The Historical Development of Biblical Mariology Pre- and Post- Vatican II," James Joseph Tibbetts; an S.T.L. thesis at the International Marian Research Institute, Dayton, Ohio, 1995. Also in "Biblical Theology on Mary and Vatican II", James J. Tibbetts, Two Hearts Productions.

[2]      Dominic J. Unger, O.F.M. Cap., "Mary's Privileges in Proper Perspective," *Marianum Annus* XXXVIII (1976): 1-18., p. 2. Citing *New Catholic Encyclopedia*, vol. 16, Supplement for 1967-1974, p. 275.

[3]      Ibid., p. 12. Citing n. Apostolic letter by which the Virgin of the Annunciation was declared principle patron of the diocese of Stockholm, Aug. 8, 1963 (*AAS* 56 [1964] p. 294).

[4]      Ibid. Citing Homily, Aug. 15, 1967 (*L'Osservatore Romano*, Aug. 20, 1967); General audience, Aug. 15, 1971 (*L'Osservatore Romano*, Aug. 17/18, 1971).

[5]      Ibid. Citing n. Address for the blessing of the golden rose designated for the shrine of de Aparecida, Brazil, Mar. 5, 1967 (*L'Osservatore Romano*, Mar. 6/7, 1967).

[6]      Ibid. Citing n. General audience, May 26, 1971 (*L'Osservatore Romano*, May 27, 1971); Address to the Council Fathers in the Basilica of St. Mary Major, Oct. 11, 1963 (*AAS* 35 [1963] p. 873); Homily, Aug. 15, 1966 (*L'Osservatore Romano*, Aug. 17/18, 1966).

[7]      Ibid. Citing n. At the *Angelus*, Dec. 8, 1967 (*L'Osservatore Romano*, Dec. 11, 1967). He had a similar thought that same day at the Piazza di Spagna (*L'Osservatore Romano*, Dec. 9/10, 1967).

[8]      Ibid. Citing n. To the Clergy of the Roman Diocese, Feb. 20, 1971 (*AAS* 63 [1971] p. 222).

[9]      Ibid. Citing General audience, May 29, 1968 (*L'Osservatore Romano*, May 30, 1968).

[10]      Ibid., p. 18.

[11]      William H. Marshner. "Criteria for Doctrinal Development in the Marian Dogmas: An Essay in Metatheology", *Marian Studies* XXVIII (January 1977): 47.

[12]      Rev. Theodore A. Koehler, S.M., "Mary's Spiritual Maternity After the Second Vatican Council," *Marian Studies,* 23 (1972): 43.

[13]      Ibid., p. 39. Citing Card. L. Suenens, *Marie et le monde d'aujourd'hui,* in DC (Oct., 1971) 878-879.

[14]      Ibid. Koehler.

[15]      Ibid. n. 53: Mary is the Mother of the member of Christ (St. Augustine)
n. 54: The Mother of men, most of all, of the faithful.
n. 56: The Mother of the living (St. Epiphanius)
n. 61: Our Mother in the order of grace.
n. 62: The Maternity of Mary in the economy of grace remains without ceasing...;
n. 63: Mary, Mother and Virgin, is the type (figure) of the Church, Mother and Virgin;
n. 65: She is an example of the maternal affection...
n. 67: We moved by a filial love toward our Mother.
n. 69: We invoke the Mother of God and the Mother of men.

[16]      Ibid. As is summarized in No. 67, "the true devotion proceeds...from true faith, by which we are led to acknowledge by excellence of Mary as the Mother of God, and we are moved to a filial love toward our Mother and to the imitation of her virtues." Also, in the decree on the Ministry and Life of Priests, "Let priests love and venerate with filial devotion and veneration this Mother..." (n. 18), and for seminarians, "They should love and venerate with a filial trust the most Blessed Virgin Mary," (n. 18). Finally, the decree for the Laity "explains how Mary is the perfect example for their life, and invites them to commend their life and apostolate to her maternal care (n. 4).

[17]      Ibid., p. 40-41. Citing Texts analyzed by G. Shea, *Mary in the Documents of Vatican II*, in *MS* 17 (1966) 20-26.

[18]      Ibid., p. 43. Citing G. Philips, *Les problemes actuels de la theologie mariale,* in *Mm* 11 (1949) 31ff. A Mexican Committee prepared a doctrinal study to promote the dogmatic definition of Mary's Spiritual Maternity: *Commision Nacional Mejicana pro Definicion dogmatica de la Maternidad*

*Espiritual de Maria. Conferencias...*(1957 y 1960)(Mexico, 1961).

[19]      Rev. Charles W. Neumann, S.M., "The Decline of Interest in Mariology..., Ibid. p. 65.

[20]      Ibid., p. 21-22. Citing Cf. Philips, *L'Eglise et Son mystere au deuxieme Concile du Vatican,* 2 (Paris, 1968) 210; *La Vierge...*75.

[21]      Ibid., p. 22.

[22]      Ibid. Citing Karl Rahner, "Zur konziliaren Mariologie," *Stimmen der Zeit* 174 (1964) 87-101; and Rene Laurentin, *La Vierge au Concile,* 20-21.

[23]      Ibid.

[24]      Ibid., p. 20.

[25]      Ibid., p. 38. Citing Philips, *La Vierge....*84.

[26]      P. Eamon Carroll, O. Carm., "Reflections of a Dogmatic Theologian About Exegesis", *Maria in Sacra Scriptura, Vol. II,* Exegesis Et Theologia Biblico-Dogmatica (Romae, Pontificia Academia Mariana Internationalis, 1967): 60. Citing Cf. example of Laurentin R., *Structure et theologie de Luc 1-2,* (Paris, 1957).

[27]      Ibid., p. 62. Citing Cf. Cardinal Newman, *Essay on Development of Christian Doctrine.*

[28]      Pope Paul VI, Address to the International Mariological Congress, May 1975. (Dayton, Ohio: *Marian Studies,* The Mariological Society of America).

-Chapter 2-

# BIBLICAL TITLES OF MARY, MOTHER OF JESUS
*by James Tibbetts, S.T.L.* [1]

When Jesus was on the road to Emmaus he walked with two disciples and discussed Scriptures with them (Lk 24:13-35). He strung together the various Biblical passages that referred to him. "Beginning with Moses and all the prophets, he interpreted for them every passage of Scripture which referred to him...When he had seated himself with them to eat, he took bread, pronounced the blessing, then broke the bread and began to distribute it to them. With that their eyes were opened and they recognized him; whereupon he vanished from their sight. They said to one another, 'Were not our hearts burning inside us as he talked to us on the road and explained the Scriptures to us?'"

In this chapter Scriptures are woven together in a tapestry often referred to as "stringing pearls." The Scriptures are strung together according to a Biblical theme. Some of the Biblical texts have also been arranged on the page in a poetic fashion for ease of reading and understanding. This chapter is basically a combination of two approaches to Scripture: the scholarly (the Way of Truth) and the artistic (the Way of Beauty). It is a theological exegesis and a poetic meditation; a Scriptural science and a Biblical art. Numerous different translations have been used to bring out the beauty of the text. These are a few of Mary's many Biblical titles.

Today, interpretation of the Bible can become very complex with the different methods and scholarly tools in theology. But two thousand years ago the Jews were a very simple people and only a few could read the scrolls of the Torah and prophets.

Memorizing and quoting these sacred texts is found in the Hebrew writings, and they would make parallels and connections between the texts of Sacred Scripture. Parallelism is one of the literary techniques used throughout the Bible. Some of this collection uses parallelism and also the "stringing of pearls," of the Scripture verses, as the early Christians did, to express Biblical themes and insights concerning Jesus and Mary. After each Biblical section on a theme is one or two quotes from either the "Catechism of the Catholic Church" (CCC)[2] or from *Lumen Gentium*, Chapter 8 (Our Lady), "Documents of Vatican II" (LG).[3]

## 1. Mary, The Daughter Zion

For example, the Holy Spirit inspired Luke to equate the expression "Daughter of Zion" or "Daughter Zion" with Mary because she qualifies as a personification of the elect people. Zion becomes a symbol for the presence of God in Israel.

In 2 Sm 5:7: "But David did take the stronghold of Zion which is the City of David" (cf. 1 Chr 11:5). This rock fortress with a water source was made the center, the stronghold and symbol for an emerging nation under David, its messianic king. David brought the Ark of the Covenant there making it a sacred city. Later Solomon built a temple in Jerusalem and "at Solomon's order the elders of Israel and all the leaders of the tribes, the princes of the Israelite ancestral houses, came to Jerusalem to bring up the Ark of the Lord's Covenant from the City of David (which is Zion)" (2 Chr 5:2). Luke referred to the prophecies of Zephaniah 3:14-17; Joel 2:21-27, and Zechariah 9:9-10. All three address the Daughter of Zion (Israel personified); announce messianic joy via. the expression "Rejoice!" The message is followed by "Do not fear." The message is about Yahweh coming to dwell within Zion - as King and as Savior. All three of these are found in the annunciation; Daughter Zion is equated with Mary as full of grace and Yahweh Savior is equated with Jesus.

| The Announcement of the Prophet to Israel (Zep 3:14-17) | The Announcement of the Angel to Mary (Lk 1:29-33) |
|---|---|

Rejoice,
Daughter of Zion,
The King of Israel, Yahweh,
is in you.
Do not fear, Zion.
Yahweh, your God,
is in your womb

"Yahweh Savior."

Rejoice,
Full of Grace,
the Lord
is with you.
Do not fear, Mary.
Behold,
you will conceive in
your womb
and bring forth a Son
and you will give him
the name as Valiant
Savior.

He will reign.

Rejoice greatly, O Daughter Zion! Shout for joy, Daughter Jerusalem! See, your King shall come to you; a just savior is he.

Zec 9:9

Sing and rejoice, O Daughter Zion; for lo, I come and I will dwell in the midst of you, says the Lord.

Zec 2:14

Tell the Daughter Zion: Behold, thy King comes to thee.

Mt 21:4-5

Let Israel rejoice in his maker, and Zion's children exult in their King.

Jl 2:23

"Here so and so was born," men say. But all call Zion "Mother," since all were born in her. It is he who makes her what she is, he, the Most High, Yahweh.

Ps 87:4,5

For Yahweh has chosen Zion, desiring this to be his home;

Ps 132:13

from Zion, perfect in beauty, God shines forth.

Ps 50:2

Oh, that out of Zion would come the salvation of Israel!

Ps 53:7

About Zion I will not be silent, about Jerusalem I will not grow weary, until her integrity shines out like the dawn and her salvation flames like a torch.

Is 62:1

Praise is rightfully yours, God in Zion.

Ps 65:1

[Mary] stands out among the poor and humble of the Lord, who confidently hope for and receive salvation from him. After a long period of waiting the times are fulfilled in her, the exalted Daughter of Zion, and the new plan of salvation is established. (*LG* 55)

CCC 489

It was quite correct for the angel Gabriel to greet her as the "Daughter of Zion": "Rejoice." (cf. Zep 3:14; Zec 2:14) It is the thanksgiving of the whole people of God, and thus of the Church which Mary, in her canticle (cf. Lk 1:46-55), lifts up to the Father in the Holy Spirit while carrying within her the eternal Son.

CCC 722

## 2. Mary, The Ark Of The Covenant

The use of the same terms in Zephaniah 3 and Luke 1 in the above passages show parallelism. And they concern identical themes – the new coming of God to his people in the New Ark of the Covenant, the ancient ark having disappeared (Zephaniah is situated during the exile).

By taking this New Testament point of view, the evangelist Luke also identifies Mary with the Ark of the Covenant, which is confirmed by the following comparison. And then in Revelation

11:19, the apostle John, aware of Luke's parallel, also uses the image of the Ark of the Covenant with the solemn title "woman" (Jn 2:4; 19:26). Both Luke and John salute Mary as Israel personified.

| | |
|---|---|
| The Tabernacle's Overshadowing | Mary's Overshadowing |
| Exodus 40:35 | Luke 1:35 |
| The cloud | The power of the Most High |
| overshadowed | will overshadow |
| the tabernacle. | you [Mary]. |
| | |
| The Joy of David | The Joy of Elizabeth |
| 2 Sm 6:9 | Lk 1:43 |
| How is it to be done | How has it happened to me |
| that the Ark of the Lord | that the Mother of my Lord |
| comes to my house? | comes to my house? |
| | |
| The Ark of Yahweh | Mary |
| remained | remained |
| at Obededom | with her |
| three months. | around three months. |
| 2 Sm 6:11 | Lk 1:56 |

Then God's temple in heaven opened and in the temple could be seen the Ark of his Covenant. There were flashes of lightning and peals of thunder, an earthquake, and a violent hailstorm.

Rv 11:19

A great sign appeared in heaven, a woman clothed with the sun, with the moon under her feet, and on her head a crown of twelve stars.

Rv 12:1

The same imagery is found in Revelation 4:5. "From the throne came flashes of lightning and peals of thunder." This imagery precedes the time when God entrusts the future of the world to the Lamb. The Ark of the Covenant in Revelation 11:9 announces the "Woman clothed with the sun" in Revelation 12:1.

And similarly the lightning and thunder in Revelation 11:9 precedes the time when God entrusts the future of the world to the 'Woman' until the time when her Son's hour has come (Jn 2).

As with the Ark of the Covenant, Mary's presence brings us the Lord's presence,

Lk 1:28

who is with her, surrounds her, and is enclosed in her as the Son of God.

Lk 1:31,35

In the ark was the golden jar containing the manna.

Heb 9:4

Mary, in whom the Lord himself has just made his dwelling, is the daughter of Zion in person, the Ark of the Covenant, the place where the glory of the Lord dwells. She is "the dwelling of God...with men" (Lk 1:45).                                    CCC 2676

*Full of Grace, the Lord is with thee:* these two phrases of the angel's greeting shed light on one another. Mary is full of grace because the Lord is with her. The grace with which she is filled is the presence of him who is the source of all grace. "Rejoice...O Daughter of Jerusalem...the Lord your God is in your midst." (Zep 3:14, 17a) Mary, in whom the Lord himself has just made his dwelling, is the daughter of Zion in person, the Ark of the Covenant, the place where the glory of the Lord dwells. She is "the dwelling of God...with men." (Rv 21:3) Full of grace, Mary is wholly given over to him who has come to dwell in her and whom she is about to give to the world.                                    CCC 2676

## 3. Mary, The New Eve

God called the dry land "earth," and the mass of waters "seas," ("Maria") and God saw that it was good (Gn 1:10). God created man in the image of himself, in the image of God he created him. Male and female he created them (Gn 1:27). The first-born of all creation (Col 1:15). And she gave birth to a Son, her first-born (Lk 1:6). A great sign appeared in the sky, a woman clothed with the sun (Rv 12:1).

The great dragon, the ancient serpent,...who had deceived all the world (Rv 12:9). I will put enmity between you and the woman, and between your offspring and hers (Gn 3:15); The dragon...pursued the woman (Rv 12:13). And he went away to wage war on the rest of her offspring (Rv 12:17). He/she will crush your head and you will strike its heel (Gn 3:15). The dragon...was defeated and driven out of heaven (Rv 12:7). They have triumphed over him by the blood of the Lamb (Rv 12:11).

Now the man called his wife's name Eve because she was the mother of all the living (Gn 3:20). The Virgin's name was Mary (Lk 1:28), mother of Jesus, mother of all Christians (cf. Acts 1:14). The post-apostolic Fathers St. Justin (155) and St. Irenaeus (circa 177) both write on the Eve-Mary parallel, which indicates that it is a traditional teaching of the Church. Irenaeus also knew St. Polycarp who was a disciple of St. John. The schema of the parallelism of Irenaeus (in Haereses III, 22,4) is thus:

| Eve | Mary |
|---|---|
| still a virgin | the virgin |
| the spouse of Adam | already betrothed |
| was disobedient | through her obedience |
| became both for herself | became both for herself |
| and all the human race | and all the human race |
| the cause of death | the cause of salvation |
| what the virgin Eve | the Virgin Mary |
| had bound | unbound |
| by her belief... | by her faith... |

For, as St. Irenaeus says, she "being obedient, became the cause of salvation for herself and for the whole human race." Hence not a few of the early fathers gladly assert with him in their preaching: "the knot of Eve's disobedience was untied by Mary's obedience: what the virgin Eve bound through her disbelief, Mary loosened by her faith." Comparing Mary with Eve, they call her "Mother of the living." (St. Epiphanius) and frequently claim: "death through Eve, life through Mary" (St. Jerome, St. Augustine, St. Cyril of Jerusalem, St. John Chryostom, St. John Damascene)

*LG 56; CCC 494.*

# 4. Mary, The Immaculate Conception

Before I formed you in the womb, I knew you;
before you were born, I dedicated you.

Jer 1:5

Without human hands the stone was quarried from
out of the mountain.

Dn 2:45

And the Lord said to the serpent...I will put enmities
between thee and the woman between thy seed
and her seed; he [the woman's seed] shall crush
thyhead and thou shalt lie in wait for his heel.

Gn 3:15

Open to me, my sister, my love, my dove, my
immaculate one.

Song 5:2

Yahweh created me when his purpose first unfolded,
before the oldest of his works.

Pr 8:22

The Most High hath sanctified his own tabernacle.

Ps 46:5

There is One who is able to preserve you without sin,
will present you immaculatebefore the presence of his
glory.

Jdt 24

For God formed man to be imperishable; the image of
his own nature he made him.

Wis 2:23

Naught defiled shall come upon her...For she is the
unspotted mirror of God's majesty.

Wis 7:26

You are all beautiful, my love, and there is no blemish
in you.

Song 4:7

Hail Mary, full of grace, the Lord is with you.

Lk 1:28

Before the world was made, he chose us, chose us in Christ, to be holy and immaculate, and to live through love in his presence.

Eph 1:4

A glorious church, holy and immaculate, without stain or wrinkle or anything of that sort.

Eph 5:27

God who is mighty has done great things for me; holy is his name.

Lk 1:49

God who is omnipotent girded me with strength; and he made my way to be immaculate.

Ps 18:33

The virgin shall be with child and give birth to a Son, and they shall call him Emmanuel, and they shall call her Immaculate.

Is 7:14

The Lord sanctified his own mother, as the potter has the power to form an honorable vessel from a lump of clay,

Rom 9:21

as the painter paints a beautiful icon on an empty canvas, God is inside the city; she can never fall.

Ps 46:5

As a bad tree cannot bring forth good fruit neither could a sinful nature bring forth the sinless one.

Mt 7:17

Coming forth as the morning rising, fair as the moon, bright as the sun, shining in the temple of God.

Song 6:10

As the dawn heralds the day, the unstained conception heralds the incarnation.  God is in the midst of her, she shall not be moved.

Ps 46:5

The perfect Redeemer needs at least one person to be perfectly redeemed (totally preserved from sin) to be a perfect Redeemer.  This at last is bone from my bones, and flesh from my flesh. She shall be called Woman.

Cf. Gn 2:23

Woman, "You are all beautiful, my love, and there is no spot in you."

Song 4:7

For nothing is impossible with God.

Lk 1:37

Through the centuries the Church has become ever more aware that Mary, "full of grace" through God, (Lk 1:28) was redeemed from the moment of her conception. That is what the dogma of the Immaculate Conception confesses, as Pope Pius IX proclaimed in 1854: "the most Blessed Virgin Mary was, from the first moment of her conception, by a singular grace and privilege of almighty God and by virtue of the merits of Jesus Christ, Savior of the human race, preserved immune from all stain of original sin" (Pius IX, *Ineffabilis Deus,* 1854).

CCC 491

## 5. Mary, The All-Holy One

The Law of Preparation is found in Abraham, Isaac, Joseph (Gn 12; 17; 30); Moses, Samson, Samuel (Ex 2; Jgs 13); David, Isaiah, Jeremiah, and Daniel (1 Kgs 1; Ps 71; Is 4; Jer 1; Dn 1), to the climax in Mary, the Sanctified One, the Sinless One, the All-Holy One (Lk 1-2). "Before I formed you in the womb, I knew you" (Jer 1:5).

The Law of Exception is found in the three young men in the king's furnace (Dn 3), the burning bush of Moses (Ex 3:2), the waters of Jordan held back (Jos 3:13-16), the birth through Sarah in old age (Gn 21:2), the exception of the law of death (Gn 5:2); in Enoch and Elias (2 Kgs 2:2), the exception of the law of the king granted to Esther (Est 15), "Fear not. Thou shalt not die. This law is not made for thee, but for all others" (Est 15:12,13). The exception from the law of sin for Mary, is when he sanctified his own mother, immaculately.

The Law of Gradation in Perfection is found in nature: all flesh of men, another of beasts, another of birds, and another of fishes (1 Cor 16:29-40), is found in spiritual gifts: tongues, interpretation, prophecy, knowledge, wisdom, discernment of spirits, healing, miracles, and faith; (1 Cor 12:4-14) is found in the womb: David was strengthened in the womb (Ps 71:6), Jeremiah was sanctified in the womb (Jer 1:5), John the Baptist was filled with the Holy Spirit in the womb (Jn 1:15,41), Mary was conceived immaculately in the womb and filled with grace (cf. Lk 1:28); as with the words of the Holy Spirit unto the spouse, "One is my love, my perfect one is but one, the Faultless One, the perfectly redeemed one" (Song 6:8).

The Law of Primacy is found in the beginning, since through him all things came to be (Jn 1:2), all things in heaven and on earth (Col 1:15), so that he should be first in every way (Col 1:18). The Lord begot me, the firstborn of his ways, the forerunner of his prodigies of long ago (Prv 8:22). Before the world was made (Eph 1:4) Christ chose us (his Mother) to be sinless, to be all-holy and spotless, and to live through love in his presence (Eph 1:4). Greater love has no man (Jn 15:13).

All the glory of the King's daughter is within.

Ps 44:74

God is in the inmost Heart and shall not depart therefrom.

Ps 45:6

Mary kept all these words (things, deeds), pondering them in her heart.

Lk 2:51

God who is mighty has done great things for me,

Lk 1:49

For nothing is impossible with God.

Lk 1:37

A glorious church, holy and immaculate, without stain
or wrinkle.

Eph 5:27

He who created me hath rested in my tabernacle.

Eccl 24:12

The Most High hath sanctified his Tabernacle.

Ps 46:4

Thus Yahweh speaks out, "Reverence my sanctuary."

Lv 26:12

The fathers of the Eastern tradition call the mother of God "the All-Holy" (*Panagia*) and celebrate her as "free from any stain of sin, as though fashioned by the Holy Spirit and formed as a new creature" (*LG* 56). By the grace of God Mary remained free of every personal sin her whole life long.

CCC 493

The Church is holy: the Most Holy God is her author; Christ, her bridegroom, gave himself up to make her holy; the Spirit of holiness gives her life. Since she still includes sinners, she is "the sinless one made up of sinners." Her holiness shines in the saints; in Mary she is already all-holy.

CCC 867

## 6. Our Lady's Pentecost

In Mary's home: (Lk 1:28) "The Holy Spirit will come upon you and the power of the Most High will overshadow you" (Lk 1:35). Mary set out to visit Elizabeth (Lk 1:39), who was filled with the Holy Spirit (Lk 1:41) and prophesied, "Blest are you among women and blest is the fruit of your womb" (Lk 1:42).

In the upper room (Acts 1:13): "You will receive power when the Holy Spirit comes upon you" (Acts 1:8); and the apostles went out to their mission (Acts 2:14) and "all of them were filled with the Holy Spirit and began to speak in other tongues, and make bold proclamations" (Acts 2:4).

At Pentecost, Mary, mother of Jesus, leads the others, with a single heart in prayer (Acts 1:14), and all were filled with the Holy Spirit and they began to express themselves in foreign tongues (Acts 2:4). Even on my servants and handmaids I will pour out a portion of my spirit (Acts 2:18). All...began to express themselves with the gift of tongues...as the Spirit prompted them (Acts 2:4). All...(including Mary) prayed in tongues (glossolalia).

At the end of this mission of the Spirit, Mary became the Woman, the new Eve ("mother of the living"), the mother of the "whole Christ" (cf. Jn 19:25-27). As such, she was present with the Twelve, who "with one accord devoted themselves to prayer," (Acts 1:14) at the dawn of the "end time" which the Spirit was to inaugurate on the morning of Pentecost with the manifestation of the Church.

*CCC 726*

## 7. Our Lady's Assumption

Where will the Lord find one endowed with the meekness of Moses, the faith of Abraham, the zeal of Elijah, the patience of Job, the wisdom of Solomon, the humility of David.

For all have turned aside, all alike are tainted. There is not one good man left, not a single one.

*Ps 53:3*

Enoch walked with God in purity of heart, and was seen no more for God took him.

*Gn 5:24*

Elijah also burning with the great fire of charity, was carried away by a chariot and horses of fire.

*2 Kg 2:11*

Yet who will be found worthy to conceive true God from true God?

She is full of grace, and blessed among women,

Lk 2:28

Queen of Prophets, Handmaiden of the King, Daughter of the Father,

cf. Lk 1:35

Mother of the Son,

Lk 1:35

Spouse of the Holy Spirit!

Mt 1:20

I have placed the Lord before me continually; because he is at my right hand, I shall not be moved. Therefore my heart was glad and my soul rejoiced; my body too shall dwell securely. For thou wilt not leave my soul in the realm of the dead nor allow thy Holy One to see corruption.

Ps 16:8-10

As Elijah and Elisha walked on conversing, a flaming chariot and flaming horsescame between them, and Elijah went up to heaven in a whirlwind.

2 Kg 2:11

As with Elijah, so much more with Mary, "Nor will thou give thy holy one to see corruption."

Ps 16:10

What is shown in the earth is subject to decay, what rises is incorruptible. What rises is glorious. This corruptible body must be clothed with incorruptibility, this mortal body with immortality.

1 Cor 15:42,43,53

Many bodies of saints who had fallen asleep were raised. After Jesus' resurrection, they came forth from their tombs and entered the holy city and appeared to many.

Mt 27:53

May the God of peace make you perfect in holiness.
May he preserve you whole and entire, spirit, soul, and
body, at the coming of our Lord Jesus Christ.

1 Th 5:23

Fear not, thou shalt not die; not for thee but for these
has the law been  made.

Est 15:12-13

I will put enmity between you and the woman.

Gn 3:15

I stayed in your presence, you held my right hand; now
guide me with advice and in the end receive me into
glory.

Ps 73:23,24

And behold, the glory of God of Israel came in by the
way of the east....and the earth shown with his majesty.

Ez 43:2

My Beloved lifts up his voice; he says to me, "Come
then, my love, my beautiful one, come. For see, winter
is past, the rains are over and gone."

Song 2:10,11

You are wholly beautiful, my love, and without a
blemish. Come from Lebanon, my promised bride;
come from Lebanon, come on your way."

Song 4:7,8

But my dove is unique, mine, unique and perfect. She
is the darling of her mother, the favorite of the one who
bore her. The maidens saw her, and proclaimed her
blessed, queens and concubines sang her praises; "Who
is this arising like the dawn, fair as the moon,
resplendent as the sun."

Song 6:8,9,10

The queen takes her place at your right hand in gold of

Ophir. All glorious is the King's daughter as she enters; her raiment is threaded with spun gold. In embroidered apparel she is borne in to the King.

Ps 45:10,14,15

And the King rose to meet her, and bowed down to her; then he sat on his throne, and had a seat brought for the King's mother; and she sat on his right.

1 Kg 1:29

and nothing is impossible with God.

Lk 1:37

"Finally the Immaculate Virgin, preserved free from all stain of original sin, when the course of her earthly life was finished, was taken up body and soul into heavenly glory, and exalted by the Lord as Queen over all things, so that she might be the more fully conformed to her Son, the Lord of lords and conqueror of sin and death" (LG 59; cf. Pius XII, *Munificentissimus Deus* (1950); cf. Rev 19:16). The assumption of the Blessed Virgin is a singular participation in her Son's resurrection and an anticipation of the resurrection of other Christians: "In giving birth you kept your virginity; in your dormition you did not leave the world, O Mother of God, but were joined to the source of Life. You conceived the living God and, by your prayers, will deliver our souls from death" (Byzantine Liturgy).

CCC 966

## 8. Mary And The Communion Of Saints

Mary, the mother of Jesus, was present and in communion at the first community of Jerusalem, bound by common life, prayer (cf. Acts 1:14), the breaking of the bread (Acts 1:24; 2:42-47); and mutual love (4:32-35; 5:12-14). And they communed with her, also (1 Kgs 22:14).

In addition, the Church is a communion (Acts 2:42-47), a fellowship (Acts 4:32-35; 5:12-16), a cloud of witnesses (Heb 12:1), a body (Acts 2:46), a group of believers united in heart and soul (Acts 4:32), who are called (Jas 5:16), to pray for one another, (cf. Heb 13:18, Eph 6:19-20; 1 Thes 5:25), for the body of Christ (Eph

1:23; Col 1:24), for the reign of Christ (cf. Mt 3:2; 4:23; 9:35; 13:1-53; Mt 21:43; Mk 1:14; Lk 1:32,33; 16:16). So that primacy may be his in everything, it pleased God to make absolute fullness reside in him (Col 1:18,19), thus it is no longer I that live but Christ lives in me (Gal 2:20).

In this communion of saints, the saints together make a unity in the work of service, building up the body of Christ (Eph 4:12). If one member suffers, all the members suffer with it; if one member is honored, all the members share its joy (1 Cor 12:20-22,26). Thus join the saints and the prayers of God's people (Col 1:12; Rv 5:8), that they may receive you into everlasting dwellings (Lk 16:9), for only faith can prove the existence of the realities that at present remain unseen (Heb 11:1).

I have given them the glory you gave me that they may
be one, as we are one - I am living in them, you living
in me - that their unity may be complete.

Jn 17:22,23

Having passed through gate after gate, she found herself

Est 4:2

in the presence of the King.

1 Kg 1:28

"We believe in the communion of all the faithful of Christ, those who are pilgrims on earth, the dead who are being purified, and the blessed in heaven, all together forming one Church; and we believe that in this communion, the merciful love of God and his saints is always [attentive] to our prayers" (Paul VI CPG,30).

CCC 962

## 9. Our Lady, The Advocate Through Intercession

Moses, Aaron (cf. Ex 32:11) and Samuel, among others (Nm 17:11-13; Ps 106:23), were great intercessors (1 Sm 7:5-10). Abraham prayed to spare Sodom and Gomorrah (Gn 18:22-23). Samuel prayed for Israel (1 Sm 7:5-10). Moses prayed in time of battle (Ex 17:8-16). Nehemiah prayed for Jerusalem (Neh 1:4-11). Elijah prayed for the widow's Son (1 Kg 17:17-24). Elijah prayed to call down fire and rain from heaven (1 Kgs 18:20-46, Jas 5:17-18). Elisha prayed to raise a woman's dead Son (2 Kgs 4:32-37).

Following in the footsteps of her Jewish roots, Mary is a great intercessor, an advocate as with Cana's newlyweds (Jn 2). Since you are dependable in small matters, I will put you in charge of larger affairs (Mt 25:21). Through intercession Yahweh gives authority to the faithful: Yahweh Lord obeyed the voice of a man (Jos 10:14).

In Our Lady, the Father gives the same authority: "My mother, make your request, for I will not refuse you" (1 Kgs 2:20). Thus we can ask of Mary, "You are a devout woman, pray to the Lord for us" (Jdt 8:29). As St. Paul asked of his brethren, "I beseech you therefore brethren that you help me in your prayers for me to God" (Rom 15:30).

God never takes back his gifts or revokes his choice (Rom 11:29). He who is able to understand, let him understand (Mt 19:12). Mary as Queen Mother is advocate (1 Kgs 2:19; 15:9-13); to the King (2 Kgs 11:3; Jer 13:18,20). The King said, "Make your request, my mother; for I will not refuse you" (1 Kgs 2:20).

Thus says the Lord, "My house will be a house of prayer for all nations." (Is 56:4,7) All these joined in continuous prayer, including Mary, the mother of Jesus (Acts 1:14). With a "single heart" you led others in prayer (Acts 1:14) and thy heart rejoiced as the Spirit filled everyone (Acts 2).

Since Yahweh Lord obeyed the voice of a man.

Jos 10:14

And the King said to her, "My mother, make your request, for I will not refuse you."

1 Kg 2:20

Thus can we ask of Mary, like of Judith, "You are a devout woman, pray to the Lord for us";

Jdt 8:29

for wide is his dominion,

Is 9:6

and nothing is impossible with God.

Lk 1:37

Mary is the perfect *Orans* (pray-er), a figure of the Church. When we pray to her, we are adhering with her to the plan of the Father, who sends his Son to save all men. Like the beloved disciple we welcome Jesus' mother into our homes, (cf. Jn 19:27) for she has become the mother of all the living. We can pray with and to her. The prayer of the Church is sustained by the prayer of Mary and united with it in hope. (cf. *LG* 68-69)

CCC 2679

## 10. Our Lady's Rosary And Meditation

Meditation in Hebrew means to ponder, to murmur, to reflect, to pray, to meditate, to pre-meditate (cf. Gn 24:63, Jos 1:8; 1 Kgs 18:27; Is 33:18; Sir 6:37; 14:20, 39:7; 50:28; Jb 15:4; Ps 1:2, 5:1, 19:14, 49:3, 63:6, 77:3,6,12, 104:34, 119:12, 119:15,23,27,48,78, 119:97,99,148, 143:5, 145:5, Lk 2:19,53, Lk 21:14, 1 Tm 4:15).

Mary meditated on and followed Jesus' example. Jesus finds strength in meditating and prayer before dawn (Mk 1:35) and he went up into the mountain to pray, and continued all night in prayer to God (Lk 6:12). He prays regularly in the Synagogue (Lk 4:16). He prays and meditates in solitude (Mk 6:46). He prays twice a day (Mt 14:23; Lk 3:21, 5:16, 6:12, 9:18,28f) the basic Jewish Creed of faith: "and you shall love the Lord, your God, with all your heart, and with all your soul and with all your might" (Dt 6:5-7).

Jesus thanks his Father, God (Mt 11:25-30; Jn 11:41); he praises his Father, God (Lk 10:21; Jn 17), he is transfigured while he was praying before the Father (Lk 9:28), he prays for his disciples (Jn 17), he acts as an intercessor (Heb 4:14-16), and he teaches to "Ask....Seek....Knock," (Lk 11:9-13) and to "pray always" (Lk 18:1).

The Jewish practice of liturgical prayer (cf. Dn 6:11, 14) was three times a day: (Ps 55:17), morning, noon and evening (Acts 3:1; 10:3,30). During these three hours of prayer, as his custom was (Lk 4:16), young Jesus brought up in a devout home, meditated on the mysteries of Yahweh (Lk 2, 4:16).

The disciples went off to get into their boat. All through the night they caught nothing (Jn 21:3) Jesus came at daybreak and said, "Cast your nets off to the starboard side ("star of the sea," is the interpretation for Mary's Jewish name) and you will find something. So they made a cast, and took so many fish they could not haul the net in (Jn 21:6).

They hauled ashore the net loaded with sizable fish – one hundred and fifty-three of them! (there are 153 Hail Mary's in the rosary). In spite of the great number, the net was not torn (Jn 21:10). After they finished their meal (Jn 21:15 – bread and fish an early symbol of the Eucharist), Jesus spoke with Peter, the first Pope of the Church, and said to him, "Follow me" (Jn 21:19).

In Monasticism the Book of Psalms is called the three fifties. A rosary is three sets of a chaplet of fifty beads, or prayers. The first three beads commemorate the three courts of the temple: the outer, the inner, and the Holy of Holies (1 Kgs 6).

The centerpiece connecting the three chains is the Tabernacle proper, "the Mishcan," the shape of a triangle over the tent erected by Moses in Sinai, immediately after the law was given (Ex 26:7; 36:14). The ten beads commemorate the Ten Commandments (Ex 20). The five decades honor the first five books (Gn, Ex, Lv, Num, Dt), the Pentateuch.

Into this tent with Our Lady, she meditates on the mystery of salvation, which is beyond her (Lk 2:19,51). Thus meditating on the Torah, God's Word, she treasured all these things, pondering them in her heart (Lk 2:18).

How I love your law, O Lord! It is my meditation all the day.

Ps 119:97

At Bethlehem, Mary kept all these things, pondering (meditating) them in her heart.

Lk 2:19

At Jerusalem, the child's father and mother were marveling (pondering) at what was being said about him.

Lk 2:33

At Nazareth, his mother pondered (or meditated), all
these things in her heart.

Lk 2:51

The angel Gabriel was the first one to venerate Mary
with his salutation, "Hail, Full of Grace, the Lord is with
thee."

Lk 1:28

Elizabeth was the second one to venerate Mary, with
her exulted greeting, "Blessed are you among women
and blessed is the fruit of your womb."

Lk 1:42

Meditation engages thought, imagination, emotion, and desire.
This mobilization of faculties is necessary in order to deepen our
convictions of faith, prompt the conversion of our heart, and
strengthen our will to follow Christ. Christian prayer tries above
all to meditate on the mysteries of Christ, as in *lectio divina* or the
rosary. This form of prayerful reflection is of great value, but
Christian prayer should go further: to the knowledge of the love of
the Lord Jesus, to union with him.

CCC 2708

## 11. The Queen-Mother And Queen Of The Angels

For the Jewish people the father was considered the head
of the family, legally and ritually. But in the ethical relation
involving the reverence due her from the children she stood on
the same plane as the father. Disrespect for the mother entailed
the same punishment as disrespect for the father (cf. Ex 21:15,17;
Lv 20:9; Dt 27:16). Children are commanded to fear both parents
(Lv 19:2) and to honor the mother as the father (Ex 20:12; Dt 5:16).
In both the home life and training the mother is of equal importance
to the father (Dt 21:18,19; 1 Kgs 19:20; Jer 16:7; Prv 30:17).

The Queen-mother has an important position in ancient
Israel. Their names were preserved with care in the books of Kings:
1 Kgs 14:21; 15:2,10; 22:42 cf. 53; 2 Kgs 9:6; 12:2; 14:2; 15:2,33;

18:2; 22:1; 23:31,36; 24:18. They found themselves closely tied up with the honor and with the position of the monarchy (Jer 13:18; 22:26). The mother of the King enjoys a special place of honor before the reigning prince. She is called the great lady as was Bathsheba (1 Kgs 15:13; cf. 2:19) or the mother of King Asa (2 Chr 15:16). Thus the Old Testament brings positive support to the doctrine of the royalty of Mary as Queen. Mary is the Queen-Mother and Jesus is the King-Son.

Mary is Queen of the heavens and the earth, thus she is Queen of the angels. There are nine choirs of angels: the supreme hierarchy: Seraphim, Cherubim, Thrones; the middle hierarchy: Dominations, Virtues, Powers; and the lower hierarchy: Principalities, Archangels and Angels. And Mary is also Queen of the guardian angels. Every human being has his own guardian angel (Ex 23:20,23; Gn 32:1; Jdt 13:20; Tb 5,6,7; Ps 33:8; Mt 18:10; Jn 14:3; Acts 12:5-11, 13-16). "It is his angel" (Heb 1:14).

"I myself will send an angel before you, to guard you as you go and to bring you to the place that I have prepared. Give him reverence and listen to all that he says. Do not rebel against him, for he will not forgive your sin. My authority resides in him. If you listen carefully to his voice and do all that I say, I shall be an enemy to your enemies, foe to your foes. My angel will go before you..." (Ex 23:20-23). "Are they not all ministering spirits, sent to serve those who are to inherit salvation?" (Heb 1:14).

Mary has by grace been exalted above all angels and men to a place second only to her Son, as the most holy mother of God who was involved in the mysteries of Christ: she is rightly honored by a special cult in the Church. From the earliest times the Blessed Virgin is honored under the title of Mother of God, whose protection the faithful take refuge together in prayer in all their perils and needs.

*LG 66*

## 12. Our Lady, The Woman Of Apparitions

Elijah climbed to the top of Carmel, crouched down to the earth and put his head between his knees. Six times he looked out to the seas and saw nothing. And the seventh time the youth reported, "There is a cloud as small as a man's foot rising from the sea" (1 Kgs 18:42-44).

Apparitions of the dead appeared: with Samuel (1 Sm 28:11), with Moses and Elijah on Mount Tabor (Mt 17:1-8) and with Christ (Jn 20f). The angelic apparitions announced: Jesus' birth (Mt 1-2; Lk 1:11,26; 2:9) and Jesus' resurrection (Mt 28:2; Mk 16:5; Lk 24:4; Jn 20:12), the answered prayers of Cornelius (Acts 10:11-12), and those of Peter in prison (Acts 12:7-11).

The private apparitions of Jesus: to Mary, to the women (Jn 20:11; Mt 28:9-10; Mk 12f), to the disciples on the road to Emmaus (Lk 24:13-35; Mk 12f), and to the seven at the lakeside (Jn 21:1-23). The public apparitions of Jesus: to Simon (Lk 24:34), and to the eleven, (Mt 28:16-20; Mk 16:14-18; Jn 20:19-29), together with several other disciples (Lk 24:33-50), and the five hundred brothers at once (1 Cor 15:6). The apparitions after the ascension: the vision of Christ by Stephen (Acts 7:56), the vision of Christ by Paul (Acts 9:5), the vision of Christ by Ananias (Acts 9:10).

In Revelations, the Ark of the Covenant appeared (Rv 11:19); there appeared a sign in the sky, a woman clothed with the sun, the moon under her feet, and on her head a crown of twelve stars (Rv 12:1). For nothing is impossible with God (Lk 1:37). Blessed are those who have believed without having seen (Jn 20:29).

After her Son's ascension, Mary "aided the beginnings of the Church by her prayers" (*LG* 69). In her association with the apostles and several women, "we also see Mary by her prayers imploring the gift of the Spirit, who had already overshadowed her in the Annunciation" (*LG* 59).

                                                        CCC 965

\* \* \* \* \* \* \* \* \*

# Endnotes

[1]      This chapter is taken from "Biblical Meditations on Mary Mother of Jesus," James Joseph Tibbetts, Two Hearts Productions, 1996.

[2]      "Catechism of the Catholic Church," 1994 Libreria Editrice Vaticana, Citta del Vaticano. (Liguori, Missouri: Liguori Publications).

[3]      "Documents of Vatican II," "*Lumen Gentium,*" Chapter 8, The Blessed Virgin Mary, Mother of God in the Mystery of Christ and the Church. 1963-5. (Austin P. Flannery, Editor, Grand Rapids, Michigan: William B. Eerdmans Publishing Co., 1975).

-Chapter 3-

# LUMEN GENTIUM

In this section, we have two magnificent documents: the Second Vatican Council's teaching on Mary which comprises Section 8 on the Constitution of the Church entitled *Lumen Gentium*; and also a discourse that Pope John Paul II gave concerning it in his General Audience dated 21 November, 1964.

It is no exaggeration that the hundred years from 1854 to the close of the Second Vatican Council were the most prolific in doctrinal development in Mariology. Nothing like it was seen in any comparable period of Catholic history.

One reason for the sudden upsurge was the reaction against rationalism in modern times. When critics of the faith challenged the foundations of belief in Christ's divinity, the response of the Church would understandably be in defense of Nicea and Chalcedon, with special concern to safeguard the dignity of Mary, mother of God.

Devotion to Mary also grew apace as the role of women became more prominent in private and professional life, and their unique position was threatened by a rampant secularism that wants to exploit them for its own ends. Writers in every tradition have described the ennobling influence of faith in Mary's dignity on the life and literature of Western thought. What mainly distinguishes an advanced civilization is its reverence for womanhood. By this norm, the honor paid to Mary as the ideal of her sex has done more to elevate the status of women than any other postulate of the Christian religion.

Devotion, however, is not yet doctrine, and Mary's role as the highest symbol of womanhood is significant but, from the Catholic standpoint, valuable only if firmly rooted in Christian revelation.

It was at this juncture of history that a series of Marian doctrines was presented to the Church's faithful to assure them that what they had been practicing was divinely authorized and that their piety was founded on the principles of faith.

As prolific as these 110 years were, they were not as prolific as what has happened from the Second Vatican Council until now, for there has been an explosion of official papal teaching on Mary from the Second Vatican Council to the present moment, including this conciliar section on Mary, two papal encyclicals on Mary, a 70-part catechesis on Mary, plus innumerable other papal teachings. The entire exposition on Mary in Section 8 of *Lumen Gentium* shows that a marvelous course was taken between an over-exaggeration and an under-exaggeration of Marian dogma. In fact, the Council explicitly taught, "This synod earnestly exhorts theologians and preachers of the Divine Word that in treating of the unique dignity of the mother of God, they carefully and equally avoid the falsity of exaggeration on the one hand and the excess of narrow-mindedness on the other. Let them rightly explain the offices and privileges of the Blessed Virgin which are always related to Christ, the source of all truth, sanctity and piety."

## COUNCIL'S TEACHING ON MARY IS RICH AND POSITIVE

*The treatment of Mary by the Fathers of the Second Vatican Council was the subject of the Holy Father's weekly address at the General Audience of Wednesday, 13 December, 1995. The entire exposition in the eighth chapter of the Dogmatic Constitution on the Church clearly shows that terminological precautions did not prevent a very rich and positive presentation of basic doctrine, an expression of faith and love for her whom the Church acknowledges as Mother and Model", the Pope said. Here is a translation of his catechesis, which was the ninth in the series on the Blessed Virgin and was given in Italian.*

1. Today I would like to reflect on the particular presence of the Mother of the Church at what was certainly the most important ecclesial event of our century: the Second Vatican Ecumenical Council, opened by Pope John XXIII on the morning of 11 October 1962 and closed by Pope Paul VI on 8 December 1965.

An extraordinary Marian tone actually marked the Council from its indiction. In the Apostolic letter Celebrandi Concihi Oecumenici, my venerable predecessor, the Servant of God John XXIII had already recommended recourse to the powerful intercession of Mary, "Mother of grace and heavenly patroness of the Council" (11 April 1961, *AAS* 53 [1961] 242).

## Treatment Of Mary Placed In Constitution On The Church

Subsequently, in 1962, on the feast of the Purification of Mary, Pope John set the opening of the Council for 11 October, explaining that he had chosen this date in memory of the great Council of Ephesus, which precisely on that date had proclaimed Mary "Theotokos", Mother of God (Motu, proprio Concilium; *AAS* 54 [1962] 67-68). Later, in his opening address, the Pope entrusted the Council itself to the "Help of Christians, Help of Bishops", imploring her motherly assistance for the successful outcome of the Council's work (*AAS* 54 [1962] 795).

The Council Fathers also turned their thoughts expressly to Mary in their message to the world at the opening of the Council's sessions, saying: "We successors of the Apostles, joined together in prayer with Mary, the Mother of Jesus, form one apostolic body" (Acta Synodalia, I, I, 254), thus linking themselves, in communion with Mary, to the early Church awaiting the Holy Spirit (cf. Acts 1:14).

2. At the second session of the Council it was proposed that the treatment of the Blessed Virgin Mary be put into the Constitution on the Church. This initiative, although expressly recommended by the Theological Commission, prompted a variety of opinions.

Some, who considered this proposal inadequate for emphasizing the very special mission of Jesus' Mother in the Church, maintained that only a separate document could express Mary's dignity, pre-eminence, exceptional holiness and unique role in the Redemption accomplished by the Son. Furthermore, regarding Mary as above the Church in a certain way, they were afraid that the decision to put the Marian teaching in the treatment of the Church would not sufficiently emphasize Mary's privileges and would reduce her role to the level of other members of the Church (Acta Synodalia, II, III, 338-342).

Others, however, spoke in favor of the Theological Commission's proposal to put the doctrinal treatment of Mary and the Church in a single document. According to them, these realities could not be separated at a Council which, in airing to rediscover the identity and mission of the People of God, had to show its close connection with her who is the type and exemplar of the Church in her virginity and motherhood. Indeed, as an eminent member of the ecclesial community, the Blessed Virgin has a special place in the Church's doctrine. Furthermore, by stressing the link between Mary and the Church, Christians of the Reformation could better understand the Marian teaching presented by the Council (Acta Synodalia, II, III, 343-345).

The Council Fathers, moved by the same love for Mary, thus tended, in their expression of different doctrinal positions, to favor various aspects of her person. Some reflected on Mary primarily in her relationship to Christ, others considered her more as a member of the Church.

3. After an intense doctrinal discussion attentive to the dignity of the Mother of God and to her particular presence in the Church's life, it was decided that the treatment of Mary would be situated in the Council's document on the Church (cf. Acta Synodalia, II, III, 627).

The new schema on the Blessed Virgin, drafted so as to be included in the Dogmatic Constitution on the Church, shows real doctrinal progress. The stress placed on Mary's faith and a more systematic concern to base Marian doctrine on Scripture are significant and useful elements for enriching the piety and esteem of the Christian people for the Blessed Mother of God.

Moreover, with the passing of time the danger of reductionism, feared by some Fathers, proved to be unfounded: Mary's mission and privileges were amply reaffirmed; her cooperation in the divine plan of salvation was highlighted; the harmony of this cooperation with Christ's unique mediation appeared more evident. For the first time, the conciliar Magisterium offered the Church a doctrinal exposition of Mary's role in Christ's redemptive work and in the life of the Church.

Thus, we must consider the Council Fathers' choice, which proved very fruitful for later doctrinal work, to have been a truly providential decision.

4. During the Council sessions, many Fathers wished further to enrich Marian doctrine with other statements of Mary's role in the work of salvation The particular context in which Vatican II's Mariological debate took place did not allow these wishes, although substantial and widespread, to be accepted, but the Council's entire discussion of Mary remains vigorous and balanced, and the topics themselves, though not fully defined, received significant attention in the overall treatment.

## A Balanced Presentation Of Marian Doctrine

Thus, the hesitation of some Fathers regarding the title of Mediatrix did not prevent the Council from using this title once, and from stating in other terms Mary's mediating role from her consent to the Angel's message to her motherhood in the order of grace (cf. *Lumen Gentium*, n. 62). Furthermore, the Council asserts her cooperation "in a wholly singular way" in the work of restoring supernatural life to souls (ibid., n. 61). Lastly, even if it avoided using the title "Mother of the Church", the text of *Lumen Gentium* clearly underscores the Church's veneration for Mary as a most loving Mother.

The entire exposition in the eighth chapter of the Dogmatic Constitution on the Church clearly shows that terminological precautions did not prevent a very rich and positive presentation of basic doctrine, an expression of faith and love for her whom the Church acknowledges as Mother and Model.

On the other hand, the Fathers' differing points of view, as they emerged during the conciliar debate, turned out to be providential, because, on the basis of their harmonious relationship, they have afforded the faith and devotion of the Christian people a more complete and balanced presentation of the marvelous identity of the Lord's Mother and of her exceptional role in the work of Redemption.

# LUMEN GENTIUM
## Dogmatic Constitution on the Church, Vatican Council II

## Chapter VIII

## The Role Of The Blessed Virgin Mary, Mother Of God, In The Mystery Of Christ And The Church[257]

# I. Preface

52. Wishing in his supreme goodness and wisdom to effect the redemption of the world, "when the fullness of time came, God sent his Son, born of a woman, ..that we might receive the adoption of sons" (Gal 4:4-5). "He for us men, and for our salvation, came down from heaven, and was incarnate by the Holy Spirit from the Virgin Mary."[258] This divine mystery of salvation is revealed to us and continued in the Church, which the Lord established as his body. Joined to Christ the Head and in the unity of fellowship with all his saints, the faithful must in the first place reverence the memory "of the glorious ever Virgin Mary, Mother of our God and Lord Jesus Christ".[259]

53. The Virgin Mary, who at the message of the angel received the Word of God in her heart and in her body and gave Life to the world, is acknowledged and honored as being truly the Mother of God and Mother of the Redeemer. Redeemed by reason

of the merits of her Son and united to him by a close and indissoluble tie, she is endowed with the high office and dignity of being the Mother of the Son of God,[260] by which account she is also the beloved daughter of the Father and the temple of the Holy Spirit. Because of this gift of sublime grace she far surpasses all creatures, both in heaven and on earth. At the same time, however, because she belongs to the offspring of Adam she is one with all those who are to be saved. She is "the mother of the members of Christ... having cooperated by charity that faithful might be born in the Church, who are members of that Head."[261] Wherefore she is hailed as a pre-eminent and singular member of the Church, and as its type and excellent exemplar in faith and charity. The Catholic Church, taught by the Holy Spirit, honors her with filial affection and piety as a most beloved mother.[262]

54. Wherefore this Holy Synod, in expounding the doctrine on the Church, in which the divine Redeemer works salvation, intends to describe with diligence both the role of the Blessed Virgin in the mystery of the Incarnate Word and the Mystical Body, and the duties of redeemed mankind toward the Mother of God, who is mother of Christ and mother of men, particularly of the faithful.[263] It does not, however, have it in mind to give a complete doctrine on Mary, nor does it wish to decide those questions which the work of theologians has not yet fully clarified. Those opinions therefore may be lawfully retained which are propounded in Catholic schools concerning her, who occupies a place in the Church which is the highest after Christ and yet very close to us.[264]

# II. The Role Of The Blessed Mother In The Economy Of Salvation

55. The Sacred Scriptures of both the Old and the New Testament, as well as ancient Tradition show the role of the Mother of the Savior in the economy of salvation in an ever clearer light and draw attention to it.[265] The books of the Old Testament describe the history of salvation, by which the coming of Christ into the world was slowly prepared. These earliest documents, as they are

read in the Church and are understood in the light of a further and full revelation, bring the figure of the woman, Mother of the Redeemer, into a gradually clearer light. When it is looked at in this way, she is already prophetically foreshadowed in the promise of victory over the serpent which was given to our first parents after their fall into sin (cf. Gn 3:15). Likewise she is the Virgin who shall conceive and bear a Son, whose name will be called Emmanuel (cf. Is 7:14; Mi 5:23; Mt 1:22-23). She stands out among the poor and humble of the Lord, who confidently hope for and receive salvation from him. With her the exalted Daughter of Zion, and after a long expectation of the promise, the times are fulfilled and the new Economy established, when the Son of God took a human nature from her, that he might in the mysteries of his flesh free man from sin.

56. The Father of mercies willed that the incarnation should be preceded by the acceptance of her who was predestined to be the mother of his Son, so that just as a woman contributed to death, so also a woman should contribute to life. That is true in outstanding fashion of the mother of Jesus, who gave to the world him who is Life itself and who renews all things, and who was enriched by God with the gifts which befit such a role. It is no wonder therefore that the usage prevailed among the Fathers whereby they called the Mother of God entirely holy and free from all stain of sin, as though fashioned by the Holy Spirit and formed as a new creature.[266] Adorned from the first instant of her conception with the radiance of an entirely unique holiness, the Virgin of Nazareth is greeted, on God's command, by an angel messenger as "full of grace", (cf. Lk 1:28) and to the heavenly messenger she replies: "Behold the handmaid of the Lord, be it done unto me according to thy word" (Lk 1:38). Thus Mary, a daughter of Adam, consenting to the divine Word, became the mother of Jesus, the one and only Mediator. Embracing God's salvific will with a full heart and impeded by no sin, she devoted herself totally as a handmaid of the Lord to the person and work of her Son, under him and with him, by the grace of almighty God, serving the mystery of redemption. Rightly therefore the holy Fathers see her as used by God not merely in a passive way, but as freely cooperating in the work of human salvation through faith

and obedience. For, as St. Irenaeus says, she "being obedient, became the cause of salvation for herself and for the whole human race."[267] Hence not a few of the early Fathers gladly assert in their preaching, "The knot of Eve's disobedience was untied by Mary's obedience; what the virgin Eve bound through her unbelief, the Virgin Mary loosened by her faith."[268] Comparing Mary with Eve, they call her "the Mother of the living,"[269] and still more often they say: "death through Eve, life through Mary."[270]

57. This union of the Mother with the Son in the work of salvation is made manifest from the time of Christ's virginal conception up to his death it is shown first of all when Mary, arising in haste to go to visit Elizabeth, is greeted by her as blessed because of her belief in the promise of salvation and the precursor leaped with joy in the womb of his mother (cf. Lk 1:41-45). This union is manifest also at the birth of Our Lord, who did not diminish his mother's virginal integrity but sanctified it,[271] when the Mother of God joyfully showed her firstborn Son to the shepherds and Magi. When she presented him to the Lord in the temple, making the offering of the poor, she heard Simeon foretelling at the same time that her Son would be a sign of contradiction and that a sword would pierce the mother's soul, that out of many hearts thoughts might be revealed (cf. Lk 2:34-35). When the Child Jesus was lost and they had sought him sorrowing, his parents found him in the temple, taken up with the things that were his Father's business; and they did not understand the word of their Son. His Mother indeed kept these things to be pondered over in her heart (cf. Lk 2:41-51).

58. In the public life of Jesus, Mary makes significant appearances. This is so even at the very beginning, when at the marriage feast of Cana, moved with pity, she brought about by her intercession the beginning of miracles of Jesus the Messiah (cf. Jn 2:1-11). In the course of her Son's preaching she received the words whereby in extolling a kingdom beyond the calculations and bonds of flesh and blood, he declared blessed (cf. Mk 3:35; Lk 11:27-28) those who heard and kept the word of God, as she was faithfully doing (cf. Lk 2:19, 51). After this manner the Blessed Virgin advanced in her pilgrimage of faith, and faithfully persevered in her union with her Son unto the cross, where she stood, in

keeping with the divine plan, (cf. Jn 19:25) grieving exceedingly with her only begotten Son, uniting herself with a maternal heart with his sacrifice, and lovingly consenting to the immolation of this Victim which she herself had brought forth. Finally, she was given by the same Christ Jesus dying on the cross as a mother to his disciple with these words: "Woman, behold thy Son" (Jn 19:26-27).[272]

59. But since it has pleased God not to manifest solemnly the mystery of the salvation of the human race before he would pour forth the Spirit promised by Christ, we see the apostles before the day of Pentecost "persevering with one mind in prayer with the women and Mary the Mother of Jesus, and with his brethren", (Acts 1:14) and Mary by her prayers imploring the gift of the Spirit, who had already overshadowed her in the Annunciation. Finally, the Immaculate Virgin, preserved free from all guilt of original sin,[273] on the completion of her earthly sojourn, was taken up body and soul into heavenly glory,[274] and exalted by the Lord as Queen of the universe, that she might be the more fully conformed to her Son, the Lord of lords (cf. Rv 19:16) and the conqueror of sin and death.[275]

# III. On The Blessed Virgin And The Church

60. There is but one Mediator as we know from the words of the apostle, "for there is one God and one mediator of God and men, the man Christ Jesus, who gave himself a redemption for all" (1 Tm 2:5-6).[276] The maternal duty of Mary toward men in no wise obscures or diminishes this unique mediation of Christ, but rather shows his power. For all the salvific influence of the Blessed Virgin on men originates, not from some inner necessity, but from the divine pleasure. It flows forth from the superabundance of the merits of Christ, rests on his mediation, depends entirely on it and draws all its power from it. In no way does it impede, but rather does it foster the immediate union of the faithful with Christ.

61. Predestined from eternity by that decree of divine providence which determined the incarnation of the Word to be

the Mother of God, the Blessed Virgin was in this earth the virgin Mother of the Redeemer, and above all others and in a singular way the generous associate and humble handmaid of the Lord. She conceived, brought forth and nourished Christ. She presented him to the Father in the temple, and was united with him by compassion as he died on the Cross. In this singular way she cooperated by her obedience, faith, hope and burning charity in the work of the Savior in giving back supernatural life to souls. Wherefore she is our mother in the order of grace.

62. This maternity of Mary in the order of grace began with the consent which she gave in faith at the Annunciation and which she sustained without wavering beneath the cross, and lasts until The eternal fulfillment of all the elect. Taken up to heaven she did not lay aside this salvific duty, but by her constant intercession continued to bring us the gifts of eternal salvation.[277] By her maternal charity, she cares for the brethren of her Son, who still journey on earth surrounded by dangers and cultics, until they are led into the happiness of their true home. Therefore the Blessed Virgin is invoked by the Church under the titles of Advocate, Auxiliatrix, Adjutrix, and Mediatrix.[278] This, however, is to be so understood[279] that it neither takes away from nor adds anything to the dignity and efficaciousness of Christ the one Mediator.[280]

For no creature could ever be counted as equal with the Incarnate Word and Redeemer. Just as the priesthood of Christ is shared in various ways both by the ministers and by the faithful, and as the one goodness of God is really communicated in different ways to his creatures, so also the unique mediation of the Redeemer does not exclude but rather gives rise to a manifold cooperation which is but a sharing in this one source.

The Church does not hesitate to profess this subordinate role of Mary. It knows it through unfailing experience of it and commends it to the hearts of the faithful, so that encouraged by this maternal help they may the more intimately adhere to the Mediator and Redeemer.

63. By reason of the gift and role of divine maternity, by which she is united with her Son, the Redeemer, and with his singular graces and functions, the Blessed Virgin is also intimately

united with the Church. As St. Ambrose taught, the Mother of God is a type of the Church in the order of faith,[281] charity and perfect union with Christ.[282] For in the mystery of the Church, which is itself rightly called mother and virgin, the Blessed Virgin stands out in eminent and singular fashion as exemplar both of virgin and mother.[283] By her belief and obedience, not knowing man but overshadowed by the Holy Spirit, as the new Eve she brought forth on earth the very Son of the Father, showing an undefiled faith, not in the word of the ancient serpent, but in that of God's messenger. The Son whom she brought forth is he whom God placed as the first-born among many brethren, (cf. Rom 8:29) namely the faithful, in whose birth and education she cooperates with a maternal love.

64. The Church indeed, contemplating her hidden sanctity, imitating her charity and faithfully fulfilling the Father's will, by receiving the word of God in faith becomes herself a mother. By her preaching she brings forth to a new and immortal life the sons who are born to her in baptism, conceived of the Holy Spirit and born of God. She herself is a virgin, who keeps the faith given to her by her Spouse whole and entire. Imitating the mother of her Lord, and by the power of the Holy Spirit, she keeps with virginal purity an entire faith, a firm hope and a sincere charity.[284]

65. But while in the most holy Virgin the Church has already reached that perfection whereby she is without spot or wrinkle, the followers of Christ still strive to increase in holiness by conquering sin (cf. Eph 5:27). And so they turn their eyes to Mary who shines forth to the whole community of the elect as the model of virtues. Piously meditating on her and contemplating her in the light of the Word made man, the Church with reverence enters more intimately into the great mystery of the Incarnation and becomes more and more like her Spouse. For Mary, who since her entry into salvation history unites in herself and re-echoes the greatest teachings of the faith as she is proclaimed and venerated, calls the faithful to her Son and his sacrifice and to the love of the Father. Seeking after the glory of Christ, the Church becomes more like her exalted Type, and continually progresses in faith, hope and charity, seeking and doing the will of God in all things. Hence

the Church, in her apostolic work also, justly looks to her, who, conceived of the Holy Spirit, brought forth Christ, who was born of the Virgin that through the Church he may be born and may increase in the hearts of the faithful also. The Virgin in her own life lived an example of that maternal love, by which it behooves that all should be animated who cooperate in the apostolic mission of the Church for the regeneration of men.

## IV. The Cult Of The Blessed Virgin In The Church

66. Placed by the grace of God, as God's Mother, next to her Son, and exalted above all angels and men, Mary intervened in the mysteries of Christ and is justly honored by a special cult in the Church.[285] Clearly from earliest times the Blessed Virgin is honored under the title of Mother of God, under whose protection the faithful took refuge in all their dangers and necessities.[286] Hence after the Synod of Ephesus the cult of the people of God toward Mary wonderfully increased in veneration and love, in invocation and imitation, according to her own prophetic words: "All generations shall call me blessed, because he that is mighty hath done great things to me" (Lk 1:48). This cult, as it always existed, although it is altogether singular, differs essentially from the cult of adoration which is offered to the Incarnate Word, as well to the Father and the Holy Spirit, and it is most favorable to it. The various forms of piety toward the Mother of God, which the Church within the limits of sound and orthodox doctrine, according to the conditions of time and place, and the nature and ingenuity of the faithful has approved, bring it about that while the Mother is honored, the Son, through whom all things have their being (cf. Col 1:15-16) and in whom it has pleased the Father that all fullness should dwell, (Col 1:19) is rightly known, loved and glorified and that all his commands are observed.

67. This most Holy Synod deliberately teaches this Catholic doctrine and at the same time admonishes all the sons of the Church that the cult, especially the liturgical cult, of the Blessed Virgin, be generously fostered, and the practices and exercises of piety, recommended by the magisterium of the Church toward

her in the course of centuries be made of great moment, and those decrees, which have been given in the early days regarding the cult of images of Christ, the Blessed Virgin and the saints, be religiously observed.[287] But it exhorts theologians and preachers of the divine word to abstain zealously both from all gross exaggerations as well as from petty narrow-mindedness in considering the singular dignity of the Mother of God.[288] Following the study of Sacred Scripture, the Holy Fathers, the doctors and liturgy of the Church, and under the guidance of the Church's magisterium, let them rightly illustrate the duties and privileges of the Blessed Virgin which always look to Christ, the source of all truth, sanctity and piety. Let them assiduously keep away from whatever, either by word or deed, could lead separated brethren or any other into error regarding the true doctrine of the Church. Let the faithful remember moreover that true devotion consists neither in sterile or transitory affection, nor in a certain vain credulity, but proceeds from true faith, by which we are led to know the excellence of the Mother of God, and we are moved to a filial love toward our mother and to the imitation of her virtues.

## V. Mary The Sign Of Created Hope And Solace To The Wandering People Of God

68. In the interim just as the Mother of Jesus, glorified in body and soul in heaven, is the image and beginning of the Church as it is to be perfected is the world to come, so too does she shine forth on earth, until the day of the Lord shall come, (cf. 2 Pt 3:10) as a sign of sure hope and solace to the people of God during its sojourn on earth.

69. It gives great joy and comfort to this holy and general Synod that even among the separated brethren there are some who give due honor to the Mother of our Lord and Savior, especially among the Orientals, who with devout mind and fervent impulse give honor to the Mother of God, ever virgin.[289] The entire body of the faithful pours forth instant supplications to the Mother of God and Mother of men that she, who aided the beginnings of the Church by her prayers, may now, exalted as she is above all

the angels and saints, intercede before her Son in the fellowship of all the saints, until all families of people, whether they are honored with the title of Christian or whether they still do not know the Savior, may be happily gathered together in peace and harmony into one people of God, for the glory of the Most Holy and Undivided Trinity.[290]

Each and all these items which are set forth in this dogmatic Constitution have met with the approval of the Council Fathers. And We by the apostolic power given us by Christ together with the Venerable Fathers in the Holy Spirit, approve, decree and establish it and command that what has thus been decided in the Council be promulgated for the glory of God.

Given in Rome at St. Peter's on November 21, 1964.

\* \* \* \* \* \* \* \* \* \*

## Endnotes

[257] This eighth chapter was appended to the Constitution on the Church as a result of a vote in the Council on Oct. 29, 1963, in which the Fathers, by a small majority, decided not to issue a separate document on the Blessed Virgin, as had originally been planned. The present chapter, while it treats of Mary's relationship to the Church, speaks also of her relation to Christ, as indicated in the title of the chapter. The entire text represents a skillful and prudent compromise between two tendencies in modern Catholic theology, one of which would emphasize Mary's unique connection with Christ the Redeemer; the other, her close connection with the Church and all the redeemed. This is the only chapter with official headings; and the headings clearly indicate the structure.

[258] *The Creed in the Roman Mass: the Constantinopolitan creed: Mansi, 3, 566. Cf. Council of Ephesus: Mansi, 4 1130 ( as well as Mansi, 2, 665, and 4, 1071); the Council of Chalcedon: Mansi, 7, III-6; and the Council of Constantinople II: Mansi, 9, 375-96.*

[259] *Canon of the Roman Mass.*

[260] The foundation of all Mary's other privileges is her dignity as Mother of the Son of God.

²⁶¹     *St. Augustine, "De s. virginitate," 6: PL 40, 399.*

²⁶²     The Council comes very close here to calling Mary "Mother of the Church." This title, while not bestowed by the Council itself, was actually conferred by Paul VI in his closing allocution at the end of the third session, Nov. 21, 1964.

²⁶³     This paragraph succinctly states the purposes of the whole chapter.

²⁶⁴     *Cf. Paul VI, allocution, the Council, Dec. 4, 1963: AAS 56 (1964), p. 37.*

²⁶⁵     The first sentence gives the topic of the next five articles (55-59), which summarize, in language generally close to that of the Bible itself, Mary's role in the economy of salvation. Throughout this section her proximity to Christ is strongly emphasized.

²⁶⁶     *Cf. St. Germanus of Constantinople, "Hom. in Annunt. Deiparae": PG 98, 328 A and his "Hom. in Dorm.",, 2: PG 98, 357; St. Anastasius of Antioch, "Serm. 2 de Annunt." 2 PG 89, 1377 AB and his "Serm 3 de Annunt.," 2 PG 89, 1388 C; St. Andrew of Crete, "Can. in B.V. Nat.," 4: PG 97, 1321 B and his "In B.V. Nat.," I: PG 97, 812 A, as well as his "Hom. in dorm.," I: PG 97, 1068 C: and St. Sophronius, "Or. 2 in Annunt.," 18: PG 87 (3), 3237 BD.*

²⁶⁷     *St. Irenaeus, "Adv. haer.," III, 22,4: PG 7, 959, A (Harvey, 2, 123).*

²⁶⁸     *St. Irenaeus, as cited in the preceding footnote (Harvey, 2, 123).*

²⁶⁹     *St. Epiphanius, "Haer.," 78, 18: PG 42, 728 CD-729 AB.*

²⁷⁰     *St. Jerome, "Epist.," 22, 21: PL 22, 408. Cf. St. Augustine, "Serm.," 51, 2 ,3: PL 38, 335 and his "Serm." 232, 2: PL 38, 1108; St. Cyril of Jerusalem, "Catech.," 12, 15: PG 33, 741 AB; St. John Chrysostom, "In Ps.," 44, 6: PG 55, 193; and St. John of Damascus, "Hom. 2 in dorm. B.M.V.," 3: PG 96, 728.*

²⁷¹     *Cf. Lateran Council of the year 649, can. 3: Mansi, 10, 1151; St. Leo the Great, "Epist. ad Flav.": PL 54 759; Council of Chalcedon: Mansi, 7, 462; and St. Ambrose, "De inst. virg.": PL 16, 320.*

²⁷²     *Cf. Pius XII, encyclical "Mystici Corporis, June 29, 1943: AAS 35 (1943), pp. 247-8.*

²⁷³     *Cf. Pius IX, bull "ineffabilis," Dec. 8, 1854: "Acta Pii IX," 1,1, p. 616; Denz. 1641 (2803).*

274      *Cf. Pius XII, Apostolic constitution "Munificentissimus," Nov. 1, 1950: AAS 42 (1950), p. 770 (Denz. 2333 [3903]). Cf. St. John of Damascus, "Enc. in dorm. Dei genitricis," Hom. 1 and 3: PG 96, 721-61 especially 728 B; St. Germanus of Constantinople, "In S. Dei gen. dorm.," Serm. I: PG 98 (6), 340-8 as well as his Serm. 3: PG 98 (6), 361; and St. Modestus of Jerusalem, "In dorm SS. Deiparae": PG 86 (2), 3277-3312.*

275      *Cf. Pius XII, encyclical "Ad Caeli Reginam," Oct. 11, 1954: AAS 46 (1954), pp. 633-6 (Denz. 3913 ff.). Cf. St. Andrew of Crete, "Hom. 3 in dorm. SS. Deiparae": PG 97, 1089-1109; and St. John of Damascus, "De fide orth.," IV, 14: PG 94, 1153-61.*

276      The following six articles (60-65) stress the second facet of Mary's role, her solidarity with the redeemed.

277      *Cf. Kleutgen, the revised text of "De mysterio Verbi incarnati," c. IV: Mansi, 53, 290. Cf. St. Andrew of Crete, "In nat. Mariae," Sermo 4: PG 97, 865 A; St. Germanus of Constantinople, "In annunt Deiparae": PG 98, 321 BC and his "In dorm Deiparae," III: PG 98, 361 D; and St. John of Damascus, "In dorm B.V. Mariae," Hom. I, 9: PG 96, 712 BC-712A.*

278      *Cf. Leo XIII, encyclical "Adiutricem populi," Sept. 5, 1895: Acta Sanctae Sedis 15 (1895-6), p. 303; St. Pius X, encyclical "Ad diem illum," Feb. 2, 1904: "Pii X Pontificis Maximi Acta," I, p. 154 (Denz. 1978 a [3370]), Pius XI, encyclical "Miserentissimus," May 8, 1928: AAS 20 (1928), p. 178; Pius XII, radio message, May 13, 1946: AAS 38 (1946), p. 266.*

279      The Council applies to the Blessed Virgin the title of Mediatrix, but carefully explains this so as to remove any impression that it could detract from the uniqueness an sufficiency of Christ's position as Mediator (cf. 1 Tim. 2:5), already referred to in Chap. I (Art 8).

280      *St. Ambrose, "Epist.," 63: PL 15, 1218.*

281      The theme of Mary as type of the Church, developed in this and the following two articles, is central to the chapter and partly accounts for the decision of the Council to treat Mariology in the Constitution on the Church.

282      *St. Ambrose, "Expos. Lc.," II, 7: PL 15, 1555.*

283      *Cf. pseudo-Peter Damian, "Serm.," 63: PL 144, 861 AB; Godfrey of St. Victor, "In nat. B.M.," Ms. Paris, Mazarine, 1002, fol 109r; Gerhoh of Reichersberg, "De gloria et honore Filii hominis," 10: PL 194, 1105 AB.*

284      *St. Ambrose as cited in footnote 282, as well as his "Expos. Lc.," X,*

*24-5: PL 15, 1810; St. Augustine, "In Io.," tr. 13, 12: PL 35, 1499, and see also his "serm.," 191, 2, 3: PL 38, 1010 as well as other of his texts. Cf. Venerable Bede, "In Lc. expos.," I, c. 2: PL 92, 330; and Isaac of Stella, "Serm.," 51: PL 194, 1863 A.*

[285]      The last major division of the chapter deals with the way in which the Church venerates Mary. The Council commends a generous devotion to her which is at the same time Christ-centered and free from all exaggeration. Here as elsewhere, the Council in its choice of language and emphasis tries to avoid anything which might unnecessarily offend the sensibilities of the separated brethren.

[286]      *"We fly to thy patronage."*

[287]      *Council of Nicaea II in the year 787: Mansi, 13, 378-9 (Denz. 302 [600-1]); Council of Trent, Session 25: Mansi, 33, 171-2.*

[288]      *Cf. Pius XII, radio message, Oct. 24, 1954: AAS 46 (1954), p. 679; and the same Pontiff's encyclical "Ad Caeli Reginam," Oct. 11, 1954: AAS 46 (1954), p. 637.*

[289]      *Cf. Pius XI, encyclical "Ecclesiam Dei," Nov. 12, 1923: AAS 15 (1923), p. 581; and Pius XII, encyclical, "Fulgens Corona," Sept. 8, 1953: AAS 45 (1953), pp. 590-1.*

[290]      This last sentence, returning to the theme of the People of God, eloquently sums up the goal for which the Church unceasingly prays and labors

# -Chapter 4-

# MARIALIS CULTUS

The encyclical Marialis Cultus of Pope Paul VI, issued 2 February, 1974, is in reality a liturgical document and not a dogmatic one. Its primary aim is the right ordering of liturgical devotions to the Mother of God. Pope Paul VI stated that he has constantly striven not only to enhance devotion to Mary, the Mother of God, but also to integrate this devotion into the whole sphere of Christian liturgy. The purpose is precisely to restore and enhance Marian elements in the liturgy in order to make a more fruitful participation of the laity in these devotions. Pope Paul VI's aim was actually a wider one, namely the improvement of all liturgical worship and function, as the Constitution on the Sacred Liturgy had called for. The liturgy must always be the summit toward which the activity of the Church is directed. At the same time, it is the fountain from which all her powers flow. Mary's role in the liturgy must always be as mother of the Church to bring all her children to her Son Jesus and through him to the Father. Her liturgical role and her maternal role form one and the same function: to make sure that Christ is formed in us so that we too can be sons and daughters of the Father, who worship him in spirit and in truth. Mary also has an intercessory role as mother of the whole Church and mother of all. The development desirable by Pope Paul VI of devotion to the Blessed Virgin Mary is an indication of the Church's genuine piety. This devotion must fit into the only worship that is rightly called Christian because it takes its origin and effectiveness from Christ, finds its complete expression in Christ, and leads through Christ in the Spirit to the Father. All true Mariology must be Christ-centered, for Mary is always pointing towards Christ and saying to all her children, "Do whatever he tells you."

# MARIALIS CULTUS
**February 2, 1974**

## For the Right Ordering and Development of Devotion to the Blessed Virgin Mary

**Solemnly Promulgated by His Holiness, Pope Paul VI**

**To All Bishops in Peace and Communion with the Apostolic See**

# Introduction

## Division of the Treatise Occasion and Purpose of the Document

### Venerable Brothers: Health and the Apostolic Blessing

From the moment when we were called to the See of Peter, we have constantly striven to enhance devotion to the Blessed Virgin Mary, not only with the intention of interpreting the sentiments of the Church and our own personal inclination but also because, as is well known, this devotion forms a very noble part of the whole sphere of that sacred worship in which there intermingle the highest expressions of wisdom and of religion[1] and which is therefore the primary task of the People of God.

Precisely with a view to this task, we have always favored and encouraged the great work of liturgical reform promoted by the Second Vatican Ecumenical Council, and it has certainly come about not without a particular design of divine Providence that the first conciliar document which together with the venerable Fathers we approved and signed in Spiritu Sancto was the Constitution Sacrosanctum Concilium. The purpose of this document was precisely to restore and enhance the liturgy and to make more fruitful the participation of the faithful in the sacred mysteries.[2] From that time onwards, many acts of our pontificate have been directed towards the improvement of divine worship, as is demonstrated by the fact that we have promulgated in these recent years numerous books of the Roman Rite, restored according to the principles and norms of the same Council. For this we profoundly thank the Lord, the giver of all good things, and we are grateful to the episcopal conferences and individual bishops who in various ways have collaborated with us in the preparation of these books.

We contemplate with joy and gratitude the work so far accomplished and the first positive results of the liturgical renewal, destined as they are to increase as this renewal comes to be understood in its basic purposes and correctly applied. At the same time we do not cease with vigilant solicitude to concern ourselves with whatever can give orderly fulfillment to the renewal of the worship with which the Church in spirit and truth (cf. Jn 4:24) adores the Father and the Son and the Holy Spirit, "venerates with special love Mary the most holy Mother of God"[3] and honors with religious devotion the memory of the martyrs and the other saints.

The development, desired by us, of devotion to the Blessed Virgin Mary is an indication of the Church's genuine piety. This devotion fits, as we have indicated above, into the only worship that is rightly called "Christian," because it takes its origin and effectiveness from Christ, finds its complete expression in Christ, and leads through Christ in the Spirit to the Father. In the sphere of worship this devotion necessarily reflects God's redemptive plan, in which a special form of veneration is appropriate to the singular place which Mary occupies in that plan.[4] Indeed every authentic development of Christian worship is necessarily followed by a fitting increase of veneration for the Mother of the Lord. Moreover, the history of piety shows how "the various forms of devotion towards the Mother of God that the Church has approved within the limits of wholesome and orthodox doctrine"[5] have developed in harmonious subordination to the worship of Christ, and have gravitated towards this worship as to their natural and necessary point of reference. The same is happening in our own time. The Church's reflection today on the mystery of Christ and on her own nature has led her to find at the root of the former and is a culmination of the latter the same figure of a woman: the Virgin Mary, the Mother of Christ and the Mother of the Church. And the increased knowledge of Mary's mission has become joyful veneration of her and adoring respect for the wise plan of God, who has placed within his family (the Church), as in every home, the figure of a Woman, who in a hidden manner and in a spirit of service watches over that family "and carefully looks after it until the glorious day of the Lord."[6]

In our time, the changes that have occurred in social behavior, people's sensibilities, manners of expression in art and letters and in the forms of social communication have also influenced the manifestations of religious sentiment. Certain practices of piety that not long ago seemed suitable for expressing the religious sentiment of individuals and of Christian communities seem today inadequate or unsuitable because they are linked with social and cultural patterns of the past. On the other hand in many places people are seeking new ways of expressing the unchangeable relationship of creatures with their Creator, of children with their Father. In some people this may cause temporary confusion. But anyone who, with trust in God reflects upon these phenomena discovers that many tendencies of modern piety (for example, the interiorization of religious sentiment) are meant to play their part in the development of Christian piety in general and devotion to the Blessed Virgin in particular. Thus our own time, faithfully attentive to tradition and to the progress of theology and the sciences, will make its contribution of praise to her whom, according to her own prophetical words, all generations will call blessed (cf. Lk 1:48).

We therefore judge it in keeping with our apostolic service, venerable Brothers, to deal, in a sort of dialogue, with a number of themes connected with the place that the Blessed Virgin occupies in the Church's worship. These themes have already been partly touched upon by the Second Vatican Council[7] and also by ourselves,[8] but it is useful to return to them in order to remove doubts and, especially, to help the development of that devotion to the Blessed Virgin which in the Church is motivated by the Word of God and practiced in the Spirit of Christ.

We therefore wish to dwell upon a number of questions

concerning the relationship between the sacred liturgy and devotion to the Blessed Virgin (I), to offer considerations and directives suitable for favoring the development of that devotion (II) and finally to put forward a number of reflections intended to encourage the restoration, in a dynamic and more informed manner, of the recitation of the Rosary, the practice of which was so strongly recommended by our predecessors and is so widely diffused among the Christian people (III).

# Part One

## Devotion To The Blessed Virgin Mary In The Liturgy

1. As we prepare to discuss the place which the Blessed Virgin Mary occupies in Christian worship, we must first turn our attention to the sacred liturgy. In addition to its rich doctrinal content, the liturgy has an incomparable pastoral effectiveness and a recognized exemplary conduct for the other forms of worship. We would have liked to take into consideration the various liturgies of the East and the West, but for the purpose of this document we shall dwell almost exclusively on the books of the Roman Rite. In fact, in accordance with the practical norms issued by the Second Vatican Council,[9] it is this Rite alone which has been the object of profound renewal. This is true also in regard to expressions of veneration for Mary. This Rite therefore deserves to be carefully considered and evaluated.

# Section One

## The Blessed Virgin In The Revised Roman Liturgy

2. The reform of the Roman liturgy presupposed a careful restoration of its General Calendar. This Calendar is arranged in such a way as to give fitting prominence to the celebration on appropriate days of the work of salvation. It distributes throughout the year the whole mastery of Christ, from the Incarnation to the expectation of his return in glory,[10] and thus makes it possible in a

more organic and closely-knit fashion to include the commemoration of Christ's Mother in the annual cycle of the mysteries of her Son.

3. For example, during Advent there are many liturgical references to Mary besides the Solemnity of December 8, which is a joint celebration of the Immaculate Conception of Mary, of the basic preparation (cf. Is 11:1-10) for the coming of the Savior and of the happy beginning of the Church without spot or wrinkle.[11] Such liturgical references are found especially on the days from December 17 to 24, and more particularly on the Sunday before Christmas, which recalls the ancient prophecies concerning the Virgin Mother and the Messiah[12] and includes readings from the Gospel concerning the imminent birth of Christ and his precursor.[13]

4. In this way the faithful, living in the liturgy the spirit of Advent, by thinking about the inexpressible love with which the Virgin Mother awaited her Son,[14] are invited to take her as a model and to prepare themselves to meet the Savior who is to come. They must be "vigilant in prayer and joyful in...praise."[15] We would also remark that the Advent liturgy, by linking the awaiting of the Messiah and the awaiting of the glorious return of Christ with the admirable commemoration of his Mother, presents a happy balance in worship. This balance can be taken as a norm for preventing any tendency (as has happened at times in certain forms of popular piety) to separate devotion to the Blessed Virgin from its necessary point of reference, Christ. It also ensures that this season, as liturgy experts have noted, should be considered as a time particularly suited to devotion to the Mother of the Lord. This is an orientation that we confirm and which we hope to see accepted and followed everywhere.

5. The Christmas season is a prolonged commemoration of the divine, virginal and salvific motherhood of her whose "inviolate virginity brought the Savior into the world."[16] In fact, on the Solemnity of the Birth of Christ the Church both adores the Savior and venerates his glorious Mother. On the Epiphany, when she celebrates the universal call to salvation, the Church contemplates the Blessed Virgin, the true Seat of Wisdom and true Mother of the King, who presents to the Wise Men, for their adoration, the Redeemer of all peoples (cf. Mt 2:11). On the Feast

of the Holy Family of Jesus, Mary and Joseph (the Sunday within the octave of Christmas) the Church meditates with profound reverence upon the holy life led in the house at Nazareth by Jesus, the Son of God and Son of Man, Mary his Mother, and Joseph the just man (cf. Mt 1:19).

In the revised ordering of the Christmas period it seems to us that the attention of all should be directed towards the restored Solemnity of Mary the holy Mother of God. This celebration, placed on January 1 in conformity with the ancient indication of the liturgy of the City of Rome, is meant to commemorate the part played by Mary in this mystery of salvation. It is meant also to exalt the singular dignity which this mystery brings to the "holy Mother ... through whom we were found worthy to receive the Author of life."[17] It is likewise a fitting occasion for renewing adoration of the newborn Prince of Peace, for listening once more to the glad tidings of the angels (cf. Lk 2:14), and for imploring from God, through the Queen of Peace, the supreme gift of peace. It is for this reason that, in the happy concurrence of the Octave of Christmas and the first day of the year, we have instituted the World Day of Peace, an occasion that is gaining increasing support and already bringing forth fruits of peace in the hearts of many.

6. To the two solemnities already mentioned (the Immaculate Conception and the Divine Motherhood) should be added the ancient and venerable celebrations of March 25 and August 15.

For the Solemnity of the Incarnation of the Word, in the Roman Calendar the ancient title, the Annunciation of the Lord, has been deliberately restored, but the feast was and is a joint one of Christ and of the Blessed Virgin: of the Word, who becomes Son of Mary (Mk 6:3), and of the Virgin, who becomes Mother of God. With regard to Christ, the East and the West, in the inexhaustible riches of their liturgies, celebrate this solemnity as the commemoration of the salvific "fiat" of the Incarnate Word, who, entering the world, said: "God, here I am! I am coming to obey Your will" (cf. Heb 10:7; Ps 39:8-9). They commemorate it as the beginning of the redemption and of the indissoluble and wedded union of the divine nature with human nature in the one Person of the Word. With regard to Mary, these liturgies celebrate it as a feast of the new Eve, the obedient and faithful virgin, who with her generous "fiat" (cf. Lk 1:38) became through the working of the Spirit the Mother of God, but also the true Mother of the living, and, by receiving into her womb the one Mediator (cf. 1 Tm 2:5), became the true Ark of the Covenant and true Temple of God. These liturgies celebrate it as a culminating moment in the salvific dialogue between God and man, and as a commemoration of the Blessed Virgin's free consent and cooperation in the plan of redemption.

The Solemnity of August 15 celebrates the glorious assumption of Mary into heaven. It is a feast of her destiny of fullness and blessedness, of the glorification of her immaculate soul and of her virginal body, of her perfect configuration to the Risen Christ; a feast that sets before the eyes of the Church and of all mankind the image and the consoling proof of the fulfillment of their final hope, namely, that this full glorification is the destiny of all those whom Christ has made his brothers, having "flesh and blood in common with them" (Heb 2:14; cf. Gal 4:4). The Solemnity of the Assumption is prolonged in the celebration of the Queenship of the Blessed Virgin Mary, which occurs seven days later. On this occasion we contemplate her who, seated beside the King of ages, shines forth as Queen and intercedes as Mother.[18] These four solemnities therefore, mark with the highest liturgical rank the main dogmatic truths concerning the handmaid of the lord.

7. After the solemnities just mentioned, particular consideration must be given to those celebrations that commemorate salvific events in which the Blessed Virgin was closely associated with her Son. Such are the feasts of the Nativity of Our Lady (September 8), "the hope of the entire world and the dawn of salvation"[19]; and the Visitation (May 31), in which the liturgy recalls the "Blessed Virgin Mary carrying her Son within her,"[20] and visiting Elizabeth to offer charitable assistance and to proclaim the mercy of God the Savior.[21] Then there is the commemoration of Our Lady of Sorrows (September 15), a fitting occasion for reliving a decisive moment in the history of salvation and for venerating, together with the Son "lifted up on the cross, his suffering Mother."[22]

The feast of February 2, which has been given back its

ancient name, the Presentation of the Lord, should also be considered as a joint commemoration of the Son and of the Mother, if we are fully to appreciate its rich content. It is the celebration of a mystery of salvation accomplished by Christ, a mystery with which the Blessed virgin was intimately associated as the Mother of the Suffering Servant of Yahweh, as the one who performs a mission belonging to ancient Israel, and as the model for the new People of God, which is ever being tested in its faith and hope by suffering and persecution (cf. Lk 2:21-35).

8. The restored Roman Calendar gives particular prominence to the celebrations listed above, but it also includes other kinds of commemorations connected with local devotions and which have acquired a wider popularity and interest (e.g., February 11, Our Lady of Lourdes August 5, the Dedication of the Basilica of St. Mary Major). Then there are others, originally celebrated by particular religious families but which today, by reason of the popularity they have gained, can truly be considered ecclesial (e.g., July 16, Our Lady of Mount Carmel; October 7, Our Lady of the Rosary). There are still others which, apart from their apocryphal content, present lofty and exemplary values and carry on venerable traditions having their origin especially in the East (e.g., the Immaculate Heart of the Blessed Virgin, celebrated on the Saturday following the second Sunday after Pentecost).

9. Nor must one forget that the General Roman Calendar does not include all celebrations in honor of the Blessed Virgin. Rather, it is for individual Calendars to include, with fidelity to liturgical norms but with sincere endorsement, the Marian feasts proper to the different local Churches. Lastly, it should be noted that frequent commemorations of the Blessed Virgin are possible through the use of the Saturday Masses of our Lady. This is an ancient and simple commemoration and one that is made very adaptable and varied by the flexibility of the modern Calendar and the number of formulas provided by the Missal.

10. In this Apostolic Exhortation we do not intend to examine the whole content of the new Roman Missal. But by reason of the work of evaluation that we have undertaken to carry out in regard to the revised books of the Roman Rite,[23] we would like to mention some of the aspects and themes of the Missal. In

the first place, we are pleased to note how the Eucharistic Prayers of the Missal, in admirable harmony with the Eastern liturgies,[24] contain a significant commemoration of the Blessed Virgin. For example, the ancient Roman Canon, which commemorates the Mother of the Lord in terms full of doctrine and devotional inspiration: "In union with the whole Church we honor Mary, the ever-virgin Mother of Jesus Christ our Lord and God." In a similar way the recent Eucharistic Prayer III expresses with intense supplication the desire of those praying to share with the Mother the inheritance of sons: "May he make us an everlasting gift to you (the Father) and enable us to share in the inheritance of your saints, with Mary, the Virgin Mother of God." This daily commemoration, by reason of its place at the heart of the divine Sacrifice, should be considered a particularly expressive form of the veneration that the Church pays to the "Blessed of the Most High" (cf. Lk 1:28).

    11. As we examine the texts of the revised Missal we see how the great Marian themes of the Roman prayer book have been accepted in perfect doctrinal continuity with the past. Thus, for example, we have the themes of Mary's Immaculate Conception and fullness of grace, the divine motherhood, the unblemished and fruitful virginity, the Temple of the Holy Spirit, Mary's cooperation in the work of her Son, her exemplary sanctity, merciful intercession, assumption into heaven, maternal Queenship and many other themes. We also see how other themes, in a certain sense new ones, have been introduced in equally perfect harmony with the theological developments of the present day. Thus, for example, we have the theme of Mary and the Church, which has been inserted into the texts of the Missal in a variety of aspects, a variety that matches the many and varied relations that exist between the Mother of Christ and the Church. For example, in the celebration of the Immaculate Conception which texts recognize the beginning of the Church, the spotless Bride of Christ.[25] In the assumption they recognize the beginning that has already been made and the image of what, for the whole Church, must still come to pass.[26] In the mystery of Mary's motherhood they confess that she is the Mother of the Head and of the members, the holy Mother of God and therefore the provident Mother of the

Church.[27]

When the liturgy turns its gaze either to the primitive Church or to the Church of our own days it always finds Mary. In the primitive Church she is seen praying with the apostles,[28] in our own day she is actively present, and the Church desires to live the mystery of Christ with her: "Grant that your Church which with Mary shared Christ's passion may be worthy to share also in his resurrection."[29] She is also seen represented as a voice of praise in unison with which the Church wishes to give glory to God: "...with her [Mary] may we always praise you."[30] And since the liturgy is worship that requires as way of living consistent with it, it asks that devotion to the Blessed Virgin should become a concrete and deeply felt love for the Church, as is wonderfully expressed in the prayer after Communion in the Mass of September: "... that as we recall the sufferings shared by the Blessed Virgin Mary, we may with the Church fulfill in ourselves what is lacking in the sufferings of Christ."

12. The Lectionary is one of the books of the Roman Rite that has greatly benefited from the post-conciliar reform, by reason both of its added texts and of the intrinsic value of these texts, which contain the ever-living and efficacious word of God (cf. Heb 4:12). This rich collection of Biblical texts has made it possible to arrange the whole history of salvation in an orderly three year cycle and to set forth more completely the mystery of Christ. The logical consequence has been that the Lectionary contains a larger number of Old and New Testament readings concerning the Blessed Virgin. This numerical increase has not however been based on random choice: only those readings have been accepted which in different ways and degrees can be considered Marian, either from the evidence of their content or from the results of careful exegesis, supported by the teachings of the magisterium or by solid Tradition. It is also right to observe that these readings occur not only on feasts of the Blessed Virgin but are read on many other occasions, for example on certain Sundays during the liturgical year[31], in the celebration of rites that deeply concern the Christian's sacramental life and the choices confronting him,[32] as also in the joyful or sad experiences of his life on earth.[33]

13. The Liturgy of the Hours, the revised book of the Office,

also contains outstanding examples of devotion to the Mother of the Lord. These are to be found in the hymns, which include several masterpieces of universal literature, such as Dante's sublime prayer to the Blessed Virgin[34] and in the antiphons that complete the daily Office. To these lyrical invocations there has been added the well-known prayer Sub tuum praesidium, venerable for its antiquity and admirable for its content. Other examples occur in the prayers of intercession at Lauds and Vespers, prayers which frequently express trusting recourse to the Mother of mercy. Finally there are selections from the vast treasury of writings on our Lady composed by authors of the first Christian centuries, of the Middle Ages and of modern times.

14. The commemoration of the Blessed Virgin occurs often in the Missal, the Lectionary and the Liturgy of the Hours, the hinges of the liturgical prayer of the Roman Rite. In the other revised liturgical books also expressions of love and suppliant veneration addressed to the Theotokos are not lacking. Thus the Church invokes her, the Mother of grace, before immersing candidates in the saving waters of baptism[35]; the Church invokes her intercession for mothers who, full of gratitude for the gift of motherhood, come to Church to express their joy[36]; the Church holds her up as a model to those who follow Christ by embracing the religious life[37] or who receive the Consecration of Virgins.[38] For these people the Church asks Mary's motherly assistance.[39] The Church prays fervently to Mary on behalf of her children who have come to the hour of their death.[40] The Church asks Mary's intercession for those who have closed their eyes to the light of this world and appeared before Christ, the eternal Light",[41] and the Church, through Mary's prayers, invokes comfort upon those who in sorrow mourn with faith the departure of their loved ones.[42]

15. The examination of the revised liturgical books leads us to the comforting observation that the postconciliar renewal has, as was previously desired by the liturgical movement, properly considered the Blessed Virgin in the mystery of Christ, and, in harmony with tradition, has recognized the singular place that belongs to her in Christian worship as the holy Mother of God and the worthy Associate of the Redeemer.

It could not have been otherwise. If one studies the history of Christian worship, in fact, one notes that both in the East and in the West the highest and purest expressions of devotion to the Blessed Virgin have sprung from the liturgy or have been incorporated into it.

We wish to emphasize the fact that the veneration which the universal Church today accords to blessed Mary is a derivation from and an extension and unceasing increase of the devotion that the Church of every age has paid to her, with careful attention to truth and with an ever watchful nobility of expression. From perennial Tradition kept alive by reason of the uninterrupted presence of the Spirit and continual attention to the Word, the Church of our time draws motives, arguments and incentives for the veneration that she pays to the Blessed Virgin. And the liturgy, which receives approval and strength from the magisterium, is a most lofty expression and an evident proof of this living Tradition.

# Section Two

## The Blessed Virgin As The Model
## Of The Church In Divine Worship

16. In accordance with some of the guidelines of the Council's teaching on Mary and the Church, we now wish to examine more closely a particular aspect of the relationship between Mary and the liturgy, namely, Mary as a model of the spiritual attitude with which the Church celebrates and lives the divine mysteries. That the Blessed virgin is an exemplar in this field derives from the fact that she is recognized as a most excellent exemplar of the Church in the order of faith, charity and perfect union with Christ,[43] that is, of that interior disposition with which the Church, the beloved spouse, closely associated with her Lord, invokes Christ and through him worships the eternal Father.[44]

17. Mary is the attentive Virgin, who receives the word of God with faith, that faith which in her case was the gateway and path to divine motherhood, for, as Saint Augustine realized, "Blessed Mary by believing conceived him (Jesus) whom believing she brought forth."[45] In fact, when she received from the angel the

answer to her doubt (cf. Lk 1:34-37), "full of faith, and conceiving Christ in her mind before conceiving him in her womb, she said, 'I am the handmaid of the Lord, let what you have said be done to me' (Lk 1:38)."[46] It was faith that was for her the cause of blessedness and certainty in the fulfillment of he promise: "Blessed is she who believed that the promise made her by the Lord would be fulfilled" (Lk 1:45). Similarly, it was faith with which she, who played a part in the Incarnation and was a unique witness to it, thinking back on the events of the infancy of Christ, meditated upon these events in her heart (cf. Lk 2:19 ,51). The Church also acts in this way, especially in the liturgy, when with faith she listens, accepts, proclaims and venerates the word of God, distributes it to the faithful as the bread of life[47] and in the light of that word examines the signs of the times and interprets and lives the events of history.

18. Mary is also the Virgin in prayer. She appears as such in the visit to the mother of the precursor, when she pours out her soul in expressions glorifying God, and expressions of humility, faith and hope. This prayer is the Magnificat (cf. Lk 1:46-55), Mary's prayer par excellence, the song of the messianic times in which there mingles the joy of the ancient and the new Israel. As St. Irenaeus seems to suggest, it is in Mary's canticle that there was heard once more the rejoicing of Abraham who foresaw the Messiah (cf. Jn 8:56)[48] and there rang out in prophetic anticipation the voice of the Church: "In her exultation Mary prophetically declared in the name of the Church: 'My soul proclaims the glory of the Lord... '"[49] And in fact Mary's hymn has spread far and wide and has become the prayer of the whole Church in all ages.

At Cana, Mary appears once more as the Virgin in prayer: when she tactfully told her Son of a temporal need she also obtained an effect of grace, namely, that Jesus, in working the first of his "signs," confirmed his disciples' faith in him (cf. Jn 2:1-12).

Likewise, the last description of Mary's life presents her as praying. The apostles "joined in continuous prayer, together with several women, including Mary the mother of Jesus, and with his brothers" (Acts 1:14). We have here the prayerful presence of Mary in the early Church and in the Church throughout all ages, for, having been assumed into heaven, she has not abandoned her mission of intercession and salvation.[50] The title Virgin in prayer also fits the Church, which day by day presents to the Father the needs of her children, "praises the Lord unceasingly and intercedes for the salvation of the world."[51]

19. Mary is also the Virgin-Mother, she who "believing and obeying...brought forth on earth the Father's Son. This she did, not knowing man but overshadowed by the Holy Spirit."[52] This was a miraculous motherhood, set up by God as the type and exemplar of the fruitfulness of the Virgin-Church, which "becomes herself a mother.... For by her preaching and by baptism she brings forth to a new and immortal life children who are conceived by the power of the Holy Spirit and born of God."[53] The ancient Fathers rightly taught that the Church prolongs in the sacrament of Baptism the virginal motherhood of Mary. Among such references we like to recall that of our illustrious predecessor, Saint Leo the Great, who in a Christmas homily says: "The origin which (Christ took in the womb of the Virgin he has given to the baptismal font: he has given to water what he had given to his Mother, the power of the Most High and the overshadowing of the Holy Spirit (cf. Lk 1:35), which was responsible for Mary's bringing forth the Savior, has the same effect, so that water may regenerate the believer."[54] If we wished to go to liturgical sources, we could quote the beautiful Illatio of the Mozarabic liturgy: "The former [Mary] carried Life in her womb; the latter [the Church] bears Life in the waters of baptism. In Mary's members Christ was formed; in the waters of the Church Christ is put on."[55]

20. Mary is, finally, the Virgin presenting offerings. In the episode of the Presentation of Jesus in the Temple (cf. Lk 2:22-35), the Church, guided by the Spirit, has detected, over and above the fulfillment of the laws regarding the offering of the firstborn (cf. Ex 13:11-16) and the purification of the mother (cf. Lv 12:6-8), a mystery of salvation related to the history of salvation. That is, she has noted the continuity of the fundamental offering that the Incarnate Word made to the Father when he entered the world (cf. Heb 13:5-7). The Church has seen the universal nature of salvation proclaimed, for Simeon, greeting in the Child the light to enlighten the peoples and the glory of the people Israel (cf. Lk 2:32), recognized in him the Messiah, the Savior of all. The Church has understood the prophetic reference to the Passion of Christ: the

fact that Simeon's words, which linked in one prophecy the Son as "the sign of contradiction" (Lk 2:34) and the Mother, whose soul would be pierced by a sword (cf. Lk 2:35), came true on Calvary. A mystery of salvation, therefore, that in its various aspects orients the episode of the Presentation in the Temple to the salvific event of the cross. But the Church herself, in particular from the Middle Ages onwards, has detected In the heart of the Virgin taking her Son to Jerusalem to present him to the Lord (cf. Lk 2:22) a desire to make an offering, a desire that exceeds the ordinary meaning of the rite. A witness to this intuition is found in the loving prayer of Saint Bernard "Offer your Son, holy Virgin, and present to the Lord the blessed fruit of your womb. Offer for the reconciliation of us all the holy Victim which is pleasing to God."[56]

This union of the Mother and the Son in the work of redemption[57] reaches its climax on Calvary, where Christ "offered himself as the perfect sacrifice to God" (Heb 9:14) and where Mary stood by the cross (cf. Jn 19:25), "suffering grievously with her only-begotten Son. There she united herself with a maternal heart to his sacrifice, and lovingly consented to the immolation of this victim which she herself had brought forth"[58] and also was offering to the eternal Father."[59] To perpetuate down the centuries the Sacrifice of the Cross, the divine Savior instituted the Eucharistic sacrifice, the memorial of his death and resurrection, and entrusted it to his spouse the Church,[60] which, especially on Sundays, calls the faithful together to celebrate the Passover of the Lord until he comes again.[61] This the Church does in union with the saints in heaven and in particular with the Blessed Virgin,[62] whose burning charity and unshakable faith she imitates.

21. Mary is not only an example for the whole Church in the exercise of divine worship but is also, clearly, a teacher of the spiritual life for individual Christians. The faithful at a very early date began to look to Mary and to imitate her in making their lives an act of worship of God and making their worship a commitment of their lives. As early as the fourth century, St. Ambrose, speaking to the people, expressed the hope that each of them would have the spirit of Mary in order to glory God May the heart of Mary be in each Christian to proclaim the greatness of the Lord; may her spirit be in everyone to exult in God."[63] But Mary is above all the

example of that worship that consists in making one's life an offering to God. This is an ancient and ever new doctrine that each individual can hear again by heeding the Church's teaching, but also by heeding the very voice of the Virgin as she, anticipating in herself the wonderful petition of the Lord's Prayer, "Your will be done" (Mt 6:10), replied to God's messenger: "I am the handmaid of the Lord. Let what you have said be done to me" (Lk 1:38). And Mary's "yes" is for all Christians a lesson and example of obedience to the will of the Father, which is the, way and means of one's own sanctification.

22. It is also important to note how the Church expresses in various effective attitudes of devotion the many relationships that bind her to Mary: in profound veneration, when she reflects on the singular dignity of the Virgin who, through the action of the Holy Spirit has become Mother of the Incarnate Word; in burning love, when she considers the spiritual motherhood of Mary towards all members of the Mystical Body; in trusting invocation; when she experiences the intercession of her advocate and helper;[64] in loving service, when she sees in the humble handmaid of the Lord the queen of mercy and the mother of grace; in zealots imitation, when she contemplates the holiness and virtues of her who is "full of grace" (Lk 1:28); in profound wonder, when she sees in her, "as in a faultless model, that which she herself wholly desires and hopes to be"[65]; in attentive study, when she recognizes in the associate of the Redeemer, who already shares fully in the fruits of the Paschal Mystery, the prophetic fulfillment of her own future, until the day on which, when she has been purified of every spot and wrinkle (cf. Eph 5:27), she will become like a bride arrayed for the bridegroom, Jesus Christ (cf. Rv 21:2).

23. Therefore, venerable Brothers, as we consider the piety that the liturgical Tradition of the universal Church and the renewed Roman Rite expresses towards the holy Mother of God, and as we remember that the liturgy through its pre-eminent value as worship constitutes the golden norm for Christian piety, and finally as we observe how the Church when she celebrates the sacred mysteries assumes an attitude of faith and love similar to that of the Virgin, we realize the rightness of the exhortation that the Second Vatican Council addresses to all the children of the Church, namely "that

the cult, especially the liturgical cult, of the Blessed Virgin be generously fostered."[66] This is an exhortation that we would like to see accepted everywhere without reservation and put into zealous practice.

# Part Two

## The Renewal Of Devotion To Mary

24. The Second Vatican Council also exhorts us to promote other forms of piety side by side with liturgical worship, especially those recommended by the magisterium.[67] However, as is well known, the piety of the faithful and their veneration of the Mother of God has taken on many forms according to circumstances of time and place, the different sensibilities of peoples and their different cultural traditions. Hence it is that the forms in which this devotion is expressed, being subject to the ravages of time, show the need for a renewal that will permit them to substitute elements that are transient, to emphasize the elements that are ever new and to incorporate the doctrinal data obtained from theological reflection and the proposals of the Church's magisterium. This shows the need for episcopal conferences, local churches, religious families and Community of the faithful to promote a genuine creative activity and at the same time to proceed to a careful revision of expressions and exercises of piety directed towards the Blessed Virgin. We would like this revision to be respectful of wholesome tradition and open to the legitimate requests of the people of our time. It seems fitting therefore, venerable Brothers, to put forward some principles for action in this field.

# Section One

## Trinitarian, Christological And Ecclesial Aspects Of Devotion To The Blessed Virgin

25. In the first place it is supremely fitting that exercises of

piety directed towards the Virgin Mary should clearly express the Trinitarian and Christological note that is intrinsic and essential to them. Christian worship in fact is of itself worship offered to the Father and to the Son and to the Holy Spirit, or, as the liturgy puts it, to the Father through Christ in the Spirit. From this point of view worship is rightly extended, though in a substantially different way, first and foremost and in a special manner, to the Mother of the Lord and then to the saints, in whom the Church proclaims the Paschal Mystery, for they have suffered with Christ and have been glorified with him.[68] In the Virgin Mary everything is relative to Christ and dependent upon him. It was with a view to Christ that God the Father from all eternity chose her to be the all-holy Mother and adorned her with gifts of the Spirit granted to no one else. Certainly genuine Christian piety has never failed to highlight the indissoluble link and essential relationship of the Virgin to the divine Savior.[69] Yet it seems to us particularly in conformity with the spiritual orientation of our time. which is dominated and absorbed by the "question of Christ,"[70] that in the expressions of devotion to the Virgin the Christological aspect should have particular prominence. It likewise seems to us fitting that these expressions of devotion should reflect God's plan, which laid down "with one single decree the origin of Mary and the Incarnation of the divine Wisdom."[71] This will without doubt contribute to making piety towards the Mother of Jesus more solid, and to making it an effective instrument for attaining to full "knowledge of the Son of God, until we become the perfect man, fully mature with the fullness of Christ himself" (Eph 4:13). It will also contribute to increasing the worship due to Christ himself, since, according to the perennial mind of the Church authoritatively repeated in our own day,[72] "what is given to the handmaid is referred to the Lord; thus what is given to the Mother redounds to the Son; ... and thus what is given as humble tribute to the Queen becomes honor rendered to the King."[73]

26. It seems to us useful to add to this mention of the Christological orientation of devotion to the Blessed Virgin a reminder of the fittingness of giving prominence in this devotion to one of the essential facts of the Faith: the person and work of the Holy Spirit. Theological reflection and the liturgy have in fact

noted how the sanctifying intervention of the Spirit in the Virgin of Nazareth was a culminating moment of the Spirit's action in the history of salvation. Thus, for example, some fathers and writers of the Church attributed to the work of the Spirit the original holiness of Mary, who was as it were "fashioned by the Holy Spirit into a kind of new substance and new creature."[74] Reflecting on the Gospel texts, "The Holy Spirit will come upon you and the power of the Most High will cover you with his shadow" (Lk 1:35) and "[Mary] was found to be with child through the Holy Spirit.... She has conceived what is in her by the Holy Spirit" (Mt 1:18, 20), they saw in the Spirit's intervention an action that consecrated and made fruitful Mary's virginity[75] and transformed her into the "Abode of the King" or "Bridal Chamber of the Word,"[76] the "Temple" or "Tabernacle of the Lord,"[77] the "Ark of the Covenant" or "the Ark of Holiness,"[78] titles rich in Biblical echoes. Examining more deeply still the mystery of the Incarnation, they saw in the mysterious relationship between the Spirit and Mary an aspect redolent of marriage, poetically portrayed by Prudentius: "The unwed Virgin espoused the Spirit,"[79] and they called her the "Temple of the Holy Spirit,"[80] an expression that emphasizes the sacred character of the Virgin, now the permanent dwelling of the Spirit of God. Delving deeply into the doctrine of the Paraclete, they saw that from him as from a spring there flowed forth the fullness of grace (cf. Lk 1:28) and the abundance of gifts that adorned her. Thus they attributed to the Spirit the faith, hope and charity that animated the Virgin's heart, the strength that sustained her acceptance of the will of God, and the vigor that upheld her in her suffering at the foot of the cross.[81] In Mary's prophetic canticle (cf. Lk 1:46-55) they saw a special working of the Spirit who had spoken through the mouths of the prophets.[82] Considering, finally, the presence of the Mother of Jesus in the Upper Room, where the Spirit came down upon the infant Church (cf. Acts 1:12-14; 2:1-4), they enriched with new developments the ancient theme of Mary and the Church.[83] Above all they had recourse to the Virgin's intercession in order to obtain from the Spirit the capacity for engendering Christ in their own soul, as is attested to by Saint Ildephonsus in a prayer of supplication, amazing in its doctrine and prayerful power: "I beg you, holy Virgin, that I may have Jesus from the Holy Spirit, by whom you brought Jesus forth. May my soul receive Jesus through the Holy Spirit by whom your flesh conceived Jesus.... May I love Jesus in the Holy Spirit in whom you adore Jesus as Lord and gaze upon him as your Son."[84]

27. It is sometimes said that many spiritual writings today do not sufficiently reflect the whole doctrine concerning the Holy Spirit. It is the task of specialists to verify and weigh the truth of this assertion, but it is our task to exhort everyone, especially those in the pastoral ministry and also theologians, to meditate more deeply on the working of the Holy Spirit in the history of salvation, and to ensure that Christian spiritual writings give due prominence to his life-giving action. Such a study will bring out in particular the hidden relationship between the Spirit of God and the Virgin of Nazareth, and show the influence they exert on the Church. From a more profound meditation on the truths of the Faith will flow a more vital piety.

28. It is also necessary that exercises of piety with which the faithful honor the Mother of the Lord should clearly show the place she occupies in the Church: "the highest place and the closest to us after Christ."[85] The liturgical buildings of Byzantine rite, both in the architectural structure itself and in the use of images, show clearly Mary's place in the Church. On the central door of the iconostasis there is a representation of the Annunciation and in the apse an image of the glorious Theotokos. In this way one perceives how through the assent of the humble handmaid of the Lord mankind begins its return to God and sees in the glory of the all-holy Virgin the goal towards which it is journeying. The symbolism by which a church building demonstrates Mary's place in the mystery of the Church is full of significance and gives grounds for hoping that the different forms of devotion to the Blessed Virgin may everywhere be open to ecclesial perspectives.

The faithful will be able to appreciate more easily Mary's mission in the mystery of the Church and her preeminent place in the communion of saints if attention is drawn to the Second Vatican Council's references to the fundamental concepts of the nature of the Church as the Family of God, the People of God, the Kingdom of God and the Mystical Body of Christ.[86] This will also bring the faithful to a deeper realization of the brotherhood which unites all of them as sons and daughters of the Virgin Mary, "who with a mother's love has cooperated in their rebirth and spiritual formation,"[87] and as sons and daughters of the Church, since "we are born from the Church's womb we are nurtured by the Church's milk, we are given life by the Church's Spirit."[88] They will also realize that both the Church and Mary collaborate to give birth to the Mystical Body of Christ since "both of them are the Mother of Christ, but neither brings forth the whole (body) independently of the other."[89] Similarly the faithful will appreciate more clearly that the action of the Church in the world can be likened to an extension of Mary's concern. The active love she showed at Nazareth, in the house of Elizabeth, at Cana and on Golgotha, all salvific episodes having vast ecclesial importance, finds its extension in the Church's maternal concern that all men should come to knowledge of the truth (cf. 1 Tm 2:4), in the Church's concern for people in lowly circumstances and for the poor and weak, and in her constant commitment to peace and social harmony, as well as in her untiring efforts to ensure that all men will share in the salvation which was merited for them by Christ's death. Thus love for the Church will become love for Mary, and vice versa, since the one cannot exist without the other, as St. Chromatius of Aquileia observed with keen discernment: "The Church was united... in the Upper Room with Mary the Mother of Jesus and with his brethren. The Church therefore cannot be referred to as such unless it includes Mary the Mother of our Lord, together with his brethren."[90] In conclusion, therefore, we repeat that devotion to the Blessed Virgin must explicitly show its intrinsic and ecclesiological content: thus it will be enabled to revise its forms and texts in a fitting way.

# Section Two

## Four Guidelines For Devotion To The Blessed Virgin: Biblical, Liturgical, Ecumenical And

# Anthropological

29. The above considerations spring from an examination of the Virgin Mary's relationship with God, the Father and the Son and the Holy Spirit, and with the Church. Following the path traced by conciliar teaching,[91] we wish to add some further guidelines from Scripture, liturgy, ecumenism and anthropology. These are to be borne in mind in any revision of exercises of piety or in the creation of new ones, in order to emphasize and accentuate the bond which unites us to her who is the Mother of Christ and our Mother in the communion of saints.

30. Today it is recognized as a general need of Christian piety that every form of worship should have a Biblical imprint. The progress made in Biblical studies, the increasing dissemination of the Sacred Scriptures, and above all the example of Tradition and the interior action of the Holy Spirit are tending to cause the modern Christian to use the Bible ever increasingly as the basic prayer book, and to draw from it genuine inspiration and unsurpassable examples. Devotion to the Blessed Virgin cannot be exempt from this general orientation of Christian piety[92]; indeed it should draw inspiration in a special way from this orientation in order to gain new vigor and sure help. In its wonderful presentation of God's plan for man's salvation, the Bible is replete with the mystery of the Savior, and from Genesis to the Book of Revelation, also contains clear references to her who was the Mother and associate of the Savior. We would not, however, wish this Biblical imprint to be merely a diligent use of texts and symbols skillfully selected from the Sacred Scriptures. More than this is necessary. What is needed is that texts of prayers and chants should draw their inspiration and their wording from the Bible, and above all that devotion to the Virgin should be imbued with the great themes of the Christian message. This will ensure that, as they venerate the Seat of Wisdom, the faithful in their turn will be enlightened by the divine word, and be inspired to live their lives in accordance with the precepts of Incarnate Wisdom.

31. We have already spoken of the veneration which the Church gives to the Mother of God in the celebration of the sacred

liturgy. However, speaking of the other forms of devotion and of the criteria on which they should be based we wish to recall the norm laid down in the Constitution Sacrosanctum Concilium. This document, while wholeheartedly approving of the practices of piety of the Christian people, goes on to say:"... it is necessary however that such devotions with consideration for the liturgical seasons should be so arranged as to be in harmony with the sacred liturgy. They should somehow derive their inspiration from it, and because of its pre-eminence they should orient the Christian people towards it."[93] Although this is a wise and clear rule, its application is not an easy matter, especially in regard to Marian devotions, which are so varied in their formal expressions. What is needed on the part of the leaders of the local communities is effort, pastoral sensitivity and perseverance, while the faithful on their part must show a willingness to accept guidelines and ideas drawn from the true nature of Christian worship; this sometimes makes it necessary to change long-standing customs wherein the real nature of this Christian worship has become somewhat obscured.

In this context we wish to mention two attitudes which in pastoral practice could nullify the norm of the Second Vatican Council. In the first place there are certain persons concerned with the care of souls who scorn a priori, devotions of piety which, in their correct forms have been recommended by the magisterium, who leave them aside and in this way create a vacuum which they do not fill. They forget that the Council has said that devotions of piety should harmonize with the liturgy, not be suppressed. Secondly there are those who, without wholesome liturgical and pastoral criteria, mix practices of piety and liturgical acts in hybrid celebrations. It sometimes happens that novenas or similar practices of piety are inserted into the very celebration of the Eucharistic Sacrifice. This creates the danger that the Lord's Memorial Rite, instead of being the culmination of the meeting of the Christian community, becomes the occasion, as it were, for devotional practices. For those who act in this way we wish to recall the rule laid down by the Council prescribing that exercises of piety should be harmonized with the liturgy not merged into it. Wise pastoral action should, on the one hand, point out and emphasize the proper nature of the liturgical acts, while on the other hand it should enhance the value of practices of piety in order to adapt them to the needs of individual communities in the Church and to make them valuable aids to the liturgy.

32. Because of its ecclesial character, devotion to the Blessed Virgin reflects the preoccupation of the Church herself. Among these especially in our day is her anxiety for the re-establishment of Christian unity. In this way devotion to the Mother of the Lord is in accord with the deep desires and aims of the ecumenical movement, that is, it acquires an ecumenical aspect. This is so for a number of reasons.

In the first place, in venerating with particular love the glorious Theotokos and in acclaiming her as the 'Hope of Christians,'[94] Catholics unite themselves with their brethren of the Orthodox Churches, in which devotion to the Blessed Virgin finds its expression in a beautiful lyricism and in solid doctrine. Catholics are also united with Anglicans, whose classical theologians have already drawn attention to the sound Scriptural basis for devotion to the Mother of our Lord, while those of the present day increasingly underline the importance of Mary's place in the Christian life. Praising God with the very words of the Virgin (cf. Lk 1:46-55), they are united, too, with their brethren in the Churches of the Reform, where love for the Sacred Scriptures flourishes.

For Catholics, devotion to the Mother of Christ and Mother of Christians is also a natural and frequent opportunity for seeking her intercession with her Son in order to obtain the union of all the baptized within a single People of God.[95] Yet again, the ecumenical aspect of Marian devotion is shown in the Catholic Church's desire that, without in any way detracting from the unique character of this devotion,[96] every care should be taken to avoid any exaggeration which could mislead other Christian brethren about the true doctrine of the Catholic Church.[97] Similarly, the Church desires that any manifestation of cult which is opposed to correct Catholic practice should be eliminated.

Finally, since it is natural that in true devotion to the Blessed Virgin "the Son should be duly known, loved and glorified...when the Mother is honored,"[98] such devotion is an approach to Christ, the source and center of ecclesiastical communion, in which all

who openly confess that he is God and Lord, Savior and sole
Mediator (cf. 1 Tm 2:5) are called to be one, with one another,
with Christ and with the Father in the unity of the Holy Spirit.[99]

33. We realize that there exist important differences between
the thought of many of our brethren in other Churches and
ecclesial communities and the Catholic doctrine on "Mary's role
in the work of salvation."[100] In consequence there are likewise
differences of opinion on the devotion which should be shown to
her. Nevertheless, since it is the same power of the Most High
which overshadowed the Virgin of Nazareth (cf. Lk 1:35) and
which today is at work within the ecumenical movement and
making it fruitful, we wish to express our confidence that devotion
to the humble handmaid of the Lord, in Whom the Almighty has
done great things (cf. Lk 1:49), will become, even if only slowly,
not an obstacle but a path and a rallying point for the union of all
who believe in Christ. We are glad to see that, in fact, a better
understanding of Mary's place in the mystery of Christ and of the
Church on the part also of our separated brethren is smoothing
the path to union. Just as at Cana the Blessed Virgin's intervention
resulted in Christ's performing his first miracle (cf. Jn 2:1-12), so
today her intercession can help to bring to realization the time
when the disciples of Christ will again find full communion in
faith. This hope of ours is strengthened by a remark of our
predecessor Leo XIII, who wrote that the cause of Christian unity
"properly pertains to the role of Mary's spiritual motherhood. For
Mary did not and cannot engender those who belong to Christ,
except in one faith and one love: for 'Is Christ divided?' (1 Cor
1:13) We must all live together the life of Christ, so that in one and
the same body 'we may bear fruit for God' (Rom 7:4)."[101]

34. Devotion to the Blessed Virgin must also pay close
attention to certain findings of the human sciences. This will help
to eliminate one of the causes of the difficulties experienced in
devotion to the Mother of the Lord, namely, the discrepancy
existing between some aspects of this devotion and modern
anthropological discoveries and the profound changes which have
occurred in the psychosociological field in which modern man
lives and works. The picture of the Blessed Virgin presented in a
certain type of devotional literature cannot easily be reconciled

with today's lifestyle, especially the way women live today. In the home, woman's equality and coresponsibility with man in the running of the family are being justly recognized by laws and the evolution of customs. In the sphere of politics women have in many countries gained a position in public life equal to that of men. In the social field women are at work in a whole range of different employments, getting further away every day from the restricted surroundings of the home. In the cultural field new possibilities are opening up for women in scientific research and intellectual activities.

In consequence of these phenomena some people are becoming disenchanted with devotion to the Blessed Virgin and finding it difficult to take as an example Mary of Nazareth because the horizons of her life, so they say, seem rather restricted in comparison with the vast spheres of activity open to mankind today. In this regard we exhort theologians, those responsible for the local Christian communities and the faithful themselves to examine these difficulties with due care. At the same time we wish to take the opportunity of offering our own contribution to their solution by making a few observations.

35. First, the Virgin Mary has always been proposed to the faithful by the Church as an example to be imitated, not precisely in the type of life she led, and much less for the socio-cultural background in which she lived and which today scarcely exists anywhere. She is held up as an example to the faithful rather for the way in which, in her own particular life, she fully and responsibly accepted the will of God (cf. Lk 1:38), because she heard the word of God and acted on it, and because charity and a spirit of service were the driving force of her actions. She is worthy of imitation because she was the first and the most perfect of Christ's disciples. All of this has a permanent and universal exemplary value.

36. Secondly, we would like to point out that the difficulties alluded to above are closely related to certain aspects of the image of Mary found in popular writings. They are not connected with the Gospel image of Mary nor with the doctrinal data which have been made explicit through a slow and conscientious process of drawing from Revelation. It should be considered quite normal

for succeeding generations of Christians in differing socio-cultural contexts to have expressed their sentiments about the Mother of Jesus in a way and manner which reflected their own age. In contemplating Mary and her mission these different generations of Christians, looking on her as the New Woman and perfect Christian, found in her as a virgin, wife and mother the outstanding type of womanhood and the preeminent exemplar of life lived in accordance with the Gospels and summing up the most characteristic situations in the life of a woman. When the Church considers the long history of Marian devotion she rejoices at the continuity of the element of cult which it shows, but she does not bind herself to any particular expression of an individual cultural epoch or to the particular anthropological ideas underlying such expressions. The Church understands that certain outward religious expressions, while perfectly valid in themselves, may be less suitable to men and women of different ages and cultures.

37. Finally, we wish to point out that our own time, no less than former times, is called upon to verify its knowledge of reality with the word of God, and, keeping to the matter at present under consideration, to compare its anthropological ideas and the problems springing therefrom with the figure of the Virgin Mary as presented by the Gospel. The reading of the divine Scriptures, carried out under the guidance of the Holy Spirit, and with the discoveries of the human sciences and the different situations in the world today being taken into account, will help us to see how Mary can be considered a mirror of the expectations of the men and women of our time. Thus, the modern woman, anxious to participate with decision-making power in the affairs of the community, will contemplate with intimate joy Mary who, taken into dialogue with God, gives her active and responsible consent,[102] not to the solution of a contingent problem, but to that "event of world importance," as the Incarnation of the Word has been rightly called.[103] The modern woman will appreciate that Mary's choice of the state of virginity, which in God's plan prepared her for the mystery of the Incarnation, was not a rejection of any of the values of the married state but a courageous choice which she made in order to consecrate herself totally to the love of God. The modern woman will note with pleasant surprise that Mary of Nazareth,

while completely devoted to the will of God, was far from being a timidly submissive woman or one whose piety was repellent to others; on the contrary, she was a woman who did not hesitate to proclaim that God vindicates the humble and the oppressed, and removes the powerful people of this world from their privileged positions (cf. Lk 1:51-53). The modern woman will recognize in Mary, who "stands out among the poor and humble of the Lord,"[104] a woman of strength, who experienced poverty and suffering, flight and exile (cf. Mt 2:13-23). These are situations that cannot escape the attention of those who wish to support, with the Gospel spirit, the liberating energies of man and of society. And Mary will appear not as a Mother exclusively concerned with her own divine Son, but rather as a woman whose action helped to strengthen the apostolic community's faith in Christ (cf. Jn 2:1-12), and whose maternal role was extended and became universal on Calvary.[105] These are but examples, but examples which show clearly that the figure of the Blessed Virgin does not disillusion any of the profound expectations of the men and women of our time but offers them the perfect model of the disciple of the Lord: the disciple who builds up the earthly and temporal city while being a diligent pilgrim towards the heavenly and eternal city; the disciple who works for that justice which sets free the oppressed and for that charity which assists the needy; but above all, the disciple who is the active witness of that love which builds up Christ in people's hearts.

38. Having offered these directives, which are intended to favor the harmonious development of devotion to the Mother of the Lord, we consider it opportune to draw attention to certain attitudes of piety which are incorrect. The Second Vatican Council has already authoritatively denounced both the exaggeration of content and form which even falsifies doctrine and likewise the small-mindedness which obscures the figure and mission of Mary. The Council has also denounced certain devotional deviations, such as vain credulity, which substitutes reliance on merely external practices for serious commitment. Another deviation is sterile and ephemeral sentimentality, so alien to the spirit of the Gospel that demands persevering and practical action.[106] We reaffirm the Council's reprobation of such attitudes and practices.

They are not in harmony with the Catholic Faith and therefore they must have no place in Catholic worship. Careful defense against these errors and deviations will render devotion to the Blessed Virgin more vigorous and more authentic. It will make this devotion solidly based, with the consequence that study of the sources of Revelation and attention to the documents of the magisterium will prevail over the exaggerated search for novelties or extraordinary phenomena. It will ensure that this devotion is objective in its historical seeing, and for this reason everything that is obviously legendary or false must be eliminated. It will ensure that this devotion matches its doctrinal content, hence the necessity of avoiding a one-sided presentation of the figure of Mary, which by overstressing one element compromises the overall picture given by the Gospel. It will make this devotion clear in its motivation; hence every unworthy self-interest is to be carefully banned from the area of what is sacred.

39. Finally, insofar as it may be necessary we would like to repeat that the ultimate purpose of devotion to the Blessed Virgin is to glorify God and to lead Christians to commit themselves to a life which is in absolute conformity with his will. When the children of the Church unite their voices with the voice of the unknown woman in the Gospel and glorify the Mother of Jesus by saying to him: "Blessed is the womb that bore you and the breasts that you sucked" (Lk 11:27), they will be led to ponder the Divine Master's serious reply: "Blessed rather are those who hear the word of God and keep it!" (Lk 11:28). While it is true that this reply is in itself lively praise of Mary, as various Fathers of the Church interpreted it[107] and the Second Vatican Council has confirmed,[108] it is also an admonition to us to live our lives in accordance with God's commandments. It is also an echo of other words of the Savior: "Not every one who says to me 'Lord, Lord,' will enter the kingdom of heaven, but he who does the will of my Father who is in heaven" (Mt 7:21); and again: "You are my friends if you do what I command you" (Jn 15:14).

# Part Three

# Observations On Two Exercises Of Piety: The Angelus And The Rosary

40. We have indicated a number of principles which can help to give fresh vigor to devotion to the Mother of the Lord. It is now up to episcopal conferences, to those in charge of local communities and to the various religious congregations prudently to revise practices and exercises of piety in honor of the Blessed Virgin, and to encourage the creative impulse of those who through genuine religious inspiration or pastoral sensitivity wish to establish new forms of piety. For different reasons we nevertheless feel it is opportune to consider here two practices which are widespread in the West, and with which this Apostolic See has concerned itself on various occasions: the Angelus and the Rosary.

## The Angelus

41. What we have to say about the Angelus is meant to be only a simple but earnest exhortation to continue its traditional recitation wherever and whenever possible. The Angelus does not need to be revised, because of its simple structure, its Biblical character, its historical origin which links it to the prayer for peace and safety, and its quasi-liturgical rhythm which sanctifies different moments during the day, and because it reminds us of the Paschal Mystery, in which recalling the Incarnation of the Son of God we pray that we may be led "through his passion and cross to the glory of his resurrection."[109] These factors ensure that the Angelus despite the passing of centuries retains an unaltered value and an intact freshness. It is true that certain customs traditionally linked with the recitation of the Angelus have disappeared or can continue only with difficulty in modern life. But these are marginal elements. The value of contemplation on the mystery of the Incarnation of the Word, of the greeting to the Virgin, and of recourse to her merciful intercession remains unchanged. And despite the changed conditions of the times, for the majority of people there remain unaltered the characteristic periods of the day, morning,

noon and evening, which mark the periods of their activity and constitute an invitation to pause in prayer.

## The Rosary

42. We wish now, venerable Brothers, to dwell for a moment on the renewal of the pious practice which has been called "the compendium of the entire Gospel"[110]: the Rosary. To this our predecessors have devoted close attention and care. On many occasions they have recommended its frequent recitation, encouraged its diffusion, explained its nature, recognized its suitability for fostering contemplative prayer, prayer of both praise and petition, and recalled its intrinsic effectiveness for promoting Christian life and apostolic commitment.

We, too, from the first general audience of our pontificate on July 13, 1963, have shown our great esteem for the pious practice of the Rosary.[111] Since that time we have underlined its value on many different occasions, some ordinary, some grave. Thus, at a moment of anguish and uncertainty, we published the Letter Christi Matri (September 15, 1966), in order to obtain prayers to Our Lady of the Rosary and to implore from God the supreme benefit of peace.[112] "We renewed this appeal in our Apostolic Exhortation Recurrens mensis October (October 7 1969), in which we also commemorated the fourth centenary of the Apostolic Letter Consueverunt Romani pontifices of our predecessor Saint Pius V, who in that document explained and in a certain sense established the traditional form of the Rosary.[113]

43. Our assiduous and affectionate interest in the Rosary has led us to follow very attentively the numerous meetings which in recent years have been devoted to the pastoral role of the Rosary in the modern world, meetings arranged by associations and individuals profoundly attached to the Rosary and attended by bishops, priests, religious and lay people of proven experience and recognized ecclesial awareness. Among these people special mention should be made of the sons of Saint Dominic, by tradition the guardians and promoters of this very salutary practice. Parallel with such meetings has been the research work of historians, work

aimed not at defining in a sort of archaeological fashion the primitive form of the Rosary but at uncovering the original inspiration and driving force behind it and its essential structure. The fundamental characteristics of the Rosary, its essential elements and their mutual relationship have all emerged more clearly from these congresses and from the research carried out.

44. Thus, for instance, the Gospel inspiration of the Rosary has appeared more clearly: the Rosary draws from the Gospel the presentation of the mysteries and its main formulas. As it moves from the angel's joyful greeting and the Virgin's pious assent, the Rosary takes its inspiration from the Gospel to suggest the attitude with which the faithful should recite it. In the harmonious succession of Hail Mary's the Rosary puts before us once more a fundamental mystery of the Gospel, the Incarnation of the Word, contemplated at the decisive moment of the Annunciation to Mary. The Rosary is thus a Gospel prayer, as pastors and scholars like to define it, more today perhaps than in the past.

45. It has also been more easily seen how the orderly and gradual unfolding of the Rosary reflects the very way in which the Word of God, mercifully entering into human affairs, brought about the Redemption. The Rosary considers in harmonious succession the principal salvific events accomplished in Christ, from his virginal conception and the mysteries of his childhood to the culminating moments of the Passover, the blessed passion and the glorious resurrection, and to the effects of this on the infant Church on the day of Pentecost, and on the Virgin Mary when at the end of her earthly life she was assumed body and soul into her heavenly home. It has also been observed that the division of the mysteries of the Rosary into three parts not only adheres strictly to the chronological order of the facts but above all reflects the plan of the original proclamation of the Faith and sets forth once more the mystery of Christ in the very way in which it is seen by Saint Paul in the celebrated "hymn" of the Letter to the Philippians, kenosis, death and exaltation (cf. Phil 2:6-11).

46. As a Gospel prayer, centered on the mystery of the redemptive Incarnation, the Rosary is therefore a prayer with a clearly Christological orientation. Its most characteristic element, in fact, the litany-like succession of Hail Mary's, becomes in itself

an unceasing praise of Christ, who is the ultimate object both of the angel's announcement and of the greeting of the mother of John the Baptist: "Blessed is the fruit of your womb" (Lk 1:42). We would go further and say that the succession of Hail Mary's constitutes the warp on which is woven the contemplation of the mysteries. The Jesus that each Hail Mary recalls is the same Jesus whom the succession of the mysteries proposes to us, now as the Son of God, now as the Son of the Virgin, at his birth in a stable at Bethlehem, at his presentation by his Mother in the Temple, as a youth full of zeal for his Father's affairs, as the Redeemer in agony in the garden, scourged and crowned with thorns, carrying the cross and dying on Calvary, risen from the dead and ascended to the glory of the Father to send forth the gift of the Spirit. As is well known, at one time there was a custom, still preserved in certain places, of adding to the name of Jesus in each Hail Mary reference to the mystery being contemplated. And this was done precisely in order to help contemplation and to make the mind and the voice act in unison.

47. There has also been felt with greater urgency the need to point out once more the importance of a further essential element in the Rosary, in addition to the value of the elements of praise and petition, namely the element of contemplation. Without this the Rosary is a body without a soul, and its recitation is in danger of becoming a mechanical repetition of formulas and of going counter to the warning of Christ: "And in praying do not heap up empty phrases as the Gentiles do; for they think that they will be heard for their many words" (Mt 6:7). By its nature the recitation of the Rosary calls for a quiet rhythm and a lingering pace, helping the individual to meditate on the mysteries of the Lord's life as seen through the eyes of her who was closest to the Lord. In this way the unfathomable riches of these mysteries are unfolded.

48. Finally, as a result of modern reflection the relationships between the liturgy and the Rosary have been more clearly understood. On the one hand it has been emphasized that the Rosary is, as it were, a branch sprung from the ancient trunk of the Christian liturgy, the Psalter of the Blessed Virgin, whereby the humble were associated in the Church's hymn of praise and

universal intercession. On the other hand it has been noted that this development occurred at a time, the last period of the Middle Ages, when the liturgical spirit was in decline and the faithful were turning from the liturgy towards a devotion to Christ's humanity and to the Blessed Virgin Mary, a devotion favoring a certain external sentiment of piety. Not many years ago some people began to express the desire to see the Rosary included among the rites of the liturgy, while other people, anxious to avoid repetition of former pastoral mistakes, unjustifiably disregarded the Rosary. Today the problem can easily be solved in the light of the principles of the Constitution Sacrosanctum Concilium. Liturgical celebrations and the pious practice of the Rosary must be neither set in opposition to one another nor considered as being identical.[114] The more an expression of prayer preserves its own true nature and individual characteristics the more fruitful it becomes. Once the pre-eminent value of liturgical rites has been reaffirmed it will not be difficult to appreciate the fact that the Rosary is a practice of piety which easily harmonizes with the liturgy. In fact, like the liturgy, it is of a community nature, draws its inspiration from Sacred Scripture and is oriented towards the mystery of Christ. The commemoration in the liturgy and the contemplative remembrance proper to the Rosary, although existing on essentially different planes of reality, have as their object the same salvific events wrought by Christ. The former presents new, under the veil of signs and operative in a hidden way, the great mysteries of our Redemption. The latter, by means of devout contemplation, recalls these same mysteries to the mind of the person praying and stimulates the will to draw from them the norms of living. Once this substantial difference has been established, it is not difficult to understand that the Rosary is an exercise of piety that draws its motivating force from the liturgy and leads naturally back to it, if practiced in conformity with its original inspiration.; It does not, however, become part of the liturgy. In fact, meditation on the mysteries of the Rosary, by familiarizing the hearts and minds of the faithful with the mysteries of Christ, can be an excellent preparation for the creation of those same mysteries in the liturgical action and an also become a continuing echo thereof. However, it is a mistake to recite the Rosary during the celebration of the liturgy, though unfortunately this practice still persists here and there.

49. The Rosary of the Blessed Virgin Mary, according to the tradition accepted by our predecessor St. Pius V and authoritatively taught by him, consists of various elements disposed in an organic fashion:

a) Contemplation in communion with Mary, of a series of mysteries of salvation, wisely distributed into three cycles. These mysteries express the joy of the messianic times, the salvific suffering of Christ and the glory of the Risen Lord which fills the Church. This contemplation by its very nature encourages practical reflection and provides stimulating norms for living.

b) The Lord's Prayer, or Our Father, which by reason of its immense value is at the basis of Christian prayer and ennobles that prayer in its various expressions.

c) The litany-like succession of the Hail Mary, which is made up of the angel's greeting to the Virgin (cf. Lk 1:28), and of Elizabeth's greeting (cf. Lk 1:42), followed by the ecclesial supplication, Holy Mary. The continued series of Hail Mary's is the special characteristic of the Rosary, and their number, in the full and typical number of one hundred and fifty, presents a certain analogy with the Psalter and is an element that goes back to the very origin of the exercise of piety. But this number, divided, according to a well-tried custom, into decades attached to the individual mysteries, is distributed in the three cycles already mentioned, thus giving rise to the Rosary of fifty Hail Mary's as we know it. This latter has entered into use as the normal measure of the pious exercise and as such has been adopted by popular piety and approved by papal authority, which also enriched it with numerous indulgences.

d) The doxology Glory be to the Father which, in conformity with an orientation common to Christian piety concludes the prayer with the glorifying of God who is one and three, from whom, through whom and in whom all things have their being (cf. Rom 11:36).

50. These are the elements of the Rosary. Each has its own particular character which, wisely understood and appreciated, should be reflected in the recitation in order that the Rosary may

express all its richness and variety. Thus the recitation will be grave and suppliant during the Lord's Prayer, lyrical and full of praise during the tranquil succession of Hail Mary's, contemplative in the recollected meditation on the mysteries and full of adoration during the doxology. This applies to all the ways in which the Rosary is usually recited: privately, in intimate recollection with the Lord; in community, in the family or in groups of the faithful gathered together to ensure the special presence of the Lord (cf. Mt 18:20); or publicly, in assemblies to which the ecclesial community is invited.

51. In recent times certain exercises of piety have been created which take their inspiration from the Rosary. Among such exercises we wish to draw attention to and recommend those which insert into the ordinary celebration of the word of God some elements of the Rosary, such as meditation on the mysteries and litany-like repetition of the angel's greeting to Mary. In this way these elements gain in importance, since they are found in the context of Bible readings, illustrated with a homily, accompanied by silent pauses and emphasized with song. We are happy to know that such practices have helped to promote a more complete understanding of the spiritual riches of the Rosary itself and have served to restore esteem for its recitation among youth associations and movements.

52. We now desire, as a continuation of the thought of our predecessors, to recommend strongly the recitation of the family Rosary. The Second Vatican Council has pointed out how the family, the primary and vital cell of society, "shows itself to be the domestic sanctuary of the Church through the mutual affection of its members and the common prayer they offer to God."[115] The Christian family is thus seen to be a domestic Church"[116] if its members, each according to his proper place and tasks, all together promote justice, practice works of mercy, devote themselves to helping their brethren, take part in the apostolate of the wider local community and play their part in its liturgical worship.[117] This will be all the more true if together they offer up prayers to God. If this element of common prayer were missing, the family would lack its very character as a domestic Church. Thus there must logically follow a concrete effort to reinstate communal prayer in family life

if there is to be a restoration of the theological concept of the family as the domestic Church.

53. In accordance with the directives of the Council the Institutio Generulis de Liturgia Horarum rightly numbers the family among the groups in which the Divine Office can suitably be celebrated in community: "It is fitting...that the family, as a domestic sanctuary of the Church, should not only offer prayers to God in common, but also, according to circumstances, should recite parts of the Liturgy of the Hours, in order to be more intimately linked with the Church."[118] No avenue should be left unexplored to ensure that this clear and practical recommendation finds within Christian families growing and joyful acceptance.

54. But there is no doubt that, after the celebration of the Liturgy of the Hours, the high point which family prayer can reach, the Rosary should be considered as one of the best and most efficacious prayers in common that the Christian family is invited to recite. We like to think, and sincerely hope, that when the family gathering becomes a time of prayer, the Rosary is a frequent and favored manner of praying. We are well aware that the changed conditions of life today do not make family gatherings easy, and that even when such a gathering is possible many circumstances make it difficult to turn it into an occasion of prayer. There is no doubt of the difficulty. But it is characteristic of the Christian in his manner of life not to give in to circumstances but to overcome them, not to succumb but to make an effort. Families which want to live in full measure the vocation and spirituality proper to the Christian family must therefore devote all their energies to overcoming the pressures that hinder family gatherings and prayer in common.

55. In concluding these observations, which give proof of the concern and esteem which the Apostolic See has for the Rosary of the Blessed Virgin, we desire at the same time to recommend that this very worthy devotion should not be propagated in a way that is too one-sided or exclusive. The Rosary is an excellent prayer, but the faithful should feel serenely free in its regard. They should be drawn to its calm recitation by its intrinsic appeal.

# Conclusion

## Theological And Pastoral Value Of Devotion To The Blessed Virgin

56. Venerable Brothers, as we come to the end of this our Apostolic Exhortation we wish to sum up and emphasize the theological value of devotion to the Blessed Virgin and to recall briefly its pastoral effectiveness for renewing the Christian way of life.

The Church's devotion to the Blessed Virgin is an intrinsic element of Christian worship. The honor which the Church has always and everywhere shown to the Mother of the Lord, from the blessing with which Elizabeth greeted Mary (cf. Lk 1:42-45) right up to the expressions of praise and petition used today, is a very strong witness to the Church's norm of prayer and an invitation to become more deeply conscious of her norm of faith. And the converse is likewise true. The Church's norm of faith requires that her norm of prayer should everywhere blossom forth with regard to the Mother of Christ. Such devotion to the Blessed Virgin is firmly rooted in the revealed word and has solid dogmatic foundations. It is based on the singular dignity of Mary, "Mother of the Son of God, and therefore beloved daughter of the Father and Temple of the Holy Spirit, Mary, who, because of this extraordinary grace, is far greater than any other creature on earth or in heaven."[119] This devotion takes into account the part she played at decisive moments in the history of the salvation which her Son accomplished, and her holiness, already full at her Immaculate Conception yet increasing all the time as she obeyed the will of the Father and accepted the path of suffering (cf. Lk 2:34-35, 41-52; Jn 19:25-27), growing constantly in faith, hope and charity. Devotion to Mary recalls too her mission and the special position she holds within the People of God, of which she is the preeminent member, a shining example and the loving Mother; it recalls her unceasing and efficacious intercession which, although she is assumed into heaven, draws her close to those who ask her help, including those who do not realize that they are her children. It recalls Mary's glory which ennobles the whole of mankind, as the outstanding phrase of Dante recalls: "You have so ennobled human nature that its very Creator did not disdain to share in it."[120] Mary, in fact, is one of our race, a true daughter of Eve, though free of that mother's sin, and truly our sister, who as a poor and humble woman fully shared our lot.

We would add further that devotion to the Blessed Virgin finds its ultimate justification in the unfathomable and free will of God who, being eternal and divine charity (cf. 1 Jn 4:7-8, 16), accomplishes all things according to a loving design. He loved her and did great things for her (cf. Lk 1:49). He loved her for his own sake, and he loved her for our sake, too; he gave her to himself and he gave her also to us.

57. Christ is the only way to the Father (cf. Jn 14:4-11), and the ultimate example to whom the disciple must conform his own conduct (cf. Jn 13:15), to the extent of sharing Christ's sentiments (cf. Phil 2:5), living his life and possessing his Spirit (cf. Gal 2:20; Rom 8:10-11). The Church has always taught this and nothing in pastoral activity should obscure this doctrine. But the Church, taught by the Holy Spirit and benefiting from centuries of experience, recognizes that devotion to the Blessed Virgin, subordinated to worship of the divine Savior and in connection with it, also has a great pastoral effectiveness and constitutes a force for renewing Christian living. It is easy to see the reason for this effectiveness Mary's many-sided mission to the People of God is a super natural reality which operates and bears fruit within the body of the Church. One finds cause for joy in considering the different aspects of this mission, and seeing how each of these aspects with its individual effectiveness is directed towards the same end, namely, producing in the children the spiritual characteristics of the first-born Son. The Virgin's maternal intercession, her exemplary holiness and the divine grace which is in her become for the human race a reason for divine hope.

The Blessed Virgin's role as Mother leads the People of God to turn with filial confidence to her who is ever ready to listen with a mother's affection and efficacious assistance.[121] Thus the People of God have learned to call on her as the Consoler of the afflicted, the Health of the sick, and the Refuge of sinners, that they may find comfort in tribulation, relief in sickness and liberating strength in guilt. For she, who is free from sin, leads her children to combat sin with energy and resoluteness.[122] This liberation from sin and evil (cf. Mt 6:13), it must be repeated, is the necessary premise for any renewal of Christian living.

The Blessed Virgin's exemplary holiness encourages the faithful to "raise their eyes to Mary who shines forth before the whole community of the elect as a model of the virtues."[123] It is a question of solid, evangelical virtues: faith and the docile acceptance of the Word of God (cf. Lk 1:26-38, 1:45, 11:27-28; Jn 2:5); generous obedience (cf. Lk 1:38); genuine humility (cf. Lk 1:48); solicitous charity (cf. Lk 1:39-56); profound wisdom (cf. Lk 1:29, 34; 2:19); worship of God manifested in alacrity in the fulfillment of religious duties (cf. Lk 2:21-41), in gratitude for gifts received (cf. Lk 1:46-49), in her offering in the Temple (cf. Lk 2:22-24) and in her prayer in the midst of the apostolic community (cf. Acts 1:12-14); her fortitude in exile (cf. Mt 2:13-23) and in suffering (cf. Lk 2:34-35, 49; Jn 19:25); her poverty reflecting dignity and trust in God (cf. Lk 1:48, 2:24) her attentive care for her Son, from his humble birth to the ignominy of the cross (cf. Lk 2:1-7; Jn 19:25-27); her delicate forethought (cf. Jn 2:1-11); her virginal purity (cf. Mt 1:18-25; Lk 1:26-38); her strong and chaste married love. These virtues of the Mother will also adorn her children who steadfastly study her example in order to reflect it in their own lives. And this progress in virtue will appear as the consequence and the already mature fruit of that pastoral zeal which springs from devotion to the Blessed Virgin.

Devotion to the Mother of the Lord becomes for the faithful an opportunity for growing in divine grace, and this is the ultimate aim of all pastoral activity. For it is impossible to honor her who is "full of grace" (Lk 1:28) without thereby honoring in oneself the state of grace, which is friendship with God, communion with him and the indwelling of the Holy Spirit. It is this divine grace which takes possession of the whole man and conforms him to the image of the Son of God (cf. Rom 8:29; Col 1:18). The Catholic Church, endowed with centuries of experience, recognizes in devotion to the Blessed Virgin a powerful aid for man as he strives for fulfillment. Mary, the New Woman, stands at the side of Christ, the New Man, within whose mystery the mystery of man[124] alone finds true light; she is given to its as a pledge and guarantee that God's plan in Christ for the salvation of the whole man has already achieved realization in a creature: in her. Contemplated in the episodes of the Gospels and in the reality which she already possesses in the City of God, the Blessed Virgin Mary offers a calm vision and a reassuring word to modern man, torn as he often is between anguish and hope, defeated by the sense of his own limitations and assailed by limitless aspirations, troubled in his mind and divided in his heart, uncertain before the riddle of death, oppressed by loneliness while yearning for fellowship, a prey to boredom and disgust. She shows forth the victory of hope over anguish, of fellowship over solitude, of peace over anxiety, of joy and beauty over boredom and disgust, of eternal visions over earthly ones, of life over death.

Let the very words that she spoke to the servants at the marriage feast of Cana, "Do whatever he tells you" (Jn 2:5), be a seal on our Exhortation and a further reason in favor of the pastoral value of devotion to the Blessed Virgin as a means of leading men to Christ. Those words, which at first sight were limited to the desire to remedy an embarrassment at the feast, are seen in the context of Saint John's Gospel to re-echo the words used by the people of Israel to give approval to the Covenant at Sinai (cf. Ex 19:8, 24:3, 7; Dt 5:27) and to renew their commitments (cf. Jos 24:24; Ezr 10:12; Neh 5:12). And they are words which harmonize wonderfully with those spoken by the Father at the theophany on Mount Tabor: "Listen to him" (Mt 17:5).

# Epilogue

58. Venerable Brothers, we have dealt at length with an integral element of Christian worship: devotion to the Mother of the Lord. This has been called for by the nature of the subject, one which in these recent years has been the object of study and revision and at times the cause of some perplexity. We are consoled to think that the work done by this Apostolic See and by yourselves

in order to carry out the norms of the Council, particularly the liturgical reform, is a stepping-stone to an ever more lively and adoring worship of God, the Father and the Son and the Holy Spirit, and to an increase of the Christian life of the faithful. We are filled with confidence when we note that the renewed Roman liturgy, also taken as a whole, is a splendid illustration of the Church's devotion to the Blessed Virgin. We are upheld by the hope that the directives issued in order to render this devotion ever more pure and vigorous will be applied with sincerity. We rejoice that the Lord has given us the opportunity of putting forward some points for reflection in order to renew and confirm esteem for the practice of the rosary. Comfort, confidence, hope and joy are the sentiments which we wish to transform into fervent praise and thanksgiving to the Lord as we unite our voice with that of the Blessed Virgin in accordance with the prayer of the Roman Liturgy.

Dear Brothers, while we express the hope that thanks to your generous commitment, there will be among the clergy and among the people entrusted to your care a salutary increase of devotion to Mary with undoubted profit for the Church and for society, we cordially impart our special apostolic blessing to yourselves and to all the faithful people to whom you devote your pastoral zeal.

Given in Rome, at Saint Peter's, on the second day of February, the Feast of the Presentation of the Lord, in the year 1974, the eleventh of our Pontificate.

Paulus PP. VI

\* \* \* \* \* \* \* \* \* \*

## Endnotes

[1]    Cf. Lactantius, *Divinae Institutiones* IV, 4, 6-10: *CSEL* 19, p. 279.

[2]    Cf. II Vatican Council, Constitution on the Sacred Liturgy, *Sacrosanctum Concilium*, 1-3, 11, 21, 48. *AAS* 56 (1964), pp. 97-98, 102-

103, 105-106, 113.

³       II Vatican Council, Constitution on the Sacred Liturgy, *Sacrosanctum Concilium*, 103: *AAS* 56 (1964), p. 125.

⁴       Cf. II Vatican Council, Dogmatic Constitution on the Church, *Lumen Gentium*, 66: *AAS* 57 (1965), p.65.

⁵       *Ibid.*

⁶       Votive Mass of the Blessed Virgin Mary, Mother of the Church, Preface.

⁷       Cf. II Vatican Council, Dogmatic Constitution on the Church, *Lumen Gentium*, 66-67: *AAS* 57 (1965), pp. 65-66, Constitution on the Sacred Liturgy, *Sacrosanctum Concilium*, 103: *AAS* 56 (1964), p. 125.

⁸       Apostolic Exhortation, *Signum Magnum*: *AAS* 59 (1967), pp. 465-475.

⁹       Cf. II Vatican Council, Constitution on the Sacred Liturgy, *Sacrosanctum Concilium*, 3: *AAS* 56 (1964), p. 98.

¹⁰      Cf. II Vatican Council *ibid.*, 102: *AAS* 56 (1964), p. 125.

¹¹      Cf. Roman Missal restored by Decree of the Sacred Ecumenical II Vatican Council, promulgated by authority of Pope Paul VI typical edition, MCMLXX, 8 December, Preface.

¹²      Roman Missal, restored by Decree of the Sacred Ecumenical II Vatican Council promulgated by authority of Pope Paul VI. *Ordo Lectionum Missae*, typical edition MCMLXIX, p. 8. First Reading (Year A: Is 7:10-14: "Behold a Virgin shall conceive"; Year B: 2 Sam 7:1-15; 8b-11, 16: "The throne of David shall be established for ever before the face of the Lord"; Year C: Mic 5:2-5a [Heb 1-4a]: "Out of you will be born for me the one who is to rule over Israel.).

¹³      *Ibid.*, p. 8. Gospel (Year A: Mt 1:18-24: "Jesus is born of Mary who was espoused to Joseph, the Son of David"; Year B: Lk 1:26-38: "You are to conceive and bear a Son"; Year C: Lk 1:39-45: "Why should I be honored with a visit from the Mother of my Lord?").

¹⁴      Cf. Roman Missal, Advent Preface, II.

¹⁵      Roman Missal, *ibid.*

[16]     Roman Missal, Eucharistic Prayer, *Communicantes* for Christmas and its octave.

[17]     Roman Missal, 1 January, Entry antiphon and Collect.

[18]     Cf. Roman Missal, 22 August, Collect.

[19]     Roman Missal, 8 September, Prayer after Communion.

[20]     Roman Missal, 31 May, Collect.

[21]     Cf. *Ibid.*, Collect and Prayer over the gifts.

[22]     Cf. Roman Missal, 15 September, Collect.

[23]     Cf. 1, p. 15.

[24]     From among the many anaphoras cf. the following which are held in special honor by the Eastern rites: *Anaphora Marci Evangelistae: Prex Eucharistica*, ed. A. Hanggi-I. Pahl, Fribourg *Editions Universitaires*, 1968, p. 107; *Anaphora Iacobi fratris Domini graeca*, ibid., p. 257; *Anaphora Ioannis Chrysostomi, ibid.*, p. 229.

[25]     Cf. Roman Missal, 8 December, Preface.

[26]     Cf. Roman Missal, 15 August, Preface.

[27]     Cf. Roman Missal, 1 January, Prayer after Communion.

[28]     Cf. Roman Missal, Common of the Blessed Virgin Mary, 6, Paschaltide, Collect.

[29]     Roman Missal, 15 September, Collect.

[30]     Roman Missal, 31 May Collect. On the same lines is the Preface of the Blessed Virgin Mary, II: "We do well... in celebrating the memory of the Virgin Mary... to glorify your love for us in the words of her song of thanksgiving."

[31]     Cf. Lectionary, III Sunday of Advent (Year C: Zeph 3:14-18a); IV Sunday of Advent (cf. above footnote 12); Sunday within the octave of Christmas (Year A: Mt 2:13-15; 19-23; Year B: Lk 2:22-40; Year C: Lk 2: 41-52); II Sunday after Christmas (Jn 1:1-18); VII Sunday after Easter (Year A: Acts 1:12-14); II Sunday of the Year C: (Jn 1:1-12); X Sunday of the Year

(Year B: Gn 3:9-15); XIV Sunday of the Year (Year B: Mk 6:1-6).

[32]    Cf. Lectionary, the catechumenate and baptism of adults; the Lord's Prayer (Second Reading, 2 Gal 4:4-7); Christian initiation outside the Easter Vigil (Gospel, 7, Jn 1:1-5; 9-16; 16-18); Nuptial Mass (Gospel, 7, Jn 2: 1-11); Consecration of Virgins and religious profession (First Reading 7, Is 61:9-11; Gospel, 6, Mk 3:31-35; Lk 1:26-38 [cf. Ordo Consecrationis Virginum, 130; Ordo Professionis religiosae, Pars altera, 145]).

[33]    Cf. Lectionary, For refugees and exiles (Gospel, 1, Mt 2:13-15; 19-23); In thanksgiving (First Reading, 4, Zeph 3:14-15).

[34]    Cf. *La Divina Commedia, Paradiso XXXIII*, 1-9; cf. Liturgy of the Hours, remembrance of Our Lady on Saturdays, Office of Reading, Hymn.

[35]    Ordo baptismi parvulorum, 48; *Ordo initiationis christianae addultorum*, 214.

[36]    Cf. Rituale Romanum, *Tit. VII, cap. III, De benedictione mulieris post partum.*

[37]    Cf. *Ordo professionis religiosae, Pars Prior*, 57 and 67.

[38]    Cf. *Ordo consecrationis virginum*, 16.

[39]    Cf. *Ordo professionis religiosae, Pars Prior*, 62 and 142; *Pars Altera*, 68 and 158; *Ordo consecrationis virginum*, 18 and 20.

[40]    Cf. *Ordo unctionis infirmorum eorumque pastoralis curae*, 143, 146, 147, 150.

[41]    Cf. Roman Missal, Masses for the Dead, For dead brothers and sisters, relations and benefactors, Collect.

[42]    Cf. *Ordo exsequiarum* 226.

[43]    Cf. II Vatican Council, Dogmatic Constitution on the Church, *Lumen Gentium*, 63: *AAS* 57 (1965), p. 64.

[44]    Cf. II Vatican Council, Constitution on the Sacred Liturgy, *Sacrosanctum Concilium*, 7: *AAS* 56 (1964), pp. 100-101.

[45]    *Sermo* 215, 4: *PL* 38, 1074.

[46]    *Ibid.*

[47]     Cf. II Vatican Council, Dogmatic Constitution on Divine Revelation, *Dei Verbum*, 21: *AAS* 58 (1966) pp. 827-828.

[48]     Cf. *Adversus Haereses* IV, 7, 1: *PG* 7,1, 990-991; *SCh* 100, t, II, pp. 454-458.

[49]     Cf. *Adversus Haereses* III, 10, 2: *PG* 7,1, 873; *SCh* 34, p. 164.

[50]     Cf. II Vatican Council, Dogmatic Constitution on the Church, *Lumen Gentium*, 62: *AAS* 57 (1965), p. 63.

[51]     II Vatican Council, Constitution on the Sacred Liturgy *Sacrosanctum Concilium*, 83: *AAS* 56 (1964), p. 121.

[52]     II Vatican Council, Dogmatic Constitution on the Church, *Lumen Gentium*, 63: *AAS* 57 (1965), p. 64.

[53]     *Ibid.*, 64: *AAS* 57 (1965), p. 64.

[54]     *Tractatus XXV (In Nativitate Domini)*, 5: *CCL* 138, p. 123; *SCh* 22, p. 132; cf. also *Tractatus XXIX (In Nativitate Domine)* 1: *CCL ibid.*, p. 147; *SCh* p. 178; *Tractatus LXIII (De Passione Domini)* 6: *CCL ibid.*, p. 386: *SCh* 74, p. 82.

[55]     M. Ferotin, *"Le Liber Mozarabicus Sacramentorum"*, col. 56.

[56]     *In Purificatione B. Mariae, Sermo III, 2: PL* 183, 370; *Sancti Bernardi Opera*, ed. J. Leclercq-H. Rochais, vol. IV, Rome 1966, p. 342.

[57]     Cf. II Vatican Council, Dogmatic Constitution on the Church, *Lumen Gentium*, 57: *AAS* 57 (1965), p. 61.

[58]     *Ibid.*, 58: *AAS* 57 (1965) p. 61.

[59]     Cf. Pius XII, Encyclical Letter *Mystici Corporis*: *AAS* 35 (1943), p. 247.

[60]     Cf. II Vatican Council, Constitution on the Sacred Liturgy *Sacrosanctum Concilium*, 47: *AAS* 56 (1964), p. 113.

[61]     *Ibid.*, 102, 106: *AAS* 56 (1964), pp. 125-126.

[62]     "...Deign to remember all who have been pleasing to you throughout the ages the holy Fathers, the Patriarchs, Prophets, Apostles... and the holy

and glorious Mother of God and all the saints... may they remember our misery and poverty, and together with us may they offer you this great and unbloody sacrifice": *Anaphora Iacobi fratris Domini syriaca: Prex Eucharistica*, ed. A. Hanggi-I, Pahl, Fribourg, *Editions Universitaires*, 1968, p. 274.

[63]     *Expositio Evangelii secundum Lucam*, 11 26: *CSEL* 32, IV, p. 55; *SCh* 45, pp. 83-84.

[64]     Cf. II Vatican Council, Dogmatic Constitution on the Church *Lumen Gentium*, 62: *AAS* 57 (1965), p. 63.

[65]     II Vatican Council, Constitution on the Sacred Liturgy *Sacrosanctum Concilium*, 103: *AAS* 56 (1964), p. 125.

[66]     II Vatican Council, Dogmatic Constitution on the Church, *Lumen Gentium*, 67: *AAS* 57 (1965), pp. 65-66.

[67]     Cf. *ibid*.

[68]     Cf. II Vatican Council, Constitution on the Sacred Liturgy *Sacrosanctum Concilium*, 104: *AAS* 56 (1964), pp. 125-126.

[69]     II Vatican Council, Dogmatic Constitution on the Church, *Lumen Gentium*, 66: *AAS* 57 (1965), p. 65.

[70]     Cf. Paul VI, Talk of 24 April 1970, in the Church of Our Lady of Bonaria in Cagliari: *AAS* 62 (1970), p. 300.

[71]     Pius IX, Apostolic Letter *Ineffabilis Deus: Pii IX Pontificis Maximi Acta*, I, 1, Rome 1854, p. 599. Cf. also *V. Sardi, La solemne definizione del dogma dell'Immacolato concepimento di Maria Santissima. Atti e documenti...*, Rome 1904-1905, vol. II, p. 302.

[72]     Cf. II Vatican Council, Dogmatic Constitution on the Church, *Lumen Gentium*, 66: *AAS* 57 (1965), p. 65.

[73]     S. Ildephonsus, *De virginitate perpetua sanctae Mariae*, chapter XII: *PL* 96, 108.

[74]     Cf. II Vatican Council, Dogmatic Constitution on the Church, *Lumen Gentium*, 56: *AAS* 57 (1965), p. 60 and the authors mentioned in note 176 of the document.

[75]     Cf. St. Ambrose, *De Spiritu Sancto II*, 37-38; *CSEL* 79 pp. 100-101; Cassian, *De incarnatione Domini II*, chapter II: *CSEL* 17, pp. 247-249; St.

Bede, *Homilia I*, 3: *CCL* 122, p. 18 and p. 20.

[76]      Cf. St. Ambrose, *De institutione virginis*, chapter XII, 79; *PL* 16 (ed. 1880), 339; *Epistula* 30, 3 and *Epistula* 42, 7: *ibid.*, 1107 and 1175; *Expositio evangelii secundum Lucam* X, 132: *SCh* 52, p. 200; S. Proclus of Constantinople, *Oratio I*, 1 and *Oratio V*, 3: *PG* 65, 681 and 720; St. Basil of Selcucia, *Oratio XXXIX*, 3: *PG* 85, 433; St. Andrew of Crete, *Oratio IV*: *PG* 97, 868; St. Germanus of Constantinople, *Oratio III*, 15: *PG* 98, 305.

[77]      Cf. St. Jerome, *Adversus Iovinianum* I, 33: *PL* 23, 267; St. Ambrose, *Epistula* 63, 33: *PL* 16 (ed. 1880), 1249; *De institutione virginis*, chapter XVII, 105: *ibid.*, 346; *De Spiritu Sancto* III, 79-80: *CSEL* 79, pp. 182-183; Sedulius, Hymn *"A solis ortus cardine"*, verses 13-14 *CSEL* 10, p. 164; *Hymnus Acathistos, Str.* 23: ed. I. B. Pitra, *Analecta Sacra*, I, p. 261; St. Proclus of Constantinople, *Oratio I*, 3: *PG* 65, 648; *Oratio II*, 6: *ibid.*, 700; St. Basil of Seleucia, *Oratio IV, In Nativitatem B. Mariae*: *PG* 97, 868; St. John Damascene, *Oratio IV*, 10: *PG* 96, 677.

[78]      Cf. Severus of Antioch, *Homilia* 57; PO 8, pp. 357-358; Hesychius of Jerusalem, *Homilia de sancta Maria Deipura*; *PG* 93, 1464; Chrysippus of Jerusalem, *Oratio in sanctam Mariam Deiparam*, 2 *PO* 19, p. 338; St. Andrew of Crete, *Oratio V*: *PG* 97, 896; St. John Damascene, *Oratio VI*, 6: *PG* 96, 972.

[79]      *Liber Apotheosis*, verses 571-572: *CCL* 126, p. 97.

[80]      Cf. S. Isidore, *De ortu et obitu Patrum*, chapter LXVII, 111: *PL* 83, 148; St. Ildephonsus, *De virginitate perpetua sanctae Mariae*, chapter X: *PL* 96, 95; St. Bernard, *In Assumptione B. Virginis Mariae: Sermo IV*, 4: *PL* 183, 428; *In Nativitate B. Virginis Mariae: ibid.*, 442; St. Peter Damien, *Carmina sacra et preces II, Oratio ad Deum Filium: PL* 145, 921; Antiphon *"Beata Dei Genetrix Maria"*: *Corpus antiphonalium officii*, ed. R. J. Hesbert, Rome 1970, vol IV, n. 6314, p. 80.

[81]      Cf. Paulus Diaconus, *Homilia I, In Assumptione B. Mariae Virginis*: *PL* 95, 1567; *De Assumptione sanctae Mariae Virginis*: Paschasio Radherto trib., 31, 42, 57, 83: ed. A. Ripberger, in *"Spicilegium Friburgense"*, 9, 1962, pp. 72, 76, 84, 96-97; Eadmer of Canterbury, *De excellentia Virginis Mariae*, chapters IV-V: *PL* 159, 562-567; St. Bernard, *In laudibus Virginis Matris, Homilia IV*, 3: *Sancti Bernardi Opera*, ed. J. Leclercq-H. Rochais, IV, Rome 1966, pp. 49-50.

[82]      Cf. Origen, *In Lucam Homilia* VII, 3: *PG* 13, 1817; *SCh* 87, p. 156; St. Cyril of Alexandria, *Commentarius in Aggaeum prophetam*, Chapter XIX: *PG* 71, 1060; St. Ambrose, *De fide* IV 9, 113-114: *CSEL* 78, pp. 197-198;

*Expositio evangelii secundum Lucam II*, 23 and 27-28: *CSEL* 32, IV, pp. 53-54 and 55-56; Severianus Gabalensis, *In mundi creationem, Oratio VI*, 10: *PG* 56 497-498; Antipater of Bostra, *Homilia in Sanctissimae Deiparae Annuntiationem*, 16: *PG* 85, 1785.

83    Cf. Eadmer of Canterbury, *De excellentia Virginis Mariae*, chapter VII: *PL* 159, 571; St. Amedeus of Lausanne, *De Maria Virginea Matre, Homilia VII*: *PL* 188, 1337; *SCh* 72, p. 184.

84    *De virginitate perpetua sanctae Mariae*, chapter XII: *PL* 96, 106.

85    II Vatican Council, Dogmatic Constitution on the Church *Lumen Gentium*, 54: *AAS* 57 (1965), p. 59; cf. Paulus VI, *Allocutio ad Patres Conciliares habita altera exacta Concilii Oecumenici Vaticani Secundi Sessione*, 4 December, 1963: *AAS* 56 (1964), p. 37.

86    Cf. II Vatican Council, Dogmatic Constitution on the Church *Lumen Gentium*, 6, 7-8, 9-11: *AAS* 57 (1965), pp. 8-9, 9-12, 12-21.

87    *Ibid.*, 63: *AAS* 57 (1965) p. 64.

88    St. Cyprian, *De Catholicae Ecclesiae unitate*, 5: *CSEL* 3, p. 214.

89    Isaac de Stella, *Sermo LI, In Assumptione B. Mariae*: *PL* 194, 1863.

90    *Sermo XXX*, I: *SCh* 164, p. 134.

91    Cf. II Vatican Council, Dogmatic Constitution on the Church *Lumen Gentium*, 66-69: *AAS* 57 (1965), pp. 65-67.

92    Cf. II Vatican Council, Dogmatic Constitution on Divine Revelation *Dei Verbum*, 25: *AAS* 58 (1966), pp. 829-830.

93    *Op. cit.*, 13: *AAS* 56 (1964), p. 103.

94    Cf. *Officum magni canonis paracletici, Magnum Orologion*, Athens 1963, p. 558; passim in liturgical canons and prayers; cf. Sophronius Eustradiadou, *Theotokarion*, Chennevieres-sur Marne 1931, pp. 9, 19.

95    Cf. II Vatican Council, Dogmatic Constitution on the Church *Lumen Gentium*, 69: *AAS* 57 (1965), pp. 66-67.

96    Cf. *ibid.*, 66: *AAS* 57 (1965), p. 65; Constitution on the Sacred Liturgy *Sacrosanctum Concilium*, 103: *AAS* 56 (1964), p. 125.

[97]     Cf. II Vatican Council, Dogmatic Constitution on the Church *Lumen Gentium*, 67: *AAS* 57 (1965), pp. 65-66.

[98]     *Ibid.*, 66: *AAS* 57 (1965), p. 65.

[99]     Cf. Paul VI, Address in the Vatican Basilica to the Fathers of the Council, 21 November, 1964: *AAS* 56 (1964), p. 1017.

[100]     II Vatican Council, Decree on Ecumenism *Unitatis Redintegratio*, 20: *AAS* 57 (1965), p. 105.

[101]     Encyclical Letter, *Adiutricem Populi*: *AAS* 28 (1895-1896), p. 135.

[102]     Cf. II Vatican Council, Dogmatic Constitution on the Church *Lumen Gentium*, 56: *AAS* 57 (1965), p. 60.

[103]     Cf. St. Peter Chrysologus, *Sermo CXLIII*: *PL* 52, 583.

[104]     II Vatican Council, Dogmatic Constitution on the Church *Lumen Gentium*, 55: *AAS* 57 (1965), pp. 59-60.

[105]     Cf. Paul VI, Apostolic Constitution, *Signum Magnum*, I: *AAS* 59 (1967), pp. 467-468; Roman Missal, 15 September, Prayer over the gifts.

[106]     Cf. II Vatican Council, Dogmatic Constitution on the Church *Lumen Gentium*, 67: *AAS* 57 (1965), pp. 65-66.

[107]     St. Augustine, *In Johannis Evangelium, Tractatus X*, 3; *CCL* 36, pp. 101-102; *Epistula* 243, *Ad Laetum*, 9: *CSEL* 57, pp. 575-576; St. Bede, *In Lucae Evangelium expositio*, IV, XI, 28: *CCL* 120, p. 237; *Homilia I*, 4: *CCL* 122, pp. 26-27.

[108]     Cf. II Vatican Council, Dogmatic Constitution on the Church *Lumen Gentium*, 58: *AAS* 57 (1965), p. 61.

[109]     Roman Missal, IV Sunday of Advent, Collect. Similarly the Collect of 25 March, which may be used in place of the previous one in the recitation of the Angelus.

[110]     Pius XII, Letter to the Archbishop of Manila, *"Philippinas Insulas"*: *AAS* 38 (1946), p. 419.

[111]     Discourse to the participants in the III Dominican International Rosary Congress: *Insegnamenti di Paolo VI* 1, (1963), pp. 463-464.

112    In *AAS* 58 (1966), pp. 745-749.

113    In *AAS* 61 (1969), pp. 649-654.

114    Cf. 13: *AAS* 56 (1964), p. 103.

115    Decree on the Lay Apostolate, *Apostolicam Actuositatem*, 11: *AAS* 58 (1966), p. 848.

116    Cf. II Vatican Council, Dogmatic Constitution on the Church *Lumen Gentium*, 11: *AAS* 57 (1965), p. 16.

117    Cf. II Vatican Council, Decree on the Lay Apostolate, *Apostolicam Actuositatem*, 11: *AAS* 58 (1966), p. 848.

118    Op. cit., 27.

119    II Vatican Council, Dogmatic Constitution on the Church *Lumen Gentium*, 53: *AAS* 57 (1965), pp. 58-59.

120    *La Divina Commedia, Paradiso XXXIII*, 4-6.

121    Cf. II Vatican Council, Dogmatic Constitution on the Church *Lumen Gentium*, 60-63: *AAS* 57 (1965), pp. 62-64.

122    Cf. *ibid.*, 65: *AAS* 57 (1965), pp. 64-65.

123    *Ibid.*, 65: *AAS* 57 (1965), p. 64.

124    Cf. II Vatican Council, Pastoral Constitution on the Church in the Modern World *Gaudium et Spes*, 22: *AAS* 58 (1966) pp. 1042-1044.

# -Chapter 5-

# REDEMPTORIS MATER

Pope John Paul II has totally dedicated his life according to the pattern recommended by St. Louis Marie de Montfort to Our Blessed Mother. He has taken for his coat of arms the words "Totus Tuus," meaning "I am all yours" (O Mary). His life is centered on Jesus through Mary. He received recommendations from a Fatima conference on Mary to take the position papers offered there and put them in an encyclical on Mary. Then on March 25, 1987, the feast of the Annunciation, he introduced this magnificent encyclical on Mary with the words, "I have been thinking of it for a long time. I have pondered it at length in my heart" (L'Osservatore Romano, 13 [1987], 23), words certainly reminiscent of Mary, "She pondered these things in her heart." John Paul has already completed his Trinitarian trilogy: one on the Father, "Dives in Miserecordia", 1988; one on the Son, "Redemptor Hominus (1979); and one on the Spirit, "Dominum et Vivificantem" (1986). He now wrote the companion encyclical on Mary, daughter of the Father, mother of the Son, spouse of the Spirit and mother of the Church.

A second inspiration for his encyclical was the Marian holy year which was to begin on Pentecost, 1987 and end on the Solemnity of the Assumption, 1988. Always looking forward to the millennium year 2000, the year of jubilee, he wanted to commemorate the two thousandth anniversary of Mary's birth. The Marian year was in his words to call notice of "the special presence of the mother of God in the mystery of Christ and his Church" (48.2).

This encyclical is more scriptural than his others, possibly for ecumenical reasons as well. He offers no exegesis of the Marian texts. He searches for the meaning which the tests reveal by examining the inherent relationships of the texts themselves, a practice that, as we shall see, he will continue in his seventy-part catechesis of Mary. By comparing the texts themselves he brings all of us to a more fruitful understanding of Mary's role in salvation history.

Reflecting also on section 8 of *Lumen Gentium* he says that this chapter offers "a clear summary of the Church's doctrine on the mother of Christ" (2.2) and hopes that this encyclical will "promote a new and more careful reading of what the Council has said about the Blessed Virgin Mary" (48.3).

The encyclical is divided into three parts: Mary is the Mystery of Christ (7-24); The Mother of God at the Center of the Pilgrim Church (25-37); and Maternal Mediation (38-50).

The key text of his encyclical is Gal 4:4, the same text that was the focus of section 8 of *Lumen Gentium*. He shows that Christology, Mariology and ecclesiology are interactions. Mary is mother of Christ, who is head of the Church, his Mystical Body. She is, therefore, the mother of Christ in us.

Referring to Eph 1:3-12, John Paul shows that Christ "chose us in him before the foundation of the world to be holy and blameless in his sight," a sanctification just wrought in his own mother.

At Cana, she is seen where "in a significant way she contributes to that beginning of the signs which reveal the Messianic power of her Son" (Jn 2: 1-2). John Paul does not ignore the more confusing and difficult texts of the synoptic Gospel, Mt 12:46-50: "Who is my mother? Who are my brothers? Whoever does the will of my Father..." (cf. also Mk 3:31-35; Lk 8 19-21).

According to the Pope, these passages serve to divert attention "from motherhood understood only as a fleshly bond, in order to divert it toward the mysterious bonds of the Spirit which develop from hearing and keeping God's word (20.3). Thus Mary is the first and greatest disciple who heard the call, "Follow me" (20.8).

At Calvary, Mary is "perfectly united with Christ in his self-emptying" act of offering himself for us (18:3). Jesus gives his mother "to every single individual and to all mankind" (23:2).

From Nazareth to the upper room she is present "as an exceptional witness to the mystery of Christ" (27:1).

# Mary And The Church

The Pope writes "Mary, as the mother of Christ, is in a particular way united with the Church" (5:1). Mary is "an effective and is exploring more deeply the truth concerning the Church" (47:2). Mary is the mother of Jesus, who lives in the Church and whose head he is. Thus, Mary's motherhood continues in and through the Church. According to the Pope, there is "a unique correspondence between the moment of the Incarnation of the Word and the moment of the birth of the Church. The person who links these two moments is Mary... In both cases her discrete yet essential presence indicates the part of both for the Holy Spirit" (24:4). As the Church makes her pilgrimage to the Father, she "proceeds along the path already trodden by the Virgin Mary" (2:1).

## The Woman: Mary - Mother; Church - Mother

In Chapter 3, Pope John Paul uses the most spiritually enriched title of Mary as the Woman (Gn 3:14; Jn 2:4; Jn 19:26; Eph 4:4; Rv 12:1-17) to describe Mary as the mother, the member and the model of the Church. He says, "From Mary, the Church learns her own motherhood. For just as Mary is at the service of the mystery of adoption to sonship through grace (43:2), with a mother's love Mary cooperates in the birth and development of the children of mother Church (44:1).

Mysteriously present in God's plan even before the creation of the world, the "Woman" who brings salvation was already promised "in the beginning" to our first parents (Gn 3:15). As "the woman clothed with the sun" (Rv 12:1), Mary accompanies the pilgrim Church until her final consummation in the glory of the heavenly Jerusalem. In the great struggle which even today is being waged against the powers of darkness, Mary takes part as a mother who watches over her children (cf. §§11, 47.3). She continues to make present for humanity the mystery of Christ, a mystery brought to life in her womb by her consent to the Incarnation. Mary's divine motherhood is ceaselessly "poured out upon the Church" (§40.1).

The Church's pilgrim journey through history takes place in time and space. Mary's presence in the Church expresses itself in many different ways, not least of which is in the "specific 'geography' of faith and Marian devotion, which includes all these special places of pilgrimage where the people of God seek to meet the mother of God... [for] a strengthening of their own faith" (§28.4). Despite the undeniable significance of this exterior Marian dimension, the Church's life is essentially an interior pilgrimage of faith. It is above all in the story of souls that Mary continues her mission. She has a unique and unrepeatable relationship with the heart of each of God's children. Like the beloved disciple, all Christians are to welcome her into their own home (cf. Jn 19:27), bringing her into the depths of their inner life, so that she can bring them to her Son.

God has confided to Mary the role of "introducing into the world the *Kingdom of her Son*" (§28.3). Just as Christ is present in the Church through the power of the Holy Spirit, so too is Mary. She carries out her maternal role from heaven, where she remains united with Christ in his continuing work of salvation. For Mary, to reign is to serve the disciples of her Son. As the handmaid of the Lord, "she wishes to act upon all those who entrust themselves to her as her children" (§46.1). Mary shares "in the many complicated problems which *today* beset the lives of individuals, families and nations" (§52.5).According to the Pope, she carries out her mission primarily by leading the faithful to the Eucharist; here "Christ, *his true body born of the Virgin Mary*, becomes present" (§44.3).

## Mary - Virgin; Church - Virgin

The Church also is virgin, as Mary is Virgin. The Church, like Mary, has a motherhood which is "a result of her total self-giving to God in virginity (39:1). Like a faithful spouse, as Mary is faithful, so the Church is also virgin, bride, and mother and each of her children are called to have the purity and the simplicity of a virgin, the fidelity and the steadfastness of a bride and the warmth and the love of a mother.

# REDEMPTORIS MATER
## Mother of the Redeemer
## March 25, 1987

## On The Blessed Virgin Mary
## In The Life Of The Pilgrim Church

## Solemnly Promulgated by His Holiness,
## Pope John Paul II

**Venerable Brothers and Dear Sons and Daughters,
Health and the Apostolic Blessing.**

# Introduction

1. The Mother of the Redeemer has a precise place in the plan of salvation, for "when the time had fully come, God sent forth his Son, born of woman, born under the law, to redeem those who were under the law, so that we might receive adoption as sons. And because you are sons, God has sent the Spirit of his Son into our hearts, crying, 'Abba! Father!'" (Gal 4:4-6).

With these words of the Apostle Paul, which the Second Vatican Council takes up at the beginning of its treatment of the Blessed Virgin Mary,[1] I too wish to begin my reflection on the role of Mary in the mystery of Christ and on her active and exemplary presence in the life of the Church. For they are words which celebrate together the love of the Father, the mission of the Son, the gift of the Spirit, the role of the woman from whom the Redeemer was born, and our own divine filiation, in the mystery of the "fullness of time."[2]

This "fullness" indicates the moment fixed from all eternity when the Father sent his Son "that whoever believes in him should not perish but have eternal life" (Jn 3:16). It denotes the blessed moment when the Word that "was with God... became flesh and dwelt among us" (Jn 1:1, 14), and made himself our brother. It marks the moment when the Holy Spirit, who had already infused the fullness of grace into Mary of Nazareth, formed in her virginal womb the human nature of Christ. This "fullness" marks the moment when, with the entrance of the eternal into time, time itself is redeemed, and being filled with the mystery of Christ becomes definitively "salvation time." Finally, this "fullness" designates the hidden beginning of the Church's journey. In the liturgy the Church salutes Mary of Nazareth as the Church's own beginning,[3] for in the event of the Immaculate Conception the Church sees projected, and anticipated in her most noble member, the saving grace of Easter. And above all, in the Incarnation she encounters Christ and Mary indissolubly joined: he who is the Church's Lord and Head and she who, uttering the first fiat of the New Covenant, prefigures the Church's condition as spouse and mother.

2. Strengthened by the presence of Christ (cf. Mt 28:20), the Church journeys through time towards the consummation of the ages and goes to meet the Lord who comes. But on this journey- and I wish to make this point straight-away - she proceeds along the path already trodden by the Virgin Mary, who "advanced in her pilgrimage of faith, and loyally persevered in her union with her Son unto the cross."[4]

I take these very rich and evocative words from the Constitution *Lumen Gentium*, which in its concluding part offers a clear summary of the Church's doctrine on the Mother of Christ, whom she venerates as her beloved Mother and as her model in faith hope and charity.

Shortly after the Council, my great predecessor Paul VI decided to speak further of the Blessed Virgin. In the Encyclical Epistle Christi Matri and subsequently in the Apostolic Exhortations Signum Magnum and Marialis Cultus[5] he expounded the foundations and criteria of the special veneration which the Mother of Christ receives in the Church, as well as the various forms of Marian devotion-liturgical, popular and private-which respond to the spirit of faith.

3. The circumstance which now moves me to take up this subject once more is the prospect of the year 2000, now drawing near, in which the Bimillennial Jubilee of the birth of Jesus Christ

at the same time directs our gaze towards his Mother. In recent years, various opinions have been voiced suggesting that it would be fitting to precede that anniversary by a similar Jubilee in celebration of the birth of Mary.

In fact, even though it is not possible to establish an exact chronological point for identifying the date of Mary's birth, the Church has constantly been aware that Mary appeared on the horizon of salvation history before Christ.[6] It is a fact that when "the fullness of time" was definitively drawing near-the saving advent of Emmanuel-he who was from eternity destined to be his Mother already existed on earth. The fact that she "preceded" the coming of Christ is reflected every year in the liturgy of Advent. Therefore, if to that ancient historical expectation of the Savior we compare these years which are bringing us closer to the end of the second Millennium after Christ and to the beginning of the third, it becomes fully comprehensible that in this present period we wish to turn in a special way to her, the one who in the "night" of the Advent expectation began to shine like a true "Morning Star" (Stella Matutina). For just as this star, together with the "dawn," precedes the rising of the sun, so Mary from the time of her Immaculate Conception preceded the coming of the Savior, the rising of the "Sun of Justice" in the history of the human race.[7]

Her presence in the midst of Israel-a presence so discreet as to pass almost unnoticed by the eyes of her contemporaries-shone very clearly before the Eternal One, who had associated this hidden "daughter of Zion" (cf. Zep 3:14; Zep 2:10) with the plan of salvation embracing the whole history of humanity. With good reason, then, at the end of this Millennium, we Christians who know that the providential plan of the Most Holy Trinity is the central reality of Revelation and of faith feel the need to emphasize the unique presence of the Mother of Christ in history, especially during these last years leading up to the year 2000.

4. The Second Vatican Council prepares us for this by presenting in its teaching the Mother of God in the mystery of Christ and of the Church. If it is true, as the Council itself proclaims,[8] that "only in the mystery of the Incarnate Word does the mystery of man take on light," then this principle must be applied in a very particular way to that exceptional "daughter of the human race,"

that extraordinary "woman" who became the Mother of Christ. Only in the mystery of Christ is her mystery fully made clear. Thus has the Church sought to interpret it from the very beginning: the mystery of the Incarnation has enabled her to penetrate and to make ever clearer the mystery of the Mother of the Incarnate Word. The Council of Ephesus (431) was of decisive importance in clarifying this, for during that Council, to the great joy of Christians, the truth of the divine motherhood of Mary was solemnly confirmed as a truth of the Church's faith. Mary is the Mother of God (Theotokos), since by the power of the Holy Spirit she conceived in her virginal womb and brought into the world Jesus Christ, the Son of God, who is of one being with the Father.[9] "The Son of God... born of the Virgin Mary... has truly been made one of us,"[10] has been made man. Thus, through the mystery of Christ, on the horizon of the Church's faith there shines in its fullness the mystery of his Mother. In turn, the dogma of the divine motherhood of Mary was for the Council of Ephesus and is for the Church like a seal upon the dogma of the Incarnation, in which the Word truly assumes human nature into the unity of his person, without canceling out that nature.

5. The Second Vatican Council, by presenting Mary in the mystery of Christ, also finds the path to a deeper understanding of the mystery of the Church. Mary, as the Mother of Christ, is in a particular way united with the Church, "which the Lord established as his own body."[11] It is significant that the conciliar text places this truth about the Church as the Body of Christ (according to the teaching of the Pauline Letters) in close proximity to the truth that the Son of God "through the power of the Holy Spirit was born of the Virgin Mary." The reality of the Incarnation finds a sort of extension in the mystery of the Church-the Body of Christ. And one cannot think of the reality of the Incarnation without referring to Mary, the Mother of the Incarnate Word.

In these reflections, however, I wish to consider primarily that "pilgrimage of faith" in which "the Blessed Virgin advanced," faithfully preserving her union with Christ.[12] In this way the "twofold bond" which unites the Mother of God with Christ and with the Church takes on historical significance. Nor is it just a question of the Virgin Mother's life-story, of her personal journey of faith and "the better part" which is hers in the mystery of salvation; it is also a question of the history of the whole People of God, of all those who take part in the same "pilgrimage of faith."

The Council expresses this when it states in another passage that Mary "has gone before," becoming "a model of the Church in the matter of faith, charity and perfect union with Christ."[13] This "going before" as a figure or model is in reference to the intimate mystery of the Church, as she actuates and accomplishes her own saving mission by uniting in herself-as Mary did-the qualities of mother and virgin. She is a virgin who "keeps whole and pure the fidelity she has pledged to her Spouse" and "becomes herself a mother," for "she brings forth to a new and immortal life children who are conceived of the Holy Spirit and born of God."[14]

6. All this is accomplished in a great historical process, comparable "to a journey." The pilgrimage of faith indicates the interior history, that is, the story of souls. But it is also the story of all human beings, subject here on earth to transitoriness, and part of the historical dimension. In the following reflections we wish to concentrate first of all on the present, which in itself is not yet history, but which nevertheless is constantly forming it, also in the sense of the history of salvation. Here there opens up a broad prospect, within which the Blessed Virgin Mary continues to "go before" the People of God. Her exceptional pilgrimage of faith represents a constant point of reference for the Church, for individuals and for communities, for peoples and nations and, in a sense, for all humanity. It is indeed difficult to encompass and measure its range.

The Council emphasizes that the Mother of God is already the eschatological fulfillment of the Church: "In the most holy Virgin the Church has already reached that perfection whereby she exists without spot or wrinkle (cf. Eph 5:27)"; and at the same time the Council says that "the followers of Christ still strive to increase in holiness by conquering sin, and so they raise their eyes to Mary, who shines forth to the whole community of the elect as a model of the virtues."[15] The pilgrimage of faith no longer belongs to the Mother of the Son of God: glorified at the side of her Son in heaven, Mary has already crossed the threshold between faith and that vision which is "face to face" (1 Cor 13:12). At the same time, however, in this eschatological fulfillment, Mary does not cease to be the "Star of the Sea" (Maris Stella)[16] for all those who are still on the journey of faith. If they lift their eyes to her from their earthly existence, they do so because "the Son whom she brought forth is he whom God placed as the first-born among many brethren (Rom 8:29),"[17] and also because "in the birth and development" of these brothers and sisters "she cooperates with a maternal love."[18]

# Part I

## Mary In The Mystery Of Christ

### 1. Full Of Grace

7. "Blessed be the God and Father of our Lord Jesus Christ, who has blessed us in Christ with every spiritual blessing in the heavenly places" (Eph 1:3). These words of the Letter to the Ephesians reveal the eternal design of God the Father, his plan of man's salvation in Christ. It is a universal plan, which concerns all men and women created in the image and likeness of God (cf. Gn 1:26). Just as all are included in the creative work of God "in the beginning," so all are eternally included in the divine plan of salvation, which is to be completely revealed, in the "fullness of time," with the final coming of Christ. In fact, the God who is the "Father of our Lord Jesus Christ"-these are the next words of the same Letter-"chose us in him before the foundation of the world, that we should be holy and blameless before him. He destined us in love to be his sons through Jesus Christ, according to the purpose of his will, to the praise of his glorious grace, which he freely bestowed on us in the Beloved. In him we have redemption through his blood, the forgiveness of our trespasses, according to the riches of his grace" (Eph 1:4-7).

The divine plan of salvation-which was fully revealed to us with the coming of Christ-is eternal. And according to the teaching contained in the Letter just quoted and in other Pauline Letters (cf. Col 1:12-14; Rom 3:24; Gal 3:13; 2 Cor 5:18-29), it is also eternally linked to Christ. It includes everyone, but it reserves a special place for the "woman" who is the Mother of him to whom the Father has entrusted the work of salvation.[19] As the Second Vatican Council says, "she is already prophetically foreshadowed in that promise made to our first parents after their fall into sin"- according to the Book of Genesis (cf. 3:15). "Likewise she is the Virgin who is to conceive and bear a Son, whose name will be called Emmanuel"-according to the words of Isaiah (cf. 7:14).[20] In this way the Old Testament prepares that "fullness of time" when God "sent forth his Son, born of woman... so that we might receive adoption as sons." The coming into the world of the Son of God is an event recorded in the first chapters of the Gospels according to Luke and Matthew.

8. Mary is definitively introduced into the mystery of Christ through this event: the Annunciation by the angel. This takes place at Nazareth, within the concrete circumstances of the history of Israel, the people which first received God's promises. The divine messenger says to the Virgin: "Hail, full of grace, the Lord is with you" (Lk 1:28). Mary "was greatly troubled at the saying, and considered in her mind what sort of greeting this might be" (Lk 1:29): what could those extraordinary words mean, and in particular the expression "full of grace" (kecharitomene).[21]

If we wish to meditate together with Mary on these words, and especially on the expression "full of grace," we can find a significant echo in the very passage from the Letter to the Ephesians quoted above. And if after the announcement of the heavenly messenger the Virgin of Nazareth is also called "blessed among women" (cf. Lk 1:42), it is because of that blessing with which "God the Father" has filled us "in the heavenly places, in Christ." It is a spiritual blessing which is meant for all people and which bears in itself fullness and universality ("every blessing"). It flows from that love which, in the Holy Spirit, unites the consubstantial Son to the Father. At the same time, it is a blessing poured out through Jesus Christ upon human history until the end: upon all people. This blessing, however, refers to Mary in a special and exceptional degree: for she was greeted by Elizabeth as "blessed among women."

The double greeting is due to the fact that in the soul of this "daughter of Zion" there is manifested, in a sense, all the "glory of grace," that grace which "the Father... has given us in his beloved Son." For the messenger greets Mary as "full of grace"; he calls her thus as if it were her real name. He does not call her by her proper earthly name: Miryam (Mary), but by this new name: "full of grace." What does this name mean? Why does the archangel address the Virgin of Nazareth in this way?

In the language of the Bible "grace" means a special gift, which according to the New Testament has its source precisely in the Trinitarian life of God himself, God who is love (cf. 1 Jn 4:8). The fruit of this love is "the election" of which the Letter to the Ephesians speaks. On the part of God, this election is the eternal desire to save man through a sharing in his own life (cf. 2 Pt 1:4) in Christ: it is salvation through a sharing in supernatural life. The effect of this eternal gift, of this grace of man's election by God, is like a seed of holiness, or a spring which rises in the soul as a gift from God himself, who through grace gives life and holiness to those who are chosen. In this way there is fulfilled, that is to say there comes about, that "blessing" of man "with every spiritual blessing," that "being his adopted sons and daughters... in Christ," in him who is eternally the "beloved Son" of the Father.

When we read that the messenger addresses Mary as "full of grace," the Gospel context, which mingles revelations and ancient promises, enables us to understand that among all the "spiritual blessings in Christ" this is a special "blessing." In the mystery of Christ she is present even "before the creation of the world," as the one whom the Father "has chosen" as Mother of his Son in the Incarnation. And, what is more, together with the Father, the Son has chosen her, entrusting her eternally to the Spirit of holiness. In an entirely special and exceptional way Mary is united to Christ, and similarly she is eternally loved in this "beloved Son," this Son who is of one being with the Father, in whom is concentrated all the "glory of grace." At the same time, she is and remains perfectly open to this "gift from above" (cf. Jas 1:17). As the Council teaches, Mary "stands out among the poor and humble of the Lord, who confidently await and receive salvation from him."[22]

9. If the greeting and the name "full of grace" say all this, in the context of the angel's announcement they refer first of all to the election of Mary as Mother of the Son of God. But at the same time the "fullness of grace" indicates all the supernatural munificence from which Mary benefits by being chosen and destined to be the Mother of Christ. If this election is fundamental for the accomplishment of God's salvific designs for humanity, and if the eternal choice in Christ and the vocation to the dignity of adopted children is the destiny of everyone, then the election of Mary is wholly exceptional and unique. Hence also the singularity and uniqueness of her place in the mystery of Christ.

The divine messenger says to her: "Do not be afraid, Mary, for you have found favor with God. And behold, you will conceive in your womb and bear a Son, and you shall call his name Jesus. He will be great, and will be called the Son of the Most High" (Lk 1:30-32). And when the Virgin, disturbed by that extraordinary greeting, asks: "How shall this be, since I have no husband?" she receives from the angel the confirmation and explanation of the preceding words. Gabriel says to her: "The Holy Spirit will come upon you, and the power of the Most High will overshadow you; therefore the child to be born will be called holy, the Son of God" (Lk 1:35).

The Annunciation, therefore, is the revelation of the mystery of the Incarnation at the very beginning of its fulfillment on earth. God's salvific giving of himself and his life, in some way to all creation but directly to man, reaches one of its high points in the mystery of the Incarnation. This is indeed a high point among all the gifts of grace conferred in the history of man and of the universe: Mary is "full of grace," because it is precisely in her that the Incarnation of the Word, the hypostatic union of the Son of God with human nature, is accomplished and fulfilled. As the Council says, Mary is "the Mother of the Son of God. As a result she is also the favorite daughter of the Father and the temple of the Holy Spirit. Because of this gift of sublime grace, she far surpasses all other creatures, both in heaven and on earth."[23]

10. The Letter to the Ephesians, speaking of the "glory of grace" that "God, the Father... has bestowed on us in his beloved Son," adds: "In him we have redemption through his blood" (Eph

1:7). According to the belief formulated in solemn documents of the Church, this "glory of grace" is manifested in the Mother of God through the fact that she has been "redeemed in a more sublime manner."[24] By virtue of the richness of the grace of the beloved Son, by reason of the redemptive merits of him who willed to become her Son, Mary was preserved from the inheritance of original sin.[25] In this way, from the first moment of her conception-which is to say of her existence-she belonged to Christ, sharing in the salvific and sanctifying grace and in that love which has its beginning in the "Beloved," the Son of the Eternal Father, who through the Incarnation became her own Son. Consequently, through the power of the Holy Spirit, in the order of grace, which is a participation in the divine nature, Mary receives life from him to whom she herself, in the order of earthly generation, gave life as a mother. The liturgy does not hesitate to call her "mother of her Creator"[26] and to hail her with the words which Dante Alighieri places on the lips of St. Bernard: "daughter of your Son."[27] And since Mary receives this "new life" with a fullness corresponding to the Son's love for the Mother, and thus corresponding to the dignity of the divine motherhood, the angel at the Annunciation calls her "full of grace."

11. In the salvific design of the Most Holy Trinity, the mystery of the Incarnation constitutes the superabundant fulfillment of the promise made by God to man after original sin, after that first sin whose effects oppress the whole earthly history of man (cf. Gn 3:15). And so, there comes into the world a Son, "the seed of the woman" who will crush the evil of sin in its very origins: "he will crush the head of the serpent." As we see from the words of the Proto-gospel, the victory of the woman's Son will not take place without a hard struggle, a struggle that is to extend through the whole of human history. The "enmity," foretold at the beginning, is confirmed in the Apocalypse (the book of the final events of the Church and the world), in which there recurs the sign of the "woman," this time "clothed with the sun" (Rv 12:1).

Mary, Mother of the Incarnate Word, is placed at the very center of that enmity, that struggle which accompanies the history of humanity on earth and the history of salvation itself. In this central place, she who belongs to the "weak and poor of the Lord" bears in herself, like no other member of the human race, that "glory of grace" which the Father "has bestowed on us in his beloved Son," and this grace determines the extraordinary greatness and beauty of her whole being. Mary thus remains before God, and also before the whole of humanity, as the unchangeable and inviolable sign of God's election, spoken of in Paul's Letter: "in Christ... he chose us... before the foundation of the world, ... he destined us... to be his sons" (Eph 1:4, 5). This election is more powerful than any experience of evil and sin, than all that "enmity" which marks the history of man. In this history Mary remains a sign of sure hope.

## 2. Blessed Is She Who Believed

12. Immediately after the narration of the Annunciation, the Evangelist Luke guides us in the footsteps of the Virgin of Nazareth towards "a city of Judah" (Lk 1:39). According to scholars this city would be the modern Ein Karim, situated in the mountains, not far from Jerusalem. Mary arrived there "in haste," to visit Elizabeth her kinswoman. The reason for her visit is also to be found in the fact that at the Annunciation Gabriel had made special mention of Elizabeth, who in her old age had conceived a Son by her husband Zechariah, through the power of God: "your kinswoman Elizabeth in her old age has also conceived a Son; and this is the sixth month with her who was called barren. For with God nothing will be impossible" (Lk 1:36-37). The divine messenger had spoken of what had been accomplished in Elizabeth in order to answer Mary's question. "How shall this be, since I have no husband?" (Lk 1:34). It is to come to pass precisely through the "power of the Most High," just as it happened in the case of Elizabeth, and even more so.

Moved by charity, therefore, Mary goes to the house of her kinswoman. When Mary enters, Elizabeth replies to her greeting and feels the child leap in her womb, and being "filled with the Holy Spirit" she greets Mary with a loud cry: "Blessed are you among women, and blessed is the fruit of your womb!" (cf. Lk 1:40-42). Elizabeth's exclamation or acclamation was subsequently to become part of the Hail Mary, as a continuation of the angel's greeting, thus becoming one of the Church's most frequently used prayers. But still more significant are the words of Elizabeth in the question which follows: "And why is this granted me, that the mother of my Lord should come to me?" (Lk 1:43). Elizabeth bears witness to Mary: she recognizes and proclaims that before her stands the Mother of the Lord, the Mother of the Messiah. The Son whom Elizabeth is carrying in her womb also shares in this witness: "The babe in my womb leaped for joy" (Lk 1:44). This child is the future John the Baptist, who at the Jordan will point out Jesus as the Messiah.

While every word of Elizabeth's greeting is filled with meaning, her final words would seem to have fundamental importance: "And blessed is she who believed that there would be a fulfillment of what was spoken to her from the Lord" (Lk 1:45).[28] These words can be linked with the little "full of grace" of the angel's greeting. Both of these texts reveal an essential Mariological content, namely the truth about Mary, who has become really present in the mystery of Christ precisely because she "has believed." The fullness of grace announced by the angel means the gift of God himself. Mary's faith, proclaimed by Elizabeth at the Visitation, indicates how the Virgin of Nazareth responded to this gift.

13. As the Council teaches, "'The obedience of faith' (Rom 16:26; cf. Rom 1:5; 2 Cor 10:5-6) must be given to God who reveals, an obedience by which man entrusts his whole self freely to God."[29] This description of faith found perfect realization in Mary. The "decisive" moment was the Annunciation, and the very words of Elizabeth: "And blessed is she who believed" refer primarily to that very moment.[30]

Indeed, at the Annunciation Mary entrusted herself to God completely, with the "full submission of intellect and will," manifesting "the obedience of faith" to him who spoke to her through his messenger.[31] She responded, therefore, with all her human and feminine "I," and this response of faith included both perfect cooperation with "the grace of God that precedes and assists" and perfect openness to the action of the Holy Spirit, who "constantly brings faith to completion by his gifts."[32]

The word of the living God, announced to Mary by the angel, referred to her: "And behold, you will conceive in your womb and bear a Son" (Lk 1:31). By accepting this announcement, Mary was to become the "Mother of the Lord," and the divine mystery of the Incarnation was to be accomplished in her: "The Father of mercies willed that the consent of the predestined Mother should precede the Incarnation."[33] And Mary gives this consent, after she has heard everything the messenger has to say. She says: "Behold, I am the handmaid of the Lord; let it be to me according to your word" (Lk 1:38). This fiat of Mary-"let it be to me"-was decisive, on the human level, for the accomplishment of the divine mystery. There is a complete harmony with the words of the Son, who, according to the Letter to the Hebrews, says to the Father as he comes into the world: "Sacrifices and offering you have not desired, but a body you have prepared for me.... Lo, I have come to do your will, O God" (Heb 10:5-7). The mystery of the Incarnation was accomplished when Mary uttered her fiat: "Let it be to me according to your word," which made possible, as far as it depended upon her in the divine plan, the granting of her Son's desire.

Mary uttered this fiat in faith. In faith she entrusted herself to God without reserve and "devoted herself totally as the handmaid of the Lord to the person and work of her Son."[34] And as the Fathers of the Church teach-she conceived this Son in her mind before she conceived him in her womb: precisely in faith![35] Rightly therefore does Elizabeth praise Mary: "And blessed is she who believed that there would be a fulfillment of what was spoken to her from the Lord." These words have already been fulfilled: Mary of Nazareth presents herself at the threshold of Elizabeth and Zechariah's house as the Mother of the Son of God. This is Elizabeth's joyful discovery: "The mother of my Lord comes to me"!

14. Mary's faith can also be compared to that of Abraham, whom St. Paul calls "our father in faith" (cf. Rom 4:12). In the salvific economy of God's revelation, Abraham's faith constitutes the beginning of the Old Covenant; Mary's faith at the Annunciation inaugurates the New Covenant. Just as Abraham

"in hope believed against hope, that he should become the father of many nations" (cf. Rom 4:18), so Mary, at the Annunciation, having professed her virginity ("How shall this be, since I have no husband?") believed that through the power of the Most High, by the power of the Holy Spirit, she would become the Mother of God's Son in accordance with the angel's revelation: "The child to be born will be called holy, the Son of God" (Lk 1:35).

However, Elizabeth's words "And blessed is she who believed" do not apply only to that particular moment of the Annunciation. Certainly the Annunciation is the culminating moment of Mary's faith in her awaiting of Christ, but it is also the point of departure from which her whole "journey towards God" begins, her whole pilgrimage of faith. And on this road, in an eminent and truly heroic manner-indeed with an ever greater heroism of faith-the "obedience" which she professes to the word of divine revelation will be fulfilled. Mary's "obedience of faith" during the whole of her pilgrimage wili show surprising similarities to the faith of Abraham. Just like the Patriarch of the People of God, so too Mary, during the pilgrimage of her filial and maternal fiat, "in hope believed against hope." Especially during certain stages of this journey the blessing granted to her "who believed" will be revealed with particular vividness. To believe means "to abandon oneself" to the truth of the word of the living God, knowing and humbly recognizing "how unsearchable are his judgments and how inscrutable his ways" (Rom 11:33). Mary, who by the eternal will of the Most High stands, one may say, at the very center of those "inscrutable ways" and "unsearchable judgments" of God, conforms herself to them in the dim light of faith, accepting fully and with a ready heart everything that is decreed in the divine plan.

15. When at the Annunciation Mary hears of the Son whose Mother she is to become and to whom "she will give the name Jesus" (Savior), she also learns that "the Lord God will give to him the throne of his father David," and that "he will reign over the house of Jacob for ever and of his kingdom there will be no end" (Lk 1:32-33). The hope of the whole of Israel was directed towards this. The promised Messiah is to be "great," and the heavenly

messenger also announces that "he will be great"-great both by bearing the name of Son of the Most High and by the fact that he is to assume the inheritance of David. He is therefore to be a king, he is to reign "over the house of Jacob." Mary had grown up in the midst of these expectations of her people: could she guess, at the moment of the Annunciation, the vital significance of the angel's words? And how is one to understand that "kingdom" which "will have no end"?

Although through faith she may have perceived in that instant the was the mother of the "Messiah King," nevertheless she replied: "Behold, I am the handmaid of the Lord; let it be to me according to your word" (Lk 1:38). From the first moment Mary professed above all the "obedience of faith," abandoning herself to the meaning which was given to the words of the Annunciation by him from whom they proceeded: God himself.

16. Later, a little further along this way of the "obedience of faith," Mary hears other words: those uttered by Simeon in the Temple of Jerusalem. It was now forty days after the birth of Jesus when, in accordance with the precepts of the Law of Moses, Mary and Joseph "brought him up to Jerusalem to present him to the Lord" (Lk 2:22). The birth had taken place in conditions of extreme poverty. We know from Luke that when, on the occasion of the census ordered by the Roman authorities, Mary went with Joseph to Bethlehem, having found "no place in the inn," she gave birth to her Son in a stable and "laid him in a manger" (cf. Lk 2:7).

A just and God-fearing man, called Simeon, appears at this beginning of Mary's "journey" of faith. His words, suggested by the Holy Spirit (cf. Lk 2:25-27), confirm the truth of the Annunciation. For we read that he took up in his arms the child to whom-in accordance with the angel's command-the name Jesus was given (cf. Lk 2:21). Simeon's words match the meaning of this name, which is Savior: "God is salvation." Turning to the Lord, he says: "For my eyes have seen your salvation which you have prepared in the presence of all peoples, a light for revelation to the Gentiles, and for glory to your people Israel" (Lk 2:30-32). At the same time, however, Simeon addresses Mary with the following words: "Behold, this child is set for the fall and rising of many in

Israel, and for a sign that is spoken against, that thoughts out of many hearts may be revealed"; and he adds with direct reference to her: "and a sword will pierce through your own soul also" (cf. Lk 2:34-35). Simeon's words cast new light on the announcement which Mary had heard from the angel: Jesus is the Savior, he is "a light for revelation" to mankind. Is not this what was manifested in a way on Christmas night, when the shepherds come to the stable (cf. Lk 2:8-20)? Is not this what was to be manifested even more clearly in the coming of the Magi from the East (cf. Mt 2:1-12)? But at the same time, at the very beginning of his life, the Son of Mary, and his Mother with him, will experience in themselves the truth of those other words of Simeon: "a sign that is spoken against" (Lk 2:34). Simeon's words seem like a second Annunciation to Mary, for they tell her of the actual historical situation in which the Son is to accomplish his mission, namely, in misunderstanding and sorrow. While this announcement on the one hand confirms her faith in the accomplishment of the divine promises of salvation, on the other hand it also reveals to her that she will have to live her obedience of faith in suffering, at the side of the suffering Savior, and that her motherhood will be mysterious and sorrowful. Thus, after the visit of the Magi who came from the East, after their homage ("they fell down and worshipped him") and after they had offered gifts (cf. Mt 2:11), Mary together with the child has to flee into Egypt in the protective care of Joseph, for "Herod is about to search for the child, to destroy him" (cf. Mt 2:13). And until the death of Herod they will have to remain in Egypt (cf. Mt 2:15).

17. When the Holy Family returns to Nazareth after Herod's death, there begins the long period of the hidden life. She "who believed that there would be a fulfillment of what was spoken to her from the Lord" (Lk 1:45) lives the reality of these words day by day. And daily at her side is the Son to whom "she gave the name Jesus"; therefore in contact with him she certainly uses this name, a fact which would have surprised no one, since the name had long been in use in Israel. Nevertheless, Mary knows that he who bears the name Jesus has been called by the angel "the Son of the Most High" (cf. Lk 1:32). Mary knows she has conceived and given birth to him "without having a husband," by the power of the Holy Spirit, by the power of the Most High who overshadowed

her (cf. Lk 1:35), just as at the time of Moses and the Patriarchs the cloud covered the presence of God (cf. Ex 24:16; 40:34-35; 1 Kgs 8:10-12). Therefore Mary knows that the Son to whom she gave birth in a virginal manner is precisely that "Holy One," the Son of God, of whom the angel spoke to her.

During the years of Jesus' hidden life in the house at Nazareth, Mary's life too is "hid with Christ in God" (cf. Col 3:3) through faith. For faith is contact with the mystery of God. Every day Mary is in constant contact with the ineffable mystery of God made man, a mystery that surpasses everything revealed in the Old Covenant. From the moment of the Annunciation, the mind of the Virgin-Mother has been initiated into the radical "newness" of God's self-revelation and has been made aware of the mystery. She is the first of those "little ones" of whom Jesus will say one day: "Father, ... you have hidden these things from the wise and understanding and revealed them to babes" (Mt 11:25). For "no one knows the Son except the Father" (Mt 11:27). If this is the case, how can Mary "know the Son"? Of course she does not know him as the Father does; and yet she is the first of those to whom the Father "has chosen to reveal him" (cf. Mt 11:26-27; 1 Cor 2:11). If though, from the moment of the Annunciation, the Son-whom only the Father knows completely, as the one who begets him in the eternal "today" (cf. Ps 2:7) was revealed to Mary, she, his Mother, is in contact with the truth about her Son only in faith and through faith! She is therefore blessed, because "she has believed," and continues to believe day after day amidst all the trials and the adversities of Jesus' infancy and then during the years of the hidden life at Nazareth, where he "was obedient to them" (Lk 2:51). He was obedient both to Mary and also to Joseph, since Joseph took the place of his father in people's eyes; for this reason, the Son of Mary was regarded by the people as "the carpenter's Son" (Mt 13:55).

The Mother of that Son, therefore, mindful of what has been told her at the Annunciation and in subsequent events, bears within herself the radical "newness" of faith: the beginning of the New Covenant. This is the beginning of the Gospel, the joyful Good News. However, it is not difficult to see in that beginning a particular heaviness of heart, linked with a sort of night of faith"-to use the words of St. John of the Cross-a kind of "veil" through which one has to draw near to the Invisible One and to live in intimacy with the mystery.[36] And this is the way that Mary, for many years, lived in intimacy with the mystery of her Son, and went forward in her "pilgrimage of faith," while Jesus "increased in wisdom... and in favor with God and man" (Lk 2:52). God's predilection for him was manifested ever more clearly to people's eyes. The first human creature thus permitted to discover Christ was Mary, who lived with Joseph in the same house at Nazareth.

However, when he had been found in the Temple, and his Mother asked him, "Son, why have you treated us so?" the twelve-year-old Jesus answered: "Did you not know that I must be in my Father's house?" And the Evangelist adds: "And they (Joseph and Mary) did not understand the saying which he spoke to them" (Lk 2:48-50). Jesus was aware that "no one knows the Son except the Father" (cf. Mt 11:27); thus even his Mother, to whom had been revealed most completely the mystery of his divine sonship, lived in intimacy with this mystery only through faith! Living side by side with her Son under the same roof, and faithfully persevering "in her union with her Son," she "advanced in her pilgrimage of faith," as the Council emphasizes.[37] And so it was during Christ's public life too (cf. Mk 3:21-35) that day by day there was fulfilled in her the blessing uttered by Elizabeth at the Visitation: "Blessed is she who believed."

18. This blessing reaches its full meaning when Mary stands beneath the Cross of her Son (cf. Jn 19:25). The Council says that this happened "not without a divine plan": by "suffering deeply with her only-begotten Son and joining herself with her maternal spirit to his sacrifice, lovingly consenting to the immolation of the victim to whom she had given birth," in this way Mary "faithfully preserved her union with her Son even to the Cross."[38] It is a union through faith-the same faith with which she had received the angel's revelation at the Annunciation. At that moment she had also heard the words: "He will be great ... and the Lord God will give to him the throne of his father David, and he will reign over the house of Jacob for ever; and of his kingdom there will be no end" (Lk 1:32-33).

And now, standing at the foot of the Cross, Mary is the

witness, humanly speaking, of the complete negation of these words. On that wood of the Cross her Son hangs in agony as one condemned. "He was despised and rejected by men; a man of sorrows... he was despised, and we esteemed him not": as one destroyed (cf. Is 53:3-5). How great, how heroic then is the obedience of faith shown by Mary in the face of God's "unsearchable judgments"! How completely she "abandons herself to God" without reserve, offering the full assent of the intellect and the will"[39] to him whose "ways are inscrutable" (cf. Rom 11:33)! And how powerful too is the action of grace in her soul, how all-pervading is the influence of the Holy Spirit and of his light and power!

Through this faith Mary is perfectly united with Christ in his self-emptying. For "Christ Jesus, who, though he was in the form of God, did not count equality with God a thing to be grasped, but emptied himself, taking the form of a servant, being born in the likeness of men": precisely on Golgotha "humbled himself and became obedient unto death, even death on a cross" (cf. Phil. 2:5-8). At the foot of the Cross Mary shares through faith in the shocking mystery of this self-emptying. This is perhaps the deepest "kenosis" of faith in human history. Through faith the Mother shares in the death of her Son, in his redeeming death; but in contrast with the faith of the disciples who fled, hers was far more enlightened. On Golgotha, Jesus through the Cross definitively confirmed that he was the "sign of contradiction" foretold by Simeon. At the same time, there were also fulfilled on Golgotha the words which Simeon had addressed to Mary: "and a sword will pierce through your own soul also."[40]

19. Yes, truly "blessed is she who believed"! These words, spoken by Elizabeth after the Annunciation, here at the foot of the Cross seem to re-echo with supreme eloquence, and the power contained within them becomes something penetrating. From the Cross, that is to say from the very heart of the mystery of Redemption, there radiates and spreads out the prospect of that blessing of faith It goes right hack to "the beginning." and as a sharing in the sacrifice of Christ-the new Adam-it becomes in a certain sense the counterpoise to the disobedience and disbelief embodied in the sin of our first parents. Thus teach the Fathers of

the Church and especially St. Irenaeus, quoted by the Constitution *Lumen Gentium*: "The knot of Eve's disobedience was untied by Mary's obedience; what the virgin Eve bound through her unbelief, the Virgin Mary loosened by her faith."[41] In the light of this comparison with Eve, the Fathers of the Church-as the Council also says-call Mary the "mother of the living" and often speak of "death through Eve, life through Mary."[42]

In the expression "Blessed is she who believed," we can therefore rightly find a kind of "key" which unlocks for us the innermost reality of Mary, whom the angel hailed as "full of grace." If as "full of grace" she has been eternally present in the mystery of Christ, through faith she became a sharer in that mystery in every extension of her earthly journey. She "advanced in her pilgrimage of faith" and at the same time, in a discreet yet direct and effective way, she made present to humanity the mystery of Christ. And she still continues to do so. Through the mystery of Christ, she too is present within mankind. Thus through the mystery of the Son the mystery of the Mother is also made clear.

## 3. Behold Your Mother

20. The Gospel of Luke records the moment when "a woman in the crowd raised her voice" and said to Jesus: "Blessed is the womb that bore you, and the breasts that you sucked!" (Lk 11:27). These words were an expression of praise of Mary as Jesus' mother according to the flesh. Probably the Mother of Jesus was not personally known to this woman; in fact, when Jesus began his messianic activity Mary did not accompany him but continued to remain at Nazareth. One could say that the words of that unknown woman in a way brought Mary out of her hiddenness.

Through these words, there flashed out in the midst of the crowd, at least for an instant, the Gospel of Jesus' infancy. This is the Gospel in which Mary is present as the mother who conceives Jesus in her womb, gives him birth and nurses him: the nursing mother referred to by the woman in the crowd. Thanks to this motherhood, Jesus, the Son of the Most High (cf. Lk 1:32), is a true Son of man. He is "flesh," like every other man: he is "the Word (who) became flesh" (cf. Jn 1:14). He is of the flesh and blood of Mary![43]

But to the blessing uttered by that woman upon her who was his mother according to the flesh, Jesus replies in a significant way: "Blessed rather are those who hear the word of God and keep it" (Lk 11:28). He wishes to divert attention from motherhood understood only as a fleshly bond, in order to direct it towards those mysterious bonds of the spirit which develop from hearing and keeping God's word.

This same shift into the sphere of spiritual values is seen even more clearly in another response of Jesus reported by all the Synoptics. When Jesus is told that "his mother and brothers are standing outside and wish to see him," he replies: "My mother and my brothers are those who hear the word of God and do it" (cf. Lk 8:20-21). This he said "looking around on those who sat about him," as we read in Mark (3:34) or, according to Matthew (12:49), "stretching out his hand towards his disciples."

These statements seem to fit in with the reply which the twelve-year-old Jesus gave to Mary and Joseph when he was found after three days in the Temple at Jerusalem. Now, when Jesus left Nazareth and began his public life throughout Palestine, he was completely and exclusively "concerned with his Father's business" (cf. Lk 2:49). He announced the Kingdom: the "Kingdom of God" and "his Father's business," which add a new dimension and meaning to everything human, and therefore to every human bond, insofar as these things relate to the goals and tasks assigned to every human being. Within this new dimension, also a bond such as that of "brotherhood" means something different from "brotherhood according to the flesh" deriving from a common origin from the same set of parents. "Motherhood," too, in the dimension of the Kingdom of God and in the radius of the fatherhood of God himself, takes on another meaning. In the words reported by Luke, Jesus teaches precisely this new meaning of motherhood.

Is Jesus thereby distancing himself from his mother according to the flesh? Does he perhaps wish to leave her in the hidden obscurity which she herself has chosen? If this seems to be the case from the tone of those words, one must nevertheless note that the new and different motherhood which Jesus speaks of to his disciples refers precisely to Mary in a very special way. Is not Mary the first of "those who hear the word of God and do it"? And therefore does not the blessing uttered by Jesus in response to the woman in the crowd refer primarily to her? Without any doubt, Mary is worthy of blessing by the very fact that she became the mother of Jesus according to the flesh ("Blessed is the womb that bore you, and the breasts that you sucked"), but also and especially because already at the Annunciation she accepted the word of God, because she believed it, because she was obedient to God, and because she "kept" the word and "pondered it in her heart" (cf. Lk 1:38, 45; 2:19, 51) and by means of her whole life accomplished it. Thus we can say that the blessing proclaimed by Jesus is not in opposition, despite appearances, to the blessing uttered by the unknown woman, but rather coincides with that blessing in the person of this Virgin Mother, who called herself only "the handmaid of the Lord" (Lk 1:38). If it is true that "all generations will call her blessed" (cf. Lk 1:48), then it can be said that the unnamed woman was the first to confirm unwittingly that prophetic phrase of Mary's Magnificat and to begin the Magnificat of the ages.

If through faith Mary became the bearer of the Son given to her by the Father through the power of the Holy Spirit, while preserving her virginity intact, in that same faith she discovered and accepted the other dimension of motherhood revealed by Jesus during his messianic mission. One can say that this dimension of motherhood belonged to Mary from the beginning, that is to say from the moment of the conception and birth of her Son. From that time she was "the one who believed." But as the messianic mission of her Son grew clearer to her eyes and spirit, she herself as a mother became ever more open to that new dimension of motherhood which was to constitute her "part" beside her Son. Had she not said from the very beginning: "Behold, I am the handmaid of the Lord; let it be to me according to your word" (Lk 1:38)? Through faith Mary continued to hear and to ponder that word, in which there became ever clearer, in a way "which surpasses knowledge" (Eph 3:19), the self-revelation of the living God. Thus in a sense Mary as Mother became the first "disciple" of her Son, the first to whom he seemed to say: "Follow me," even before he addressed this call to the Apostles or to anyone else (cf. Jn 1:43).

21. From this point of view, particularly eloquent is the passage in the Gospel of John which presents Mary at the wedding feast of Cana. She appears there as the Mother of Jesus at the beginning of his public life: "There was a marriage at Cana in Galilee, and the mother of Jesus was there; Jesus also was invited to the marriage, with his disciples" (Jn 2:1-2). From the text it appears that Jesus and his disciples were invited together with Mary, as if by reason of her presence at the celebration: the Son seems to have been invited because of his mother. We are familiar with the sequence of events which resulted from that invitation, that "beginning of the signs" wrought by Jesus-the water changed into wine-which prompts the Evangelist to say that Jesus "manifested his glory; and his disciples believed in him" (Jn 2:11).

Mary is present at Cana in Galilee as the Mother of Jesus, and in a significant way she contributes to that "beginning of the signs" which reveal the messianic power of her Son. We read: "When the wine gave out, the mother of Jesus said to him, 'They have no wine.' And Jesus said to her, 'O woman, what have you to do with me? My hour has not yet come'" (Jn 2:3-4). In John's Gospel that "hour" means the time appointed by the Father when the Son accomplishes his task and is to be glorified (cf. Jn 7:30; 8:20; 12:23, 27; 13:1; 17:1; 19:27). Even though Jesus' reply to his mother sounds like a refusal (especially if we consider the blunt statement "My hour has not yet come" rather than the question), Mary nevertheless turns to the servants and says to them: "Do whatever he tells you" (Jn 2:5). Then Jesus orders the servants to fill the stone jars with water, and the water becomes wine, better than the wine which has previously been served to the wedding guests.

What deep understanding existed between Jesus and his mother? How can we probe the mystery of their intimate spiritual union? But the fact speaks for itself. It is certain that that event already quite clearly outlines the new dimension, the new meaning of Mary's motherhood. Her motherhood has a significance which is not exclusively contained in the words of Jesus and in the various episodes reported by the Synoptics (Lk 11:27-28 and Lk 8:19-21; Mt 12:46-50; Mk 3:31-35). In these texts Jesus means above all to contrast the motherhood resulting from the fact of birth with what this "motherhood" (and also "brotherhood") is to be in the dimension of the Kingdom of God, in the salvific radius of God's fatherhood. In John's text on the other hand, the description of the Cana event outlines what is actually manifested as a new kind of motherhood according to the spirit and not just according to the flesh, that is to say Mary's solicitude for human beings, her coming to them in the wide variety of their wants and needs. At Cana in Galilee there is shown only one concrete aspect of human need, apparently a small one of little importance ("They have no wine"). But it has a symbolic value: this coming to the aid of human needs means, at the same time, bringing those needs within the radius of Christ's messianic mission and salvific power. Thus there is a mediation: Mary places herself between her Son and mankind in the reality of their wants, needs and sufferings. She puts herself "in the middle," that is to say she acts as a mediatrix not as an outsider, but in her position as mother. She knows that as such she can point out to her Son the needs of mankind, and in fact, she "has the right" to do so. Her mediation is thus in the nature of intercession: Mary "intercedes" for mankind. And that is not all. As a mother she also wishes the messianic power of her Son to be manifested, that salvific power of his which is meant to help man in his misfortunes, to free him from the evil which in various forms and degrees weighs heavily upon his life. Precisely as the Prophet Isaiah had foretold about the Messiah in the famous passage which Jesus quoted before his fellow townsfolk in Nazareth: "To preach good news to the poor... to proclaim release to the captives and recovering of sight to the blind ..." (cf. Lk 4:18).

Another essential element of Mary's maternal task is found in her words to the servants: "Do whatever he tells you." The Mother of Christ presents herself as the spokeswoman of her Son's will, pointing out those things which must be done so that the salvific power of the Messiah may be manifested. At Cana, thanks to the intercession of Mary and the obedience of the servants, Jesus begins "his hour." At Cana Mary appears as believing in Jesus. Her faith evokes his first "sign" and helps to kindle the faith of the disciples.

22. We can therefore say that in this passage of John's Gospel we find as it were a first manifestation of the truth concerning Mary's maternal care. This truth has also found expression in the teaching of the Second Vatican Council. It is important to note how the Council illustrates Mary's maternal role as it relates to the mediation of Christ. Thus we read: "Mary's maternal function towards mankind in no way obscures or diminishes the unique mediation of Christ, but rather shows its efficacy," because "there is one mediator between God and men, the man Christ Jesus" (1 Tm 2:5). This maternal role of Mary flows, according to God's good pleasure, "from the superabundance of the merits of Christ; it is founded on his mediation, absolutely depends on it, and draws all its efficacy from it."[44] It is precisely in this sense that the episode at Cana in Galilee offers us a sort of first announcement of Mary's mediation, wholly oriented towards Christ and tending to the revelation of his salvific power.

From the text of John it is evident that it is a mediation which is maternal. As the Council proclaims: Mary became "a mother to us in the order of grace." This motherhood in the order of grace flows from her divine motherhood. Because she was, by the design of divine Providence, the mother who nourished the divine Redeemer, Mary became "an associate of unique nobility, and the Lord's humble handmaid," who "cooperated by her obedience, faith, hope and burning charity in the Savior's work of restoring supernatural life to souls."[45] And "this maternity of Mary in the order of grace... will last without interruption until the eternal fulfillment of all the elect."[46]

23. If John's description of the event at Cana presents Mary's caring motherhood at the beginning of Christ's messianic activity, another passage from the same Gospel confirms this motherhood in the salvific economy of grace at its crowning moment, namely when Christ's sacrifice on the Cross, his Paschal Mystery, is accomplished. John's description is concise: "Standing by the cross of Jesus were his mother, and his mother's sister, Mary the wife of Clopas, and Mary Magdalene. When Jesus saw his mother, and the disciple whom he loved standing near, he said to his mother: 'Woman, behold your Son!' Then he said to the disciple, 'Behold,

your mother!' And from that hour the disciple took her to his own home" (Jn 19:25-27).

Undoubtedly, we find here an expression of the Son's particular solicitude for his Mother, whom he is leaving in such great sorrow. And yet the "testament of Christ's Cross" says more. Jesus highlights a new relationship between Mother and Son, the whole truth and reality of which he solemnly confirms. One can say that if Mary's motherhood of the human race had already been outlined, now it is clearly stated and established. It emerges from the definitive accomplishment of the Redeemer's Paschal Mystery. The Mother of Christ, who stands at the very center of this mystery-a mystery which embraces each individual and all humanity-is given as mother to every single individual and all mankind. The man at the foot of the Cross is John, "the disciple whom he loved."[47] But it is not he alone. Following tradition, the Council does not hesitate to call Mary "the Mother of Christ and mother of mankind": since she "belongs to the offspring of Adam she is one with all human beings.... Indeed she is 'clearly the mother of the members of Christ... since she cooperated out of love so that there might be born in the Church the faithful.'"[48]

And so this "new motherhood of Mary," generated by faith, is the fruit of the "new" love which came to definitive maturity in her at the foot of the Cross, through her sharing in the redemptive love of her Son.

24. Thus we find ourselves at the very center of the fulfillment of the promise contained in the Proto-gospel: the "seed of the woman... will crush the head of the serpent" (cf. Gn 3:15). By his redemptive death Jesus Christ conquers the evil of sin and death at its very roots. It is significant that, as he speaks to his mother from the Cross, he calls her "woman" and says to her: "Woman, behold your Son!" Moreover, he had addressed her by the same term at Cana too (cf. Jn 2:4). How can one doubt that especially now, on Golgotha, this expression goes to the very heart of the mystery of Mary, and indicates the unique place which she occupies in the whole economy of salvation? As the Council teaches, in Mary "the exalted Daughter of Zion, and after a long expectation of the promise, the times were at length fulfilled and the new dispensation established. All this occurred when the Son

of God took a human nature from her, that he might in the mysteries of his flesh free man from sin."[49]

The words uttered by Jesus from the Cross signify that the motherhood of her who bore Christ finds a "new" continuation in the Church and through the Church, symbolized and represented by John. In this way, she who as the one "full of grace" was brought into the mystery of Christ in order to be his Mother and thus the Holy Mother of God, through the Church remains in that mystery as "the woman" spoken of by the Book of Genesis (3:15) at the beginning and by the Apocalypse (12:1) at the end of the history of salvation. In accordance with the eternal plan of Providence, Mary's divine motherhood is to be poured out upon the Church, as indicated by statements of Tradition, according to which Mary's "motherhood" of the Church is the reflection and extension of her motherhood of the Son of God.[50]

According to the Council the very moment of the Church's birth and full manifestation to the world enables us to glimpse this continuity of Mary's motherhood: "Since it pleased God not to manifest solemnly the mystery of the salvation of the human race until he poured forth the Spirit promised by Christ, we see the Apostles before the day of Pentecost 'continuing with one mind in prayer with the women and Mary the mother of Jesus, and with his brethren' (Acts 1:14). We see Mary prayerfully imploring the gift of the Spirit, who had already overshadowed her in the Annunciation."[51]

And so, in the redemptive economy of grace, brought about through the action of the Holy Spirit, there is a unique correspondence between the moment of the Incarnation of the Word and the moment of the birth of the Church. The person who links these two moments is Mary: Mary at Nazareth and Mary in the Upper Room at Jerusalem. In both cases her discreet yet essential presence indicates the path of "birth from the Holy Spirit." Thus she who is present in the mystery of Christ as Mother becomes-by the will of the Son and the power of the Holy Spirit-present in the mystery of the Church. In the Church too she continues to be a maternal presence, as is shown by the words spoken from the Cross: "Woman, behold your Son!"; "Behold, your mother."

# Part II

## The Mother Of God At The
## Center Of The Pilgrim Church

## 1. The Church, The People Of God Present In All
## The Nations Of The Earth

25. "The Church 'like a pilgrim in a foreign land, presses forward amid the persecutions of the world and the consolations of God,'[52] announcing the Cross and Death of the Lord until he comes (cf. 1 Cor 11:26)."[53] "Israel according to the flesh, which wandered as an exile in the desert, was already called the Church of God (cf. Neh 13:1; Num. 20:4; Dt. 23:1ff.). Likewise the new Israel... is also called the Church of Christ (cf. Mt 16:18). For he has bought it for himself with his blood (Acts 20:28), has filled it with his Spirit, and provided it with those means which befit it as a visible and social unity. God has gathered together as one all those who in faith look upon Jesus as the author of salvation and the source of unity and peace, and has established them as Church, that for each and all she may be the visible sacrament of this saving unity."[54]

The Second Vatican Council speaks of the pilgrim Church, establishing an analogy with the Israel of the Old Covenant journeying through the desert. The journey also has an external character, visible in the time and space in which it historically takes place. For the Church "is destined to extend to all regions of the earth and so to enter into the history of mankind," but at the same time "she transcends all limits of time and of space."[55] And yet the essential character of her pilgrimage is interior: it is a question of a pilgrimage through faith, by "the power of the Risen Lord,"[56] a pilgrimage in the Holy Spirit, given to the Church as the invisible Comforter (parakletos) (cf. Jn 14:26; 15:26; 16:7): "Moving forward through trial and tribulation, the Church is strengthened by the power of God's grace promised to her by the

Lord, so that... moved by the Holy Spirit, she may never cease to renew herself, until through the Cross she arrives at the light which knows no setting."[57]

It is precisely in this ecclesial journey or pilgrimage through space and time, and even more through the history of souls, that Mary is present, as the one who is "blessed because she believed," as the one who advanced on the pilgrimage of faith, sharing unlike any other creature in the mystery of Christ. The Council further says that "Mary figured profoundly in the history of salvation and in a certain way unites and mirrors within herself the central truths of the faith."[58] Among all believers she is like a "mirror" in which are reflected in the most profound and limpid way "the mighty works of God" (Acts 2:11).

26. Built by Christ upon the Apostles, the Church became fully aware of these mighty works of God on the day of Pentecost, when those gathered together in the Upper Room "were all filled with the Holy Spirit and began to speak in other tongues, as the Spirit gave them utterance" (Acts 2:4). From that moment there also begins that journey of faith, the Church's pilgrimage through the history of individuals and peoples. We know that at the beginning of this journey Mary is present. We see her in the midst of the Apostles in the Upper Room, "prayerfully imploring the gift of the Spirit."[59]

In a sense her journey of faith is longer. The Holy Spirit had already come down upon her, and she became his faithful spouse at the Annunciation, welcoming the Word of the true God, offering "the full submission of intellect and will... and freely assenting to the truth revealed by him," indeed abandoning herself totally to God through "the obedience of faith,"[60] whereby she replied to the angel: "Behold, I am the handmaid of the Lord; let it be to me according to your word." The journey of faith made by Mary, whom we see praying in the Upper Room, is thus longer than that of the others gathered there: Mary "goes before them," "leads the way" for them.[61] The moment of Pentecost in Jerusalem had been prepared for by the moment of the Annunciation in Nazareth, as well as by the Cross. In the Upper Room Mary's journey meets the Church's journey of faith. In what way?

Among those who devoted themselves to prayer in the

Upper Room, preparing to go "into the whole world" after receiving the Spirit, some had been called by Jesus gradually from the beginning of his mission in Israel. Eleven of them had been made Apostles, and to them Jesus had passed on the mission which he himself had received from the Father. "As the Father has sent me, even so I send you" (Jn 20:21), he had said to the Apostles after the resurrection. And forty days later, before returning to the Father, he had added: "when the Holy Spirit has come upon you... you shall be my witnesses... to the end of the earth" (cf. Acts 1:8). This mission of the Apostles began the moment they left the Upper Room in Jerusalem. The Church is born and then grows through the testimony that Peter and the Apostles bear to the Crucified and Risen Christ (cf. Acts 2:31-34; 3:15-18; 4:10-12; 5:30-32).

Mary did not directly receive this apostolic mission. She was not among those whom Jesus sent "to the whole world to teach all nations" (cf. Mt 28:19) when he conferred this mission on them. But she was in the Upper Room, where the Apostles were preparing to take up this mission with the coming of the Spirit of Truth: she was present with them. In their midst Mary was "devoted to prayer" as the "mother of Jesus" (cf. Acts 1:13-14), of the Crucified and Risen Christ. And that first group of those who in faith looked "upon Jesus as the author of salvation,"[62] knew that Jesus was the Son of Mary, and that she was his Mother, and that as such she was from the moment of his conception and birth a unique witness to the mystery of Jesus, that mystery which before their eyes had been disclosed and confirmed in the Cross and resurrection. Thus, from the very first moment, the Church "looked at" Mary through Jesus, just as she "looked at" Jesus through Mary. For the Church of that time and of every time Mary is a singular witness to the years of Jesus' infancy and hidden life at Nazareth, when she "kept all these things, pondering them in her heart" (Lk 2:19; cf. Lk 2:51).

But above all, in the Church of that time and of every time Mary was and is the one who is "blessed because she believed"; she was the first to believe. From the moment of the Annunciation and conception, from the moment of his birth in the stable at Bethlehem, Mary followed Jesus step by step in her maternal pilgrimage of faith. She followed him during the years of his hidden life at Nazareth; she followed him also during the time after he left home, when he began "to do and to teach" (cf. Acts 1:1) in the midst of Israel. Above all she followed him in the tragic experience of Golgotha. Now, while Mary was with the Apostles in the Upper Room in Jerusalem at the dawn of the Church, her faith, born from the words of the Annunciation, found confirmation. The angel had said to her then: "You will conceive in your womb and bear a Son, and you shall call his name Jesus. He will be great... and he will reign over the house of Jacob for ever; and of his kingdom there will be no end." The recent events on Calvary had shrouded that promise in darkness, yet not even beneath the Cross did Mary's faith fail. She had still remained the one who, like Abraham, "in hope believed against hope" (Rom 4:18). But it is only after the resurrection that hope had shown its true face and the promise had begun to be transformed into reality. For Jesus, before returning to the Father, had said to the Apostles: "Go therefore and make disciples of all nations... lo, I am with you always, to the close of the age" (cf. Mt 28:19-20). Thus had spoken the one who by his resurrection had revealed himself as the conqueror of death, as the one who possessed the kingdom of which, as the angel said, "there will be no end."

27. Now, at the first dawn of the Church, at the beginning of the long journey through faith which began at Pentecost in Jerusalem, Mary was with all those who were the seed of the "new Israel." She was present among them as an exceptional witness to the mystery of Christ. And the Church was assiduous in prayer together with her, and at the same time "contemplated her in the light of the Word made man." It was always to be so. For when the Church "enters more intimately into the supreme mystery of the Incarnation," she thinks of the Mother of Christ with profound reverence and devotion.[63] Mary belongs indissolubly to the mystery of Christ, and she belongs also to the mystery of the Church from the beginning, from the day of the Church's birth. At the basis of what the Church has been from the beginning, and of what she must continually become from generation to generation, in the midst of all the nations of the earth, we find the one "who believed that there would be a fulfillment of what was spoken to her from the Lord" (Lk 1:45). It is precisely Mary's faith which marks the

beginning of the new and eternal Covenant of God with man in Jesus Christ; this heroic faith of hers "precedes" the apostolic witness of the Church, and ever remains in the Church's heart hidden like a special heritage of God's revelation. All those who from generation to generation accept the apostolic witness of the Church share in that mysterious inheritance, and in a sense share in Mary's faith.

Elizabeth's words "Blessed is she who believed" continue to accompany the Virgin also at Pentecost; they accompany her from age to age, wherever knowledge of Christ's salvific mystery spreads, through the Church's apostolic witness and service. Thus is fulfilled the prophecy of the Magnificat: "All generations will call me blessed; for he who is mighty has done great things for me, and holy is his name" (Lk 1:48-49). For knowledge of the mystery of Christ leads us to bless his Mother, in the form of special veneration for the Theotokos. But this veneration always includes a blessing of her faith, for the Virgin of Nazareth became blessed above all through this faith, in accordance with Elizabeth's words. Those who from generation to generation among the different peoples and nations of the earth accept with faith the mystery of Christ, the Incarnate Word and Redeemer of the world, not only turn with veneration to Mary and confidently have recourse to her as his Mother, but also seek in her faith support for their own. And it is precisely this lively sharing in Mary's faith that determines her special place in the Church's pilgrimage as the new People of God throughout the earth.

28. As the Council says, "Mary figured profoundly in the history of salvation.... Hence when she is being preached and venerated, she summons the faithful to her Son and his sacrifice, and to love for the Father."[64] For this reason, Mary's faith, according to the Church's apostolic witness, in some way continues to become the faith of the pilgrim People of God: the faith of individuals and communities, of places and gatherings, and of the various groups existing in the Church. It is a faith that is passed on simultaneously through both the mind and the heart. It is gained or regained continually through prayer. Therefore, "the Church in her apostolic work also rightly looks to her who brought forth Christ, conceived by the Holy Spirit and born of the Virgin, so that through the Church Christ may be born and increase in the hearts of the

faithful also."[65]

Today, as on this pilgrimage of faith we draw near to the end of the second Christian Millennium, the Church, through the teaching of the Second Vatican Council, calls our attention to her vision of herself, as the "one People of God... among all the nations of the earth." And she reminds us of that truth according to which all the faithful, though "scattered throughout the world, are in communion with each other in the Holy Spirit."[66] We can therefore say that in this union the mystery of Pentecost is continually being accomplished. At the same time, the Lord's apostles and disciples, in all the nations of the earth, "devote themselves to prayer together with Mary, the mother of Jesus" (Acts 1:14). As they constitute from generation to generation the "sign of the Kingdom" which is not of his world,[67] they are also aware that in the midst of this world they must gather around that King to whom the nations have been given in heritage (cf. Ps 2:8), to whom the Father has given "the throne of David his father," so that he "will reign over the house of Jacob for ever, and of his kingdom there will he no end."

During this time of vigil, Mary, through the same faith which made her blessed, especially from the moment of the Annunciation, is present in the Church's mission, present in the Church's work of introducing into the world the Kingdom of her Son.[68]

This presence of Mary finds many different expressions in our day, just as it did throughout the Church's history. It also has a wide field of action. Through the faith and piety of individual believers; through the traditions of Christian families or "domestic churches," of parish and missionary communities, religious institutes and dioceses; through the radiance and attraction of the great shrines where not only individuals or local groups, but sometimes whole nations and societies, even whole continents, seek to meet the Mother of the Lord, the one who is blessed because she believed is the first among believers and therefore became the Mother of Emmanuel. This is the message of the Land of Palestine, the spiritual homeland of all Christians because it was the homeland of the Savior of the world and of his Mother. This is the message of the many churches in Rome and throughout the world which have been raised up in the course of the centuries by the faith of Christians. This is the message of centers like Guadalupe, Lourdes, Fatima and the others situated in the various countries. Among them how could I fail to mention the one in my own native land, Jasna Gora? One could perhaps speak of a specific "geography" of faith and Marian devotion, which includes all these special places of pilgrimage where the People of God seek to meet the Mother of God in order to find, within the radius of the maternal presence of her "who believed," a strengthening of their own faith. For in Mary's faith, first at the Annunciation and then fully at the foot of the Cross, an interior space was reopened within humanity which the eternal Father can fill "with every spiritual blessing." It is the space "of the new and eternal Covenant,"[69] and it continues to exist in the Church, which in Christ is "a kind of sacrament or sign of intimate union with God, and of the unity of all mankind."[70]

In the faith which Mary professed at the Annunciation as the "handmaid of the Lord" and in which she constantly "precedes" the pilgrim People of God throughout the earth, the Church "strives energetically and constantly to bring all humanity... back to Christ its Head in the unity of his Spirit."[71]

## 2. The Church's Journey And The Unity Of All Christians

29. "In all of Christ's disciples the Spirit arouses the desire to be peacefully united, in the manner determined by Christ, as one flock under one shepherd."[72] The journey of the Church, especially in our own time, is marked by the sign of ecumenism: Christians are seeking ways to restore that unity which Christ implored from the Father for his disciples on the day before his Passion: "That they may all be one; even as you, Father, are in me, and I in you that they also may be in us, so that the world may believe that you have sent me" (Jn 17:21). The unity of Christ's disciples, therefore, is a great sign given in order to kindle faith in the world while their division constitutes a scandal.[73]

The ecumenical movement, on the basis of a clearer and more widespread awareness of the urgent need to achieve the unity of all Christians, has found on the part of the Catholic Church its culminating expression in the work of the Second Vatican Council: Christians must deepen in themselves and each of their communities that "obedience of faith" of which Mary is the first and brightest example. And since she "shines forth on earth,... as a sign of sure hope and solace for the pilgrim People of God," "it gives great joy and comfort to this most holy Synod that among the divided brethren, too, there are those who live due honor to the Mother of our Lord and Savior. This is especially so among the Easterners."[74]

30. Christians know that their unity will be truly rediscovered only if it is based on the unity of their faith. They must resolve considerable discrepancies of doctrine concerning the mystery and ministry of the Church, and sometimes also concerning the role of Mary in the work of salvation.[75] The dialogues begun by the Catholic Church with the Churches and Ecclesial Communities of the West[76] are steadily converging upon these two inseparable aspects of the same mystery of salvation. If the mystery of the Word made flesh enables us to glimpse the mystery of the divine motherhood and is, in turn, contemplation of the Mother of God brings us to a more profound understanding of the mystery of the Incarnation, then the same must be said for the mystery of the Church and Mary's role in the work of salvation. By a more profound study of both Mary and the Church, clarifying each by the light of the other, Christians who are eager to do what Jesus tells them-as their Mother recommends (cf. Jn 2:5)-will be able to go forward together on this "pilgrimage of faith." Mary, who is still the model of this pilgrimage, is to lead them to the unity which is willed by their one Lord and so much desired by those who are attentively listening to what "the Spirit is saying to the Churches" today (Rv 2:7, 11, 17).

Meanwhile, it is a hopeful sign that these Churches and Ecclesial Communities are finding agreement with the Catholic Church on fundamental points of Christian belief, including matters relating to the Virgin Mary. For they recognize her as the Mother of the Lord and hold that this forms part of our faith in Christ, true God and true man. They look to her who at the foot of the Cross accepts as her Son the beloved disciple, the one who in his turn accepts her as his mother.

Therefore, why should we not all together look to her as our common Mother, who prays for the unity of God's family and who "precedes" us all at the head of the long line of witnesses of faith in the one Lord, the Son of God, who was conceived in her virginal womb by the power of the Holy Spirit?

31. On the other hand, I wish to emphasize how profoundly the Catholic Church, the Orthodox Church and the ancient Churches of the East feel united by love and praise of the Theotokos. Not only "basic dogmas of the Christian faith concerning the Trinity and God's Word made flesh of the Virgin Mary were defined in Ecumenical Councils held in the East,"[77] but also in their liturgical worship "the Orientals pay high tribute, in very beautiful hymns, to Mary ever Virgin... God's Most Holy Mother."[78]

The brethren of these Churches have experienced a complex history, but it is one that has always been marked by an intense desire for Christian commitment and apostolic activity, despite frequent persecution, even to the point of bloodshed. It is a history of fidelity to the Lord, an authentic "pilgrimage of faith" in space and time, during which Eastern Christians have always looked with boundless trust to the Mother of the Lord, celebrated her with praise and invoked her with unceasing prayer. In the difficult moments of their troubled Christian existence, "they have taken refuge under her protection,"[79] conscious of having in her a powerful aid. The Churches which profess the doctrine of Ephesus proclaim the Virgin as "true Mother of God," since "our Lord Jesus Christ, born of the Father before time began according to his divinity, in the last days, for our sake and for our salvation, was himself begotten of Mary, the Virgin Mother of God according to his humanity."[80] The Greek Fathers and the Byzantine tradition contemplating the Virgin in the light of the Word made flesh, have sought to penetrate the depth of that bond which unites Mary, as the Mother of God, to Christ and the Church: the Virgin is a permanent presence in the whole reality of the salvific mystery.

The Coptic and Ethiopian traditions were introduced to this contemplation of the mystery of Mary by St. Cyril of Alexandria, and in their turn they have celebrated it with a profuse poetic blossoming.[81] The poetic genius of St. Ephrem the Syrian, called "the lyre of the Holy Spirit," tirelessly sang of Mary, leaving a still living mark on the whole tradition of the Syriac Church.[82]

In his panegyric of the Theotokos, St. Gregory of Narek, one of the outstanding glories of Armenia, with powerful poetic inspiration ponders the different aspects of the mystery of the Incarnation, and each of them is for him an occasion to sing and extol the extraordinary dignity and magnificent beauty of the Virgin Mary, Mother of the Word made flesh.[83]

It does not surprise us therefore that Mary occupies a privileged place in the worship or the ancient Oriental Churches with an incomparable abundance of feasts and hymns.

32. In the Byzantine liturgy, in all the hours of the Divine Office, praise of the Mother is linked with praise of her Son and with the praise which, through the Son, is offered up to the Father in the Holy Spirit. In the Anaphora or Eucharistic Prayer of St. John Chrysostom, immediately after the epiclesis the assembled community sings in honor of the Mother of God: "It is truly just to proclaim you blessed, O Mother of God, who are most blessed, all pure and Mother of our God. We magnify you who are more honorable than the Cherubim and incomparably more glorious than the Seraphim. You who, without losing your virginity, gave birth to the Word of God. You who are truly the Mother of God."

These praises, which in every celebration of the Eucharistic Liturgy are offered to Mary, have molded the faith, piety and prayer of the faithful. In the course of the centuries they have permeated their whole spiritual outlook, fostering in them a profound devotion to the "All Holy Mother of God."

33. This year there occurs the twelfth centenary of the Second Ecumenical Council of Nicaea (787). Putting an end to the well-known controversy about the cult of sacred images, this Council defined that, according to the teaching of the holy Fathers and the universal tradition of the Church, there could be exposed for the veneration of the faithful, together with the Cross, also images of the Mother of God, of the angels and of the saints, in churches and houses and at the roadside.[84] This custom has been maintained in the whole of the East and also in the West. Images of the Virgin have a place of honor in churches and houses. In

them Mary is represented in a number of ways: as the throne of God carrying the Lord and giving him to humanity (Theotokos); as the way that leads to Christ and manifests him (Hodegetria); as a praying figure in an attitude of intercession and as a sign of the divine presence on the journey of the faithful until the day of the Lord (Deesis); as the protectress who stretches out her mantle over the peoples (Pokrov), or as the merciful Virgin of tenderness (Eleousa). She is usually represented with her Son, the child Jesus, in her arms: it is the relationship with the Son which glorifies the Mother. Sometimes she embraces him with tenderness (Glykophilousa); at other times she is a hieratic figure, apparently rapt in contemplation of him who is the Lord of history (cf. Rv 5:9-14).[85]

It is also appropriate to mention the icon of Our Lady of Vladimir, which continually accompanied the pilgrimage of faith of the peoples of ancient Russia'. The first Millennium of the conversion of those noble lands to Christianity is approaching: lands of humble folk, of thinkers and of saints. The Icons are still venerated in the Ukraine, in Byelorussia and in Russia under various titles. They are images which witness to the faith and spirit of prayer of that people, who sense the presence and protection of the Mother of God. In these Icons the Virgin shines as the image of divine beauty, the abode of Eternal Wisdom, the figure of the one who prays, the prototype of contemplation, the image of glory: she who even in her earthly life possessed the spiritual knowledge inaccessible to human reasoning and who attained through faith the most sublime knowledge. I also recall the Icon of the Virgin of the Cenacle, praying with the Apostles as they awaited the Holy Spirit: could she not become the sign of hope for all those who, in fraternal dialogue, wish to deepen their obedience of faith?

34. Such a wealth of praise, built up by the different forms of the Church's great tradition, could help us to hasten the day when the Church can begin once more to breathe fully with her "two lungs," the East and the West. As I have often said, this is more than ever necessary today. It would be an effective aid in furthering the progress of the dialogue already taking place between the Catholic Church and the Churches and Ecclesial

Communities of the West.[86] It would also be the way for the pilgrim Church to sing and to live more perfectly her "Magnificat."

## 3. The "Magnificat" Of The Pilgrim Church

35. At the present stage of her journey, therefore, the Church seeks to rediscover the unity of all who profess their faith in Christ, in order to show obedience to her Lord, who prayed for this unity before his Passion. "Like a pilgrim in a foreign land, the Church presses forward amid the persecutions of the world and the consolations of God, announcing the Cross and Death of the Lord until he comes."[87] "Moving forward through trial and tribulation, the Church is strengthened by the power of God's grace promised to her by the Lord, so that in the weakness of the flesh she may not waver from perfect fidelity, but remain a bride worthy of her Lord; that moved by the Holy Spirit she may never cease to renew herself, until through the Cross she arrives at the light which knows no setting."[88]

The Virgin Mother is constantly present on this journey of faith of the People of God towards the light. This is shown in a special way by the canticle of the "Magnificat," which, having welled up from the depths of Mary's faith at the Visitation, ceaselessly re-echoes in the heart of the Church down the centuries. This is proved by its daily recitation in the liturgy of Vespers and at many other moments of both personal and communal devotion.

"My soul magnifies the Lord,
and my spirit rejoices in God my Savior,
for he has looked on his servant in her lowliness.
For behold, henceforth all generations will call me blessed;
for he who is mighty has done great things for me,
and holy is his name:
And his mercy is from age to age on those who fear him.
He has shown strength with his arm.
he has scattered the proud-hearted,
he has cast down the mighty from their thrones,

and lifted up the lowly;
he has filled the hungry with good things,
sent the rich away empty.
He has helped his servant Israel,
remembering his mercy,
as he spoke to our fathers,
to Abraham and to his posterity for ever" (Lk 1:46-55).

36. When Elizabeth greeted her young kinswoman coming from Nazareth, Mary replied with the Magnificat. In her greeting, Elizabeth first called Mary "blessed" because of "the fruit of her womb," and then she called her "blessed" because of her faith (cf. Lk 1:42, 45). These two blessings referred directly to the Annunciation. Now, at the Visitation, when Elizabeth's greeting bears witness to that culminating moment, Mary's faith acquires a new consciousness and a new expression. That which remained hidden in the depths of the "obedience of faith" at the Annunciation can now be said to spring forth like a clear and life-giving flame of the spirit. The words used by Mary on the threshold of Elizabeth's house are an inspired profession of her faith, in which her response to the revealed word is expressed with the religious and poetical exultation of her whole being towards God. In these sublime words, which are simultaneously very simple and wholly inspired by the sacred texts of the people of Israel,[89] Mary's personal experience, the ecstasy of her heart, shines forth. In them shines a ray of the mystery of God, the glory of his ineffable holiness, the eternal love which, as an irrevocable gift, enters into human history.

Mary is the first to share in this new revelation of God and, within the same, in this new "self-giving" of God. Therefore she proclaims: "For he who is mighty has done great things for me, and holy is his name." Her words reflect a joy of spirit which is difficult to express: "My spirit rejoices in God my Savior." Indeed, "the deepest truth about God and the salvation of man is made clear to us in Christ, who is at the same time the mediator and the fullness of all revelation."[90] In her exultation Mary confesses that she finds herself in the very heart of this fullness of Christ. She is conscious that the promise made to the fathers, first of all "to

Abraham and to his posterity for ever," is being fulfilled in herself. She is thus aware that concentrated within herself as the mother of Christ is the whole salvific economy, in which "from age to age" is manifested he who as the God of the Covenant, "remembers his mercy."

37. The Church, which from the beginning has modeled her earthly journey on that of the Mother of God, constantly repeats after her the words of the Magnificat. From the depths of the Virgin's faith at the Annunciation and the Visitation, the Church derives the truth about the God of the Covenant: the God who is Almighty and does "great things" for man: "holy is his name." In the Magnificat the Church sees uprooted that sin which is found at the outset of the earthly history of man and woman, the sin of disbelief and of "little faith" in God. In contrast with the "suspicion" which the "father of lies" sowed in the heart of Eve the first woman, Mary, whom tradition is wont to call the "new Eve"[91] and the true "Mother of the living,"[92] boldly proclaims the undimmed truth about God: the holy and almighty God, who from the beginning is the source of all gifts, he who "has done great things" in her, as well as in the whole universe. In the act of creation God gives existence to all that is. In creating man, God gives him the dignity of the image and likeness of himself in a special way as compared with all earthly creatures. Moreover, in his desire to give God gives himself in the Son, notwithstanding man's sin: "He so loved the world that he gave his only Son" (Jn 3:16). Mary is the first witness of this marvelous truth, which will be fully accomplished through "the works and words" (cf. Acts 1:1) of her Son and definitively through his Cross and resurrection.

The Church, which even "amid trials and tribulations" does not cease repeating with Mary the words of the Magnificat, is sustained by the power of God's truth, proclaimed on that occasion with such extraordinary simplicity. At the same time, by means of this truth about God, the Church desires to shed light upon the difficult and sometimes tangled paths of man's earthly existence. The Church's journey, therefore, near the end of the second Christian Millennium, involves a renewed commitment to her mission. Following him who said of himself: "(God) has anointed me to preach good news to the poor" (cf. Lk 4:18), the Church has sought from generation to generation and still seeks today to accomplish that same mission.

The Church's love of preference for the poor is wonderfully inscribed in Mary's Magnificat. The God of the Covenant, celebrated in the exultation of her spirit by the Virgin of Nazareth, is also he who "has cast down the mighty from their thrones, and lifted up the lowly,... filled the hungry with good things, sent the rich away empty,... scattered the proud-hearted... and his mercy is from age to age on those who fear him." Mary is deeply imbued with the spirit of the "poor of Yahweh," who in the prayer of the Psalms awaited from God their salvation, placing all their trust in him (cf. Ps 25; 31; 35; 55). Mary truly proclaims the coming of the "Messiah of the poor" (cf. Is 11:4; 61:1). Drawing from Mary's heart, from the depth of her faith expressed in the words of the Magnificat, the Church renews ever more effectively in herself the awareness that the truth about God who saves, the truth about God who is the source of every gift, cannot be separated from the manifestation of his love of preference for the poor and humble, that love which, celebrated in the Magnificat, is later expressed in the words and works of Jesus.

The Church is thus aware-and at the present time this awareness is particularly vivid-not only that these two elements of the message contained in the Magnificat cannot be separated, but also that there is a duty to safeguard carefully the importance of "the poor" and of "the option in favor of the poor" in the word of the living God. These are matters and questions intimately connected with the Christian meaning of freedom and liberation. "Mary is totally dependent upon God and completely directed towards him, and at the side of her Son, she is the most perfect image of freedom and of the liberation of humanity and of the universe. It is to her as Mother and Model that the Church must look in order to understand in its completeness the meaning of her own mission."[93]

# Part III

## Maternal Mediation

### 1. Mary, The Handmaid Of The Lord

38. The Church knows and teaches with Saint Paul that there is only one mediator: "For there is one God, and there is one mediator between God and men, the man Christ Jesus, who gave himself as a ransom for all" (1 Tm 2:5-6). "The maternal role of Mary towards people in no way obscures or diminishes the unique mediation of Christ, but rather shows its power":[94] it is mediation in Christ.

The Church knows and teaches that "all the saving influences of the Blessed Virgin on mankind originate... from the divine pleasure. They flow forth from the superabundance of the merits of Christ, rest on his mediation, depend entirely on it, and draw all their power from it. In no way do they impede the immediate union of the faithful with Christ. Rather, they foster this union."[95] This saving influence is sustained by the Holy Spirit, who, just as he overshadowed the Virgin Mary when he began in her the divine motherhood, in a similar way constantly sustains her solicitude for the brothers and sisters of her Son.

In effect, Mary's mediation is intimately linked with her motherhood. It possesses a specifically maternal character, which distinguishes it from the mediation of the other creatures who in various and always subordinate ways share in the one mediation of Christ, although her own mediation is also a shared mediation.[96] In fact, while it is true that "no creature could ever be classed with the Incarnate Word and Redeemer," at the same time "the unique mediation of the Redeemer does not exclude but rather gives rise among creatures to a manifold cooperation which is but a sharing in this unique source." And thus "the one goodness of God is in reality communicated diversely to his creatures."[97]

The teaching of the Second Vatican Council presents the truth of Mary's mediation as "a sharing in the one unique source that is the mediation of Christ himself." Thus we read: "The Church does not hesitate to profess this subordinate role of Mary. She experiences it continuously and commends it to the hearts of the faithful, so that, encouraged by this maternal help, they may more closely adhere to the Mediator and Redeemer."[98] This role is at the same time special and extraordinary. It flows from her divine motherhood and can be understood and lived in faith only on the basis of the full truth of this motherhood. Since by virtue of divine election Mary is the earthly Mother of the Father's consubstantial Son and his "generous companion" in the work of redemption "she is a mother to us in the order of grace."[99] This role constitutes a real dimension of her presence in the saving mystery of Christ and the Church.

39. From this point of view we must consider once more the fundamental event in the economy of salvation, namely the Incarnation of the Word at the moment of the Annunciation. It is significant that Mary, recognizing in the words of the divine messenger the will of the Most High and submitting to his power, says: "Behold, I am the handmaid of the Lord; let it be to me according to your word" (Lk 1:38). The first moment of submission to the one mediation "between God and men"-the mediation of Jesus Christ-is the Virgin of Nazareth's acceptance of motherhood. Mary consents to God's choice, in order to become through the power of the Holy Spirit the Mother of the Son of God. It can be said that a consent to motherhood is above all a result of her total self-giving to God in virginity. Mary accepted her election as Mother of the Son of God, guided by spousal love, the love which totally "consecrates" a human being to God. By virtue of this love, Mary wished to be always and in all things "given to God," living in virginity. The words "Behold, I am the handmaid of the Lord" express the fact that from the outset she accepted and understood her own motherhood as a total gift of self, a gift of her person to the service of the saving plans of the Most High. And to the very end she lived her entire maternal sharing in the life of Jesus Christ, her Son, in a way that matched her vocation to virginity.

Mary's motherhood, completely pervaded by her spousal attitude as the "handmaid of the Lord," constitutes the first and fundamental dimension of that mediation which the Church confesses and proclaims in her regard[100] and continually "commends to the hearts of the faithful," since the Church has great trust in her. For it must be recognized that before anyone else it was God himself, the Eternal Father, who entrusted himself to the Virgin of Nazareth, giving her his own Son in the mystery of the Incarnation. Her election to the supreme office and dignity of Mother of the Son of God refers, on the ontological level, to the very reality of the union of the two natures in the person of the Word (hypostatic union). This basic fact of being the Mother of the Son of God is from the very beginning a complete openness to the person of Christ, to his whole work, to his whole mission. The words "Behold, I am the handmaid of the Lord" testify to Mary's openness of spirit: she perfectly unites in herself the love proper to virginity and the love characteristic of motherhood, which are joined and, as it were, fused together.

For this reason Mary became not only the "nursing mother" of the Son of Man but also the "associate of unique nobility"[101] of the Messiah and Redeemer. As I have already said, she advanced in her pilgrimage of faith, and in this pilgrimage to the foot of the Cross there was simultaneously accomplished her maternal cooperation with the Savior's whole mission through her actions and sufferings. Along the path of this collaboration with the work of her Son, the Redeemer, Mary's motherhood itself underwent a singular transformation, becoming ever more imbued with "burning charity" towards all those to whom Christ's mission was directed. Through this "burning charity," which sought to achieve, in union with Christ, the restoration of "supernatural life to souls,"[102] Mary entered, in a way all her own, into the one mediation "between God and men" which is the mediation of the man Christ Jesus. If she was the first to experience within herself the supernatural consequences of this one mediation-in the Annunciation she had been greeted as "full of grace"-then we must say that through this fullness of grace and supernatural life she was especially predisposed to cooperation with Christ, the one Mediator of human salvation. And such cooperation is precisely this mediation subordinated to the mediation of Christ.

In Mary's case we have a special and exceptional mediation, based upon her "fullness of grace," which was expressed in the complete willingness of the "handmaid of the Lord." In response to this interior willingness of his Mother, Jesus Christ prepared her ever more completely to become for all people their "mother in the order of grace." This is indicated, at least indirectly, by certain details noted by the Synoptics (cf. Lk 11:28; 8:20-21; Mk 3:32-35; Mt 12:47-50) and still more so by the Gospel of John (cf. 2:1-12; 19:25-27), which I have already mentioned. Particularly eloquent in this regard are the words spoken by Jesus on the Cross to Mary and John.

40. After the events of the resurrection and ascension Mary entered the Upper Room together with the Apostles to await Pentecost, and was present there as the Mother of the glorified Lord. She was not only the one who "advanced in her pilgrimage of faith" and loyally persevered in her union with her Son "unto the Cross," but she was also the "handmaid of the Lord," left by her Son as Mother in the midst of the infant Church: "Behold your mother." Thus there began to develop a special bond between this Mother and the Church. For the infant Church was the fruit of the Cross and resurrection of her Son. Mary, who from the beginning had given herself without reserve to the person and work of her Son, could not but pour out upon the Church, from the very beginning, her maternal self-giving. After her Son's departure, her motherhood remains in the Church as maternal mediation: interceding for all her children, the Mother cooperates in the saving work of her Son, the Redeemer of the world. In fact the Council teaches that the "motherhood of Mary in the order of grace... will last without interruption until the eternal fulfillment of all the elect."[103] With the redeeming death of her Son, the maternal mediation of the handmaid of the Lord took on a universal dimension, for the work of redemption embraces the whole of humanity. Thus there is manifested in a singular way the efficacy of the one and universal mediation of Christ "between God and men" Mary's cooperation shares, in its subordinate character, in the universality of the mediation of the Redeemer, the one Mediator. This is clearly indicated by the Council in the words quoted above.

"For," the text goes on, "taken up to heaven, she did not lay aside this saving role, but by her manifold acts of intercession continues to win for us gifts of eternal salvation."[104] With this character of "intercession," first manifested at Cana in Galilee, Mary's mediation continues in the history of the Church and the world. We read that Mary "by her maternal charity, cares for the brethren of her Son who still journey on earth surrounded by dangers and difficulties, until they are led to their happy homeland."[105] In this way Mary's motherhood continues unceasingly in the Church as the mediation which intercedes, and the Church expresses her faith in this truth by invoking Mary "under the titles of Advocate, Auxiliatrix, Adjutrix and Mediatrix."[106]

41. Through her mediation, subordinate to that of the Redeemer, Mary contributes in a special way to the union of the pilgrim Church on earth with the eschatological and heavenly reality of the Communion of Saints, since she has already been "assumed into heaven."[107] The truth of the assumption, defined by Pius XII, is reaffirmed by the Second Vatican Council, which thus expresses the Church's faith: "Preserved free from all guilt of original sin, the Immaculate Virgin was taken up body and soul into heavenly glory upon the completion of her earthly sojourn. She was exalted by the Lord as Queen of the Universe, in order that she might be the more thoroughly conformed to her Son, the Lord of lords (cf. Rv 19:16) and the conqueror of sin and death."[108] In this teaching Pius XII was in continuity with Tradition, which has found many different expressions in the history of the Church, both in the East and in the West.

By the mystery of the assumption into heaven there were definitively accomplished in Mary all the effects of the one mediation of Christ the Redeemer of the world and Risen Lord: "In Christ shall all be made alive. But each in his own order: Christ the first fruits, then at his coming those who belong to Christ" (1 Cor 15:22-23). In the mystery of the assumption is expressed the faith of the Church, according to which Mary is "united by a close and indissoluble bond" to Christ, for, if as Virgin and Mother she was singularly united with him in his first coming, so through her continued collaboration with him she will also be united with him in expectation of the second; "redeemed in an especially sublime manner by reason of the merits of her Son,"[109] she also has that specifically maternal role of mediatrix of mercy at his final coming, when all those who belong to Christ "shall be made alive," when "the last enemy to be destroyed is death" (1 Cor 15:26)."[110]

Connected with this exaltation of the noble "Daughter of Zion"[111] through her assumption into heaven is the mystery of her eternal glory. For the Mother of Christ is glorified as "Queen of the Universe."[112] She who at the Annunciation called herself the "handmaid of the Lord" remained throughout her earthly life faithful to what this name expresses. In this she confirmed that she was a true "disciple" of Christ, who strongly emphasized that his mission was one of service: the Son of Man came not to be served but to serve, and to give his life as a ransom for many" (Mt 20:28). In this way Mary became the first of those who, "serving Christ also in others, with humility and patience lead their brothers and sisters to that King whom to serve is to reign,"[113] and she fully obtained that "state of royal freedom" proper to Christ's disciples: to serve means to reign!

"Christ obeyed even at the cost of death, and was therefore raised up by the Father (cf. Phil 2:8-9). Thus he entered into the glory of his kingdom. To him all things are made subject until he subjects himself and all created things to the Father, that God may be all in all (cf. 1 Cor 15:27-28)."[114] Mary, the handmaid of the Lord, has a share in this Kingdom of the Son.[115] The glory of serving does not cease to be her royal exaltation: assumed into heaven, she does not cease her saving service, which expresses her maternal mediation "until the eternal fulfillment of all the elect."[116] Thus, she who here on earth "loyally preserved in her union with her Son unto the Cross," continues to remain united with him, while now "all things are subjected to him, until he subjects to the Father himself and all things." Thus in her assumption into heaven, Mary is as it were clothed by the whole reality of the Communion of Saints, and her very union with the Son in glory is wholly oriented towards the definitive fullness of the Kingdom, when "God will be all in all."

In this phase too Mary's maternal mediation does not cease to be subordinate to him who is the one Mediator, until the final realization of "the fullness of time," that is to say until "all things are united in Christ" (cf. Eph 1:10).

## 2. Mary In The Life Of The Church
## And Of Every Christian

42. Linking itself with Tradition, the Second Vatican Council brought new light to bear on the role of the Mother of Christ in the life of the Church. "Through the gift... of divine motherhood, Mary is united with her Son, the Redeemer, and with his singular graces and offices. By these, the Blessed Virgin is also intimately united with the Church: the Mother of God is a figure of the Church in the matter of faith, charity and perfect union with Christ."[117] We have already noted how, from the beginning, Mary remains with the Apostles in expectation of Pentecost and how, as "the blessed one who believed," she is present in the midst of the pilgrim Church from generation to generation through faith and as the model of the hope which does not disappoint (cf. Rom 5:5).

Mary believed in the fulfillment of what had been said to her by the Lord. As Virgin, she believed that she would conceive and bear a Son: the "Holy One," who bears the name of "Son of God," the name "Jesus" (God who saves). As handmaid of the Lord, she remained in perfect fidelity to the person and mission of this Son. As Mother, "believing and obeying... she brought forth on earth the Father's Son. This she did, knowing not man but overshadowed by the Holy Spirit."[118]

For these reasons Mary is honored in the Church "with special reverence. Indeed, from most ancient times the Blessed Virgin Mary has been venerated under the title of 'God-bearer.' In all perils and needs, the faithful have fled prayerfully to her protection."[119] This cult is altogether special: it bears in itself and expresses the profound link which exists between the Mother of Christ and the Church.[120] As Virgin and Mother, Mary remains for the Church a "permanent model." It can therefore be said that especially under this aspect, namely as a model, or rather as a "figure," Mary, present in the mystery of Christ, remains constantly present also in the mystery of the Church. For the Church too is "called mother and virgin," and these names have a profound Biblical and theological justification.[121]

43. The Church "becomes herself a mother by accepting

God's word with fidelity."[122] Like Mary, who first believed by accepting the word of God revealed to her at the Annunciation and by remaining faithful to that word in all her trials even unto the Cross, so too the Church becomes a mother when, accepting with fidelity the word of God, "by her preaching and by baptism she brings forth to a new and immortal life children who are conceived of the Holy Spirit and born of God."[123] This "maternal" characteristic of the Church was expressed in a particularly vivid way by the Apostle to the Gentiles when he wrote: "My little children, with whom I am again in travail until Christ be formed in you!" (Gal 4:19). These words of Saint Paul contain an interesting sign of the early Church's awareness of her own motherhood, linked to her apostolic service to mankind. This awareness enabled and still enables the Church to see the mystery of her life and mission modeled upon the example of the Mother of the Son, who is "the first-born among many brethren" (Rom 8:29).

It can be said that from Mary the Church also learns her own motherhood: she recognizes the maternal dimension of her vocation, which is essentially bound to her sacramental nature, in "contemplating Mary's mysterious sanctity, imitating her charity and faithfully fulfilling the Father's will."[124] If the Church is the sign and instrument of intimate union with God, she is so by reason of her motherhood, because, receiving life from the Spirit, she "generates" sons and daughters of the human race to a new life in Christ. For, just as Mary is at the service of the mystery of the Incarnation, so the Church is always at the service of the mystery of adoption to sonship through grace.

Likewise, following the example of Mary, the Church remains the virgin faithful to her spouse: The Church herself is a virgin who keeps whole and pure the fidelity she has pledged to her Spouse."[125] For the Church is the spouse of Christ, as is clear from the Pauline Letters (cf. Eph 5:21-33; 2 Cor 11:2), and from the title found in John: "bride of the Lamb" (Rv 21:9). If the Church as spouse "keeps the fidelity she has pledged to Christ," this fidelity, even though in the Apostle's teaching it has become an image of marriage (cf. Eph 5:23-33), also has value as a model of total self-giving to God in celibacy "for the kingdom of heaven," in virginity consecrated to God (cf. Mt 19:11-12; 2 Cor 11:2). Precisely such virginity, after the example of the Virgin of Nazareth, is the source of a special spiritual fruitfulness: it is the source of motherhood in the Holy Spirit.

But the Church also preserves the faith received from Christ. Following the example of Mary, who kept and pondered in her heart everything relating to her divine Son (cf. Lk 2:19, 51), the Church is committed to preserving the word of God and investigating its riches with discernment and prudence, in order to bear faithful witness to it before all mankind in every age.[126]

44. Given Mary's relationship to the Church as an exemplar, the Church is close to her and seeks to become like her: "Imitating the Mother of her Lord, and by the power of the Holy Spirit, she preserves with virginal purity an integral faith, a firm hope, and a sincere charity."[127] Mary is thus present in the mystery of the Church as a model. But the Church's mystery also consists in generating people to a new and immortal life: this is her motherhood in the Holy Spirit. And here Mary is not only the model and figure of the Church; she is much more. For, "with maternal love she cooperates in the birth and development" of the sons and daughters of Mother Church. The Church's motherhood is accomplished not only according to the model and figure of the Mother of God but also with her "cooperation." The Church draws abundantly from this cooperation, that is to say from the maternal mediation which is characteristic of Mary, insofar as already on earth she cooperated in the rebirth and development of the Church's sons and daughters, as the Mother of that Son whom the Father "placed as the first-born among many brethren."[128]

She cooperated, as the Second Vatican Council teaches, with a maternal love.[129] Here we perceive the real value of the words spoken by Jesus to his Mother at the hour of the Cross: "Woman, behold your Son" and to the disciple: "Behold your mother" (Jn 19:26-27). They are words which determine Mary's place in the life of Christ's disciples and they express-as I have already said-the new motherhood of the Mother of the Redeemer: a spiritual motherhood, born from the heart of the Paschal Mystery of the Redeemer of the world. It is a motherhood in the order of grace, for it implores the gift of the Spirit, who raises up the new children of God, redeems through the sacrifice of Christ that Spirit whom Mary too, together with the Church, received on the day of Pentecost.

Her motherhood is particularly noted and experienced by the Christian people at the Sacred Banquet-the liturgical celebration of the mystery of the Redemption-at which Christ, his true body born of the Virgin Mary, becomes present.

The piety of the Christian people has always very rightly sensed a profound link between devotion to the Blessed Virgin and worship of the Eucharist: this is a fact that can be seen in the liturgy of both the West and the East, in the traditions of the Religious Families, in the modern movements of spirituality, including those for youth, and in the pastoral practice of the Marian Shrines. Mary guides the faithful to the Eucharist.

45. Of the essence of motherhood is the fact that it concerns the person. Motherhood always establishes a unique and unrepeatable relationship between two people: between mother and child and between child and mother. Even when the same woman is the mother of many children, her personal relationship with each one of them is of the very essence of motherhood. For each child is generated in a unique and unrepeatable way, and this is true both for the mother and for the child. Each child is surrounded in the same way by that maternal love on which are based the child's development and coming to maturity as a human being.

It can be said that motherhood "in the order of grace" preserves the analogy with what "in the order of nature" characterizes the union between mother and child. In the light of this fact it becomes easier to understand why in Christ's testament on Golgotha his Mother's new motherhood is expressed in the singular, in reference to one man: "Behold your Son."

It can also be said that these same words fully show the reason for the Marian dimension of the life of Christ's disciples. This is true not only of John, who at that hour stood at the foot of the Cross together with his Master's Mother, but it is also true of every disciple of Christ, of every Christian. The Redeemer entrusts his mother to the disciple, and at the same time he gives her to him as his mother. Mary's motherhood, which becomes man's inheritance, is a gift: a gift which Christ himself makes personally to every individual. The Redeemer entrusts Mary to John because he entrusts John to Mary. At the foot of the Cross there begins that special entrusting of humanity to the Mother of Christ, which in the history of the Church has been practiced and expressed in different ways. The same Apostle and Evangelist, after reporting the words addressed by Jesus on the Cross to his Mother and to himself, adds: "And from that hour the disciple took her to his own home" (Jn 19:27). This statement certainly means that the role of Son was attributed to the disciple and that he assumed responsibility for the Mother of his beloved Master. And since Mary was given as a mother to him personally, the statement indicates, even though indirectly, everything expressed by the intimate relationship of a child with its mother. And all of this can be included in the word "entrusting." Such entrusting is the response to a person's love, and in particular to the love of a mother.

The Marian dimension of the life of a disciple of Christ is expressed in a special way precisely through this filial entrusting to the Mother of Christ, which began with the testament of the Redeemer on Golgotha. Entrusting himself to Mary in a filial manner, the Christian, like the Apostle John, "welcomes" the Mother of Christ "into his own home"[130] and brings her into everything that makes up his inner life, that is to say into his human and Christian "I": he "took her to his own home." Thus the Christian seeks to be taken into that "maternal charity" with which the Redeemer's Mother "cares for the brethren of her Son,"[131] "in whose birth and development she cooperates"[132] in the measure of the gift proper to each one through the power of Christ's Spirit. Thus also is exercised that motherhood in the Spirit which became Mary's role at the foot of the Cross and in the Upper Room.

46. This filial relationship, this self-entrusting of a child to its mother, not only has its beginning in Christ but can also be said to be definitively directed towards him. Mary can be said to continue to say to each individual the words which she spoke at Cana in Galilee: "Do whatever he tells you." For he, Christ, is the one Mediator between God and mankind; he is "the way, and the truth, and the life" (Jn 14:6); it is he whom the Father has given to the world, so that man "should not perish but have eternal life" (Jn 3:16). The Virgin of Nazareth became the first "witness" of this

saving love of the Father, and she also wishes to remain its humble handmaid always and everywhere. For every Christian, for every human being, Mary is the one who first "believed," and precisely with her faith as Spouse and Mother she wishes to act upon all those who entrust themselves to her as her children. And it is well known that the more her children persevere and progress in this attitude, the nearer Mary leads them to the "unsearchable riches of Christ" (Eph 3:8). And to the same degree they recognize more and more clearly the dignity of man in all its fullness and the definitive meaning of his vocation, for "Christ ... fully reveals man to man himself."[133]

This Marian dimension of Christian life takes on special importance in relation to women and their status. In fact, femininity has a unique relationship with the Mother of the Redeemer, a subject which can be studied in greater depth elsewhere. Here I simply wish to note that the figure of Mary of Nazareth sheds light on womanhood as such by the very fact that God, in the sublime event of the Incarnation of his Son, entrusted himself to the ministry, the free and active ministry of a woman. It can thus be said that women, by looking to Mary, find in her the secret of living their femininity with dignity and of achieving their own true advancement. In the light of Mary, the Church sees in the face of women the reflection of a beauty which mirrors the loftiest sentiments of which the human heart is capable: the self-offering totality of love; the strength that is capable of bearing the greatest sorrows; limitless fidelity and tireless devotion to work; the ability to combine penetrating intuition with words of support and encouragement.

47. At the Council Paul VI solemnly proclaimed that Mary is the Mother of the Church, "that is, Mother of the entire Christian people, both faithful and pastors."[134] Later, in 1968, in the Profession of faith known as the "Credo of the People of God." he restated this truth in an even more forceful way in these words: "We believe that the Most Holy Mother of God, the new Eve, the Mother of the Church, carries on in heaven her maternal role with regard to the members of Christ, cooperating in the birth and development of divine life in the souls of the redeemed."[135]

The Council's teaching emphasized that the truth concerning the Blessed Virgin, Mother of Christ, is an effective aid in exploring more deeply the truth concerning the Church. When speaking of the Constitution *Lumen Gentium*, which had just been approved by the Council, Paul VI said: "Knowledge of the true Catholic doctrine regarding the Blessed Virgin Mary will always be a key to the exact understanding of the mystery of Christ and of the Church."[136] Mary is present in the Church as the Mother of Christ, and at the same time as that Mother whom Christ, in the mystery of the Redemption, gave to humanity in the person of the Apostle John. Thus, in her new motherhood in the Spirit, Mary embraces each and every one in the Church, and embraces each and every one through the Church. In this sense Mary, Mother of the Church, is also the Church's model. Indeed, as Paul VI hopes and asks, the Church must draw "from the Virgin Mother of God the most authentic form of perfect imitation of Christ."[137]

Thanks to this special bond linking the Mother of Christ with the Church, there is further clarified the mystery of that "woman" who, from the first chapters of the Book of Genesis until the Book of Revelation, accompanies the revelation of God's salvific plan for humanity. For Mary, present in the Church as the Mother of the Redeemer, takes part, as a mother, in that monumental struggle; against the powers of darkness"[138] which continues throughout human history. And by her ecclesial identification as the "woman clothed with the sun" (Rv 12:1),[139] it can be said that "in the Most Holy Virgin the Church has already reached that perfection whereby she exists without spot or wrinkle." Hence, as Christians raise their eyes with faith to Mary in the course of their earthly pilgrimage, they "strive to increase in holiness."[140] Mary, the exalted Daughter of Zion, helps all her children, wherever they may be and whatever their condition, to find in Christ the path to the Father's house.

Thus, throughout her life, the Church maintains with the Mother of God a link which embraces, in the saving mystery, the past, the present and the future, and venerates her as the spiritual mother of humanity and the advocate of grace.

# 3. The Meaning Of The Marian Year

48. It is precisely the special bond between humanity and this Mother which has led me to proclaim a Marian Year in the Church, in this period before the end of the Second Millennium since Christ's birth, a similar initiative was taken in the past. when Pius XII proclaimed 1954 as a Marian Year, in order to highlight the exceptional holiness of the Mother of Christ as expressed in the mysteries of her Immaculate Conception (defined exactly a century before) and of her assumption into heaven.[141]

Now, following the line of the Second Vatican Council, I wish to emphasize the special presence of the Mother of God in the mystery of Christ and his Church. For this is a fundamental dimension emerging from the Mariology of the Council, the end of which is now more than twenty years behind us. The Extraordinary Synod of Bishops held in 1985 exhorted everyone to follow faithfully the teaching and guidelines of the Council We can say that these two events-the Council and the synod-embody what the Holy Spirit himself wishes "to say to the Church" in the present phase of history.

In this context, the Marian Year is meant to promote a new and more careful reading of what the Council said about the Blessed Virgin Mary, Mother of God, in the mystery of Christ and of the Church, the topic to which the contents of this Encyclical are devoted. Here we speak not only of the doctrine of faith but also of the life of faith, and thus of authentic "Marian spirituality," seen in the light of Tradition, and especially the spirituality to which the Council exhorts us.[142] Furthermore, Marian spirituality, like its corresponding devotion, finds a very rich source in the historical experience of individuals and of the various Christian communities present among the different peoples and nations of the world. In this regard, I would like to recall, among the many witnesses and teachers of this spirituality, the figure of Saint Louis Marie Grignion de Montfort,[143] who proposes consecration to Christ through the hands of Mary, as an effective means for Christians to live faithfully their baptismal commitments. I am pleased to note that in our own time too new manifestations of this spirituality and devotion are not lacking. There thus exist solid points of reference to look to and follow in the context of this Marian Year.

49. This Marian Year will begin on the Solemnity of Pentecost, on June 7 next. For it is a question not only of recalling that Mary "preceded" the entry of Christ the Lord into the history of the human family, but also of emphasizing, in the light of Mary, that from the moment when the mystery of the Incarnation was accomplished, human history entered "the fullness of time," and that the Church is the sign of this fullness. As the People of God, the Church makes her pilgrim way towards eternity through faith, in the midst of all the peoples and nations, beginning from the day of Pentecost. Christ's Mother-who was present at the beginning of "the time of the Church," when in expectation of the coming of the Holy Spirit she devoted herself to prayer in the midst of the Apostles and her Son's disciples-constantly "precedes" the Church in her journey through human history. She is also the one who, precisely as the "handmaid of the Lord," cooperates unceasingly with the work of salvation accomplished by Christ, her Son.

Thus by means of this Marian Year the Church is called not only to remember everything in her past that testifies to the special maternal cooperation of the Mother of God in the work of salvation in Christ the lord, but also, on her own part, to prepare for the future the paths of this cooperation. For the end of the second Christian Millennium opens up as a new prospect.

50. As has already been mentioned, also among our divided brethren many honor and celebrate the Mother of the Lord, especially among the Orientals. It is a Marian light cast upon ecumenism. In particular, I wish to mention once more that during the Marian Year there will occur the Millennium of the Baptism of Saint Vladimir, Grand Duke of Kiev [988]. This marked the beginning of Christianity in the territories of what was then called Russia, and subsequently in other territories of Eastern Europe. In this way, through the work of evangelization, Christianity spread beyond Europe, as far as the northern territories of the Asian continent. We would therefore like, especially during this Year, to join in prayer with all those who are celebrating the Millennium of this Baptism, both Orthodox and Catholics, repeating and confirming with the Council those sentiments of joy and comfort

that "the Easterners... with ardent emotion and devout mind concur in reverencing the Mother of God, ever Virgin."[144] Even though we are still experiencing the painful effects of the separation which took place some decades later [1054], we can say that in the presence of the Mother of Christ we feel that we are true brothers and sisters within that messianic People, which is called to be the one family of God on earth. As I announced at the beginning of the New Year "We desire to reconfirm this universal inheritance of all the Sons and daughters of this earth."[145]

In announcing the Year of Mary, I also indicated that it will end next year on the Solemnity of the Assumption of the Blessed Virgin into heaven, in order to emphasize the "great sign in heaven" spoken of by the Apocalypse. In this way we also wish to respond to the exhortation of the Council, which looks to Mary as "a sign of sure hope and solace for the pilgrim People of God." And the Council expresses this exhortation in the following words: "Let the entire body of the faithful pour forth persevering prayer to the Mother of God and Mother of mankind. Let them implore that she who aided the beginning of the Church by her prayers may now, exalted as she is in heaven above all the saints and angels, intercede with her Son in the fellowship of all the saints. May she do so until all the peoples of the human family, whether they are honored with the name of Christian or whether they still do not know their Savior, are happily gathered together in peace and harmony into the one People of God, for the glory of the Most Holy and Undivided Trinity."[146]

# Conclusion

51. At the end of the daily Liturgy of the Hours, among the invocations addressed to Mary by the Church is the following:

"Loving Mother of the Redeemer,
gate of heaven, star of the sea,
assist your people who have fallen yet strive to rise again.
To the wonderment of nature you bore your Creator!"

"To the wonderment of nature"! These words of the antiphon express that wonderment of faith which accompanies the mystery of Mary's divine motherhood. In a sense, it does so in the heart of the whole of creation, and, directly, in the heart of the whole People of God, in the heart of the Church. How wonderfully far God has gone, the Creator and Lord of all things, in the "revelation of himself" to man![147] How clearly he has bridged all the spaces of that infinite "distance" which separates the Creator from the creature! If in himself he remains ineffable and unsearchable, still more ineffable and unsearchable is he in the reality of the Incarnation of the Word, who became man through the Virgin of Nazareth.

If he has eternally willed to call man to share in the divine nature (cf. 2 Pt 1:4), it can be said that he has matched the "divinization" of man to humanity's historical conditions, so that even after sin he is ready to restore at a great price the eternal plan of his love through the "humanization" of his Son, who is of the same being as himself. The whole of creation, and more directly man himself, cannot fail to be amazed at this gift in which he has become a sharer, in the Holy Spirit: "God so loved the world that he gave his only Son" (Jn 3:16).

At the center of this mystery, in the midst of this wonderment of faith, stands Mary. As the loving Mother of the Redeemer, she was the first to experience it: "To the wonderment of nature you bore your Creator"!

52. The words of this liturgical antiphon also express the truth of the "great transformation" which the mystery of the Incarnation establishes for man. It is a transformation which belongs to his entire history, from that beginning which is revealed to us in the first chapters of Genesis until the final end, in the perspective of the end of the world, of which Jesus has revealed to us "neither the day nor the hour" (Mt 25:13). It is an unending and continuous transformation between falling and rising again, between the man of sin and the man of grace and justice. The Advent liturgy in particular is at the very heart of this transformation and captures its unceasing "here and now" when it exclaims: "Assist your people who have fallen yet strive to rise again"!

These words apply to every individual, every community, to nations and peoples, and to the generations and epochs of human history, to our own epoch, to these years of the Millennium which is drawing to a close: "Assist, yes assist, your people who have fallen"!

This is the invocation addressed to Mary, the "loving Mother of the Redeemer," the invocation addressed to Christ, who through Mary entered human history. Year after year the antiphon rises to Mary, evoking that moment which saw the accomplishment of this essential historical transformation, which irreversibly continues: the transformation from "falling" to "rising."

Mankind has made wonderful discoveries and achieved extraordinary results in the fields of science and technology. It has made great advances along the path of progress and civilization, and in recent times one could say that it has succeeded in speeding up the pace of history. But the fundamental transformation, the one which can be called "original," constantly accompanies man's journey, and through all the events of history accompanies each and every individual. It is the transformation from "falling" to "rising," from death to life. It is also a constant challenge to people's consciences, a challenge to man's whole historical awareness: the challenge to follow the path of "not falling" in ways that are ever old and ever new, and of "rising again" if a fall has occurred.

As she goes forward with the whole of humanity towards the frontier between the two Millennia, the Church, for her part, with the whole community of believers and in union with all men and women of good will, takes up the great challenge contained in these words of the Marian antiphon: "the people who have fallen yet strive to rise again," and she addresses both the Redeemer and his Mother with the plea: "Assist us." For, as this prayer attests, the Church sees the Blessed Mother of God in the saving mystery of Christ and in her own mystery. She sees Mary deeply rooted in humanity's history, in man's eternal vocation according to the providential plan which God has made for him from eternity She sees Mary maternally present and sharing in the many complicated problems which today beset the lives of individuals, families and nations; she sees her helping the Christian people in the constant struggle between good and evil, to ensure that it "does not fall," or, if it has fallen, that it "rises again."

I hope with all my heart that the reflections contained in the present Encyclical will also serve to renew this vision in the hearts of all believers.

As Bishop of Rome, I send to all those to whom these thoughts are addressed the kiss of peace, my greeting and my blessing in our Lord Jesus Christ. Amen.

Given in Rome, at Saint Peter's, on March 25, the Solemnity of the Annunciation of the Lord, in the year 1987, the ninth of my Pontificate.

JOANNES PAULUS PP.II

\* \* \* \* \* \* \* \* \* \*

## Endnotes

¹       Cf. Second Vatican Ecumenical Council, Dogmatic Constitution on the Church *Lumen Gentium*, 52, and the whole Chapter VIII, entitled "The Role of the Blessed Virgin Mary, Mother of God, in the Mystery of Christ and the Church."

²       The expression "fullness of time" (pleroma tou chronou) is parallel with similar expressions of Judaism, both Biblical (cf. Gn 29:21; 1 Sam 7:12; Tob 14:5) and extra-Biblical, and especially of the New Testament (cf. Mk 1:15; Lk 21:24; Jn 7:8; Eph 1:10). From the point of view of form, it means not only the conclusion of a chronological process but also and especially the coming to maturity or completion of a particularly important period, one directed toward the fulfillment of an expectation, a coming to completion which thus takes on an eschatological dimension. According to Gal 4:4 and its context, it is the coming of the Son of God that reveals that time has, so to speak, reached its limit. That is to say, the period marked by the promise made to Abraham and by the Law mediated by Moses has now reached its climax, in the sense that Christ fulfills the divine promise and supersedes the Old Law.

³       Cf. Roman Missal, Preface of December 8, Immaculate Conception of the Blessed Virgin Mary; Saint Ambrose, *De Institutione Virginis*, XV, 93-94; PL 16, 342; Second Vatican Ecumenical Council, Dogmatic Constitution on the Church *Lumen Gentium*, 68.

4       Second Vatican Ecumenical Council, Dogmatic Constitution on the Church *Lumen Gentium*, 58.

5       Paul VI, Encyclical Epistle *Christi Matri* (September 15, 1966); *AAS* 58 (1966), 745-749; Apostolic Exhortation *Signum Magnum* (May 13, 1967); *AAS* 59 (1967), 465-475; Apostolic Exhortation *Marialis Cultus* (February 2, 1974): *AAS* 66 (1974), 113-168.

6       The Old Testament foretold in many different ways the mystery of Mary: cf. Saint John Damascene, *Homilia in Dormitionem*, I, 8-9, *SCh* 80, 103-107.

7       Cf. *Insegnamenti* VI/2 (1983), 225-226; Pius IX, Apostolic Letter *Ineffabilis Deus* (December 8, 1854): *Pii IX P. M. Acta*, I, 597-599.

8       Cf. Pastoral Constitution on the Church in the Modern World *Gaudium et Spes*, 22.

9       Ecumenical Council of Ephesus: *Conciliorum Oecumenicorum Decreta*, Ed. Istituto per le Scienze Religiose, 3rd ed., Bologna, 1973, 41-44, 59-61 (DS 250-264); cf. Ecumenical Council of Chalcedon: Conciliorum Oecumenicorum Decreta, Ed. Istituto per le Scienze Religiose, 3rd ed., Bologna, 1973, 84-87 (DS 300-303).

10       Second Vatican Ecumenical Council, Pastoral Constitution on the Church in the Modern World *Gaudium et Spes,* 22.

11       Dogmatic Constitution on the Church *Lumen Gentium*, 52.

12       Cf. ibid., 58.

13       Ibid., 63; cf. Saint Ambrose, *Expositio Evangelii secundum Lucam*, II, 7: *CSEL* 32/4 45; *De Institutione Virginis*, XIV, 88-89: PL 16,.341.

14       Cf. Dogmatic Constitution on the Church *Lumen Gentium*, 64.

15       Ibid., 65.

16       "Take away this star of the sun which illuminates the world: where does the day go: Take away Mary, this Star of the Sea, of the great and boundless sea: what is left but a vast obscurity and the shadow of death and deepest Darkness?": Saint Bernard, *In Nativitate Beatae Mariae Sermo, De Aquaeductu, 6: Sancti Bernardi Opera*, V. 1968, 279; cf. *In Laudibus Virginis Matris Homilia*, II, 17: loc. cit., IV, 1966, 34-35.

[17]     Dogmatic Constitution on the Church *Lumen Gentium*, 63.

[18]     Ibid., 63.

[19]     Concerning the predestination of Mary, cf. Saint John Damascene, *Homilia in Nativitatem*, 7; 10: *SCh* 80, 65; 73; *Homilia in Dormitionem*, I, 3: *SCh* 80, 85: "For it is she, who, chosen from the ancient generations, by virtue of the predestination and benevolence of the God and Father who generated you (the Word of God) outside time without coming out of himself or suffering change, it is she who gave you birth, nourished of her flesh, in the last time."

[20]     Dogmatic Constitution on the Church *Lumen Gentium*, 55.

[21]     In patristic tradition there is a wide and varied interpretation of this expression: cf. Origen, *In Lucam Homiliae*, VI 7: *SCh* 87, 148; Severianus of Gabala, *In Mundi Creationem, Oratio* VI, 10: *PG* 56, 497-498; Saint John Chrysostom (Pseudo), *In Annuntiationem Deiparae et contra Arium Impium*: *PG* 62, 765-766; Basil of Seleucia, *Oratio* 39, *In Sanctissimae Deiparae Annuntiationem*, 5: *PG* 85, 441-446; Antipater of Bosra, *Homilia II, In Sanctissimae Deiparae Annuntiationem*, 3-11: *PG* 85, 1777-1783; Saint Sophronius of Jerusalem, *Oratio II, In Sanctissimae Deiparae Annuntiationem*, 17-19: *PG* 87/3, 3235-3240; Saint John Damascene, *Homilia in Dormitionem*, I, 70: *SCh* 80, 96-101; Saint Jerome, *Epistula* 65, 9: *PL* 22, 628; Saint Ambrose, *Expositio Evangelii secundum Lucam*, II, 9: *CSEL* 32/4, 45-46; Saint Augustine, *Sermo* 291, 4-6: *PL* 38, 1318-1319; *Enchiridion*, 36, 11: *PL* 40, 250; Saint Peter Chrysologus, *Sermo* 142: *PL* 52, 579-580; *Sermo* 143: *PL* 52, 583; Saint Fulgentius of Ruspe, *Epistula* 17, VI, 12: *PL* 65, 458; Saint Bernard, *In Laudibus Virginis Matris, Homilia*, III, 2-3: *Sancti Bernardi Opera*, IV, 1966, 36-38.

[22]     Dogmatic Constitution on the Church *Lumen Gentium*, 55

[23]     Ibid., 53.

[24]     Cf. Pius XI, Apostolic Letter *Ineffabilis Deus* (December 8, 1854): *Pii IX P. M. Acta*, I, 616; Second Vatican Ecumenical Council, Dogmatic Constitution on the Church *Lumen Gentium*, 53.

[25]     Cf. Saint Germanus of Constantinople, *In Annuntiationem Sanctissimae Deiparae Homilia*: *PG* 98, 327-328; Saint Andrew of Crete, *Canon in Beatae Mariae Natalem*, 4: *PG* 97, 1321-132; *In Nativitatem Beatae Mariae*, I: *PG* 97, 811-812; *Homilia in Dormitionem Sanctae Mariae*, I: *PG* 97, 1067-1068.

[26]      Liturgy of the Hours of August 15, Assumption of the Blessed Virgin Mary, Hymn at First and Second Vespers; Saint Peter Damian, *Carmina et Preces*, XLVII: *PL* 145, 934.

[27]      *The Divine Comedy*, Paradise, XXXIII, 1; cf. Liturgy of the Hours, Memorial of the Blessed Virgin Mary on Saturday, Hymn II in the Office of Readings.

[28]      Cf. Saint Augustine, *De Sancta Virginitate*, III, 3: *PL* 40, 398; *Sermo* 25, 7: *PL* 46.

[29]      Dogmatic Constitution on Divine Revelation *Dei Verbum*, 5.

[30]      This is a classic theme, already expounded by Saint Irenaeus: "And, as by the action of the disobedient virgin, man was afflicted and, being cast down, died, so also by the action of the Virgin who obeyed he word of God, man being regenerated received, through life, life....For it was meet and just ... that Eve should be 'recapitulated' in Mary, so that the Virgin, becoming the advocate of the virgin, should dissolve and destroy the virginal disobedience by means of virginal obedience": *Expositio Doctrinae Apostolicae*, 33: *SCh* 62, 83-86; cf. *Adversus Haereses*, V, 19, 1: *SCh* 153, 248-250.

[31]      Second Vatican Ecumenical Council, Dogmatic Constitution on Divine Revelation *Dei Verbum*, 5.

[32]      Ibid., 5; cf. Dogmatic Constitution on the Church *Lumen Gentium*, 56.

[33]      Second Vatican Ecumenical Council, Dogmatic Constitution on Divine Revelation *Dei Verbum*, 56.

[34]      Ibid., 56.

[35]      Cf. ibid., 53; Saint Augustine, *De Sancta Virginitate*, III, 3: *PL* 40, 398; *Sermo* 215, 4: *PL* 38, 1074; *Sermo* 196, 1: *PL* 38, 1019; *De Peccatorum Meritis et Remissione*, I, 29, 57: *PL* 44, 142; *Sermo* 25, 7: *PL* 46, 937-938; Saint Leo the Great, *Tractatus 21, De Natale Domini*, I: CCL 138, 86.

[36]      Cf. *The Ascent of Mount Carmel*, Book II, Chapter 3, 4-6.

[37]      Dogmatic Constitution on the Church *Lumen Gentium*, 58.

[38]      Ibid., 58.

39    Dogmatic Constitution on Divine Revelation *Dei Verbum*, 5.

40    Concerning Mary's participation of "compassion" in the death of Christ, cf. Saint Bernard, *In Dominica infra octavam Assumptionis Sermo,* 14: *Sancti Bernardi Opera*, V, 1968, 273.

41    Saint Irenaeus, *Adversus Haereses*, III, 22, 4: *SCh* 211, 438-444; cf. Dogmatic Constitution on the Church *Lumen Gentium*, 56, Note 6.

42    Cf. Dogmatic Constitution on the Church *Lumen Gentium*, 56, and the Fathers quoted there in Notes 8 and 9.

43    "Christ is truth, Christ is flesh: Christ is truth in the mind of Mary, Christ is flesh in the womb of Mary": Saint Augustine, *Sermo* 25 (*Sermones inediti*), 7: *PL* 46, 938.

44    Cf. Dogmatic Constitution on the Church *Lumen Gentium*, 60.

45    Ibid., 61.

46    Ibid., 62.

47    There is a well-known passage of Origen on the presence of Mary and John on Calvary: "The Gospels are the first fruits of all Scripture and the Gospel of John is the first of the Gospels: no one can grasp its meaning without having leaned his head on Jesus' breast and having received from Jesus Mary as Mother": *Commentarium in Ioannem*, I, 6: *PG* 14, 31; cf. Saint Ambrose, *Expositio Evangelii secundum Lucam*, X, 129-131: *CSEL* 32/4, 504-505.

48    Dogmatic Constitution on the Church *Lumen Gentium*, 54 and 53; the latter text quotes Saint Augustine, *De Sancta Virginitate*, VI, 6: *PL* 40, 399.

49    Dogmatic Constitution on the Church *Lumen Gentium*, 55.

50    Cf. Saint Leo the Great, *Tractatus* 25, *De Natale Domine*, 2: *CCL* 138, 126.

51    Dogmatic Constitution on the Church *Lumen Gentium*, 59.

52    Saint Augustine, *De Civitate Dei*, XVIII, 51: *CCL* 48, 650.

53    Second Vatican Ecumenical Council, Dogmatic Constitution on the Church *Lumen Gentium*, 8.

54        Ibid., 9.

55        Ibid., 9.

56        Ibid., 8.

57        Ibid., 9.

58        Ibid., 65.

59        Ibid., 59.

60        Cf. Second Vatican Ecumenical Council, Dogmatic Constitution on Divine Revelation *Dei Verbum*, 5.

61        Second Vatican Ecumenical Council, Dogmatic Constitution on the Church *Lumen Gentium*, 63.

62        Cf. ibid., 9.

63        Cf. ibid., 65.

64        Ibid., 65.

65        Ibid., 65.

66        Cf. ibid., 13.

67        Cf. ibid., 13.

68        Cf. ibid., 13.

69        Cf. Roman Missal, formula of the Consecration of the Chalice in the Eucharistic Prayers.

70        Second Vatican Ecumenical Council, Dogmatic Constitution on the Church *Lumen Gentium*, 1.

71        Ibid., 13.

72        Ibid., 15.

73        Cf. Second Vatican Ecumenical Council, Decree on Ecumenism *Unitatis Redintegratio*, 1.

[74]    Dogmatic Constitution on the Church *Lumen Gentium*, 68, 69. On Mary Most Holy, promoter of Christian unity, and on the cult of Mary in the East, cf. Leo XIII, Encyclical Epistle *Adiutricem Populi* (September 5, 1885): *Leonis XIII P. M. Acta, XV*, Rome, 1896, 300-312.

[75]    Cf. Second Vatican Ecumenical Council, Decree on Ecumenism *Unitatis Redintegratio*, 20.

[76]    Cf. ibid., 19.

[77]    Ibid., 14.

[78]    Ibid., 15.

[79]    Second Vatican Ecumenical Council, Dogmatic Constitution on the Church *Lumen Gentium*, 66.

[80]    Ecumenical Council of Chalcedon, *Definitio fidei: Conciliorum Oecumenicorum Decreta*, Ed. Istituto per le Scienze Religiose, 3rd ed., Bologna, 1973, 86 (DS 301).

[81]    Cf. the *Weddase Maryam (Praises of Mary)*, which follows the Ethiopian Psalter and contains hymns and prayers to Mary for each day of the week. Cf. also *the Matshafa Kidana Mehrat (Book of the Pact of Mercy)*; the importance given to Mary in the Ethiopian hymnology and liturgy deserves to be emphasized.

[82]    Cf. Saint Ephrem, *Hymni de Nativitate: Scriptores Syri, 82, CSCO,* 186.

[83]    Cf. Saint Gregory of Narek, *Le livre de Prieres*: *SCh* 78, 160-163, 428-432.

[84]    Second Ecumenical Council of Nicaea: *Conciliorum Oecumenicorum Decreta*, Ed. Istituto per le Scienze Religiose, 3rd ed., Bologna, 1973, 135-138 (DS 600-609).

[85]    Second Vatican Ecumenical Council, Dogmatic Constitution on the Church *Lumen Gentium*, 59.

[86]    Cf. Second Vatican Ecumenical Council, Decree on Ecumenism *Unitatis redintegratio*, 19.

[87]    Second Vatican Ecumenical Council, Dogmatic Constitution on the

Church *Lumen Gentium*, 8.

[88]     Ibid., 9.

[89]     As is well known, the words of the Magnificat contain or echo numerous passages of the Old Testament.

[90]     Second Vatican Ecumenical Council, Dogmatic Constitution on Divine Revelation *Dei Verbum*, 2.

[91]     Cf., for example, Saint Justin, *Dialogus cum Tryphone Iudaeo*, 100: Otto II, 358; Saint Irenaeus, *Adversus Haereses*, III, 22, 4: *SCh* 211, 439-445; Tertullian, *De Carne Christi*, 17, 4-6: *CCL* 2, 904-905.

[92]     Cf. Saint Epiphanius, *Panarion*, III, 2; *Haer.* 78, 18: *PG* 42, 727-730.

[93]     Congregation for the Doctrine of the Faith, Instruction on Christian Freedom and Liberation *Libertatis Conscientia* (March 22, 1986), 97.

[94]     Second Vatican Ecumenical Council, Dogmatic Constitution on the Church *Lumen Gentium*, 66.

[95]     Ibid., 60.

[96]     Cf. the formula of Mediatrix "ad Mediatorem" of Saint Bernard, *In Dominica infra octavam Assumptionis Sermo*, 2: *Sancti Bernardi Opera*, V, 1968, 263. Mary as a pure mirror sends back to her Son all the glory and honor which she receives: Saint Bernard, *In Nativitate Beatae Mariae Sermo, De Aquaeductu*, 12: loc. cit., 283.

[97]     Second Vatican Ecumenical Council, Dogmatic Constitution on the Church *Lumen Gentium*, 62.

[98]     Ibid., 62.

[99]     Ibid., 61.

[100]     Ibid., 62.

[101]     Ibid., 61.

[102]     Ibid., 61.

[103]     Ibid., 62.

[104] Ibid., 62.

[105] Ibid., 62; in her prayer too the Church recognizes and celebrates Mary's "maternal role": It is a role "of intercession and forgiveness, petition and grace, reconciliation and peace" (cf. Preface of the Mass of the Blessed Virgin Mary, Mother and Mediatrix of Grace, in *Collectio Missarum de Beata Maria Virgine*, editio typica, 1987, I, 120).

[106] Ibid., 62.

[107] Ibid., 62; cf. Saint John Damascene, *Homilia in Dormitionem*, I, 11; II 2; II, 14; III, 2: *SCh* 80, 111-112; 127-131; 157-161; 181-185; Saint Bernard, *In Assumptione Beatae Mariae Sermo*, 1-2: *Sancti Bernardi Opera*, V, 1968, 228-238.

[108] Dogmatic Constitution on the Church *Lumen Gentium*, 59; cf. Pius XII, Apostolic Constitution *Munificentissimus Deus* (November 1, 1950): *AAS* 42 (1950), 769-771; Saint Bernard presents Mary immersed in the splendor of the Son's glory: *In Dominica infra octavam Assumptionis Sermo*, 3; *Sancti Bernardi Opera*, V, 1968, 263-264.

[109] Dogmatic Constitution on the Church *Lumen Gentium*, 53.

[110] On this particular aspect of Mary's mediation as implorer of clemency from the "Son as Judge," cf. Saint Bernard, *In Dominica infra octavam Assumptionis Sermo*, 1-2: *Sancti Bernardi Opera*, V, 1968, 262-263; Leo XIII Encyclical Epistle *Octobri Mense* (September 22, 1891): *Leonis XIII P.M. Acta*, XI, Rome, 1892, 299-315.

[111] Second Vatican Ecumenical Council, Dogmatic Constitution on the Church *Lumen Gentium*, 55.

[112] Ibid., 59

[113] Ibid., 36.

[114] Ibid., 36.

[115] With regard to Mary as Queen, cf. Saint John Damascene, *Homilia in Nativitatem*, 6; 12; *Homilia in Dormitionem*, I, 2,12,14; II, 11; III, 4 *SCh* 80, 59-60, 77-78; 83-84, 113-114,117; 151-152; 189-193.

[116] Second Vatican Ecumenical Council, Dogmatic Constitution on the Church *Lumen Gentium*, 62.

117     Ibid., 63.

118     Ibid., 63.

119     Ibid., 66.

120     Cf. Saint Ambrose, *De Institutione Virginis*, XIV, 88-89: *PL* 16, 241; Saint Augustine, *Sermo* 215, 4: *PL* 38, 1074; *De Sancta Virginitate*, II, 2; V, 5; VI, 6; *PL* 40, 297; 398-399; *Sermo* 191, II, 3: *PL* 38, 1010-1011.

121     Cf. Second Vatican Ecumenical Council, Dogmatic Constitution on the Church *Lumen Gentium*, 63.

122     Ibid., 64.

123     Ibid., 64.

124     Ibid., 64.

125     Ibid., 64.

126     Cf. Second Vatican Ecumenical Council, Dogmatic Constitution on Divine Revelation *Dei Verbum*, 8; Saint Bonaventure, Commentarium in Evangelium Sancti Lucae: Ad Claras Aquas, VII, 53, No. 40; 68, No. 109

127     Second Vatican Ecumenical Council, Dogmatic Constitution on the Church *Lumen Gentium*, 64.

128     Ibid., 63.

129     Cf. ibid., 63.

130     Clearly, in the Greek text the expression "eis ta idia" goes beyond the mere acceptance of Mary by the disciple in the sense of material lodging and hospitality in his house; it indicates rather a *communion of life* established between the two as a result of the words of the dying Christ; cf. Saint Augustine, *In Ioannis Evangelium Tractatus*, 119, 3: *CCL* 36, 659: "He took her to himself, not into his own property, for he possessed nothing of his own, but among his own duties, which he attended to with dedication."

131     Second Vatican Ecumenical Council, Dogmatic Constitution on the Church *Lumen Gentium*, 62.

132     Ibid., 63

[133]     Second Vatican Ecumenical Council, Pastoral Constitution on the Church in the Modern World *Gaudium et Spes*, 22.

[134]     Cf. Paul VI, Address at the Closing of the Third Session of the Second Vatican Ecumenical Council (November 21, 1964): *AAS* 56 (1964), 1015.

[135]     Paul VI, Solemn Profession of Faith (June 30, 1968), 15: *AAS* 60 (1968), 438-439.

[136]     Paul VI, Address at the Closing of the Third Session of the Second Vatican Ecumenical Council (November 21, 1964): *AAS* 56 (1964), 1015.

[137]     Ibid., 1016.

[138]     Cf. Second Vatican Ecumenical Council, Pastoral Constitution on the Church in the Modern World *Gaudium et Spes*, 37.

[139]     Cf. Saint Bernard, *In Dominica infra octavam Assumptionis Sermo*: *Sancti Bernardi Opera*, V, 1968, 262-274.

[140]     Second Vatican Ecumenical Council, Dogmatic Constitution on the Church *Lumen Gentium*, 65.

[141]     Cf. Encyclical Letter *Fulgens Corona* (September 8, 1953): *AAS* 45 (1953), 577-592. Pius X with his Encyclical Letter *Ad Diem Illum* (February 2, 1904), on the occasion of the fiftieth anniversary of the dogmatic definition of the Immaculate Conception of the Blessed Virgin Mary, had proclaimed an Extraordinary Jubilee of a few months: Pii X P. M. Acta, I, 147-166.

[142]     Cf. Dogmatic Constitution on the Church *Lumen Gentium*, 66-67.

[143]     Saint Louis Marie Grignion de Montfort, *True Devotion to the Blessed Virgin Mary*. This Saint can rightly be linked with the figure of Saint Alphonsus Liguori, the second centenary of whose death occurs this year; cf. among his works *The Glories of Mary*.

[144]     Dogmatic Constitution on the Church *Lumen Gentium*, 69.

[145]     Homily (January 1, 1987), 4: *AAS* 79 (1987), 1148.

[146]     Dogmatic Constitution on the Church *Lumen Gentium*, 69.

[147]     Cf. Second Vatican Ecumenical Council, Dogmatic Constitution on Divine Revelation *Dei Verbum*, 2: "Through this revelation ... the invisible God ... out of the abundance of his love speaks to men as friends ... and

lives among them ... so that he may invite and take them into fellowship with himself."

## -Chapter 6-

# Mary In The Catechism
# Of The Catholic Church

Another powerful official Magisterial treatment of Mariology is the Catechism of the Catholic Church.

# Prologue

In the prologue John Paul II gives his vision of the Catechism of the Catholic Church and Mary's role. John Paul II promulgated the Catechism of the Catholic Church in his Apostolic constitution *Fidei Depositum* (The Deposit of Faith) on October 11, 1992. Formerly October 11 was celebrated as the Feast of the Holy Mother of God. Thirty years prior, the Council of Vatican II opened. The Pope stated:

> The principal task entrusted to the Council by Pope John XXIII was to guard and present better the precious deposit of Christian doctrine in order to make it more accessible to the Christian faithful and to people of good will.[1]

John Paul II views the Catechism as a presentation of the mysteries of God's loving kindness through the history of salvation. It is within that overarching theme that we can see the role of the Virgin Mother, the favorite title for Mary in the Catechism. In fact, she is important throughout the Catechism rather than in one concentrated section. Her presence is seen within the whole context of the Catechism and not in isolation from the four principal parts: The Profession of Faith; The Celebration of the Christian Mystery; Life in Christ; and Christian Prayer. In the Catechism there are 121 references to Mary, plus two found in the decree *Fidei Depositum* and one in the prologue presented through the earliest fresco from the catacomb of Priscilla in Rome dating from 200 AD.

In the Apostolic Constitution *Fidei Depositum*, John Paul II summarizes both how he envisions the Catechism and how he understands Mary's role:

> In reading the Proto-gospel we can perceive the wonderful unity of the mystery of God, his saving will, as well as the central place of Jesus Christ, the only-begotten Son of God, sent by the Father, made man in the womb of the Blessed Virgin Mary by the power of the Holy Spirit, to be our Savior. Having dies and risen, Christ is always present in his church, especially in the sacraments; he is the source of our faith, the model of Christian conduct, and the Teacher of our prayer.[2]

His concluding paragraph contains a prayer to Mary:

> I beseech the Blessed Virgin Mary, Mother of the Incarnate Word and Mother of the Church, to support with her powerful intercession the catechetical work of the entire Church on every level, at this time when she is called to a new effort of evangelization.[3]

In the Catechism of the Catholic Church there are five general sections on Mary:

> in relation to the Father
> in relation to Jesus
> in relation to the Spirit
> in relation to the Church
> Mary's life of faith and prayer

Daughter of the Father in relation to Trinity in general, mother of the Son and spouse of the Holy Spirit, Mary is the most perfect created image of God, fully redeemed antecedently by

her Son.
Paragraph 1024 states:

This perfect life with the Most Holy Trinity - this communication of life and love with the Trinity, with the Virgin Mary, the angels and all the blessed - is called "heaven". Heaven is the ultimate end and fulfillment of the deepest human longings, the state of supreme, definitive happiness.

# 1. In Relation To The Father

Assumed into heaven because of her unique and total holiness, she offers ongoing and perfect praise and adoration to the Father through her faith, obedience, words and example.
Paragraph 2097 states:

To adore God is to acknowledge, in respect and absolute submission, the "nothingness of the creature" who would not exist but for God. To adore God is to praise and exalt him and to humble oneself, as Mary did in the Magnificat, confessing with gratitude that he has done great things and holy is his name.[4] The worship of the one God sets man free from turning in on himself, from the slavery of sin and the idolatry of the world.

In the section on the creation of man and woman, Mary becomes an example of the human being recreated in God's image and likeness. Paragraph 369 states:

Man and woman have been *created*, which is to say, *willed* by God: on the one hand, in perfect equality as human persons; on the other, in their respective beings as man and woman. "Being man" or "being woman" is a reality which is good and willed by God: man and woman possess an inalienable dignity which comes to them immediately from God their Creator.[5] Man and woman are both with one and the same dignity "in the image of God." In their "being-man" and "being-woman," they reflect the Creator's wisdom and goodness.

Mary becomes the "new Eve," full of grace, preserved from sin and death's corruption. Paragraph 2853 states:

Victory over the "prince of this world"[6] was won once for all at the hour when Jesus freely gave himself up to death to give us his life. This is the judgment of this world, and the prince of this world is "cast out."[7]. "He pursued the woman"[8] but had no hold on her: the new Eve, "full of grace" of the Holy Spirit, is preserved from sin and the corruption of death (the Immaculate Conception and the Assumption of the Most Holy Mother of God, Mary, ever virgin). "Then the dragon was angry with the woman, and went off to make war on the rest of her offspring."[9]. Therefore the Spirit and the Church pray: "Come, Lord Jesus,"[10] since his coming will deliver us from the Evil One.

## 2. In Relation To Jesus

She who is daughter of the Father by her overshadowing of the Spirit becomes mother of the Son, who is the center and heart of belief, practice and catechesis Everything points to Christ, including Mary. "Do whatsoever he tells you." Paragraph 426 states:

"At the heart of catechesis we find, in essence, a Person, the Person of Jesus of Nazareth, the only Son from the Father ... who suffered and died for us and who now, after rising, is living with us forever."[11] To catechize is "to reveal in the Person of Christ the whole of God's eternal design reaching fulfillment in that Person. It is to seek to understand the meaning of Christ's actions and words and of the signs worked by him."[12] Catechesis aims at putting "people ... in communion ... with Jesus Christ: only he can lead us to the love of the Father in the Spirit and make us share in the life of the Holy Trinity."[13]

As mother of Jesus, she gives faith to the Redeemer and Savior of the world and through her fiat cooperates in the mystery of salvation. Paragraph 502 states:

The eyes of faith can discover in the context of the whole of Revelation the mysterious reasons why God in his saving plan wanted his Son to be born of a virgin. These reasons touch both on the person of Christ and his redemptive mission, and on the welcome Mary gave that mission on behalf of all men.

## Sola Gratia

God's saving work is a work totally and solely of grace. Everything is grace. It is totally God's unmerited gift. It is solely God's initiative. Paragraph 503 states:

Mary's virginity manifests God's absolute initiative in the Incarnation. Jesus has only God as father. "He was never estranged from the Father because of the human nature which he assumed.... He is naturally Son of the Father as to his divinity and naturally Son of his mother as to his humanity, but properly Son of the Father in both natures.

Yet God's plan is that we cooperate with him in faith, hope, surrender, obedience and love. Mary cooperated with grace fully. Paragraph 969 states:

"This motherhood of Mary in the order of grace continues uninterruptedly from the consent which she loyally gave at the Annunciation and which she sustained without wavering beneath the cross, until the eternal fulfillment of all the elect. Taken up to Heaven she did not lay aside this saving office but by her manifold intercession continues to bring us the gifts of eternal salvation....Therefore the Blessed Virgin is invoked in the Church under the titles of Advocate, Helper, Benefactress, and Mediatrix."[14]

Therefore Mary has a special place in God's redemptive plan, in union with the One Mediator, her Son Jesus and she cooperated fully.

520 In all of his life Jesus presents himself as our model. He is "the perfect man,"[15] who invites us to become his disciples and follow him. In humbling himself, he has given us an example to imitate, through his prayer he draws us to pray, and by his poverty he calls us to accept freely the privation and persecutions that may come our way.[16]

437 To the shepherds, the angel announced the birth of Jesus as the Messiah promised to Israel: "To you is born this day in the city of David a Savior, who is Christ the Lord."[17] From the beginning he was "the one whom the Father consecrated and sent into the world," conceived as "holy" in Mary's virginal womb.[18] God called Joseph to "take Mary as your wife, for that which is conceived in her is of the Holy Spirit," so that Jesus, "who is called Christ," should be born of Joseph's spouse into the messianic lineage of David.[19]

467 The Monophysites affirmed that the human nature had ceased to exist as such in Christ when the divine person of God's Son assumed it. Faced with this heresy, the fourth ecumenical council, at Chalcedon in 451 confessed:

Following the holy Fathers, we unanimously teach and confess one and the same Son, our Lord Jesus Christ: the same perfect in divinity and perfect in humanity, the same truly God and truly man, composed of rational soul and body; consubstantial with the Father as to his divinity and consubstantial with us as to his humanity; "like us in all things but sin." He was begotten from the Father before all ages as to his divinity and in these last days for us and for our salvation, was born as to his humanity of the virgin Mary, the Mother of God.[20]

We confess that one and the same Christ, Lord, and only-begotten Son, is to be acknowledged in two natures without confusion, change, division, or separation. The distinction between the natures was never abolished by their union, but rather the character proper to each of the two natures was preserved as they came together in one person (*prosopon*) and one hypostasis.[21]

469 The Church thus confesses that Jesus is inseparably true God and true man. He is truly the Son of God who, without ceasing to be God and Lord, became a man and our brother:

"What he was, he remained and what he was not, he assumed," sings the Roman Liturgy[22]. And the liturgy of St. John Chrysostom proclaims and sings: "O only-begotten Son and Word of God, immortal being, you who deigned for our salvation to become incarnate of the holy Mother of God and ever-virgin Mary, you who without change became man and were crucified, O Christ our God, you who by your death have crushed death, you who are one of the Holy Trinity, glorified with the Father and the Holy Spirit, save us!"[23]

726 At the end of this mission of the Spirit, Mary became the Woman, the new Eve ("mother of the living"), the mother of the "whole Christ."[24] As such, she was present with the Twelve, who "with one accord devoted themselves to prayer,"[25] at the dawn of the "end time" which the Spirit was to inaugurate on the morning of Pentecost with the manifestation of the Church.

1138 "Recapitulated in Christ," these are the ones who take part in the service of the praise of God and the fulfillment of his plan: the heavenly powers, all creation (the four living beings), the servants of the Old and New Covenants (the twenty-four elders), the new People of God (the one hundred and forty-four thousand),[26] especially the martyrs "slain for the word of God," and the all-holy Mother of God (the Woman), the Bride of the Lamb,[27] and finally "a great multitude which no one could number, from every nation, from all tribes and peoples and tongues."[28]

2665          The prayer of the Church, nourished by the Word of God and the celebration of the liturgy, teaches us to pray to the Lord Jesus. Even though her prayer is addressed above all to the Father, it includes in all the liturgical traditions forms of prayer addressed to Christ. Certain psalms, given their use in the Prayer of the Church, and the New Testament place on our lips and engrave in our hearts the prayer to Christ in the form of invocations: Son of God, Word of God, Lord, Savior, Lamb of God, King, Beloved Son, Son of the Virgin, Good Shepherd, our Life, our Light, our Hope our resurrection, Friend of mankind...

## Mary, Mother Of The Jewish Messiah

Jesus was the foretold and promised Messiah of the Jewish people. The first Messianic promise called the Proto Evangel is in Genesis 3:15. The citation in paragraph 469 from the Byzantine liturgy further explains Mary's cooperative role in the preeminent saving work of her Son.

As the longest and most complete section, I reproduce it here.

## Paragraph 6. Mary - Mother Of Christ, Mother Of The Church

963 Since the Virgin Mary's role in the mystery of Christ and the Spirit has been treated, it is fitting now to consider her place in the mystery of the Church. "The Virgin Mary ... is acknowledged and honored as being truly the Mother of God and of the redeemer....She is 'clearly the mother of the members of Christ' ... since she has by her charity joined in bringing about the birth of believers in the Church, who are members of its head."[29] "Mary, Mother of Christ, Mother of the Church."[30]

# I. Mary's Motherhood With Regard To The Church

## Wholly united with her Son...

964 Mary's Role in the Church is inseparable from her union with Christ and flows directly from it. "This union of the mother with the Son in the work of salvation is made manifest from the time of Christ's virginal conception up to his death,"[31] it is made manifest above all at the hour of his Passion:

Thus the Blessed Virgin advanced in her pilgrimage of faith, and faithfully persevered in her union with her Son unto the cross. There she stood, in keeping with the divine plan, enduring with her only begotten Son the intensity of his suffering, joining herself with his sacrifice in her mother's heart, and lovingly consenting to the immolation of this victim, born of her: to be given, by the same Christ Jesus dying on the cross, as a mother to his disciple, with these words: "Woman, behold your Son."[32]

965 After her Son's ascension, Mary "aided the beginnings of the Church by her prayers."[33] In her association with the apostles and several women, "we also see Mary by her prayers imploring the gift of the Spirit, who had already overshadowed her in the Annunciation."[34]

## ... also in her Assumption

966 "Finally the Immaculate Virgin, preserved free from all stain of original sin, when the course of her earthly life was finished, was taken up body and soul into heavenly glory, and exalted by the Lord as Queen over all things, so that she might be the more fully conformed to her Son, the Lord of lords and conqueror of sin and death."[35] The assumption of the Blessed Virgin is a singular participation in her Son's resurrection and an anticipation of the resurrection of other Christians:

In giving birth you kept your virginity; in your Dormition you did not leave the world, O Mother of God, but were joined to the source of Life. You conceived the living God and, by your prayers, will deliver our souls from death.[36]

## ...she is our Mother in the order of grace

967 By her complete adherence to the Father's will, to his Son's redemptive work, and to every prompting of the Holy Spirit, the Virgin Mary is the Church's model of faith and charity. Thus she is a "preeminent and .... wholly unique member of the Church"; indeed, she is the "exemplary realization" (*typus*)[37] of the Church.

968 Her role in relation to the Church and to all humanity goes still further. "In a wholly singular way she cooperated by her obedience, faith, hope, and burning charity in the Savior's work of restoring supernatural life to souls. For this reason she is a mother to us in the order of grace."[38]

969 "This motherhood of Mary in the order of grace continues uninterruptedly from the consent which she loyally gave at the Annunciation and which she sustained without wavering beneath the cross, until the eternal fulfillment of all the elect. Taken up to heaven she did not lay aside this saving office but by her manifold intercession continues to bring us the gifts of eternal salvation....Therefore the Blessed Virgin is invoked in the Church under the titles of Advocate, Helper, Benefactress, and Mediatrix."[39]

970 "Mary's function as mother of men in no way obscures or diminished this unique mediation of Christ, but rather shows its power. But the Blessed Virgin's salutary influence on men ... flows froth from the superabundance of the merits of Christ, rests on his mediation, depends entirely on it, and draws all its power from it."[40] "No creature could ever be counted along with the Incarnate Word and Redeemer; but just as the

priesthood of Christ is shared in various ways both by his ministers and the faithful, and as the one goodness of God is radiated in different ways among his creatures, so also the unique mediation of the Redeemer does not exclude but rather gives rise to a manifold cooperation which is but a sharing in this one source."[41]

## II. Devotion To The Blessed Virgin

971 "All generations will call me blessed": "The Church's devotion to the Blessed Virgin is intrinsic to Christian worship."[42] The Church rightly honors "the Blessed Virgin with special devotion. From the most ancient times the Blessed Virgin has been honored with the title of 'Mother of God,' to whose protection the faithful fly in all their dangers and needs....This very special devotion ... differs essentially from the adoration which is given to the incarnate Word and equally to the Father and the Holy Spirit, and greatly fosters this adoration."[43] The liturgical feasts dedicated to the Mother of God and Marian prayer, such as the rosary, an "epitome of the whole Gospel," express this devotion to the Virgin Mary.[44]

## III. Mary - Eschatological Icon Of The Church

972 After speaking of the Church, her origin, mission and destiny, we can find no better way to conclude than by looking to Mary. In her we contemplate what the Church already is in her mystery on her own "pilgrimage of faith," and what she will be in the homeland at the end of her journey. There, "in the glory of the Most Holy and Undivided Trinity," "in the communion of all the saints,"[45] the Church is awaited by the one she venerates as Mother of her Lord and as her own mother.

In the meantime the Mother of Jesus, in the glory which she possesses in body and soul in heaven, is the image and beginning of the Church as it is to be perfected in the world to come. Likewise she shines forth on earth, until the day of the Lord shall come, a sign of certain hope and comfort to the pilgrim People of God.[46]

## In Brief

973 By pronouncing her "fiat" at the Annunciation and giving her consent to the Incarnation, Mary was already collaborating with the whole work her Son was to accomplish. She is mother wherever he is Savior and head of the Mystical Body.

974 The Most Blessed Virgin Mary, when the course of her earthly life was completed, was taken up body and soul into the glory of heaven, where she already shares in the glory of her Son's resurrection, anticipating the resurrection of all members of his Body.

975 "We believe that the Holy Mother of God, the new Eve, Mother of the Church, continues in heaven to exercise her maternal role on behalf of the members of Christ."[47]

# 3. Mary In Relation To The Holy Spirit

There are a considerable number of references to Mary and the Holy Spirit in Part One of the Catechism (721-725). Her cooperation with the work of the Spirit is seen in her because: 1) the Father found the dwelling place where his Son and his Spirit could dwell among men (721); 2) the Holy Spirit prepared Mary by his grace (722); 3) in Mary, the Holy Spirit fulfills the plan of the Father's loving goodness (723); 4) in Mary, the Holy Spirit manifests the Son of the Father, now become the Son of the Virgin (724); and 5) finally, through Mary, the Holy Spirit begins to bring men, the object of God's merciful love, into communion with Christ (725). Several of the symbols of the Holy Spirit are also presented in a Marian dimension – especially the anointing and the symbol of the cloud and light (695, 697). Other paragraphs which mention Mary in relationship to the Holy Spirit are 485, 486, 504, 726, 744, 2673, 2676 and 2682.

Perhaps the section (par. 2, Chapter 2, Article 3) entitled "conceived by the Power of the Holy Spirit and Born of the Virgin Mary" is the centerpiece in the Marian teaching of the Catechism. Commencing with Paul's announcement of the Christ-event in the fullness of time,[48] and then showing how the Holy Spirit descends upon Mary at the Annunciation,[49] it is learned that the mission of the Holy Spirit is conjoined and ordered to that of the Son (485). Through the operation of the Holy Spirit, Mary conceives the eternal Son. The Christ, that is the Anointed One of the Holy Spirit, progressively manifests himself to the shepherds, the Magi, the Baptist, and to the disciples. "...God anointed Jesus of Nazareth with the Holy Spirit and power."[50] Mary's response to God and the action of the spirit results in the birth of Jesus. Her faith has made this possible.

Mary was already foreseen in the Divine plan. This is emphasized in the section of Vatican II's *Lumen Gentium* dedicated to Mary: "The Father of mercies willed that the Incarnation should be preceded by assent on the part of the predestined mother, so that just as a woman had a share in bringing about death, so also a woman should contribute to life."[51]

The singular grace of Mary's Immaculate Conception is also due to the presence and operation of the Holy Spirit. Her redemption is also due to her Son but in view of his merits. In the Eastern Tradition Mary is called the All-Holy one, Panagia. She is celebrated as "free from every stain of sin, as though fashioned by the Holy Spirit and formed as a new creature."[52] Moved by the Holy Spirit, Elizabeth praises Mary for her faith and professes her as "the mother of my Lord."[53]

## II. ...Born Of The Virgin Mary

487 What the Catholic faith believes about Mary is based on what it believes about Christ, and what it teaches about Mary

illumines in turn its faith in Christ.

## Mary's predestination

488 "God sent forth his Son," but to prepare a body for him[54] he wanted the free cooperation of a creature. For this, from all eternity God chose for the mother of his Son a daughter of Israel, a young Jewish woman of Nazareth in Galilee, "a virgin betrothed to a man whose name was Joseph, of the house of David; and the virgin's name was Mary."[55]

The Father of mercies willed that the Incarnation should be preceded by assent on the part of the predestined mother, so that just as a woman had a share in the coming of death, so also should a woman contribute to the coming of life.[56]

489 Throughout the Old Covenant the mission of many holy women *prepared* for that of Mary. At the very beginning there was Eve; despite her disobedience, she receives the promise of a posterity that will be victorious over the evil one, as well as the promise that she will be the mother of all the living.[57] By virtue of this promise, Sarah conceives a Son in spite of her old age.[58] Against all human expectation God chooses those who were considered powerless and weak to show forth his faithfulness to his promises: Hannah, the mother of Samuel; Deborah; Ruth; Judith and Esther; and many other women.[59] Mary "stands out among the poor and humble of the Lord, who confidently hope for and receive salvation from him. After a long period of waiting the times are fulfilled in her, the exalted Daughter of Zion, and the new plan of salvation is established."[60]

## The Immaculate Conception

490 To become the mother of the Savior, Mary "was enriched by God with gifts appropriate to such a role."[61] The angel Gabriel at the moment of the annunciation salutes her as "full of grace."[62] In fact, in order for Mary to be able to give the free

assent of her faith to the announcement of her vocation, it was necessary that she be wholly borne by God's grace.

491 Through the centuries the Church has become ever more aware that Mary, "full of grace" through God,[63] was redeemed from the moment of her conception. That is what the dogma of the Immaculate Conception confesses, as Pope Pius IX proclaimed in 1854:

The most Blessed Virgin Mary was, from the first moment of her conception, by a singular grace and privilege of almighty God and by virtue of the merits of Jesus Christ, Savior of the human race, preserved immune from all stain of original sin.[64]

492 The "splendor of an entirely unique holiness" by which Mary is "enriched from the first instant of her conception" comes wholly from Christ: she is "redeemed, in a more exalted fashion, by reason of the merits of her Son."[65] The Father blessed Mary more than any other created person "in Christ with every spiritual blessing in the heavenly places" and chose her "in Christ before the foundation of the world, to be holy and blameless before him in love."[66]

493 The Fathers of the Eastern tradition call the Mother of God "the All-Holy" (*Panagia*) and celebrate her as "free from any stain of sin, as though fashioned by the Holy Spirit and formed as a new creature."[67] By the grace of God Mary remained free of every personal sin her whole life long.

## "Let it be done to me according to your word..."

494 At the announcement that she would give birth to "the Son of the Most High" without knowing man, by the power of the Holy Spirit, Mary responded with the obedience of faith, certain that "with God nothing will be impossible": "Behold, I am the handmaid of the Lord; let it be [done] to me according to your word."[68] Thus, giving her consent to God's word, Mary becomes the mother of Jesus. Espousing the divine will for

salvation wholeheartedly, without a single sin to restrain her, she gave herself entirely to the person and to the work of her Son; she did so in order to serve the mystery of redemption with him and dependent on him, by God's grace.[69]

As St. Irenaeus says, "Being obedient she became the cause of salvation for herself and for the whole human race.[70] Hence not a few of the early Fathers gladly assert ... "The knot of Eve's disobedience was untied by Mary's obedience: what the virgin Eve bound through her disbelief, Mary loosened by her faith."[71] Comparing her with Eve, they call Mary "the Mother of the living" and frequently claim: "Death through Eve, life through Mary."[72]

## Mary's divine motherhood

495 Called in the Gospels "the mother of Jesus," Mary is acclaimed by Elizabeth, at the prompting of the Spirit and even before the birth of her Son, as "the mother of my Lord."[73] In fact, the One whom she conceived as man by the Holy Spirit, who truly became her Son according to the flesh,, was none other than the Father's eternal Son, the second person of the Holy Trinity. Hence the Church confesses that Mary is truly "Mother of God" (*Theotokos*).[74]

## Mary's virginity

496 From the first formulations of her faith, the Church has confessed that Jesus was conceived solely by the power of the Holy Spirit in the womb of the Virgin Mary, affirming also the corporeal aspect of this event: Jesus was conceived "by the Holy Spirit without human seed."[75] The Fathers see in the virginal conception the sign that it truly was the Son of God who came in a humanity like our own. Thus St. Ignatius of Antioch at the beginning of the second century says:

You are firmly convinced about our Lord, who is truly of the race of David according to the flesh, Son of God according to the will and power of God, truly born of a virgin, ... he was truly nailed to a tree for us in his flesh under Pontius Pilate ... he truly suffered, as he is also truly risen.[76]

497 The Gospel accounts understand the virginal conception of Jesus as a divine work that surpasses all human understanding and possibility:[77] "That which is conceived in her is of the Holy Spirit," said the angel to Joseph about Mary his fiancee.[78] The Church sees here the fulfillment of the divine promise given through the prophet Isaiah: "Behold, a virgin shall conceive and bear a Son."[79]

498 People are sometimes troubled by the silence of St. Mark's Gospel and the New Testament Epistles about Jesus' virginal conception. Some might wonder if we were merely dealing with legends of theological constructs not claiming to be history. To this we must respond: Faith in the virginal conception of Jesus met with the lively opposition, mockery, or incomprehension of non-believers, Jews and pagans alike;[80] so it could hardly have been motivated by pagan mythology or by some adaptation to the ideas of the age. The meaning of this event is accessible only to faith, which understands in it the "connection of these mysteries with one another"[81] in the totality of Christ's mysteries, from his Incarnation to his Passover. St. Ignatius of Antioch already bears witness to this connection: "Mary's virginity and giving birth, and even the Lord's death escaped the notice of the prince of this world: these three mysteries worthy of proclamation were accomplished in God's silence."[82]

## Mary - "ever virgin"

499 The deepening of faith in the virginal motherhood led the Church to confess Mary's real and perpetual virginity even in the act of giving birth to the Son of God made man.[83] In fact, Christ's birth "did not diminish his mother's virginal integrity

but sanctified it."[84] And so the liturgy of the Church celebrates Mary as *Aeiparthenos*, the "Ever-virgin."[85]

500 Against this doctrine the objection is sometimes raised that the Bible mentions brothers and sisters of Jesus.[86] The Church has always understood these passages as not referring to other children of the Virgin Mary In fact James and Joseph, "brothers of Jesus," are the sons of another Mary, a disciple of Christ, whom St. Matthew significantly calls "the other Mary."[87] They are close relations of Jesus according to an Old Testament expression.[88]

501 Jesus is Mary's only Son, but her spiritual motherhood extends to all men whom indeed he came to save: "The Son whom she brought forth is he whom God placed as the first-born among many brethren, that is, the faithful in whose generation and formulation she cooperates with a mother's love.[89]

## Mary's virginal motherhood in God's plan

502 The eyes of faith can discover in the context of the whole of Revelation the mysterious reasons why God in his saving plan wanted his Son to be born of a virgin. These reasons touch both on the person of Christ and his redemptive mission, and on the welcome Mary gave that mission on behalf of all men.

503 Mary's virginity manifests God's absolute initiative in the Incarnation. Jesus has only God as Father. "He was never estranged from the Father because of the human nature which he assumed....He is naturally Son of the Father as to his divinity and naturally Son of his mother as to his humanity, but properly Son of the father in both natures."[90]

504 Jesus is conceived by the Holy Spirit in the Virgin Mary's womb because he is the New Adam, who inaugurates the new creation: "The first man was from the earth, a man of dust; the second man is from heaven."[91] From his conception, Christ's

humanity is filled with the Holy Spirit, for God "gives him the Spirit without measure."[92] From "his fullness" as the head of redeemed humanity "we have all received, grace upon grace."[93]

505 By his virginal conception, Jesus, the New Adam, ushers in *the new birth* of children adopted in the Holy Spirit through faith. "How can this be?"[94] Participation in the divine life arises "not of blood nor of the will of the flesh nor of the will of man, but of God."[95] The acceptance of this life is virginal because it is entirely the Spirit's gift to man. The spousal character of the human vocation in relation to God[96] is fulfilled perfectly in Mary's virginal motherhood.

506 Mary is a virgin because her virginity is *the sign of her faith* "unadulterated by any doubt," and of her undivided gift of herself to God's will.[97] It is her faith that enables her to become the mother of the Savior: "Mary is more blessed because she embraces faith in Christ than because she conceives the flesh of Christ."[98]

507 At once virgin and mother, Mary is the symbol and the most perfect realization of the Church: "the Church indeed ... by receiving the word of God in faith becomes herself a mother. By preaching and Baptism she brings forth sons, who are conceived by the Holy Spirit and born of God, to a new and immortal life. She herself is a virgin, who keeps in its entirety and purity the faith she pledged to her spouse."[99]

# In Brief

508 From among the descendants of Eve, God chose the Virgin Mary to be the mother of his Son. "Full of grace," Mary is "the most excellent fruit of redemption:"[100] from the first instant of her conception, she was totally preserved from the stain of original sin and she remained pure from all personal sin throughout her life.

509 Mary is truly "Mother of God" since she is the mother of the eternal Son of God made man, who is God himself.

510 Mary "remained a virgin in conceiving her Son, a virgin in giving birth to him, a virgin in carrying him, a virgin in nursing him at her breast, always a virgin:"[101] with her whole being she is "the handmaid of the Lord."[102]

511 The Virgin Mary "cooperated through free faith and obedience in human salvation."[103] She uttered her yes "in the name of all human nature."[104] By her obedience she became the new Eve, mother of the living.

## The Great Marian Periscope

The Great Marian New Testament Pauline periscope is Galatians 4:4 and following, Paul's announcement of the coming of the Christ born of a woman so that we could be adopted as sons, is the central quote of Vatican II as well as the central quotation of John Paul II's Marian encyclical. It stresses four themes: the fullness of time; the sending of Jesus; born of a woman; our adoption as sons and daughters into the family of God.

## Fullness of Time

The expression "fullness of time" has Marian overtones, for when after thousands of years of men and women doing their own thing, even their own religious thing, God finally got someone to be fully open and obedient to him. Mary of Nazareth was fully open totally surrendered, absolutely virgin and empty of all self will. What was totally empty would be totally full. Since God is never willing to buy into our plans he had to wait for someone fully open to him. With Mary's full fiat, the fullness of time could come.

## Born of the Woman

Paul's use of this title of Mary, "a woman" or "the woman", contains a richness of Marian overtones, for this is the most Scriptural and Scripturally rich title of Mary. This title "the woman" is used eleven times in Scripture with deep salvation inference:

1.      Gn 3:15      I will put total enmity between you and the woman, and between your offspring and hers; he will strike at your head, while you strike at his heel.
2.      Jn 2:4      Jesus replied, ""Woman, how does this concern of yours involve me? My your has not yet come."
3.      Jn 19:26      Seeing his mother there with the disciple whom he loved, Jesus said to his mother, "Woman, there is your Son."
4.      Gal 4:4      But when the time had fully come, God sent forth his Son, born of woman...
5.      Rv 12:1      A great and wondrous sign appeared in the heaven: a woman clothed with the sun, with the moon under her feet and a crown of twelve stars on her head.
6.      Rv 12:4      The dragon stood in front of the woman who was about to give birth, so that he might devour her child the moment it was born.
7.      Rv 12:6      The woman fled into the desert to a place prepared for her by God, where she might be taken care of for 1,260 days.
8.      Rv 12:14      The woman was given the two wings of a great eagle so that she might fly to the place prepared for her in the desert, where she would be taken care of for a time, times and half a time, out of the serpent's reach.
9.      Rv 12:15      Then from his mouth the serpent spewed water like a river, to overtake the woman and sweep her away with the torrent.
10.      Rv 12:16      But the earth helped the woman by opening its mouth and swallowing the river that the dragon had spewed out of his mouth.
11.      Rv 12:17      Then the dragon was enraged at the woman and went off to make war against the rest of her children - those who obey God's commandments and hold to the testimony of Jesus.

The Father of mercies willed that the Incarnation should be preceded by assent on the part of the predestined mother so that just as a woman had a share in bringing about death, so also a woman should contribute to life.[105]

## The Holy Spirit and Her Immaculate Conception

Mary's immaculate conception due to the antecedent graces of her Son's redemptive work is due to the work also of the Holy Spirit. The Eastern Church uses the title "Panagia" (the All Holy One).

Elizabeth, moved by the Holy Spirit, cries, "Blessed is she who trusted that the Lord's word to her would be fulfilled" and humbly asks, "Who am I that the mother of my Lord should come to me?"[106]

# 4 Mary In Relation To The Church

## Mary And The Mystical Body Of Christ

Mary, who is the mother of Jesus, is therefore not only mother of the Eucharistic Christ, but also the mother of the Mystical Body of Christ, the Church. One who is mother is mother of her child wherever he is. Jesus is in his resurrected Body, his Eucharistic Body, his Mystical Body. She who is the mother of Jesus is the mother of Jesus in us. The Catechism states in paragraph 963, "She is 'clearly the mother of the members of Christ' ... since she has by her charity joined in bringing about the birth of believers in the Church, who are members of its head." As Paul VI stated, Mary, the Mother of Christ, is the mother of the Church.[107]

The basis of the Church teaching that Mary is also our mother, that is, the mother of Christ within us who form the Church is traditionally John 19:26: "Woman, behold your Son." The text has been used as the foundation of this teaching since the 4th century.

Recently many scholars are also using Rv 12:17: "Satan angry at the woman is going to war on the rest of her children," that is, those who keep the commands of Jesus and bear witness to his name. Also the fact that Mary was there at Pentecost at the birth of the Church.[108] Mary, who is the mother of Jesus, is obviously, therefore, the Mother of Jesus in us who form his Mystical Body. She is the mother of grace.

Paul VI reminds us that the Church's devotion to the Blessed Virgin is an intrinsic element of Christian worship.[109]

In *Lumen Gentium*, Mary is member, model and mother of the Church. Therefore, she is also hailed as a pre-eminent and altogether singular member of the Church, and as the Church's model and an excellent exemplar in faith and charity, taught by the Holy Spirit, the Catholic Church honors her with filial affection and piety as the most beloved mother.[110]

## Mary in the Church

In Mary the Church is all-holy. Paragraph 829 states:

> "But while in the most Blessed Virgin the Church has already reached that perfection whereby she exists without spot or wrinkle, the faithful still strive to conquer sin and increase in holiness. And so they turn their eyes to Mary:"[111] in her, the Church is already the "all-holy."

Paragraph 773 states:

> In the Church this communion of men with God, in the "love [that] never ends," is the purpose which governs everything in her that is a sacramental means, tied to this passing world.[112] "[The Church's] structure is totally ordered to the holiness of Christ's members. And holiness is measured according to the 'great mystery' in which the Bride responds with the gift of love to the gift of the Bridegroom."[113] Mary goes before us all in the holiness that is the Church's mystery as "the bride without spot

or wrinkle."[114] That is why the "Marian" dimension of the Church precedes the "Petrine."[115]

Paragraph 973 states:

973 By pronouncing her "fiat" at the Annunciation and giving her consent to the Incarnation, Mary was already collaborating with the whole work her Son was to accomplish. She is mother wherever he is Savior and head of the Mystical Body.

Mary supported the beginning of the Church by her prayers. Paragraph 965 states:

965 After her Son's ascension, Mary "aided the beginnings of the Church by her prayers."[116] In her association with the apostles and several women, "we also see Mary by her prayers imploring the gift of the Spirit, who had already overshadowed her in the Annunciation."[117]

Place of Mary in the Church (963-972):

963 Since the Virgin Mary's role in the mystery of Christ and the Spirit has been treated, it is fitting now to consider her place in the mystery of the Church. "The Virgin Mary ... is acknowledged and honored as being truly the Mother of God and of the redeemer....She is 'clearly the mother of the members of Christ' ... since she has by her charity joined in bringing about the birth of believers in the Church, who are members of its head."[118] "Mary, Mother of Christ, Mother of the Church."[119]

964 Mary's Role in the Church is inseparable from her union with Christ and flows directly from it. "This union of the mother with the Son in the work of salvation is made manifest from the time of Christ's virginal conception up to his death;"[120] it is made manifest above all at the hour of his Passion:

Thus the Blessed Virgin advanced in her pilgrimage of faith, and faithfully persevered in her union with her Son unto the cross. There she stood, in keeping with the divine plan, enduring with her only begotten Son the intensity of his suffering, joining herself with his sacrifice in her mother's heart, and lovingly consenting to the immolation of this victim, born of her: to be given, by the same Christ Jesus dying on the cross, as a mother to his disciple, with these words: "Woman, behold your Son."[121]

965 After her Son's ascension, Mary "aided the beginnings of the Church by her prayers."[122] In her association with the apostles and several women, "we also see Mary by her prayers imploring the gift of the Spirit, who had already overshadowed her in the Annunciation.[123]

966 "Finally the Immaculate Virgin, preserved free from all stain of original sin, when the course of her earthly life was finished, was taken up body and soul into heavenly glory, and exalted by the Lord as Queen over all things, so that she might be the more fully conformed to her Son, the Lord of lords and conqueror of sin and death."[124] The assumption of the Blessed Virgin is a singular participation in her Son's resurrection and an anticipation of the resurrection of other Christians:

In giving birth you kept your virginity; in your Dormition you did not leave the world, O Mother of God, but were joined to the source of Life. You conceived the living God and, by your prayers, will deliver our souls from death.[125]

967 By her complete adherence to the Father's will, to his Son's redemptive work, and to every prompting of the Holy Spirit, the Virgin Mary is the Church's model of faith and charity. Thus she is a "preeminent and .... wholly unique member of the Church"; indeed, she is the "exemplary realization" (*typus*)[126] of the Church.

968 Her role in relation to the Church and to all humanity goes still further. "In a wholly singular way she cooperated by her obedience, faith, hope, and burning charity in the Savior's work of restoring supernatural life to souls. For this reason she is a

mother to us in the order of grace."[127]

969 "This motherhood of Mary in the order of grace continues uninterruptedly from the consent which she loyally gave at the Annunciation and which she sustained without wavering beneath the cross, until the eternal fulfillment of all the elect. Taken up to heaven she did not lay aside this saving office but by her manifold intercession continues to bring us the gifts of eternal salvation....Therefore the Blessed Virgin is invoked in the Church under the titles of Advocate, Helper, Benefactress, and Mediatrix."[128]

970 "Mary's function as mother of men in no way obscures or diminished this unique mediation of Christ, but rather shows its power. But the Blessed Virgin's salutary influence on men ... flows froth from the superabundance of the merits of Christ, rests on his mediation, depends entirely on it, and draws all its power from it."[129] "No creature could ever be counted along with the Incarnate Word and Redeemer; but just as the priesthood of Christ is shared in various ways both by his ministers and the faithful, and as the one goodness of God is radiated in different ways among his creatures, so also the unique mediation of the Redeemer does not exclude but rather gives rise to a manifold cooperation which is but a sharing in this one source."[130]

971 "All generations will call me blessed": "The Church's devotion to the Blessed Virgin is intrinsic to Christian worship."[131] The Church rightly honors "the Blessed Virgin with special devotion. From the most ancient times the Blessed Virgin has been honored with the title of 'Mother of God,' to whose protection the faithful fly in all their dangers and needs....This very special devotion ... differs essentially from the adoration which is given to the incarnate Word and equally to the Father and the Holy Spirit, and greatly fosters this adoration."[132] The liturgical feasts dedicated to the Mother of God and Marian prayer, such as the rosary, an "epitome of the whole Gospel," express this devotion to the Virgin Mary.[133]

972 After speaking of the Church, her origin, mission and destiny, we can find no better way to conclude than by looking to Mary. In her we contemplate what the Church already is in her mystery on her own "pilgrimage of faith," and what she will be in the homeland at the end of her journey. There, "in the glory of the Most Holy and Undivided Trinity," "in the communion of all the saints,"[134] the Church is awaited by the one she venerates as Mother of her Lord and as her own mother.

Place of Mary inseparable from Christ:

964 Mary's Role in the Church is inseparable from her union with Christ and flows directly from it. "This union of the mother with the Son in the work of salvation is made manifest from the time of Christ's virginal conception up to his death";[135] it is made manifest above all at the hour of his Passion:

Thus the Blessed Virgin advanced in her pilgrimage of faith, and faithfully persevered in her union with her Son unto the cross. There she stood, in keeping with the divine plan, enduring with her only begotten Son the intensity of his suffering, joining herself with his sacrifice in her mother's heart, and lovingly consenting to the immolation of this victim, born of her: to be given, by the same Christ Jesus dying on the cross, as a mother to his disciple, with these words: "Woman, behold your Son."[136]

Mary, model for the Church:

2030        It is in the Church, in communion with all the baptized, that the Christian fulfills his vocation. From the Church he receives the Word of God containing the Teachings of "the law of Christ."[137] From the Church he receives the grace of the sacraments that sustains him on the "way." From the Church he learns the example of holiness and recognizes its model and source in the all-holy Virgin Mary; he discerns it in the authentic witness of those who live it; he discovers it in the spiritual tradition and long history of the saints who have gone before him and whom the liturgy celebrates in the rhythms of the sanctoral cycle.

Her faith:

> 273 Only faith can embrace the mysterious ways of God's almighty power. This faith glories in its weaknesses in order to draw to itself Christ's power.[138] The Virgin Mary is the supreme model of this faith, for she believed that "nothing will be impossible with God," and was able to magnify the Lord: "For he who is mighty has done great things for me, and holy is his name."[139]

The Catechism of the Catholic Church contains a compendium of teaching about Mary, the Mother of Jesus. Mary is present throughout the Catechism primarily as she is seen in the Scriptures and in the Conciliar document *Lumen Gentium*. It is especially through this Scriptural and conciliar image of Mary that renewed knowledge, love and devotion to Mary are enhanced and developed for the reader of the Catechism. There are no polemic overtones or innuendoes in this contextual synthesis surrounding the person of Mary. She is a courageous, generous, and loving woman and mother. Mary's total response to God makes of her a model for the believer whose response echoes her "May it be done to me according to your word."[140]

# 5 Mary's Life Of Faith And Prayer

Mary, the Virgin mother of Jesus, is introduced in the Catechism in the first reflection on the Creed. She is the most perfect realization of free submission in faith just as Abraham was presented as the model of obedient faith. The response of Mary to the Word of God through her vibrant faith shows her as a courageous woman who believes in God as the ultimate truth who guaranteed the promises made in the sacred Word of Scripture.[141] It is significant that the Creed which expresses the human response to God is first presented in the context of the decree of Vatican II on Divine

Revelation, and that the two models of such a human response to God with complete trust are found in Abraham and Mary. Twenty-five years later John Paul II introduced a similar parallel of Abraham and Mary in his encyclical *Redemptoris Mater*. This complementarity of a man of faith and a woman of faith strengthens the relationship of God's revelatory message in the Hebrew Scriptures with that of the Christian Scriptures. Abraham is the father in faith of Judaism, while Christianity is likewise modeled in Mary's great response of "yes" to God. In a word the First Testament is complemented in the Second Testament. The focusing on the persons of Mary and Abraham thus has an ecumenical nuance as well as a Scriptural basis for our imitating the faith of both of our ancestors in faith - a father and a mother.[142]

Mary is declared as blessed, that is, a happy and fortunate person because she has believed in God's word.[143] Abraham first heard the expression "nothing is impossible to God"[144] and Sarah his aged wife was so astonished that she laughed at the idea of conceiving a child. Mary had accepted and received the promise of the angel Gabriel. Mary's total decision and commitment to the word of God through the messenger is an absolutely free and unconditional response of love on the part of the servant of God.[145] Elizabeth, the cousin of Mary, is the first to call Mary blessed because of her belief.[146] The retelling of Mary's story by Luke is paralleled in the Catechism with the story of Abraham and Sarah. Again the Scriptural witness to Mary's faith is attested; the Old and the New Testaments are seen as complementary. There is also a sensitivity to the Jewish heritage of Mary of Nazareth.

Mary's faith continued to grow steadily throughout her life, and in the supreme moment of witnessing the death of Jesus her faith did not vacillate. Mary never ceased in believing in the fulfillment of God's word. This is the reason for the Church venerating the most pristine realization of faith in a person.[147] Once again the description of Mary and her faith is seen within the Scriptures.[148] Together with the most recent instruction on Mary, the Catechism approaches Mary from a Scriptural context. The Holy Scriptures are thus the soul of an authentic Mariology.

The final paragraph (165) of Article I, referring to the Apostles' Creed, returns to the faith of Abraham and Mary. Scripture again testifies to their faith: Abraham believes "hoping against hope."[149] The Virgin Mary, the preferred title for Mary in the Catechism, is a believing disciple despite the night of faith, the suffering of her Son, and the darkness of the tomb. The Catechism here is resonating the earliest Creed given in Paul's epistle to the Corinthians:

> For I handed on to you as of first importance what I also received: that Christ died for our sins in accordance with the Scriptures; that he was buried; that he was raised on the third day in accordance with the Scriptures; that he appeared to Kephas, then to the Twelve. After that, he appeared to more than five hundred brothers at once, most of whom are still living, though some have fallen asleep. After that he appeared to James, then to all the apostles Last of all, as to one born abnormally, he appeared to me.[150]

The overarching theme of Mary's courageous womanly faith continues in the context of her being under the shadow of the Holy Spirit. The section under her Immaculate Conception (pars. 490-493) underlines that it was her faith in God that enabled her to give her absolute free consent in a positive human act of loving response to her call; however, this was possible because she was given the grace of God. She was said to be "full of grace."[151] We know from the philological study done by I. de la Potterie that this fullness of grace is in reality the title the angel Gabriel calls her - you who have been transformed and favored by the grace of God.[152]

Mary is always pointing to Jesus. This is an important principle in the texts of the New Testament referring to her, especially in those texts which deal with a faith dimension. In the Cana account, Mary says, "Do whatever he [Jesus] tells you."[153]. In the Catechism (par. 165) a similar faith in Jesus is expressed through the following text:

> Therefore, since we are surrounded by so great a cloud of witnesses, let us rid ourselves of every burden and sin that clings to us and persevere in running the race that lies before us while keeping our eyes fixed on Jesus, the leader and perfecter of

faith. For the sake of the joy that lay before him he endured the cross, despising its shame, and has taken his seat at the right of the throne of God.[154]

In the paradoxical mystery of the omnipotent God seemingly lacking power in the tragedies of the world, such as war, disease, suffering and death, Mary is presented again as a model of faith drawing us to Christ in his humanness. The faith response of Mary is seen in the context of the Annunciation[155] and in her faith-filled praise of God in her Magnificat.[156] Our weaknesses are shared by Mary in the light of our relationship to Christ through faith:

> But he said to me, "My grace is sufficient for you, for power is made perfect in weakness." I will rather boast most gladly of my weaknesses, in order that the power of Christ may dwell with me.[157]

> I have the strength for everything through him who empowers me.[158]

The development of Mary's faith starts with the Annunciation narrative which is both an announcement and a vocation account. Mary responds with her obedience of faith.[159] Such a dynamic faith response is only possible through the influence of God's Holy Spirit upon Mary. This enables her to give a complete human response: "May it be done to me according to your word."[160] Again the Catechism places her response as a direct reply to the Word of God. Citing Irenaeus, the first Mariologist, Mary's obedience and her faith remove the obstacles of disobedience and incredulity.[161] Perhaps, this obedience of faith can be understood in the Hebrew expression *leb shomeah*; that is, Mary responded with a "listening heart."

The crowning reference to Mary's faith is found under the title "the prayer of the Virgin Mary" in the fourth and final part of the Catechism.[162] The experience of Mary's practical prayer is seen at Cana when her solicitude and care result in an effective request of Jesus her Son. This is also seen in the only other direct mention of Mary at the foot of the Cross, where she is seen as the "mother of the living" in the spiritual realm, that is, those who through their belief have become sons and daughters of God: "But to those who did accept him he gave power to become children of God, to those who believe in his name."[163]

The Catechism quite appropriately frames the prayer and faith of Mary with the two Marian texts of the fourth Gospel, the contemplative Gospel: Jn 2:1-22 (par. 1613) and Jn 19:25-27 (pars. 762, 2618). Other paragraphs in the Catechism touching upon the faith of Mary are: 273, 506, 511, 534, 964, 967, 968, 972, 2617, 2619, 2622.

In three paragraphs (2617-2619) within the Proto-gospel the prayer of Mary is mentioned. Once again, this Marian aspect is described in the Scriptures. The use of the revelatory texts is a guiding method for the Catechism. This is consistent with Vatican II's *Dei Verbum* (Divine Revelation), *Sacrosanctum Concilium* (Sacred Liturgy), and *Lumen Gentium* (Church).

Mary is a model for prayer within the life of the Church. The sections that describe her prayer are found in the concluding part of the Catechism: "Christian Life." Over 300 numbered articles are dedicated to prayer.

The principal section on the prayer of Mary is found in Article 2 under the title "In the Fullness of Time."[164] Mary's prayer thereby is introduced into the earliest reference to her in the New Testament: "But when the fullness of time had come, God sent his Son, born of a woman, born under the law, to ransom those under the law, so that we might receive adoption."[165] According to St. Paul, Mary's prayer coincided with the benevolent plan of God's loving mercy. At the Annunciation, Mary articulated her prayer through a heart-filled "yes." She not only ponders over the events of her life in the light of her Jewish faith,[166] she is at the center of a community gathered in prayer in the upper room prior to the coming of the Holy Spirit at Pentecost. Her prayer embraces the time of expectant waiting, the event of the Incarnation, and the birth of the Church. Mary symbolizes the prayer life of the Church at every important moment of the Christ-event. Her "let it be" (*fiat*) is the soul of Christian prayer, that is, to be entirely oriented toward the Person of God. Her magnanimous response continues in her Magnificat which we, the People of God, pray each day in the universal prayer of he Church. The Johannine image of Mary is that of a woman interceding for the needy and who stands in strong faith at the moment of death.[167]

The Catechism sums up the perfect expression of Mary's prayer:

2619      That is why the Canticle of Mary,[168] the Magnificat (Latin) or Megalynei (Byzantine) is the song both of the Mother of God and of the Church, the song of the Daughter of Zion and of the new People of God; the song of thanksgiving for the fullness of graces poured out in the economy of salvation and the song of the "poor" whose hope is met by the fulfillment of the promises made to our ancestors, "to Abraham and to his posterity for ever."

Mary is a model for the Church at prayer, and when we pray with her or to her we gather in spirit with the brothers and sisters, the apostles, and the holy women in the upper room awaiting the promise of Jesus, which is the Holy Spirit: "All these devoted themselves with one accord to prayer, together with some women, and Mary the mother of Jesus, and his brothers."[169]

In a fitting way, after the prayer to God, to the Second Person of the Trinity (Jesus), and to and through the Holy Spirit, Mary is included as one who prays with us and for us. It is Mary who is the model for the Church at prayer. In the final paragraph of the section on Marian prayer, this summary statement orients us in a Marian form of prayer:

2682      Because of Mary's singular cooperation with the action of the Holy Spirit, the Church loves to pray in communion with the Virgin Mary, to magnify with her the great things the Lord has done for her, and to entrust supplications and praises to her.

All Christian prayer is related to the prayer o Jesus Christ. This is a basic principle that influences all facets of our prayer life, including our Marian aspect of prayer and devotions. We see Christ as the way especially in our prayer life. We pray in the name of Jesus. The titles and description of Jesus both in the Scriptures and the sacred liturgy are part of our invocation of him: Son of God,

Word of God, Lord, Savior, Lamb of God, King, Beloved Son, Son of the Virgin, Good Shepherd, our Life, our Light, our Hope, our resurrection, and our Friend.(cf. par. 2665) Above all, it is the holy name Jesus which contains all humanity, divinity, creation and redemption. In the East the Jesus Prayer is essential to what we are when we pray, "Jesus, the Christ, Son of God, Lord, have pity on us sinners."[170] Among the devotions that entail this form of prayer are devotion to the Sacred Heart of Jesus and the Way of the Cross. The invocation, "Come, Holy Spirit," enables us to pray, for no one can say "Jesus is Lord" except under the power and action of the Holy Spirit. Only after carefully treating of Prayer to the Persons of the Holy Trinity does the Catechism introduce the section on prayer, entitled "In communion with the holy Mother of God." (pars. 2673-2682)

Mary is especially important in our prayer to help us understand the humanity of Jesus. Mary is totally transparent in the honor and glory she renders God in her Son Jesus. She shows us the way to Jesus as the *hodoghitria*. There is within the Church's prayer to and with Mary a double movement: the first glorifies God for the great things that have been accomplished in Mary, the devoted handmaid of the Lord, and also in us because of her role in the Incarnation, ; the second entrusts to the Mother of God the supplications and praise of the children of God because Jesus has taken his human flesh from her.

The double movement of prayer is seen in the greatest prayer dedicated to Mary, the "Hail Mary." This Biblical prayer is identified with Catholics probably more than the Lord's Prayer. The Catechism addresses both the *Ave Maria* (pars. 2676-2677) and the *Pater Noster* (pars. 2777-2802). The first section of the Hail Mary is directly from the Gospel of Luke, a Gospel which emphasizes prayer on twenty-two occasions. The *Ave Maria* is, therefore, to be seen within a prayerful context. The atmosphere that surrounds Mary during the angelic salutation is favorable to prayer and has been used as the favorite prayer within the Catholic church both through the Angelus as well as the hold rosary. In a special way the rosary is a compendium of the whole Gospel (cf. par. 971).

God through Gabriel calls Mary to her special vocation. Mary responds totally to God with openness and with joy. In fact, she is told by the angel to rejoice because she has already found favor with God. As the salutation continues, the theme of the Daughter of Zion is recalled through words similar to those of the prophet Zephaniah (3:14-16). Mary like Judith is blessed among women. She is the person in Luke's Gospel who best exemplifies the beatitudes.[171] Elizabeth, her cousin, is the first to proclaim her blessed because of her belief.[172] Just as Abraham was blessed with the promise of a progeny of believers,[173] Mary, too, is the beginning of a new line of believers in the Son she will bear.

In the conclusion of the prayer, the confidence we put in Mary's intercession is based on her own prayer: "May it be with me according to your word."[174] This is similar to Jesus prayer during the agony in the Garden of Olives.[175]. The prayer is one of profound humility in which our present status is put into the perspective of our final hour: "now and at the hour of our death." Just as the Lord's Prayer is seen as an eschatological prayer (according to R.E. Brown)[176] so, too, is the Hail Mary an eschatological prayer helping us always to look toward the final moments and purpose of our lives in union with God's will.

The Catechism takes note of the various traditions in bringing this section to a close. Not only are the Roman or Western devotions to Mary mentioned but also those of the Byzantine, Coptic, Syrian, and Armenian Churches (cf. par. 2678). Thus the universal dimension of Christian prayer prevails.

The final mention of Mary in the Catechism sees her as in image and model of the Church at prayer. This is Biblical, for the last mention of her is in the Acts of the Apostles:

Then they returned to Jerusalem from the mount called Olivet, which is near Jerusalem, a Sabbath day's journey away. When they entered the city they went to the upper room where they were staying. Peter and John and James and Andrew Philip and Thomas, Bartholomew and Matthew, James Son of Alphaeus, Simon the Zealot, and Judas Son of James. All these devoted themselves with one accord to prayer, together with some women, and Mary the mother of Jesus, and his brothers.[177]

The Catechism's description of her is a commentary on Acts 1:12-24:

2679          Mary is the perfect *Orans* (pray-er), a figure of the Church. When we pray to her, we are adhering with her to the pan of the Father, who sends his Son to save all men. Like the beloved disciple we welcome Jesus' mother into our homes,[17] for she has become the mother of all the living. We can pray with and to her. the prayer of the Church is sustained by the prayer of Mary and united with it in hope.[179]

The sources used for depicting the mysteries of the birth, early childhood and hidden life of Jesus are taken from the Infancy Narratives of Matthew and Luke. Primarily, the Catechism is developing a Christology rather than a Mariology. Mary's life is connected with that of her Child. Her life experiences are known precisely because of Jesus her Son who is the center of both Infancy Narratives, and the catechism (Par. 525) celebrates her in a hymn taken from Romanos the Melodist:

> The Virgin today brings into the world the Eternal
> And the earth offers a cave to the Inaccessible.
> The angels and shepherds praise him
> And the magi advance with the star,
> For you are born for us,
> Little Child, God eternal.[180]

The nativity is presented as a mystery which leads us to humility and acceptance of our human limits (par. 526).

Mary is related to the events of Jesus' infancy. With circumcision he is fully under the Covenant and the prescriptions of the Torah. By birth, religion, and culture Jesus is Jewish. In the Epiphany Jesus is manifested to the Gentiles who find him with Mary and Joseph in their home in Bethlehem. The magi must first seek Jesus through the Jewish leaders and people before they can understand him as the Messiah promised through the Scriptures. Jesus is recognized as the promised one by Simeon and Anna who share in the glory of Israel. Mary, however, is forewarned that Jesus will be a sign of contradiction and that a sword of sorrow will pierce her heart. The flight into Egypt and his return to Israel recall the Exodus Event. Jesus is seen as a definitive liberator (par. 530).

The experiences of the hidden life of Jesus are presented in a setting that would be typical of any Jew during this epoch – day by day chores, manual labor, and a religious conduct guided by the Torah and its prescriptions. All of this is under the tutelage of his parents[181]

Likewise, his life of living out the fourth commandment – "honor your father and your mother" – announces and anticipates his submission to the will of God during his agony in the garden in Luke 22:42 (par. 532).

Pope Paul VI in a marvelous sermon for the feast of the Holy Family sums up the hidden years of Jesus:

> The home of Nazareth is the school where we begin to understand the life of Jesus – the school of the Gospel. First, then, a lesson of silence. May esteem for *silence*, that admirable and indispensable condition of mind, revive in us.... A lesson on *family life*. May Nazareth teach us what family life is, its communion of love, its austere and simple beauty, and its sacred and inviolable character.... A lesson of *work*. Nazareth, home of the "Carpenter's Son," is you I would choose to understand and proclaim the severe and redeeming law of human work.. To conclude, I want to greet all the workers of the world, holding up to them their great pattern, their brother who is God.[182]

The only incident that breaks through the hidden life of Jesus is the finding of him in the Temple by Mary and Joseph. Here Mary's faith is again tested and strengthened by pondering over his unusual and mysterious words.[183]

The Catechism shows us Mary's life through that of Christ's; it is always within the context of what we know from the Gospels of Matthew and Luke that we learn of Mary's life in relationship and dependence on what is being said of her Son, Jesus. Her experiences are seen within the mission of the Son and Holy Spirit in the fullness of time.[184] Mary is seen as the Seat of Wisdom precisely because of her cooperative effort in the history of salvation. Texts that are from Wisdom literature are accommodated to her life experiences.[185] She is seen as the Daughter of Zion in Luke's Annunciation narrative. Her song of praise, the Magnificat, becomes the thanksgiving of the whole people of God (par. 722).

Mary continues throughout her life to be influenced and guided by God's Spirit of power and grace. This renders her virginity fruitful in the birth of Jesus. In her the Holy Spirit renders effective the merciful plan of god. The Spirit also manifests the Son of God become Son of Mary. Through her the Spirit begins to bring people into communion with Christ. The Catechism is clearly showing Mary as cooperative with all three Persons of the Holy Trinity. Through the Spirit she becomes the Woman, the new Eve, and mother of all living, the Mother of the whole Christ. We finally see her on the morning of Pentecost praying together with the Twelve as the Church is born. Mary's perfect response to God is expressed at the Annunciation and confirmed by her praise and adoration of God in the powerful sentiments of her Magnificat. This adoration renders her the absolute freedom of a liberated person who is bound by no form of slavery to sin nor any form of idolatry (Par. 2097).

* * * * * * * * *

## Endnotes

[1]  *Fidei Depositum*, in Catechism of the Catholic Church, 2.

[2]  Ibid., 5.

[3]  Ibid., 6.

[4]  Cf. Lk 1:46-49.

[5]  Cf. Gn 2:7, 22.

[6]  Jn 14:30.

[7]  Jn 12:31; Rv 12:10.

[8]   Rv 12:13-16.

[9]   Rv 12:17.

[10]   Rv 22:17, 20.

[11]   *CT* 5.

[12]   *CT* 5.

[13]   *CT* 5.

[14]   *LG* 62.

[15]   *GS* 38; cf. Rom 15:5; Phil 2:5.

[16]   Cf. Jn 13:15; Lk 11:1; Mt 5:11-12.

[17]   Lk 2:11.

[18]   Jn 10:36; cf. Lk 1:35.

[19]   Mt 1:20; cf. Mt 1:16;Rom 1:1; 2 Tim 2:8; Rv 22:16.

[20]   Council of Chalcedon (451); *DS* 301; cf. Heb 4:15.

[21]   Council of Chalcedon: *DS* 302.

[22]   *LH*, January 1, Antiphon for Morning Prayer; cf. St. Leo the Great, *Sermo in nat. Dom.* 1,2; PL 54, 191-192.

[23]   Liturgy of St. John Chrysostom, Troparion *"O monogenes."*

[24]   Cf. Jn 19:25-27.

[25]   Acts 1:14.

[26]   Cf. Rv 4-5; 7:1-8; 14:1; Is 6:2-3.

[27]   Rv 6:9-11; Rv 21:9; cf. 12.

[28]   Rv 7:9.

[29]   *LG* 53; cf. St. Augustine, *De virg.* 6: PL 40, 399.

[30] Paul VI, Discourse, November 21, 1964.

[31] *LG* 57.

[32] *LG* 58; cf. Jn 19:26-27

[33] *LG* 69.

[34] *LG* 59.

[35] *LG* 59; cf. Pius XII, *Munificentissimus Deus* (1950): DS 3903; cf. Rv 19:16.

[36] Byzantine Liturgy, *Troparion*, Feast of the Dormition, August 15th.

[37] Cf. *LG* 53; 63.

[38] *LG* 61.

[39] *LG* 62.

[40] *LG* 60.

[41] *LG* 62.

[42] Lk 1:48; Paul VI, *MC* 56.

[43] *LG* 66.

[44] Cf. Paul VI, *MC* 42; *SC* 103.

[45] *LG* 69.

[46] *LG* 68; cf. 2 Pt 3:10.

[47] Paul VI, *CPG* § 15.

[48] Gal 4:4.

[49] Lk 1:35.

[50] Acts 10:38.

[51] *LG* 56; cf. 61.

[52]  *LG* 56.

[53]  Lk 1:43.

[54]  Gal 4:4; Heb 10:5.

[55]  Lk 1:26-27.

[56]  *LG* 56; cf. 61.

[57]  Cf. Gn 3:15,20.

[58]  Cf. Gn 18:10-14; 21:1-2.

[59]  Cf. 1 Cor 1:17; 1 Sam 1.

[60]  *LG* 55.

[61]  *LG* 56.

[62]  Lk 1:28.

[63]  Lk 1:28

[64]  Pius IX, *Ineffabilis Deus*, 1854: DS 2803.

[65]  *LG* 53, 56.

[66]  Cf. Eph 1:3-4.

[67]  *LG* 56.

[68]  Lk 1:28-38; cf. Rom 1:5.

[69]  *LG* 56.

[70]  St. Irenaeus, *Adv. Haeres.* 3, 22, 4: PG 7/1, 959A.

[71]  St. Irenaeus, *Adv. Haeres.* 3, 22, 4: PG 7/1, 959A.

[72]  *LG* 56; Epiphanius, *Haer.* 78, 18: PG 42, 728CD-729AB; St. Jerome, *Ep.* 22, 21: PL 22, 408.

[73]  Lk 1:43; Jn 2:1; 19:25; cf. Mt 13:55; et al.

[74] Council of Ephesus (431): DS 251.

[75] Council of the Lateran (649): DS 503; cf. DC 10-64.

76 St. Ignatius of Antioch, Ad Smyrn. 1-2: Apostolic Fathers, ed. J. B. Lightfoot (London: Macmillan, 1889) II/2, 289-293; *SCh* 10, 154-156; cf. Rom 1:3; Jn 1:13.

[77] Cf. Mt 1:18-25; Lk 1:26-38.

[78] Mt 1:20.

[79] Is 7:14 in the LXX, quoted in Mt 1:23(Gk.).

[80] Cf. St. Justin, *Dial.*, 99,7: PG 6, 708-709; Origen, *Contra Celsum* 1, 32, 69: GP 11, 720-721; et al.

[81] *Dei Filius* 4: DS 3016.

[82] St. Ignatius of Antioch, Ad. Eph. 19,1: AF II/2, 76-80; *SCh* 10, 88; cf. 1 Cor 2:8.

[83] Cf. DS 291; 294; 427; 442; 503; 571; 1880.

[84] *LG* 57.

[85] Cf. *LG* 52.

[86] Cf. Mk 3:31-35; 6:3;1 Cor 9:5; Gal 1:19.

[87] Mt 13:55; 28:1; cf. Mt 27:56.

[88] Cf. Gn 13:8; 14:16l 29:15; etc.

[89] *LG* 63; cf. Jn 19:26-27; Rom 8:29; Rv 12:17.

[90] Council of Friuli (796): DS 619; cf. Lk 2:48-49.

[91] 1 Cor 15-45, 47.

[92] Jn 3:34.

[93] Jn 1:16; cf. Col 1:18.

[94] Lk 1:34; cf. Jn 3:9.

[95] Jn 1:13

[96] Cf. 2 Cor 11:2.

[97] *LG* 63; cf. 1 Cor 7: 34-35.

[98] St. Augustine, De virg., 3: PL 40, 398.

[99] *LG* 64; cf. 63.

[100] *SC* 103.

[101] St. Augustine, *Serm.* 186, 1: PL 38, 999.

[102] Lk 1:38.

[103] *LG* 56.

[104] St. Thomas Aquinas, STh III, 30, 1.

[105] *LG* 56; cf. 61.

[106] Lk 1:43.

[107] Disc. Nov. 21, 1964.

[108] Cf. Acts 1:14.

[109] *MC* 56.

[110] *LG* 53.

[111] *LG* 65; cf. Eph 5:26-27.

[112] 1 Cor 13:8; cf. *LG* 48.

[113] John Paul II, *MD* 27.

[114] Eph 5:27.

[115] Cf. John Paul II, *MD* 27.

[116] *LG* 59.

[117] *LG* 59.

[118] *LG* 53; cf. St. Augustine, *De virg.* 6: PL 40, 399.

[119] Paul VI, Discourse, November 21, 1964.

[120] *LG* 57.

[121] *LG* 58; cf. Jn 19:26-27.

[122] *LG* 69.

[123] *LG* 59.

[124] *LG* 59; cf. Pius XII, *Munificentissimus Deus* (1950): DS 3903; cf. Rv 19:16.

[125] Byzantine Liturgy, *Troparion*, Feast of the Dormition, August 15th.

[126] Cf. *LG* 53; 63.

[127] *LG* 61.

[128] *LG* 62.

[129] *LG* 61.

[130] *LG* 62.

[131] Lk 1:48; Paul VI, *MC* 56.

[132] *LG* 66.

[133] Cf. Paul VI, *MC* 42; *SC* 103.

[134] *LG* 69.

[135] *LG* 57.

[136] *LG* 58; cf. Jn 19:26-27.

[137] Gal 6:2.

[138] Cf. 2 Cor 12:9; Phil 4:13.

[139] Lk 1:37, 49.

[140] Lk 1:38.

[141] Cf. par. 144.

[142] Cf. pars. 145-147.

[143] Lk 1:45.

[144] Gn 18:14.

[145] Lk 1:38.

[146] Cf. par. 148.

[147] Cf. par. 149.

[148] Lk 2:35, Jn 19:25-27.

[149] Rom 4:18.

[150] 1 Cor 15:3-8.

[151] Lk 1:28.

[152] Lk 1:28.

[153] Jn 2:5.

[154] Heb 12:1-2.

[155] Lk 1:37.

[156] Lk 1:49.

[157] 2 Cor 12:9.

[158] Phil 4:13.

[159] Rom 1:5.

[160] Lk 1:38.

[161] Cf. par. 494.

[162] *CCC*, 630.

[163]  Jn 1:12.

[164]  *CCC*, 630.

[165]  Gal 4:4-5.

[166]  Lk 2:19, 51.

[167]  Cf. Jn 2:1-11; 19:25-27.

[168]  Cf. Lk 1:46-55.

[169]  Acts 1:14.

[170]  Cf. Phil 2:6-11.

[171]  Lk 6:20-22; cf. Mt 5:1-12.

[172]  Lk 1:45.

[173]  Gn 12:2-3.

[174]  Lk 1:38.

[175]  Lk 22:42.

[176]  Raymond E. Brown, New Testament Essays, (New York, Paulist, 1965), 217-253.

[177]  Acts 1:12-14.

[178]  Cf. Jn 19:27.

[179]  Cf. *LG* 68-69.

[180]  *Kontakion* of Romanos the Melodist.

[181]  Lk 2:52-62.

[182]  Paul VI at Nazareth, January 5, 1964. Cited in the Catechism, par. 533.

[183]  Lk 2:51.

[184]  Gal 4:4.

[185]  Cf. Prv 8:1-9:6; Sir 24.

-Chapter 7-

# John Paul II Catechesis On Mary

Following are a series of 70 talks on Mary given by Pope John Paul II, the greatest catechesis the Church has ever produced, between 6 September, 1995 and 12 November, 1997.

## Mary Is Pattern Of Church's Holiness

*"The Blessed Virgin is the perfect realization of the Church's holiness and its model", the Holy Father said as he began a series of reflections on Mary's role in the Church at the General Audience of Wednesday, 6 September 1995. Here is a translation of his address, which was the first in the new series and was given in Italian.*

1. After pausing in the previous catecheses to reflect more deeply on the identity and mission of the Church, I now feel the need to turn our gaze to the Blessed Virgin, she who is the perfect realization of the Church's holiness and its model.

This is exactly what the Fathers of the Second Vatican Council did: after explaining the doctrine on the reality of the People of God in salvation history, they wanted to complete it with an illustration of Mary's role in the work of salvation. In fact, the purpose of chapter eight of the conciliar Constitution *Lumen Gentium*, is to emphasize the ecclesiological significance of Marian doctrine, but likewise to shed light on the contribution that the figure of the Blessed Virgin offers to our understanding of the Church's mystery.

2. Before explaining the Council's Marian itinerary, I would like to take a reflective look at Mary just as, at the Church's beginning, she is described in the Acts of the Apostles. At the beginning of this New Testament text, which describes the life of

the first Christian community, and after recording the names of the Apostles one by one (Lk 1:13), Luke states: "All these with one accord devoted themselves to prayer, together with the women and Mary, the mother of Jesus, and with his brethren" (1:14).

The person of Mary stands out clearly in this picture; she is the only one, with the Apostles, mentioned by name. She represents one face of the Church, different from and complementary to the ministerial or hierarchical aspect.

3. In fact, Luke's statement mentions the presence in the Upper Room of some women, thus showing the importance of the feminine contribution to the Church's life from the very beginning. This presence is closely linked to the perseverance of the community in prayer and harmony. These traits perfectly express two basic aspects of women's specific contribution to ecclesial life. Better suited to outward activity, men need women's help to be brought back into personal relationships in order to progress towards the union of hearts.


## Mary's Role Had Notable Importance

"Blessed among women" (Lk 1:42), Mary eminently fills this feminine mission. Who better than Mary can encourage all believers to persevere in prayer? Who better than she can promote harmony and love?

Recognizing the pastoral mission entrusted by Jesus to the Eleven, the women in the Upper Room, with Mary in their midst, joined in their prayer and at the same time witnessed to the presence in the Church of people who, although they have not received that mission, are likewise full-fledged members of the community gathered in faith in Christ.

4. Mary's presence in the community, which was waiting in prayer for the outpouring of the Spirit (cf. Acts 1:14), calls to mind her part in the Incarnation of the Son of God by the work of the Holy Spirit (cf. Lk 1:35). The Virgin's role in that initial stage and the role she plays now, in the manifestation of the Church at Pentecost, are closely linked.

Mary's presence at the first moments of the Church's life is remarkably highlighted by comparison with her previous, very discreet participation during Jesus' public ministry. When the Son began his mission, Mary remained in Nazareth, even though this separation did not exclude significant contacts such as the one at Cana. Above all, it did not prevent her from taking part in the sacrifice of Calvary.

In the first community, however, Mary's role assumes notable importance. After the ascension and in expectation of Pentecost, Jesus' Mother is personally present at the first stages of the work begun by her Son.

5. The Acts of the Apostles stress that Mary was in the Upper Room "with his [Jesus'] brethren" (Acts 1:14), that is, with his relatives, as has always been the Church's interpretation. It was not so much a family gathering as the fact that under Mary's guidance, Jesus' natural family came to be part of Christ's spiritual family: "Whoever does the will of God", Jesus had said, "is my brother and sister, and mother" (Mk 3:35).

On the same occasion, Luke explicitly described Mary as "the mother of Jesus" (Acts 1:14), almost as if he wished to suggest that something of the presence of the Son ascended into heaven has remained in the presence of the mother. She reminded his disciples of Jesus' face and, with her presence in the community, is the symbol of the Church's fidelity to Christ the Lord.

The title of "Mother", in this context, proclaims the attitude of thoughtful closeness with which Our Lady followed the Church's life. Mary was to open her heart to the Church to show the marvels done in her by the almighty and merciful God.

## Mary Is A Teacher Of Prayer For Christians

From the very beginning, Mary carried out her role as "Mother of the Church": her action encouraged understanding between the Apostles, whom Luke describes as being of "one accord", far from the disputes that had occasionally arisen among them.

Lastly, Mary expressed her motherhood towards the community of believers not only by praying to obtain for the

Church the gifts of the Holy Spirit necessary for her formation and her future, but also by teaching the Lord's disciples about constant communion with God.

She thus became the Christian people's teacher of prayer, of encounter with God, a central and indispensable element, so that the work of the Pastors and the faithful would always have its beginning and its inner motivation in the Lord.

6. From these brief remarks it can clearly be seen how the relationship between Mary and the Church is a fascinating comparison between two mothers. It clearly reveals Mary's maternal mission and the Church's commitment ever to seek her true identity in contemplation of the face of the Theotokos.

# Mary Is The Virgin Mother Of God

*At the General Audience of Wednesday, 13 September, 1995, the Holy Father continued the catechesis he had begun the previous week on the Blessed Virgin Mary. In this talk he discussed the mystery of Mary's virginal motherhood and the title officially attributed to her by the Council of Ephesus in 431. Here is a translation of the Pope's catechesis, which was the second in the series on the Blessed Virgin and was given in Italian.*

1. In the Constitution *Lumen Gentium*, the Council states that "joined to Christ the head and in communion with all his saints, the faithful must in the first place reverence the memory 'of the glorious ever Virgin Mary, Mother of God and of our Lord Jesus Christ'" (n. 52). The conciliar Constitution uses these terms from the Roman Canon of the Mass, thereby stressing how faith in the divine motherhood of Mary has been present in Christian thought since the first centuries.

In the newborn Church Mary is remembered with the title "Mother of Jesus". It is Luke himself who gives her this title in the Acts of the Apostles, a title that corresponds moreover to what is said in the Gospels: "Is this not... the Son of Mary?", the residents of Nazareth wonder according to the Evangelist Mark's account

(6:3); "Isn't Mary known to be his mother?", is the question recorded by Matthew (13:55).

## The Motherhood Of Mary Also Concerns The Church

2. In the disciples' eyes, as they gathered after the ascension, the title "Mother of Jesus" acquires its full meaning. For them, Mary is a person unique in her kind: she received the singular grace of giving birth to the Savior of humanity; she lived for a long while at his side; and on Calvary she was called by the Crucified One to exercise a "new motherhood" in relation to the beloved disciple and, through him, to the whole Church.

For those who believe in Jesus and follow him, "Mother of Jesus" is a title of honor and veneration, and will forever remain such in the faith and life of the Church. In a particular way, by this title Christians mean to say that one cannot refer to Jesus' origins without acknowledging the role of the woman who gave him birth in the Spirit according to his human nature. Her maternal role also involves the birth and growth of the Church. In recalling the place of Mary in Jesus' life, the faithful discover each day her efficacious presence in their own spiritual journey.

3. From the beginning, the Church has acknowledged the virginal motherhood of Mary. As the infancy Gospels enable us to grasp, the first Christian communities themselves gathered together Mary's recollections about the mysterious circumstances of the Savior's conception and birth. In particular, the Annunciation account responds to the disciples' desire to have the deepest knowledge of the events connected with the beginnings of the risen Christ's earthly life. In the last analysis, Mary is at the origin of the revelation about the mystery of the virginal conception by the work of the Holy Spirit.

This truth, showing Jesus' divine origin, was immediately grasped by the first Christians for its important significance and included among the key affirmations of their faith. Son of Joseph according to the law, Jesus in fact, by an extraordinary intervention of the Holy Spirit, was in his humanity only the Son of Mary, since he was born without the intervention of man.

Mary's virginity thus acquires a unique value and casts new light on the birth of Jesus and on the mystery of his sonship, since the virginal generation is the sign that Jesus has God himself as his Father.

Acknowledged and proclaimed by the faith of the Fathers, the virginal motherhood can never be separated from the identity of Jesus, true God and true man, as "born of the Virgin Mary, as we profess in the Nicene-Constantinopolitan Creed. Mary is the only Virgin who is also a Mother. The extraordinary co-presence of these two gifts in the person of the maiden of Nazareth has led Christians to call Mary simply "the Virgin", even when they celebrate her motherhood.

The virginity of Mary thus initiates in the Christian community the spread of the virginal life, embraced by all who are called to it by the Lord. This special vocation, which reaches its apex in Christ's example, represents immeasurable spiritual wealth for the Church in every age, which finds in Mary her inspiration and model.

## 'Mother Of God' Was Expression Of Popular Piety

4. The assertion: "Jesus was born of the Virgin Mary" already implies in this event a transcendent mystery, which can find its most complete expression only in the truth of Jesus' divine sonship. The truth of Mary's divine motherhood is closely tied to this central statement of the Christian faith: she is indeed the Mother of the Incarnate Word, in whom is "God from God... true God from true God".

The title "Mother of God", already attested by Matthew in the equivalent expression "Mother of Emmanuel", God with us (cf. Mt 1:23), was explicitly attributed to Mary only after a reflection that embraced about two centuries. It is third century Christians in Egypt who begin to invoke Mary as "Theotokos", Mother of God.

With this title, which is broadly echoed in the devotion of the Christian people, Mary is seen in the true dimension of her motherhood: she is the Mother of God's Son, whom she virginally begot according to his human nature and raised him with her motherly love, thus contributing to the human growth of the divine person who came to transform the destiny of mankind.

5. In a highly significant way, the most ancient prayer to Mary ("Sub tuam praesidium...", "We fly to thy patronage...") contains the invocation: "Theotokos, Mother of God". This title did not originally come from the reflection of theologians, but from an intuition of faith of the Christian people. Those who acknowledge Jesus as God address Mary as the Mother of God and hope to obtain her powerful aid in the trials of life.

The Council of Ephesus in 431 defined the dogma of the divine motherhood, officially attributing to Mary the title "Theotokos" in reference to the one person of Christ, true God and true man.

The three expressions which the Church has used down the centuries to describe her faith in the motherhood of Mary: "Mother of Jesus", "Virgin Mother and "Mother of God", thus show that Mary's motherhood is intimately linked with the mystery of the Incarnation. They are affirmations of doctrine, connected as well with popular piety, which help define the very identity of Christ.

# Mary Was United To Jesus On The Cross

*At the General Audience of Wednesday, 25 October, 1995, the Holy Father returned to his catechesis on the Blessed Virgin Mary and her participation in her Son's saving work. "Mary is our Mother: this consoling truth, offered to us ever more clearly and profoundly by the love and faith of the Church, has sustained and sustains the spiritual life of us all, and encourages us, even in suffering, to have faith and hope". Here is a translation of the Pope's address, which was given in Italian and was the third in the series on the Blessed Virgin.*

1. Saying that "the Virgin Mary... is acknowledged and honored as being truly the Mother of God and of the Redeemer" (*Lumen Gentium*, n. 53), the Council draws attention to the link

between Mary's motherhood and Redemption.

After becoming aware of the maternal role of Mary, who was venerated in the teaching and worship of the first centuries as the virginal Mother of Jesus Christ and therefore as the Mother of God, in the Middle Ages the Church's piety and theological reflection brought to light her cooperation in the Savior's work.

This delay is explained by the fact that the efforts of the Church Fathers and of the early Ecumenical Councils, focused as they were on Christ's identity, necessarily left other aspects of dogma aside. Only gradually could the revealed truth be unfolded in all its richness. Down the centuries, Mariology would always take its direction from Christology. The divine motherhood of Mary was itself proclaimed at the Council of Ephesus primarily to affirm the oneness of Christ's person. Similarly, there was a deeper understanding of Mary's presence in salvation history.

2. At the end of the second century, St. Irenaeus, a disciple of Polycarp, already pointed out Mary's contribution to the work of salvation. He understood the value of Mary's consent at the time of the Annunciation, recognizing in the Virgin of Nazareth's obedience to and faith in the angel's message the perfect antithesis of Eve's disobedience and disbelief, with a beneficial effect on humanity's destiny. In fact, just as Eve caused death, so Mary, with her "yes", became "a cause of salvation" for herself and for all mankind (cf. Adv. Haer., III, 22,4; 5C211, 441). But this affirmation was not developed in a consistent and systematic way by the other Fathers of the Church.

## Mary Became Spiritual Mother Of Whole Human Race

Instead, this doctrine was systematically worked out for the first time at the end of the 10th century in the Life of Mary by a Byzantine monk, John the Geometer. Here Mary is united to Christ in the whole work of Redemption, sharing, according to God's plan, in the Cross and suffering for our salvation. She remained united to the Son "in every deed, attitude and wish" (cf. Life of Mary, Bol. 196, f. 122 v.). Mary's association with Jesus' saving work came about through her Mother's love, a love inspired by grace, which conferred a higher power on it: love freed of passion proves to be the most compassionate (cf. ibid., Bol. 196, f. 123 v.).

3. In the West St. Bernard, who died in 1153, turns to Mary and comments on the presentation of Jesus in the temple: "Offer your Son, sacrosanct Virgin, and present the fruit of your womb to the Lord. For our reconciliation with all, offer the heavenly victim pleasing to God" (Serm. 3 in Purif., 2: PL 183, 370).

A disciple and friend of St. Bernard, Arnold of Chartres, shed light particularly on Mary's offering in the sacrifice of Calvary. He distinguished in the Cross "two altars: one in Mary's heart, the other in Christ's body. Christ sacrificed his flesh, Mary her soul". Mary sacrificed herself spiritually in deep communion with Christ, and implored the world's salvation: "What the mother asks, the Son approves and the Father grants" (cf. De septem verbis Domini in cruce, 3: PL 189, 1694). From this age on other authors explain the doctrine of Mary's special cooperation in the redemptive sacrifice.

4. At the same time, in Christian worship and piety contemplative reflection on Mary's "compassion" developed, poignantly depicted in images of the Pieta'. Mary's sharing in the drama of the Cross makes this event more deeply human and helps the faithful to enter into the mystery: the Mother's compassion more clearly reveals the Passion of the Son.

By sharing in Christ's redemptive work, Mary's spiritual and universal motherhood is also recognized. In the East, John the Geometer told Mary: "You are our mother". Giving Mary thanks "for the sorrow and suffering she bore for us", he sheds light on her maternal affection and motherly regard for all those who receive salvation (cf. Farewell Discourse on the Dormition of Our Most Glorious Lady, Mother of God, in A. Wenger, LAssomption de la Tres Sainte Vierge dans la tradition Byzantine, p.407).

In the West too, the doctrine of the spiritual motherhood developed with St. Anselm, who asserted: "You are the mother ... of reconciliation and the reconciled, the mother of salvation and the saved" (cf. Oratio 52, 8: PL 158, 957 A). Mary does not cease to be venerated as the Mother of God, but the fact that she is our Mother gives her divine motherhood a new aspect that opens within us the way to a more intimate communion with her.

5. Mary's motherhood in our regard does not only consist of an affective bond: because of her merits and her intercession she contributes effectively to our spiritual birth and to the development of the life of grace within us. This is why Mary is called "Mother of grace" and "Mother of life".

## Mother Of The Life From Whom All Take Life

The title "Mother of life", already employed by St. Gregory of Nyssa, was explained as follows by Bl. Guerric of Igny, who died in 1157: "She is the Mother of the Life from whom all men take life: in giving birth to this life herself, she has somehow given rebirth to all those who have lived it. Only one was begotten, but we have all been reborn" (In Assumpt I, 2: PL 185, 188).

A 13th century text, the Mariale, used a vivid image in attributing this rebirth to the "painful travail" of Cavalry, by which "she became the spiritual mother of the whole human race". Indeed, "in her chaste womb she conceived by compassion the children of the Church" (0.29, par. 3).

6. The Second Vatican Council, after stating that Mary "in a wholly singular way cooperated in the work of the Savior, concludes: "for this reason she is a mother to us in the order of grace" (*Lumen Gentium*, n. 61), thus coming the Church's perception that Mary is at the side of her Son as the spiritual Mother of all humanity.

Mary is our Mother: this consoling truth, offered to us ever more clearly and profoundly by the love and faith of the Church, has sustained and sustains the spiritual life of us all, and encourages us, even in suffering, to have faith and hope.

# Church Grew In Understanding Of Mary's Role

*"The sparse information on Mary's earthly life is compensated by its quality and theological richness, which contemporary exegesis has carefully brought to light", the Holy*

*Father said at the General Audience of 8 November, 1995, as he continued his reflections on the Virgin Mary. The Pope's catechesis on Mary in Sacred Scripture and theological reflection was the fourth in the series on the Blessed Mother and was given in Italian.*

1. In our preceding catecheses we saw how the doctrine of Mary's motherhood passed from its first formula, "Mother of Jesus", to the more complete and explicit, "Mother of God", even to the affirmation of her maternal involvement in the redemption of humanity.

For other aspects of Marian doctrine as well, many centuries were necessary to arrive at the explicit definition of the revealed truths concerning Mary. Typical examples of this faith Journey towards the ever deeper discovery of Mary's role in the history of salvation are the dogma of the Immaculate Conception and the Assumption, proclaimed, as we know by two of my venerable predecessors, respectively, the Servant of God Pius IX in 1854, and the Servant of God Pius XII during the Jubilee Year of 1950.

Mariology is a particular field of theological research: in it the Christian people's love for Mary intuited, frequently in anticipation, certain aspects of the mystery of the Blessed Virgin, calling the attention of theologians and pastors to them.

## Mother Of Jesus Had Role In Salvation History

2. We must recognize that, at first sight, the Gospels offer scant information on the person and life of Mary. We would certainly like to have had fuller information about her, which would have enabled us to know the Mother of God better.

This expectation remains unsatisfied, even in the other New Testament writings where an explicit doctrinal development regarding Mary is lacking. Even St. Paul's letters, which offer us a rich reflection on Christ and his work, limit themselves to stating, in a very significant passage, that God sent his Son "born of woman" (Gal 4:4).

Very little is said about Mary's family. If we exclude the infancy narratives, in the Synoptic Gospels we find only two statements which shed some light on Mary: one concerning the attempt by his "brethren" or relatives to take Jesus back to Nazareth (cf. Mk 3:21; Mt 12:48); the other, in response to a woman's exclamation about the blessedness of Jesus' Mother (Lk 11:27).

Nevertheless, Luke, in the infancy Gospel, in the episodes of the Annunciation, the Visitation, the birth of Jesus, the presentation of the Child in the temple and his finding among the teachers at the age of 12, not only provides us with some important facts, but presents a sort of "proto-Mariology" of fundamental interest. His information is indirectly completed by Matthew in the account of the annunciation to Joseph (Mt 1:18-25), but only with regard to the virginal conception of Jesus.

Moreover, John's Gospel deepens our knowledge of the value for salvation history of the role played by the Mother of Jesus, when it records her presence at the beginning and end of his public life. Particularly significant is Mary's presence at the Cross, when she received from her dying Son the charge to be mother to the beloved disciple and, in him, to all Christians (cf. Jn 2:1-12; Jn 19:25-27).

Lastly, the Acts of the Apostles expressly numbers the Mother of Jesus among the women of the first community awaiting Pentecost (cf. Acts 1:14).

However, in the absence of farther New Testament evidence and reliable historical sources, we know nothing of Mary's life after the Pentecost event, nor of the date and circumstances of her death. We can only suppose that she continued to live with the Apostle John and that she was very closely involved in the development of the first Christian community.

3. The sparse information on Mary's earthly life is compensated by its quality and theological richness, which contemporary exegesis has carefully brought to light.

Moreover, we must remember that the Evangelists' viewpoint is totally Christological and is concerned with the Mother only in relation to the joyful proclamation of the Son. As St. Ambrose observed, the Evangelist, in expounding the mystery of the Incarnation, 'believed it was better not to seek further testimonies about Mary's virginity, in order not to seem the defender of the Virgin rather than the preacher of the mystery" (Exp. in Lucam, 2, 6: PL 15, 1555).

We can recognize in this fact a special intention of the Holy Spirit, who desired to awaken in the Church an effort of research which, preserving the centrality of the mystery of Christ, might not be caught up in details about Mary's life, but aim above all at discovering her role in the work of salvation, her personal holiness and her maternal mission in Christian life.

## Faith Of The Simple Recognized Mary's Holiness

4. The Holy Spirit guides the Church's effort, committing her to take on Mary's own attitudes. In the account of Jesus' birth, Luke noted how his mother kept all these things, "pondering them in her heart" (Lk 2:19), striving, that is, to "put together" (symballousa), in a deeper vision, all the events of which she was the privileged witness.

Similarly, the people of God are also urged by the same Spirit to understand deeply all that has been said about Mary, in order to progress in the knowledge of her mission, intimately linked to the mystery of Christ.

As Mariology develops, the particular role of the Christian people emerges. They cooperate, by the affirmation and witness of their faith, in the progress of Marian doctrine, which normally is not only the work of theologians, even if their task is indispensable to deepening and clearly explaining the datum of faith and the Christian experience itself.

The faith of the simple is admired and praised by Jesus, who recognized in it a marvelous expression of the Father's benevolence (cf. Mt 11:25; Lk 10:21). Down the centuries it continues to proclaim the marvels of the history of salvation, hidden from the wise. This faith, in harmony with the Virgin's simplicity, has led to progress in the recognition of her personal holiness and the transcendent value of her motherhood.

The mystery of Mary commits every Christian, in communion with the Church, "to pondering in his heart" what the Gospel revelation affirms about the Mother of Christ. In the logic of the Magnificat, after the example of Mary, each one will personally experience God's love and will discover a sign of God's tenderness for man in the marvels wrought by the Blessed Trinity in the woman "full of grace".

# To Honor Mary Is To Go To Jesus

*"It can be clearly seen... how the Marian dimension pervades the Church's whole life. The proclamation of the Word, the liturgy, the various charitable and cultural expressions find in Mary an occasion for enrichment and renewal", the Holy Father said at the General Audience on Wednesday, 15 November, 1995, as he continued his reflections on the Virgin Mary. The Pope's catechesis on Mary in the spiritual experience of the Church was the fifth in the series on the Blessed Mother and was given in Italian.*

1. After following in our previous catecheses how the Christian community's reflection on the figure and role of the Blessed Virgin in salvation history took shape from the earliest times, let us pause today to meditate on the Marian experience of the Church.

The development of Mariological thought and devotion to the Blessed Virgin down the centuries has contributed to revealing ever better the Church's Marian aspect. Of course, the Blessed Virgin is totally related to Christ, the foundation of faith and ecclesial experience, and she leads to him. That is why, in obedience to Jesus, who reserved a very special role for his Mother in the economy of salvation, Christians have venerated, loved and prayed to Mary in a most particular and fervent way. They have attributed to her an important place in faith and piety, recognizing her as the privileged way to Christ, the supreme Mediator.

The Church's Marian dimension is thus an undeniable element in the experience of the Christian people. It is expressed in many ways in the life of believers; testifying to the place Mary holds in their hearts. It is not a superficial sentiment but a deep and conscious emotional bond, rooted in the faith which spurs Christians of the past and present to turn habitually to Mary, to enter into a more intimate communion with Christ.

2. After the most ancient prayer, formulated in Egypt by the Christian communities of the third century, to implore "the Mother of God" for protection in danger, numerous invocations were addressed to her, whom the baptized consider most powerful in her intercession with the Lord.

## Christian People Have Expressed Deep Devotion To Mary

Today, the most common prayer is the Hail Mary, whose first part consists of words from the Gospel (cf. Lk 1:28, 42). Christians learn to recite it at home from their earliest years and receive ft as a precious gift to be preserved throughout life. This same prayer, repeated tens of times in the Rosary, helps many of the faithful to enter into prayerful contemplation of the Gospel mysteries and sometimes to remain for long intervals in intimate contact with the Mother of Jesus. Since the Middle Ages, the Hail Mary has been the most common prayer of all believers who ask the Holy Mother of the Lord to guide and, protect them on their daily journey through life (cf. Apostolic Exhortation Marialis Cultus, nn. 42-55).

Christian people have also expressed their love for Mary by multiplying expressions of their devotion: hymns, prayers and poetic compositions, simple or sometimes of great quality, imbued with that same love for her who was given to men as Mother by the Crucified One. Some of these, such as the "Akathist Hymn" and the "Salve Regina", have deeply marked the faith life of believers.

The counterpart of Marian piety is the immensely rich artistic production in the East and West, which has enabled entire generations to appreciate Mary's spiritual beauty. Painters, sculptors, musicians and poets have left us masterpieces which, in shedding light on the various aspects of the Blessed Virgin's greatness, help to give us a better understanding of the meaning and value of her lofty contribution to the work of Redemption.

In Mary, Christian art recognizes the fulfillment of a new humanity which corresponds to God's plan and is therefore a sublime sign of hope for the whole human race.

3. This message could not fail to be grasped by Christians called to a vocation of special consecration. In fact, Mary is particularly venerated in religious orders and congregations, in institutes or associations of consecrated life. Many institutes, primarily but not only female, include Mary's name in their tide. Nevertheless, over and above its external expressions, the spirituality of religious families, as well as of many ecclesial movements, some of which are specifically Marian, highlight their special bond with Mary as the guarantee of a charism fully and authentically lived.

This Marian reference in the lives of people particularly favored by the Holy Spirit has also developed the mystical dimension, which shows how the Christian can experience Mary's intervention in the innermost depths of his being.

This reference to Mary binds not only committed Christians but also simple believers and even the "distant", for whom it is frequently their only link with the life of the Church. Pilgrimages to Marian shrines, which attract large crowds of the faithful throughout the year, are a sign of the Christian people's common sentiment for the Mother of the Lord. Some of these bulwarks of Marian piety are famous, such as Lourdes, Fatima, Loreto, Pompeii, Guadalupe and Czestochowa! Others are known only at the national or local level. In all of them, the memory of events associated with recourse to Mary conveys the message of her motherly tenderness, opening our hearts to God's grace.

These places of Marian prayer are a wonderful testimony to God's mercy, which reaches man through Mary's intercession. The miracles of physical healing, spiritual redemption and conversion are the obvious sign that, with Christ and in the Spirit, Mary is continuing her work as helper and mother.

## Marian Dimension Pervades Church's Whole Life

4. Marian shrines often become centers of evangelization. Indeed, even in the Church today, as in the community awaiting Pentecost, prayer with Mary spurs many Christians to the

apostolate and to the service of their brothers and sisters. Here I would especially like to recall the great influence of Marian piety on the practice of charity and the works of mercy. Encouraged by Mary's presence, believers have often felt the need to dedicate themselves to the poor, the unfortunate and the sick, in order to be for the lowliest of the earth a sign of the motherly protection of the Blessed Virgin, the living icon of the Father's mercy.

It can be clearly seen from all this how the Marian dimension pervades the Church's whole life. The proclamation of the Word, the liturgy, the various charitable and cultural expressions find in Mary an occasion for enrichment and renewal.

The People of God, under the guidance of their Pastors, are called to discern in this fact the action of the Holy Spirit who has spurred the Christian faith onward in its discovery of Mary's face. It is he who works marvels in the centers of Marian piety. It is he who, by encouraging knowledge of and love for Mary, leads the faithful to learn from the Virgin of the Magnificat how to read the signs of God in history and to acquire a wisdom that makes every man and every woman the architects of a new humanity.

# Mary Is Model Of Preserving Silence

*"Our Lady's motherly smile, reproduced in so much Marian iconography, expresses a fullness of grace and peace that seeks to be shared. This expression of her serenity of spirit effectively contributes to giving the Church a joyful face", the Holy Father said at the General Audience on Wednesday, 22 November, 1995, as he continued his reflections on the Virgin Mary. The Pope's catechesis on Mary's influence on the Church's life was the sixth in the series on the Blessed Mother and was given in Italian.*

1. After reflecting on the Marian dimension of ecclesial life, we are now going to cast light on the immense spiritual wealth Mary communicates to the Church by her example and her intercession.

We could first like to pause and briefly reflect on some

significant aspects of Mary's personality, which offer all believers valuable guidance in accepting and fulfilling their own vocation.

Mary has gone before us on the way of faith: believing the angel's message, she was the first to welcome the mystery of the Incarnation and did so perfectly (cf. *Redemptoris Mater*, n. 13). Her journey as a believer began even earlier than her divine motherhood and developed more deeply throughout her earthly experience. Hers was a daring faith. At the Annunciation she believed in what was humanly impossible, and at Cana she urged Jesus to work his first miracle, pressing him to manifest his messianic powers (cf. Jn 2:1-5).

Mary teaches Christians to live their faith as a demanding and engaging journey, which, in every age and situation of life, requires courage and constant perseverance.

## Mary's Was A Humble And Hidden Life

2. Mary's docility to the divine will was linked to her faith. Believing in God's word, she could accept it fully in her life and, showing herself receptive to God's sovereign plan, she accepted all that was asked of her from on high.

Our Lady's presence in the Church thus encourages Christians to listen to the word of the Lord every day, to understand his loving plan in various daily events, and to cooperate faithfully in bringing it about.

3. This is how Mary teaches the community of believers to look to the future with total abandonment to God. In the Virgin's personal experience, hope is enriched with ever new reasons. Since the Annunciation, Mary concentrates the expectations of ancient Israel on the Son of God, incarnate in her virginal womb. Her hope was strengthened during the successive stages of Jesus' hidden life in Nazareth and his public ministry. Her great faith in the word of Christ, who had announced his resurrection on the third day, prevented her from wavering, even when faced with the drama of the Cross. She retained her hope in the fulfillment of the messianic work and steadfastly, after the darkness of Good Friday, awaited the morning of the resurrection.

On their difficult path through history, between the "already" of salvation received and the "not yet" of its fulfillment, the community of believers know they can count on the help of the "Mother of Hope". After experiencing Christ's victory over the powers of death, she communicates to them an ever new capacity to await God's future and to abandon themselves to the Lord's promises.

4. Mary's example enables the Church better to appreciate the value of silence. Mary's silence is not only moderation in speech, but it is especially a wise capacity for remembering and embracing in a single gaze of faith the mystery of the Word made man and the events of his earthly life.

It is this silence as acceptance of the Word, this ability to meditate on the mystery of Christ, that Mary passes on to believers. In a noisy world filled with messages of all kinds, her witness enables us to appreciate a spiritually rich silence and fosters a contemplative spirit.

Mary witnesses to the value of a humble and hidden life. Everyone usually demands, and sometimes almost claims, to be able to realize fully his own person and qualities. Everyone is sensitive to esteem and honor. The Gospels frequently mention that the Apostles were ambitious for the most important places in the kingdom and they argued among themselves as to which of them was the greatest. In this matter Jesus had to teach them the need for humility and service (cf. Mt 18:1-5; 20:20-28; Mk 9:33-37; 10:35-45; Lk 9:46-48; 22:24-27). Mary, on the contrary, never sought honor or the advantages of a privileged position; she always tried to fulfill God's will, leading a life according to the Father's plan of salvation.

To all those who often feel the burden of a seemingly insignificant life, Mary reveals how valuable life can be if t it is lived for love of Christ and one's brothers and sisters.

5. Mary, moreover, witnesses to the , value of a life that is pure and full of tenderness for all men. The beauty of her soul, totally offered to the Lord, is an object of admiration for the Christian people. In Mary, the Christian community has always seen the ideal woman, a full of love and tenderness because she lived in purity of mind and body. Faced with the cynicism of a certain

contemporary culture, which too often seems not to recognize the value of chastity and degrades sexuality by separating it from personal dignity and God's plan, the Virgin Mary holds up the witness of a purity that illumines the conscience and leads to a greater love for creatures and for the Lord.

6. Furthermore, Mary appears to Christians of all times as the one who feels deep compassion for the sufferings of humanity. This compassion does not consist only in an emotional sympathy, but is expressed in effective and concrete help when confronted with humanity's material and moral misery.

In following Mary, the Church is called to take on the same attitude towards all the earth's poor and suffering. The maternal attention of the Lord's Mother to the tears, sorrows and hardships of the men and women of all ages must spur Christians, particularly at the dawn of the new millennium, to increase the concrete and visible signs of a love that will enable today's humble and suffering people to share in the promises and hopes of the new world which is born from Easter.

7. Human affection for and devotion to the Mother of Jesus surpasses the Church's visible boundaries and fosters sentiments of reconciliation. As a mother, Mary desires the union of all her children. Her presence in the Church is an invitation to preserve the unanimity of heart which reigned in the first community (cf. Acts 1:14) and, consequently, to seek ways of unity and peace among all men and women of goodwill.

In interceding with her Son, Mary asks the grace of unity for all humanity, in view of building a civilization of love, overcoming tendencies to division, temptations to revenge and hatred, and the perverse fascination of violence.

## Mary Is The Cause Of Our Joy

8. Our Lady's motherly smile, reproduced in so much Marian iconography, expresses a fullness of grace and peace that seeks to be shared. This expression of her serenity of spirit effectively contributes to giving the Church a joyful face.

Welcoming, in the Annunciation, the angel's invitation to "rejoice" (khaire - rejoice: Lk 1:28), Mary was the first to share in the messianic joy foretold by the Prophets for the "daughter of Zion" (cf. Is 12:6; Zep 3:14-15; Zec 9:9), and she passes it on to humanity in every age.

Invoking her as "causa nostrae laetitiae", the Christian people find in her the capacity to communicate the joy that is born of hope, even in the midst of life's trials, and to guide those who commend themselves to her to the joy that knows no end.

# Mary Shows Us God's Respect For Women

*The figure of Mary shows that God has such esteem for woman that any form of discrimination lacks a theoretical basis", the Holy Father said at the General Audience of Wednesday, 29 November, 1995, as he continued his reflections on the Virgin Mary. The Pope's catechesis on Mary and the value of woman was the seventh in the series on the Blessed Mother and was given in Italian.*

1. The theological and spiritual aspects of the Church's teaching on Mary, which have been amply developed in our century, have recently acquired a new importance from the sociological and pastoral standpoint, due also to a clearer understanding of woman's role in the Christian community and in society, as we see in many significant interventions of the Magisterium.

The message to women addressed by the Fathers at the conclusion of the Second Vatican Council on 8 December 1965 are well known: "But the hour is coming, in fact has come, when the vocation of woman is being achieved in its fullness, the hour in which woman acquires in the world an influence, an effect and a power never hitherto achieved" (Enchiridion Val, I, 307).

I confirmed these affirmations a few years later in the Encyclical Mulieris dignitatem: "The dignity and the vocation of women, a subject of constant human and Christian reflection, have gained exceptional prominence in recent years" (n. 1).

The role and dignity of woman have been particularly

championed this century by the feminist movement, which has sought to react, sometimes in forceful ways, against everything in the past and present that has hindered the full appreciation and development of the feminine personality as well as her participation in the many expressions of social and political life.

These demands were in large part legitimate and contributed to building up a more balanced view of the feminine question in the contemporary world. The Church, especially in recent times, has paid special attention to these demands, encouraged by the fact that the figure of Mary, if seen in the light of her Gospel life, is a valid response to woman's desire for emancipation: Mary is the only human person who eminently fulfills God's plan of love for humanity.

## Every Woman Shares In Mary's Sublime Dignity

2. This plan is already manifest in the Old Testament, with the creation narrative that introduces the first couple created in the image of God himself: "So God created man in his own image, in the image of God he created him; male and female he created them" (Gn 1:27). Thus woman, no less than man, bears God's image in herself. This means that, since her appearance on the earth as a result of the divine action, she too is appreciated: "God saw everything that he had made, and behold, it was very good" (Gn 1:31). According to this view, the difference between man and woman does not imply the inferiority of the latter nor her inequality, but is a new element which enriches God's plan, and is "very good".

However, God's intention goes well beyond what is revealed in the Book of Genesis. In fact, in Mary God created a feminine personality which greatly surpasses the ordinary condition of woman as it appears in the creation of Eve. Mary's unique excellence in the world of grace and her perfection are fruits of the particular divine benevolence which seeks to raise everyone, men and women, to the moral perfection and holiness which are proper to the adopted children of God. Mary is "blessed among women"; however, every woman shares in some way in her sublime dignity in the divine plan.

3. The remarkable gift to the Mother of the Lord not only testifies to what we could call God's respect for woman, but also emphasizes the profound regard in God's plans for her irreplaceable role in human history.

Women need to discover this divine esteem in order to be ever more aware of their lofty dignity. The historical and social situations which caused the reaction of feminism were marked by a lack of appreciation of woman's worth; frequently she was relegated to a second-rate or even marginal role. This did not allow her to express fully the wealth of intelligence and wisdom contained in her femininity. Indeed, throughout history women have not infrequently suffered from scant esteem for their abilities, and sometimes even scorn and unjust prejudice. This is a state of affairs that, despite important changes, unfortunately continues even today in many nations and in many parts of the world.

4. The figure of Mary shows that God has such esteem for woman that any form of discrimination lacks a theoretical basis. The marvelous work which the Creator achieved in Mary gives men and women the possibility to discover dimensions of their condition which before were not sufficiently perceived. In beholding the Mother of the Lord, women will be able to understand better their dignity and the greatness of their mission. But men too, in the light of the Virgin Mother, will be able to acquire a fuller and more balanced view of their identity, of the family and of society.

Attentive consideration of the figure of Mary, as she is presented to us in Sacred Scripture as read in faith by the Church, is still more necessary in view of the disparagement she sometimes receives from certain feminist currents. The Virgin of Nazareth has, in some cases, been presented as the symbol of the female personality imprisoned in a narrow, confining domesticity.

Mary, on the contrary, is the model of the full development of woman's vocation, since, despite the objective limits imposed by her social condition, she exercised a vast influence on the destiny of humanity and the transformation of society.

## In Mary All Are Called To Trust The Lord

5. Moreover Marian doctrine can shed light on the multiple ways in which the life of grace promotes woman's spiritual beauty.

In view of the shameful exploitation that sometimes makes woman an object without dignity, destined for the satisfaction of base passions, Mary reaffirms the sublime meaning of feminine beauty, a gift and reflection of God's beauty.

It is true that feminine perfection, as it was fully realized in Mary, can at first sight seem to be an exceptional case and impossible to imitate, a model too lofty for imitation. In fact, the unique holiness of her who from the very first moment received the privilege of the Immaculate Conception is sometimes considered unreachably distant.

However, far from being a restraint on the way of following the Lord, Mary's exalted holiness is, on the contrary, destined in God's plan to encourage all Christians to open themselves to the sanctifying power of the grace of God, for whom nothing is impossible. Therefore in Mary all are called to put total trust in the divine omnipotence, which transforms hearts, guiding them towards full receptivity to his providential plan of love.

# Mary Sheds Light On Role Of Women

*At the General Audience of Wednesday, 6 December, 1995, the Holy Father continued his catechesis on the Virgin Mary, calling particular attention to her as the model for woman's role in the contemporary world. Here is a translation of his address, which was the eighth in the series on the Blessed Virgin and was given in Italian.*

1. As I have already explained in the preceding catecheses, the role entrusted to Mary by the divine plan of salvation sheds light on the vocation of woman in the life of the Church and society by defining its difference in relation to man. The model represented by Mary clearly shows what is specific to the feminine personality.

In recent times some trends in the feminist movement, in order to advance women's emancipation, have sought to make her like man in every way. However, the divine intention manifested in creation, though desiring woman to be man's equal in dignity and worth, at the same time clearly affirms her diversity and specific features. Woman's identity cannot consist in being a copy of man, since she is endowed with her own qualities and prerogatives, which give her a particular uniqueness that is always to be fostered and encouraged. These prerogatives and particular features of the feminine personality attained their full development in Mary. The fullness of divine grace actually fostered in her all the natural abilities typical of woman.

## Let It Be Done To Me According To Your Word

Mary's role in the work of salvation is totally dependent on Christ's. It is a unique function, required by the fulfillment of the mystery of the Incarnation: Mary's motherhood was necessary to give the world its Savior, the true Son of God, but also perfectly man.

The importance of woman's cooperation in the coming of Christ is emphasized by the initiative of God, who, through the angel, communicates his plan of salvation to the Virgin of Nazareth so that she can consciously and freely cooperate by giving her own generous consent. Here the loftiest model of woman's collaboration in the Redemption of man every man is led; this model represents the transcendent reference point for every affirmation of woman's role and function in history.

2. In carrying out this sublime form of cooperation, Mary also shows the style in which woman must concretely express her mission.

With regard to the angel's message, the Virgin makes no proud demands nor does she seek to satisfy personal ambitions. Luke presents her to us as wanting only to offer her humble service with total and trusting acceptance of the divine plan of salvation. This is the meaning of her response: Behold, I am the handmaid of the Lord; let it be done to me according to your word" (Lk 1:38).

It is not a question of a purely passive acceptance, since her consent is given only after she has expressed the difficulty that arose from her intent to remain a virgin, inspired by her will to belong more completely to the Lord.

Having received the angel's response, Mary immediately expresses her readiness, maintaining an attitude of humble service.

It is the humble, valuable service that so many women, following Mary's example, have offered and continue to offer in the Church for the growth of Christ's kingdom.

3. The figure of Mary reminds women today of the value of motherhood. In the contemporary world the appropriate and balanced importance is not always given to this value. In some cases, the need for women to work in order to provide for the needs of their family and an erroneous concept of freedom, which sees child-care as a hindrance to woman's autonomy and opportunities, have obscured the significance of motherhood for the development of the feminine personality. On the contrary, in other cases the biological aspect of childbirth becomes so important as to overshadow the other significant opportunities woman has for expressing her innate vocation to being a mother.

In Mary we have been given to understand the true meaning of motherhood, which attains its loftiest dimension in the divine plan of salvation. For her, being a mother not only endows her feminine personality, directed towards the gift of life, with its full level but also represents an answer of faith to woman's own vocation,
which assumes its truest value only in the light of God's covenant (cf. Mulieris dignitatem, n. 19).

4. In looking attentively at Mary, we also discover in her the model of virginity lived for the kingdom. The Virgin par excellence, in her heart she grew in her desire to live in this state in order to achieve an ever deeper intimacy with God. For women called to virginal chastity, Mary reveals the lofty meaning of so special a vocation and thus draws attention to the spiritual fruitfulness which it produces in the divine plan: a higher order of motherhood, a motherhood according to the Spirit (cf. Mulieris dignitatem, n. 21).

## Women Sow The Seeds Of The Civilization Of Love

Mary's maternal heart, open to all human misfortune, also reminds women that the development of the feminine personality calls for a commitment to charity. More sensitive to the values of the heart, woman shows a high capacity for personal self-giving. To all in our age who offer selfish models for affirming the feminine personality, the luminous and holy figure of the Lord's Mother shows how only by self-giving and self-forgetfulness towards others is it possible to attain authentic fulfillment of the divine plan for one's own life. Mary's presence therefore encourages sentiments of mercy and solidarity in women for situations of human distress and arouses a desire to alleviate the pain of those who suffer: the poor, the sick and all in need of help. In virtue of her special bond with Mary, woman has often in the course of history represented God's closeness to the expectations of goodness and tenderness of a humanity wounded by hatred and sin, by sowing in the world seeds of a civilization that can respond to violence with love.

# Council's Teaching On Mary Is Rich and Positive

*The treatment of Mary by the Fathers of the Second Vatican Council was the subject of the Holy Father's weekly address at the General Audience of Wednesday, 13 December, 1995. The entire exposition in the eighth chapter of the Dogmatic Constitution on the Church clearly shows that terminological precautions did not prevent a very rich and positive presentation of basic doctrine, an expression of faith and love for her whom the Church acknowledges as Mother and Model", the Pope said. Here is a translation of his catechesis, which was the ninth in the series on the Blessed Virgin and was given in Italian.*

1. Today I would like to reflect on the particular presence of the Mother of the Church at what was certainly the most important ecclesial event of our century: the Second Vatican

Ecumenical Council, opened by Pope John XXIII on the morning of 11 October 1962 and closed by Pope Paul VI on 8 December 1965.

An extraordinary Marian tone actually marked the Council from its indiction. In the Apostolic letter Celebrandi Concihi Oecumenici, my venerable predecessor, the Servant of God John XXIII had already recommended recourse to the powerful intercession of Mary, "Mother of grace and heavenly patroness of the Council" (11 April 1961, *AAS* 53 [1961] 242).

## Treatment Of Mary Placed In Constitution On The Church

Subsequently, in 1962, on the feast of the Purification of Mary, Pope John set the opening of the Council for 11 October, explaining that he had chosen this date in memory of the great Council of Ephesus, which precisely on that date had proclaimed Mary "Theotokos", Mother of God (Motu, proprio Concilium; *AAS* 54 [1962] 67-68). Later, in his opening address, the Pope entrusted the Council itself to the "Help of Christians, Help of Bishops", imploring her motherly assistance for the successful outcome of the Council's work (*AAS* 54 [1962] 795).

The Council Fathers also turned their thoughts expressly to Mary in their message to the world at the opening of the Council's sessions, saying: "We successors of the Apostles, joined together in prayer with Mary, the Mother of Jesus, form one apostolic body" (Acta Synodalia, I, I, 254), thus linking themselves, in communion with Mary, to the early Church awaiting the Holy Spirit (cf. Acts 1:14).

2. At the second session of the Council it was proposed that the treatment of the Blessed Virgin Mary be put into the Constitution on the Church. This initiative, although expressly recommended by the Theological Commission, prompted a variety of opinions.

Some, who considered this proposal inadequate for emphasizing the very special mission of Jesus' Mother in the Church, maintained that only a separate document could express

Mary's dignity, pre-eminence, exceptional holiness and unique role in the Redemption accomplished by the Son. Furthermore, regarding Mary as above the Church in a certain way, they were afraid that the decision to put the Marian teaching in the treatment of the Church would not sufficiently emphasize Mary's privileges and would reduce her role to the level of other members of the Church (Acta Synodalia, II, III, 338-342).

Others, however, spoke in favor of the Theological Commission's proposal to put the doctrinal treatment of Mary and the Church in a single document. According to them, these realities could not be separated at a Council which, in airing to rediscover the identity and mission of the People of God, had to show its close connection with her who is the type and exemplar of the Church in her virginity and motherhood. Indeed, as an eminent member of the ecclesial community, the Blessed Virgin has a special place in the Church's doctrine. Furthermore, by stressing the link between Mary and the Church, Christians of the Reformation could better understand the Marian teaching presented by the Council (Acta Synodalia, II, III, 343-345).

The Council Fathers, moved by the same love for Mary, thus tended, in their expression of different doctrinal positions, to favor various aspects of her person. Some reflected on Mary primarily in her relationship to Christ, others considered her more as a member of the Church.

3. After an intense doctrinal discussion attentive to the dignity of the Mother of God and to her particular presence in the Church's life, it was decided that the treatment of Mary would be situated in the Council's document on the Church (cf. Acta Synodalia, II, III, 627).

The new schema on the Blessed Virgin, drafted so as to be included in the Dogmatic Constitution on the Church, shows real doctrinal progress. The stress placed on Mary's faith and a more systematic concern to base Marian doctrine on Scripture are significant and useful elements for enriching the piety and esteem of the Christian people for the Blessed Mother of God.

Moreover, with the passing of time the danger of reductionism, feared by some Fathers, proved to be unfounded: Mary's mission and privileges were amply reaffirmed; her cooperation in the divine plan of salvation was highlighted; the harmony of this cooperation with Christ's unique mediation appeared more evident. For the first time, the conciliar Magisterium offered the Church a doctrinal exposition of Mary's role in Christ's redemptive work and in the life of the Church.

Thus, we must consider the Council Fathers' choice, which proved very fruitful for later doctrinal work, to have been a truly providential decision.

4. During the Council sessions, many Fathers wished further to enrich Marian doctrine with other statements of Mary's role in the work of salvation The particular context in which Vatican II's Mariological debate took place did not allow these wishes, although substantial and widespread, to be accepted, but the Council's entire discussion of Mary remains vigorous and balanced, and the topics themselves, though not fully defined, received significant attention in the overall treatment.

## A Balanced Presentation Of Marian Doctrine

Thus, the hesitation of some Fathers regarding the title of Mediatrix did not prevent the Council from using this title once, and from stating in other terms Mary's mediating role from her consent to the Angel's message to her motherhood in the order of grace (cf. *Lumen Gentium*, n. 62). Furthermore, the Council asserts her cooperation "in a wholly singular way" in the work of restoring supernatural life to souls (ibid., n. 61). Lastly, even if it avoided using the title "Mother of the Church", the text of *Lumen Gentium* clearly underscores the Church's veneration for Mary as a most loving Mother.

The entire exposition in the eighth chapter of the Dogmatic Constitution on the Church clearly shows that terminological precautions did not prevent a very rich and positive presentation of basic doctrine, an expression of faith and love for her whom the Church acknowledges as Mother and Model.

On the other hand, the Fathers' differing points of view, as they emerged during the conciliar debate, turned out to be providential, because, on the basis of their harmonious relationship, they have afforded the faith and devotion of the Christian people a more complete and balanced presentation of the marvelous identity of the Lord's Mother and of her exceptional role in the work of Redemption.

# Mary's Place Is Highest After Christ

*The proper way to explain Marian doctrine was the topic of the Holy Father's weekly catechesis at the General Audience of Wednesday, 3 January, 1996. Here is a translation of his address, which was the 10th in the series on the Blessed Virgin and was given in Italian.*

1. Following the Dogmatic Constitution *Lumen Gentium*, which in chapter eight set forth painstakingly both the role of the Blessed Virgin in the mystery of the Incarnate Word and the Mystical Body, and the duties of the redeemed towards the Mother of God", in this catechesis I would like to offer a basic summary of the Church's faith in Mary, while reaffirming with the Council that I do not intend 'to give a complete doctrine on Mary", nor "to decide those questions which the work of theologians has not yet fully clarified" (*Lumen Gentium*, n. 54).

It is my intention first of all to describe "the role of the Blessed Virgin in the mystery of the Incarnate Word and the Mystical Body" (ibid.), by returning to data from Scripture and the Apostolic Tradition, and taking into account the doctrinal development that has taken place in the Church up to our day.

Moreover, since Mary's role in the history of salvation is closely linked to the mystery of Christ and the Church, I will not lose sight of these essential reference points which, by offering Marian doctrine the proper context, enable us to discover its vast and inexhaustible riches.

Exploring the mystery of the Lord's Mother is truly vast and has occupied many Pastors and theologians down the centuries. Some, in their endeavor to point out the central aspects of

Mariology, have sometimes treated it together with Christology or ecclesiology. However, taking into account her relationship with all the mysteries of faith, Mary deserves a specific treatment which highlights her person and role in the history of salvation, in the light of the Bible and of ecclesiastical tradition.

2. It also seems useful, following the Council's directives, to explain accurately "the duties of the redeemed towards the Mother of God, who is Mother of Christ and Mother of men, and most of all of those who believe" (ibid.).

Indeed, the part assigned to Mary by the divine plan of salvation requires of Christians not only acceptance and attention, but also concrete choices which express in life the Gospel attitudes of her who goes before the Church in faith and holiness. The Mother of the Lord is thus destined to exercise a special influence on believers' way of praying. The Church's liturgy itself recognizes her singular place in the devotion and life of every believer.

It is necessary to emphasize that Marian teaching and devotion are not the Fruit of sentimentality. The mystery of Mary is a revealed truth which imposes itself on the intellect of believers and requires of those in the Church who have the task of studying and teaching a method of doctrinal reflection no less rigorous than that used in all theology.

Moreover, Jesus himself had invited his contemporaries not to be led by enthusiasm in considering his Mother, recognizing in Mary especially the one who is blessed because she listens to the word of God and keeps it (cf. Lk 11:28).

Not only affection but particularly the light of the Spirit must guide us in understanding the Mother of Jesus and her contribution to the work of salvation.

3. With regard to the measure and balance to be maintained in both Marian doctrine and devotion, the Council strongly urges theologians and preachers of the divine word to be "careful to refrain... from all false exaggeration" (*Lumen Gentium,*. n. 67).

This exaggeration comes from those who adopt a maximalist attitude, which seeks to extend systematically to Mary the prerogatives of Christ and all the charisms of the Church.

Instead, it is always necessary in Marian doctrine to

safeguard the infinite difference existing between the human person of Mary and the divine person of Jesus. To attribute the "maximum" to Mary cannot become a norm of Mariology, which must make constant reference to the testimony of Revelation regarding God's gifts to the Virgin on account of her sublime mission.

Likewise, the Council exhorts theologians and preachers to "refrain... from too summary an attitude" (ibid.), that is, from the danger of a minimalism that can be manifest in doctrinal positions, in exegetical interpretations and in acts of devotion which tend to reduce and almost deny Mary's importance in the history of salvation, her perpetual virginity and her holiness.

Such extreme positions should always be avoided through a consistent and sincere fidelity to revealed truth as expressed in Scripture and in the Apostolic Tradition.

4. The Council itself offers us a criterion for discerning authentic Marian doctrine: Mary "occupies a place in the Church which is the highest after Christ and also closest to us" (*Lumen Gentium*, n. 54).

The highest place: we must discover this lofty position granted to Mary in the mystery of salvation. However, it is a question of a vocation totally in relationship to Christ.

The place closest to us: our life is profoundly influenced by Mary's example and intercession. Nonetheless we must ask ourselves about our effort to be close to her. The entire teaching of salvation history invites us to look to the Virgin. Christian asceticism in every age invites us to think of her as a model of perfect adherence to the Lord's will. The chosen model of holiness, Mary guides the steps of believers on their journey to heaven.

Through her closeness to the events of our daily history, Mary sustains us in trials; she encourages us in difficulty, always pointing out to us the goal of eternal salvation. Thus her role as Mother is seen ever more clearly: Mother of her Son Jesus, tender and vigil ant Mother to each one of us, to whom, from the Cross, the Redeemer entrusted her, that we might welcome her as children in faith.

# Mary's Relationship With The Trinity

*Mary "is endowed with the high office and dignity of the Mother of the Son of God, and therefore she is also the beloved daughter of the Father and the temple of the Holy Spirit" (Lumen Gentium, n. 53). With this quote from the Second Vatican Council, the Holy Father expressed in concise form the Trinitarian dimension of Marian doctrine, which was the subject of his catechesis at the General Audience of Wednesday, 10 January, 1996. Here is a translation of his address, which was the 11th in the series on the Blessed Virgin and was given in Italian.*

1. The eighth chapter of the Constitution *Lumen Gentium* shows in the mystery of Christ the absolutely necessary reference to Marian doctrine. In this regard, the first words of the Introduction are significant: "Wishing in his supreme goodness and wisdom to effect the redemption of the world, 'when the fullness of time came, God sent his Son, born of a woman ... that we might receive the adoption of sons' (Gal 4:4-5)" (*Lumen Gentium*, n. 52). This Son is the Messiah awaited by the people of the Old Covenant, sent by the Father at a decisive moment of history, the "fullness of time" (Gal 4:4), which coincides with his birth in our world from a woman. She who brought the eternal Son of God to humanity can never be separated from him who is found at the center of the divine plan carried out in history.

The primacy of Christ is shown forth in the Church, his Mystical Body: in her "the faithful are joined to Christ the Head and are in communion with all his saints" (cf. *Lumen Gentium*, n. 52): It is Christ who draws all men to himself. Since in her maternal role she is closely united with her Son, Mary helps direct the gaze and heart of believers towards him.

She is the way that leads to Christ: indeed, she who "at the message of the angel received the Word of God in her heart and in her body" (*Lumen Gentium*, n. 53) shows us how to receive into our lives the Son come down from heaven; teaching us to make Jesus the center and the supreme "law" of our existence.

# A Unique Bond Between Mary And The Holy Spirit

2. Mary also helps us discover, at the origin of the whole work of salvation, the sovereign action of the Father who calls men to become sons in the one Son. Recalling the very beautiful expressions of the Letter to the Ephesians: "God, who is rich in mercy, out of the great love with which he loved us, even when we were dead through our trespasses, made us alive together with Christ" (Eph 2:4), the Council gives God the title "most merciful": the Son "born of a woman" is thus seen as the fruit of the Father's mercy and enables us to understand better how this Woman is the "mother of mercy".

In the same context, the Council also calls God "most wise", suggesting a particular attention to the close link between Mary and the divine wisdom, which in its mysterious plan willed the Virgin's motherhood.

3. The Council's text also reminds us of the unique bond uniting Mary with the Holy Spirit, using the 'words of the Nicene-Constantinopolitan Creed which we recite in the Eucharistic liturgy: "For us men and for our salvation he came down from heaven: by the power of the Holy Spirit he was born of the Virgin Mary, and became man".

In expressing the unchanging faith of the Church, the Council reminds us that the marvelous incarnation of the Son took place in the Virgin Mary's womb without man's cooperation, by the power of the Holy Spirit.

The Introduction to the eighth chapter of *Lumen Gentium* thus shows in a Trinitarian perspective an essential dimension of Marian doctrine. Everything in fact comes from the will of the Father, who has sent his Son into the world, revealing him to men and establishing him as the Head of the Church and the center of history. This is a plan that was fulfilled by the Incarnation, the work of the Holy Spirit, but with the essential cooperation of a woman, the Virgin Mary, who thus became an integral part in the economy of communicating the Trinity to mankind

4. Mary's threefold relationship with the divine Persons is confirmed in precise words and with a description of the characteristic relationship which links the Mother of the Lord to

the Church: "She is endowed with the high office and dignity of the Mother of the Son of God, and therefore she is also the beloved daughter of the Father and the temple of the Holy Spirit" (*Lumen Gentium*, n. 53).

Mary's fundamental dignity is that of being "Mother of the Son", which is expressed in Christian doctrine and devotion with the title "Mother of God".

This is a surprising term, which shows the humility of God's only-begotten Son in his Incarnation and, in connection with it, the most high privilege granted a creature who was called to give him birth in the flesh.

Mother of the Son, Mary is the "beloved daughter of the Father" in a unique way. She has been granted an utterly special likeness between her motherhood and the divine fatherhood. And again: every Christian is a "temple of the Holy Spirit", according to the Apostle Paul's expression (1 Cor 6:19). But this assertion takes on an extraordinary meaning in Mary: in her the relationship with the Holy Spirit is enriched with a spousal dimension. I recalled this in the Encyclical *Redemptoris Mater*: "The Holy Spirit had already come down upon her, and she became his faithful spouse at the Annunciation, welcoming the Word of the true God ..." (n. 26).

## Mary's Dignity Surpasses That Of Every Creature

5. Mary's privileged relationship with the Trinity therefore confers on her a dignity which far surpasses that of every other creature. The Council recalls this explicitly: because of this "gift of sublime grace" Mary "far surpasses all creatures" (*Lumen Gentium*, n. 53). However, this most high dignity does not hinder Mary's solidarity with each of us. The Constitution *Lumen Gentium* goes on to say: "But, being of the race of Adam, she is at the same time also united to all those who are to be saved" and she has been "redeemed, in a more exalted fashion, by reason of the merits of her Son" (ibid.).

Here we see the authentic meaning of Mary's privileges and of her extraordinary relationship with the Trinity: their purpose is to enable her to cooperate in the salvation of the human race.

The immeasurable greatness of the Lord's Mother therefore remains a gift of God's love for all men. By proclaiming her "blessed" (Lk 1:48), generations praise the "great things" (Lk 1:49) the Almighty has done in her for humanity, "in remembrance of his mercy" (Lk 1:54).

# Victory Over Sin Comes Through A Woman

*"Mary's unique vocation is inseparable from humanity's vocation and, in particular, from that of every woman, on which light has been shed by the mission of Mary, proclaimed God's first ally against Satan and evil', the Holy Father said at the General Audience on Wednesday 24 January, 1996, as he returned to his catechesis on the Blessed Virgin. Here is a translation of his address, which was the 12th in the series and was given in Italian.*

1. "The books of the Old Testament describe the history of salvation, by which the coming of Christ into the world was slowly prepared. The earliest documents, as they are read in the Church and are understood in the light of a further and full revelation, bring the figure of a woman, Mother of the Redeemer, into a gradually clearer light" (*Lumen Gentium*, n. 55).

With these statements the Second Vatican Council reminds us how the figure of Mary gradually took shape from the very beginning of salvation history. She is already glimpsed in the Old Testament texts but is fully understood only when these "are read in the Church" and understood in the light of the New Testament.

The Holy Spirit, by inspiring the various human authors, oriented Old Testament Revelation to Christ, who was to come into the world from the Virgin Mary's womb.

2. Among the Biblical accounts which foretold the Mother of the Redeemer, the Council particularly cites those in which God revealed his plan of salvation after the fall of Adam and Eve. The Lord says to the serpent, the personification of the spirit of evil: "I will put enmity between you and the woman, and between your seed and her seed; he shall bruise your head, and you shall

bruise his heel" (Gn 3.15).

These statements, called the Proto-gospel, i.e., the first Good News, by Christian tradition since the 16th century, enable us to see God's saving will from the very origins of humanity. Indeed according to the sacred author's narrative, the Lord's first reaction to sin was not to punish the guilty but to offer them the hope of salvation and to involve them actively in the work of redemption, showing his great generosity even to those who had offended him.

The Proto-gospel's words also reveal the unique destiny of the woman who, although yielding to the serpent's temptation before the man did, in virtue of the divine plan later becomes God's first ally. Eve was the serpent's accomplice in enticing man to sin. Overturning this situation, God declares that he will make the woman the serpent's enemy.

3. Exegetes now agree in recognizing that the text of Genesis, according to the original Hebrew, does not attribute action against the serpent directly to the woman, but to her offspring. Nevertheless, the text gives great prominence to the role she will play in the struggle against the tempter: in fact the one who defeats the serpent will be her offspring.

Who is this woman? The Biblical text does not mention her personal name but allows us to glimpse a new woman, desired by God to atone for Eve's fall; in fact, she is called to restore woman's role and dignity, and to contribute to changing humanity's destiny, cooperating through her maternal mission in God's victory over Satan.

4. In the light of the New Testament and the Church's tradition, we know that the new woman announced by the Proto-gospel is Mary, and in "her seed" we recognize her Son, Jesus, who triumphed over Satan's power in the paschal mystery.

We also observe that in Mary the enmity God put between the serpent and the woman is fulfilled in two ways. God's perfect ally and the devil's enemy, she was completely removed from Satan's domination in the Immaculate Conception, when she was fashioned in grace by the Holy Spirit and preserved from every stain of sin. In addition, associated with her Son's saving work, Mary was fully involved in the fight against the spirit of evil.

Thus the titles "Immaculate Conception" and "Cooperator

of the Redeemer", attributed by the Church's faith to Mary, in order to proclaim her spiritual beauty and her intimate participation in the wonderful work of Redemption, show the lasting antagonism between the serpent and the New Eve.

5. Exegetes and theologians claim that the light of the New Eve, Mary, shines from the pages of Genesis onto the whole economy of salvation. In that text they already see the bond between Mary and the Church. Here we point out with joy that the term "woman", used in its generic form in the Genesis text, spurs women especially to join the Virgin of Nazareth and her task in the work of salvation for they are called to take part in the fight against the spirit of evil.

Women who, like Eve, could succumb to Satan's seduction, through solidarity with Mary receive superior strength to combat the enemy, becoming God's first allies on the way of salvation.

God's mysterious alliance with woman can also be seen in a variety of ways in our day: in women's assiduous personal prayer and liturgical devotion, in their catechetical service and in their witness to charity, in the many feminine vocations to the consecrated life, in religious education in the family, etc.

All these signs are a very concrete fulfillment of the Proto-gospel's prediction. Indeed, by suggesting a universal extension of the word "woman" within and beyond the visible confines of the Church, the Proto-gospel shows that Mary's unique vocation is inseparable from humanity's vocation and, in particular, from that of every woman, on which light has been shed by the mission of Mary, proclaimed God's first ally against Satan and evil.

# Isaiah's Prophecy Fulfilled In Incarnation

*"Therefore the Lord himself will give you a sign. Behold, a virgin shall conceive and bear a Son, and shall call his name Emmanuel" (Is 7:13-14). These well-known words from the prophet Isaiah were the subject of the Holy Father's catechesis at the General Audience of Wednesday, 31 January, 1996, as he continued his reflections on Mary's role in salvation history. Here*

*is a translation of his talk, which was the 13th in the series on the Blessed Virgin and was given in Italian.*

1. In discussing the figure of Mary in the Old Testament, the Council (*Lumen Gentium*, n. 55) refers to the well-known text of Isaiah, which caught the particular attention of the early Christians: "Behold, a virgin shall conceive and bear a Son, and shall call his name Emmanuel" (Is 7:14).

During the annunciation of the angel, who invites Joseph to take to himself Mary, his wife, "for that which is conceived in her is of the Holy Spirit", Matthew gives a Christological and Marian significance to the prophecy. In fact, he adds: "All this took place to fulfill what the Lord had spoken by the prophet: 'Behold, a virgin shall conceive and bear a Son, and his name shall be called Emmanuel (which means God with us)" (Mt 1:22-23).

2. In the Hebrew text this prophecy does not explicitly foretell the virginal birth of Emmanuel: the word used (almah), in fact, simply means "a young woman", not necessarily a virgin. Moreover, we know that Jewish tradition did not hold up the idea of perpetual virginity, nor did it ever express the idea of virginal motherhood.

## The Lord Himself Will Give You A Sign

In the Greek tradition, however, the Hebrew word was translated "parthenos", "virgin". In this fact, which could seem merely a peculiarity of translation, we must recognize a mysterious orientation given by the Holy Spirit to Isaiah's words in order to prepare for the understanding of the Messiah's extraordinary birth. The translation of the word as "virgin" is explained by the fact that Isaiah's text very solemnly prepares for the announcement of the conception and presents it as a divine sign (Is 7:10-14), arousing the expectation of not something extraordinary for a young woman to conceive a Son after being joined to her husband. However, the prophecy makes no reference to the husband. Such a formulation, then, suggested the interpretation given later in the Greek version.

3. In the original context, the prophecy of Is 7:14 was the divine reply to a lack of faith on the part of King Ahaz, who, threatened with an invasion from the armies of the neighboring kings, sought his own salvation and that of his kingdom in Assyria's protection. In advising him to put his trust solely in God and to reject the dreadful Assyrian intervention, the prophet Isaiah invites him on the Lord's behalf to make an act of faith in God's power: "Ask a sign of the Lord your God". At the king's refusal, for he preferred to seek salvation in human aid, the prophet made the famous prediction: "Hear then, O house of David! Is it too little for you to weary men, that you weary my God also? Therefore the Lord himself will give you a sign. Behold, a virgin shall conceive in and bear a Son, and shall call his name Emmanuel" (Is 7:13-14).

The announcement of the sign of Emmanuel, "God with us", implies the promise of God's presence in history, which will find its full meaning in the mystery of the Incarnation of the Word.

4. In the announcement of the wondrous birth of Emmanuel, the indication of the woman who conceives and gives birth shows a certain intention to associate the mother with the destiny of the Son, a prince destined to establish an ideal kingdom, the "messianic" kingdom, and offers a glimpse of a special divine plan, which highlights the woman's role.

The sign, in fact, is not only the child, but the extraordinary conception revealed later in the birth itself, a hope-filled event, which stresses the central role of the mother.

The prophecy of Emmanuel must also be understood in the horizon opened by the promise made to David, a promise we read about in the Second Book of Samuel. Here the prophet Nathan promises the king God's favor towards his descendent: "He shall build a house for my name, and I will establish the throne of his kingdom forever. I will be his father, and he shall be my Son" (2 Sam 7:13-14).

God wants to exercise a paternal role towards David's offspring, a role that will reveal its full, authentic meaning in the New Testament with the Incarnation of the Son of God in the family of David (cf. Rom 1:3).

5. The same prophet Isaiah, in another very familiar text, confirms the unusual nature of Emmanuel's birth. Here are his words: "For to us a child is born, to us a Son is given; and the government will be upon his shoulder, and he will be called 'Wonderful Counselor, Mighty God, Everlasting Father, Prince I of Peace'" (9:5). Thus the prophet expresses, in the series of names given the child, the qualities of his royal office: wisdom, might, fatherly kindness, peacemaking.

The mother is no longer mentioned, but the exaltation of the Son, who brings the people all they can hope for in the messianic kingdom, is also reflected in the woman who conceived him and gave him birth.

6. A famous prophecy of Micah also alludes to the birth of Emmanuel. The prophet says: "But you, O Bethlehem Ephrathah, who are little to be among the clans of Judah, from you shall come forth for me one who is to be ruler in Israel, whose origin is from of old, from ancient days. Therefore the Lord shall give them up until the time when she who is in travail has brought forth..." (5:2-3). These words re-echo the expectation of a birth full of messianic hope, in which once again the mother's role is stressed, the mother explicitly remembered and ennobled by the wondrous event that brings joy and salvation.

## Prophecy Prepares Revelation Of Virginal Motherhood

7. Mary's virginal motherhood was prepared for in a more general way by God's favor to the humble and the poor (cf. *Lumen Gentium*, n. 55).

By their attitude of placing all their trust in the Lord, they anticipated the profound meaning of Mary's virginity. By renouncing the richness of human motherhood, she awaited from God all the fruitfulness of her own life.

The Old Testament then does not contain a formal announcement of the virginal motherhood, which was fully revealed only by the New Testament. Nevertheless, Isaiah's prophecy (Is 7:14) prepares for the revelation of this mystery and was construed so in the Greek translation of the Old Testament. By quoting the prophecy thus translated, Matthew's Gospel proclaims its perfect fulfillment through the conception of Jesus in Mary's virginal womb.

# Motherhood Is God's Special Gift

*"The Bible's message regarding motherhood reveals important and ever timely aspects: indeed, it sheds light on the dimension of gratuitousness, which is especially apparent in the case of barren women, God's particular covenant with woman and the special bond between the destiny of the mother and that of the Son", the Holy Father said at the General Audience on Wednesday, 6 March, 1996, focusing on the Old Testament's treatment of motherhood. Here is a translation of the Pope's catechesis, which was the 14th in the series on the Blessed Virgin and was given in Italian.*

1. Motherhood is a gift of God. "I have gotten a man with the help of the Lord!" (Gn 4:1), Eve exclaims after giving birth to Cain, her first-born Son. With these words, the Book of Genesis presents the first motherhood in human history as a grace and joy that spring from the Creator's goodness.

2. The birth of Isaac is similarly described, at the origin of the chosen people.

God promises Abraham, who has been deprived of children and is now advanced in years, descendants as numerous as the stars of heaven (cf. Gn 15:5). The promise is welcomed by the patriarch with the faith that reveals God's plan to this man: "He believed the Lord; and he reckoned it to him as righteousness" (Gn 15:6).

This promise was confirmed in the words spoken by the Lord on the occasion of the covenant he made with Abraham: "Behold, my covenant is with you, and you shall be the father of a multitude of nations" (Gn 17:4).

Extraordinary and mysterious events emphasize how Sarah's motherhood was primarily the fruit of the mercy of God, who gives life beyond all human expectation: "I will bless her, and moreover I will give you a Son by her; I will bless her, and she shall be a mother of nations; kings of peoples shall come from her" (Gn 17:15-16).

Motherhood is presented as a decisive gift of the Lord. The patriarch and his wife will be given a new name to indicate the unexpected and marvelous transformation that God is to work in their life.

## The Lord Gladdens With The Gift Of Motherhood

3. The visit of the three mysterious persons, whom the Fathers of the Church interpreted as a prefiguration of the Trinity, announced the fulfillment of the promise to Abraham more explicitly: "The Lord appeared to him by the oaks of Mamre, as he sat at the door of his tent in the heat of the day. He lifted up his eyes and looked, and behold, three men stood in front of him" (Gn 18:1-2). Abraham objected: "Shall a child be born to a man who is a hundred years old? Shall Sarah, who is ninety years old, bear a child?" (Gn 17:17; cf. 18:11-13). The divine guest replies: "Is anything too hard for the Lord? At the appointed time I will return to you, about this time next year, and Sarah shall have a Son" (Gn 18:14; cf. Lk 1:37).

The narrative stresses the effect of the divine visit, which makes fruitful a conjugal union that had been barren until then. Believing in the promise, Abraham becomes a father against all hope, and "father in the faith" because from his faith "descends" that of the chosen people.

4. The Bible relates other stories of women released from sterility and gladdened by the Lord with the gift of motherhood. These are often situations of anguish, which God's intervention transforms into experiences of joy by receiving the heartfelt prayers of those who are humanly without hope. "When Rachel saw that she bore Jacob no children", for example, "she envied her sister; and she said to Jacob, 'Give me children, or I shall die!'. Jacob's

anger was kindled against Rachel, and he said, 'Am I in the place of God, who has withheld from you the fruit of the womb?'"(Gn 30:1-2).

But the Biblical text immediately adds: "Then God remembered Rachel, and God hearkened to her and. opened her womb. She conceived and bore a Son" (Gn 30:22-23). This Son, Joseph, would play a very important role for Israel at the time of the migration to Egypt.

In this as in other narratives, the stable intends to highlight the marvelous nature of God's intervention in these specific cases by stressing the initial condition of the woman's sterility; however, at the same time, it allows us to grasp the gratuitousness inherent in all motherhood.

5. We find a similar process in the account of the birth of Samson. The wife of Manoah; who had never been able to conceive a child, hears the Lord's announcement from the angel: "Behold, you are barren and have no children; but you shall conceive and bear a Son" (Jgs 13:3). The conception, unexpected and miraculous, announces the great things that the Lord will do through Samson.

In the case of Hannah, Samson's mother, the special role of prayer is underlined. Hannah suffers the humiliation of being barren but she is full of great trust in God, to whom she turns insistently, that he may help her to overcome this trial. One day, at the temple, she makes a vow: "Oh Lord of hosts, if you will indeed look on the affliction of your maidservant, and remember me, and not forget your maidservant, but will give to your maidservant a Son, then I will give him to the Lord all the days of his life" (1 Sm 1:11).

Her prayer was answered: "The Lord remembered her" and "Hannah conceived and bore a Son, and she called his name Samuel" (1 Sm 1:19-20). Keeping her promise, Hannah offered her Son to the Lord: "For this child I prayed; and the Lord has granted me my petition which I made to him. Therefore I have lent him to the Lord; as long as he lives, he is lent to the Lord" (1 Sm 1: 27-28). Given by God to Hannah and then given by Hannah to God, the little Samuel becomes a living bond of communion between Hannah and God.

Samuel's birth is thus an experience of joy and an occasion for thanksgiving. The First Book of Samuel contains hymn known as Hannah's Magnificat, which seems to anticipate Mary's: "My heart exults in the Lord; my strength is exalted in the Lord" (1 Sm 2:1).

The grace of motherhood that God granted to Hannah because of her ceaseless prayers filled her with a new generosity. Samuel's consecration is the grateful response of a mother who, recognizing in her child the fruit of God's mercy, returns his gift, entrusting the child she had so longed for to the Lord.

## God Intervenes In Important Moments

6. In the accounts of miraculous motherhood which we have recalled, it is easy to discover the important place the Bible assigns to mothers in the mission of their sons. In Samuel's case, Hannah has a determining role in deciding to give him to the Lord. An equally decisive role is played by another mother, Rebecca, who procures the inheritance for Jacob (Gn 27). That maternal intervention, described by the Bible, can be interpreted as the sign of being chosen as an instrument in God's sovereign plan. It is he who chooses the youngest Son, Jacob, to receive the paternal blessing and inheritance, and therefore as the shepherd and leader of his people.... It is he who by a free and wise decision, determines and governs each one's destiny (Wis 10:10-12).

The Bible's message regarding motherhood reveals important and ever timely aspects: indeed, it sheds light on the dimension of gratuitousness, which is especially apparent in the case of barren women, God's particular covenant with woman and the special bond between the destiny of the mother and that of the Son. At the same time, the intervention of God, who, at important moments in the history of his people, causes certain barren women to conceive, prepares for belief in the intervention of God who, in the fullness of time, will make a Virgin fruitful for the Incarnation of his Son.

# Women's Indispensable
# Role In Salvation History

*The role of certain Old Testament women in the salvation of God's chosen people was the theme of the Holy Father's catechesis at the General Audience of Wednesday, 27 March, 1996. The Pope considered their indispensable role as a pre figuring of Mary's mission in salvation history. Here is a translation of his talk, which was the 15th in the series on the Blessed Virgin and was given in Italian.*

1. The Old Testament holds up for our admiration some extraordinary women who, impelled by the Spirit of God, share in the struggles and triumphs of Israel or contribute to its Salvation. Their presence in the history of the people is neither marginal nor passive: they appear as true protagonists of salvation history. Here are the most significant examples.

After the crossing of the Red Sea, the sacred text emphasizes the initiative of a woman inspired to make this decisive event a festive celebration: "Then Miriam, the prophetess, the sister of Aaron, took a timbrel in her hand; and all the women went out after her with timbrels and dancing. And Miriam sang to them: 'Sing to the Lord, for he has triumphed gloriously; the horse and his rider he has thrown into the sea'" (Ex 15:20-21).

This mention of feminine enterprise in the context of a celebration stresses not only the importance of woman's role, but also her particular ability for praising and thanking God.

## Positive Contribution Of Women
## To Salvation History

2. The action of the prophetess Deborah, at the time of the Judges, is even more important. After ordering the commander of the army to go and gather his men, she guarantees by her presence the success of Israel's army, predicting that another woman, Jael, will kill their enemy's general.

To celebrate the great victory, Deborah also sings a long canticle praising Jael's action: "Most blessed of women be Jael,... of tent-dwelling women most blessed" (Jgs 5:24). In the New Testament this praise is echoed in the words Elizabeth addresses to Mary on the day of the Visitation: "Blessed are you among women..." (Lk 1:42).

The significant role of women in the salvation of their people, highlighted by the figures of Deborah and Jael, is presented again in the story of another prophetess named Huldah, who lived at the time of King Josiah. Questioned by the priest Hilkiah, she made prophecies announcing that forgiveness would be shown to the king who feared the divine wrath. Huldah thus becomes a messenger of mercy and peace (cf. 2 Kgs 22:14-20).

3. The Books of Judith and Esther, whose purpose is to idealize the positive contribution of woman to the history of the chosen people, present in a violent cultural context, two women who win victory and salvation for the Israelites.

The Book of Judith, in particular, tells of a fearsome army sent by Nebuchadnezzar to conquer Israel. Led by Holofernes, the enemy army is ready to seize the city of Bethulia, amid the desperation of its inhabitants, who, considering any resistance to be useless, ask their rulers to surrender. But the city's elders, who in the absence of immediate aid declare themselves ready to hand Bethulia over to the enemy, are rebuked by Judith for their lack of faith as she professes her complete trust in the salvation that comes from the Lord.

After a long invocation to God, she who is a symbol of fidelity to the Lord, of humble prayer and of the intention to remain chaste goes to Holofernes, the proud, idolatrous and dissolute enemy general.

Left alone with him and before striking him, Judith prays to Yahweh, saying: "Give me strength this day, O Lord God of Israel!" (Jdt 13:7). Then, taking Holofernes' sword, she cuts off his head.

Here too, as in the case of David and Goliath, the Lord used weakness to triumph over strength. On this occasion, however, it was a woman who brought victory: Judith, without being held back by the cowardice and unbelief of the people's rulers, goes to Holofernes and kills him, earning the gratitude and praise of the High Priest and the elders of Jerusalem. The latter exclaimed to the woman who had defeated the enemy: "You are the exaltation of Jerusalem, you are the great glory of Israel, you are the great pride of our nation! You have done all this single-handed; you have done great good to Israel, and God is well pleased with it. May the Almighty Lord bless you for ever!" (Jdt 15:9-10).

4. The events narrated in the Book of Esther occurred in another very difficult situation for the Jews. In the kingdom of Persia, Haman, the king's superintendent, decrees the extermination of the Jews. To remove the danger, Mordocai, a Jew living in the citadel of Susa, turns to his niece Esther, who lives in the king's palace where she has attained the rank of queen. Contrary to the law in force, she presents herself to the king without being summoned, thus risking the death penalty, and she obtains the revocation of the extermination decree. Haman is executed, Mordocai comes to power and the Jews, delivered from menace, thus get the better of their enemies.

Judith and Esther both risk their lives to win the salvation of their people. The two interventions, however, are quite different: Esther does not kill the enemy but, by playing the role of mediator, intercedes for those who are threatened with destruction.

## Holy Spirit Sketches Mary's Role In Human Salvation

5. This intercessory role is later attributed to another female figure, Abigail, the wife of Nabal, by the First Book of Samuel. Here too, it is due to her intervention that salvation is once again achieved.

She goes to meet David, who has decided to destroy Nabal's family, and asks forgiveness for her husband's sins. Thus she delivers his house from certain destruction (1 Sm 25).

As can be easily noted, the Old Testament tradition frequently emphasizes the decisive action of women in the salvation of Israel, especially in the writings closest to the coming of Christ. In this way the Holy Spirit, through the events connected with Old Testament women, sketches with ever greater precision the characteristics of Mary's mission in the work of salvation for the entire human race.

# The Ideal Woman Is A Precious Treasure

*"In these figures of woman, in whom the marvels of divine grace are manifest, we glimpse the one who will be the greatest: Mary, Mother of the Lord", the Holy Father said at the General Audience of Wednesday, 10 April, 1996, as he returned to his catechesis on the Blessed Virgin Mary. Here is a translation of his talk, which was the 16th in the series and was given in Italian.*

1. The Old Testament and the Judaic tradition are full of acknowledgments of woman's moral nobility, which is expressed above all in an attitude of trust in the Lord, in prayer to obtain the gift of motherhood and in imploring God for Israel's salvation from the assaults of its enemies. Sometimes, as in Judith's case, this quality is celebrated by the entire community, becoming the object of common admiration.

Beside the shining examples of the Biblical heroines, the negative witnesses of some women are not lacking: such as Delilah who destroys Samson's prophetic ability (Jgs 16:4-21), the foreign women who in Solomon's old age turn the king's heart away from the Lord and make him worship other gods (1 Kgs 11:1-8), Jezebel who kills all "the prophets of the Lord" (1 Kgs 18:13) and has Naboth killed, to give his vineyard to Ahab (1 Kgs 21), and Job's wife who insults him in his misfortune and spurs him to rebel (Jb 2:9). In these cases, the woman's conduct is reminiscent of Eve's. However, the prevailing outlook in the Bible is that inspired by the Proto-Gospel, which sees in woman an ally of God.

## The Feminine Figure Is A Precious Gift Of The Lord

2. In fact, if foreign women were accused of turning Solomon away from his devotion to the true God, the Book of Ruth presents us instead with the most noble figure of a foreign

woman: Ruth, the Moabite, an example of piety to her relatives and of sincere and generous humility. Sharing Israel's life and faith, she was to become David's great-grandmother and an ancestor of the Messiah. Matthew, inserting her in Jesus' genealogy (Mt 1:5), makes her a sign of universality and a proclamation of God's mercy which extends to all humanity.

Among Jesus' forebears, the first Evangelist also mentions Tamar, Rahab and Uriah's wife, three sinful but not wicked women who are listed among the female ancestors of the Messiah, in order to proclaim that divine goodness is greater than sin. Through his grace, God causes their irregular matrimonial situations to contribute to his plans of salvation, thereby also preparing for the future.

Another example of humble dedication, different from Ruth's, is represented by Jephthah's daughter, who agrees to pay for her father's victory over the Ammonites with her own death (Jgs 11:34-40). Lamenting her cruel destiny, she does not rebel but gives herself up to death in fulfillment of the thoughtless vow made by her parent in the context of primitive customs that were still prevalent (cf. Jer 7:31; Mi 6:6-8).

3. Although sapiential literature frequently alludes to woman's defects, it perceives in her a hidden treasure: "He who finds a wife finds a good thing, and obtains favor from the Lord" (Prov 18:22), says the Book of Proverbs, expressing convinced appreciation of the feminine figure, a precious gift of the Lord.

At the end of the same book the portrait of the ideal woman is sketched. Far from representing an unattainable model, she is a concrete image born from the experience of women of great value: "A good wife who can find? She is far more precious than jewels. (Prov 31:10).

Sapiential literature sees in woman's fidelity to the divine covenant the culmination of her abilities and the greatest source of admiration. Indeed, although she can sometimes disappoint, woman transcends all expectations when her heart is faithful to God: "Charm is deceitful, and beauty is vain, but a woman who fears the Lord is to be praised" (Prov 31:30).

## Mother Was Worthy Of Honorable Memory

4. In this context, the Book of the Maccabees, in the story of the mother of the seven brothers martyred during Antiochus Epiphanes' persecution, holds up to us the most admirable example of nobility in trial.

After describing the death of the seven brothers, the sacred author adds: "The mother was especially admirable and worthy of honorable memory. Though she saw her seven sons perish within a single day, she bore it with good courage because of her hope in the Lord. She encouraged each of them in the language of their fathers. Filled with a noble spirit, she fired her woman's reasoning with a man's courage", thus expressing her hope in a future resurrection: "Therefore the Creator of the world, who shaped the beginning of man and devised the origin of all things, will in his mercy give life and breath back to you again, since you now forget yourselves for the sake of his laws" (2 Mc 7:20-23).

Urging her seventh Son to submit to death rather than disobey the divine law, the mother expresses her faith in the work of God who creates all things from nothing: 'I beseech you, my child, to look at the heaven and the earth and see everything that is in them, and recognize that God did not make them out of things that existed. Thus also mankind comes into being. Do not fear this butcher, but prove worthy of your brothers. Accept death, so that in the time of mercy I may get you back again with your brothers" (2 Mc 7:28-29).

She then gives herself up to a bloody death, after suffering torture of the heart seven times, witnessing to steadfast faith, boundless hope and heroic courage.

In these figures of woman, in whom the marvels of divine grace are manifest, we glimpse the one who will be the greatest: Mary, Mother of the Lord.

# God Is Ever Faithful To His Covenant

*What is the sin of infidelity that stains Israel, Yahweh's 'wife'? It consists above all in idolatry: according to the sacred text, in the Lord's eyes recourse to idols by his chosen people is equivalent*

*to adultery", the Holy Father said at the General Audience of
Wednesday, 24 April, 1996 as he examined the relationship
between God and Israel, which is often described in the Old
Testament with the metaphors of spousal union and infidelity.
Here is a translation of his catechesis, which was the 17th in the
series on the Blessed Virgin and was given in Italian.*

1. The Bible often uses the expression "daughter of Zion" to
indicate the inhabitants of the city of Jerusalem, of which Mount
Zion is historically and religiously the most significant (cf. Mi 4:10-
13; Zep 3:14-18; Zec 2:14; 9:9-10).

This feminine personalization facilitates the spousal
interpretation of the loving relationship between God and Israel,
frequently described with the terms "betrothed" or "wife".

Salvation history is the story of God's love, but often too of
human infidelity. The word of the Lord frequently reprimands the
wife-people who break the marital Covenant established with God:
"Surely, as a faithless wife leaves her husband, so have you been
faithless to me, O house of Israel" (Jer 3:20), and invites the children
of Israel to plead with their mother: "Plead with your mother, plead,
for she is not my wife, and I am not her husband" (Hos 2:2).

What is the sin of infidelity that stains Israel, Yahweh's "wife"? It
consists above all in idolatry: according to the sacred text, in the
Lord's eyes recourse to idols by his chosen people is equivalent to
adultery.

2. The prophet Hosea develops, with strong and dramatic
images, the theme of the spousal Covenant between God and his
people and of their betrayal: his own personal experience becomes
an eloquent symbol of it. Indeed, at the birth of his children he is
ordered: "Call her name Not Pitied, for I will no more have pity on
the house of Israel, to forgive them at all", and again: "Call his
name Not My People, for you are not my people and I am not
your God" (Hos 1:6,9).

# God Announces A More Perfect
# Covenant For The Future

The Lord's rebuke and the disappointing experience of worshipping idols makes the faithless wife return to her senses and, repentant, she will say: "I will go and return to my first husband, for it was better with me then than now" (Hos 2:7). But God himself wishes to re-establish the Covenant, and then his word becomes memory, mercy and tenderness: "Therefore, behold, I will allure her, and bring her into the wilderness, and speak tenderly to her" (Hos 2:14). The wilderness, in fact, is the place where God made his definitive Covenant with his people after their deliverance from slavery.

Through these images of love, which portray the difficult relationship between God and Israel, the prophet illustrates the great tragedy of sin, the unhappiness of the way of infidelity and the efforts of divine love to speak to human hearts and bring them back to the Covenant.

3. Despite the problems of the moment, through the mouth of the prophet God announces a more perfect Covenant for the future: "And in that day, says the Lord, you will call me, 'my Baal'.... And I will betroth you to me forever; I will betroth you to me in righteousness and in justice, in steadfast love, and in mercy. I will betroth you to me in faithfulness, and you shall know the Lord" (Hos 2:16, 19-20).

The Lord is not discouraged by human weakness but responds to human infidelities by proposing a more stable and intimate union: "I will sow him for myself in the land. And I will have pity on Not Pitied, and I will say to Not My People, 'You are my people'; and he shall say, 'You are my God'" (Hos 2:23).

The same prospect of a new Covenant is presented again by Jeremiah to the people n exile: "'At that time', says the Lord, 'I will be the God of all the families of Israel, and they shall be my people'. Thus says the Lord: 'The people who survived the sword found grace in the wilderness; when Israel sought for rest, the Lord appeared to him from afar. I have loved you with an everlasting love; therefore I have continued my faithfulness to you. Again I will build you, and you shall be build, O virgin Israel!'" (Jer 31:1-4).

Despite the people's infidelity, God's eternal love is always ready to re-establish the pact of love and to offer a salvation beyond all expectation.

4. Ezekiel and Isaiah also mention the image of the unfaithful woman who is forgiven.

Through Ezekiel the Lord tells his wife: "Yet I will remember my covenant with you in the days of your youth, and I will establish with you an everlasting covenant" (Ez 16:60).

The Book of Isaiah quotes an oracle filled with tenderness: "For your Maker is your husband.... For a brief moment I forsook you, but with great compassion I will gather you. In overflowing wrath for a moment I hid my face from you, but with everlasting love I will have compassion on you, says the Lord, your Redeemer" (Is 54: 5, 7-8).

That promise to the daughter of Zion is a new and faithful love, a magnificent hope which overcomes the abandonment of the faithless wife: "Say to the daughter of Zion: 'Behold, your salvation comes; behold, his reward is with him, and his recompense before him'. And they shall be called the holy people, the redeemed of the Lord; and you shall be called Sought Out, a city not forsaken" (Is 62:11-12).

## Relationship With God Is Described In Ideal Terms

The prophet explains: "You shall no more be termed Forsaken, and your land shall no more be termed Desolate; but you shall be called My Delight is In Her and your land Married; for the Lord delights in you, and your land shall be married. For as a young man marries a virgin, your Builder shall marry you; and as the bridegroom rejoices over the bride, so shall your God rejoice over you" (Is 62:4-5).

Images and attitudes of love, which the Canticle of Canticles summarizes in the statement: "I am my beloved's and my beloved is mine" (Sg 6:3). Thus the relationship between Yahweh and his people is presented again in ideal terms.

5. When she listened to the reading of the prophecies, Mary must have thought of this perspective, which nourished messianic hope in her heart.

The rebukes addressed to the unfaithful people must have inspired in her a more ardent commitment of fidelity to the Covenant, opening her spirit to the proposal of a definitive spousal communion with the Lord in grace and love. From this new Covenant would come the salvation of the whole world.

# Mary Responds To God With Spousal Love

*"The three reasons for the invitation to joy: God's saving presence among his people, the coming of the messianic king and gratuitous and superabundant fruitfulness, find their fulfillment in Mary", the Holy Father said at the General Audience of Wednesday, 1 May, 1996, as he reflected on the angel's greeting to Mary at the Annunciation and Mary's role as the new "daughter of Zion". Here is a translation of his catechesis, which was the 18th in the series on the Blessed Virgin and was given in Italian.*

1. At the time of the Annunciation, Mary, the "exalted daughter of Zion" (*Lumen Gentium*, n. 55), is greeted by the angel as the representative of humanity, called to give her own consent to the Incarnation of the Son of God.

The first word the angel addresses to her is an invitation to joy: chaire, that is, 'rejoice'. The Greek term has been translated in Latin with 'Ave', a simple expression of greeting which does not seem to correspond fully to the divine messenger's intentions and the context in which the meeting takes place.

Of course, chaire was also a form of greeting frequently used by the Greeks, but the extraordinary circumstances in which it is uttered have nothing to do with the atmosphere of an habitual meeting. In fact, we must not forget that the angel is aware of bringing an announcement that is unique in human history: thus a simple, normal greeting would be out of place. Instead, the reference to the original meaning of the expression chaire, which is 'rejoice', seems more suitable for this exceptional occasion.

As the Greek Fathers in particular constantly pointed out, citing various prophetic oracles, the invitation to joy is especially appropriate for the announcement of the Messiah's coming.

## Rejoice, For The Lord Has Done Great Things

2. Our thoughts turn first of all to the Prophet Zephaniah. The text of the Annunciation shows a significant parallelism with his oracle: 'Sing aloud, O daughter of Zion; shout, O Israel! Rejoice and exult with all your heart, O daughter of Jerusalem!' (Zep 3:14). There is the invitation to joy: 'Rejoice and exult with all your heart' (v. 14). Mention is made of the Lord's presence: 'The King of Israel, the Lord, is in your midst' (v.15). There is the exhortation not to be afraid: 'Do not fear, O Zion, let not your hands grow weak' (v.16). Finally, there is the promise of God's saving intervention: 'The Lord your God is in your midst, a warrior who gives victory' (v.17). The comparisons are so numerous and regular that they lead one to recognize Mary as the new 'daughter of Zion', who has full reason to rejoice because God has decided to full his plan of salvation.

A similar invitation to joy, even if it is in a different context, comes from Joel's prophecy: 'Fear not, O land; be glad and rejoice, for the Lord has done great things!.... You shall know that I am in the midst of Israel' (Jl 2:21-27).

3. Also significant is the oracle of Zechariah, cited in connection with Jesus' entry into Jerusalem (Mt 21:5; Jn 12:15). In it the reason for joy is seen in the coming of the Messianic king: 'Rejoice greatly, O daughter of Zion! Shout aloud, O daughter of Jerusalem! Lo, your king comes to you; triumphant and victorious is he, humble... and he shall command peace to the nations' (Zec 9:9-10).

Finally, the announcement of joy to the new Zion springs, in the Book of Isaiah, from its numerous posterity, a sign of divine blessing: 'Sing O barren one, who did not bear; break forth into singing and cry aloud, you who have not been in travail! For the children of the desolate one will be more than the children of her that is married, says the Lord' (Is 54:1).

The three reasons for the invitation to joy: God's saving presence among his people, the coming of the messianic king and gratuitous and superabundant fruitfulness, find their fulfillment in Mary. They justify the pregnant meaning attributed by Tradition to the angel's greeting. By inviting her to give her assent to the fulfillment of the messianic promise and announcing to her the most high dignity of being Mother of the Lord, the angel could not but invite her to rejoice. Indeed, as the Council reminds us: "After a long period of waiting the times are fulfilled in her, the exalted daughter of Zion and the new plan of salvation is established, when the Son of God has taken human nature from her, that he might in the mysteries of his flesh free man from sin" (*Lumen Gentium*, n. 55).

4. The account of the Annunciation allows us to recognize in Mary the new "daughter of Zion", invited by God to deep joy. It expresses her extraordinary role as mother of the Messiah, indeed, as mother of the Son of God. The Virgin accepts the message on behalf of the people of David, but we can say that she accepts it on behalf of all humanity, because the Old Testament extended the role of the Davidic Messiah to all nations (cf. Ps 2:8; 71 [72]:8). In the divine intention, the announcement addressed to her looks to universal salvation.

## Mary Welcomes Joy Foretold By Prophets

To confirm this universal perspective of God's plan, we can recall several Old and New Testament texts which compare salvation to a great feast for all peoples on Mount Zion (cf. Is 25:6 f.) and which announce the final banquet of God's kingdom (cf. Mt 22:1-10).

As "daughter of Zion", Mary is the Virgin of the Covenant which God establishes with all humanity. Mary's representational role in this event is clear. And it is significant that it is a woman who carries out this function.

5. As the new "daughter of Zion", Mary in fact is particularly suited to entering into the spousal Covenant with God. More and better than any member of the Chosen People, she can offer the

Lord the true heart of a Bride.

With Mary, "daughter of Zion" is not merely a collective subject, but a person who represents humanity and, at the moment of the Annunciation, she responds to the proposal of divine love with her own spousal love. Thus she welcomes in a quite special way the joy foretold by the prophecies, a joy which reaches its peak here in the fulfillment of God's plan.

## Blessed Virgin Was Filled With God

*"Everything in Mary derives from a sovereign grace. All that is granted to her is not due to any claim of merit, but only to God's free and gratuitous choice", the Holy Father said at the General Audience of Wednesday, 8 May, 1996, as he examined the meaning of the title "full of grace" that Mary was given by the angel at the Annunciation. Here is a translation of his catechesis, which was the 19th in the series on the Blessed Virgin and was given in Italian.*

1. In the account of the Annunciation, the first word of the Angel's greeting, "Rejoice", is an invitation to joy which recalls the oracles of the Old Testament addressed to the "daughter of Zion". We pointed this out in our previous catecheses and also explained the reasons for this invitation: God's presence among his people, the coming of the messianic king and maternal fruitfulness. These reasons are fulfilled in Mary.

The Angel Gabriel, addressing the Virgin of Nazareth after the greeting, chaire, "rejoice", calls her kecharitomene, "full of grace" The words of the Greek text, chaire and kecharitomene, are deeply interconnected Mary is invited to rejoice primarily because God loves her and has filled her with grace in view of her divine motherhood!

The Church's faith and the experience of the saints teach us that grace is a source of joy, and that true joy comes from God. In Mary, as in Christians, the divine gift produces deep joy.

2. Kecharitomene: this term addressed to Mary seems to

be the proper way to describe the woman destined to become the mother of Jesus. *Lumen Gentium* appropriately recalls this when it : "The Virgin of Nazareth is hailed by the heralding angel, by divine command, as 'full of grace'" (*Lumen Gentium*, n. 56).

The fact that the heavenly messenger addresses her in this way enhances the value of the angelic greeting: it is a manifestation of God's mysterious saving plan in Mary's regard. As I wrote in the Encyclical *Redemptoris Mater*: "The fullness of grace" indicates all the supernatural munificence from which Mary benefits by being chosen and destined to be the Mother of Christ" (n. 9).

## God Granted Mary The Fullness Of Grace

"Full of grace" is the name Mary possesses in the eyes of God. Indeed, the angel, according to the Evangelist Luke's account, uses this expression even before he speaks the name "Mary", and thus emphasizes the predominant aspect which the Lord perceived in the Virgin of Nazareth's personality.

The expression "full of grace" is the translation of the Greek word kecharitomene, which is a passive participle. Therefore to render more exactly the nuance of the Greek word one should not say merely "full of grace", but "made full of grace", or even "filled with grace", which would clearly indicate that this was a gift given by God to the Blessed Virgin. This term, in the form of a perfect participle, enhances the image of a perfect and lasting grace which implies fullness. The same verb, in the sense of "to bestow grace", is used in the letter to the Ephesians to indicate the abundance of grace granted to us by the Father in his beloved Son (Eph 1:6), and which Mary receives as the first fruits of Redemption (cf. *Redemptoris Mater*, n. 10).

3. In the Virgin's case, God's action certainly seems surprising. Mary has no human claim to receiving the announcement of the Messiah's coming. She is not the high priest, official representative of the Hebrew religion, nor even a man, but a young woman without any influence in the society of her time. In addition, she is a native of Nazareth, a village which is never mentioned in the Old Testament. It must not have enjoyed a good reputation, as Nathaniel's question, recorded in John's Gospel,

makes clear: "Can anything good come out of Nazareth?" (Jn 1:46).

The extraordinary and gratuitous nature of God's intervention becomes even clearer in compassion with Luke's text, which recounts what happened to Zechariah. The latter's priestly status is highlighted as well as his exemplary life, which make him and his wife Elizabeth models of Old Testament righteousness: they walked "blameless in all the commandments and ordinances of the Lord" (Lk 1:6).

But we are not informed of Mary's origins either: the expression "of the house of David" (Lk 1:27) in fact refers only to Joseph. No mention is made then of Mary's behavior. With this literary choice, Luke stresses that everything in Mary derives from a sovereign grace. All that is granted to her is not due to any claim of merit, but only to God's free and gratuitous choice.

## God's Mercy Reaches The Highest Degree In Mary

4. In so doing, the Evangelist does not of course intend to downplay the outstanding personal value of the Blessed Virgin. Rather, he 'wishes to present Mary as the pure fruit of God's goodwill: he has so taken possession of her as to make her, according to the title used by the Angel, "full of grace". The abundance of grace itself is the basis of Mary's hidden spiritual richness.

In the Old Testament, Yahweh expresses the superabundance of his love in many ways and on many occasions. At the dawn of the New Testament, the gratuitousness of God's mercy reaches the highest degree in Mary. In her, God's predilection, shown to the chosen people and in particular to the humble and the poor, reaches its culmination.

Nourished by the Word of the Lord and the experience of the saints, the Church urges believers to keep their gaze fixed on the Mother of the Redeemer and to consider themselves, like her, loved by God. She invites them to share Our lady's humility and poverty, so that, after her example and through her intercession, they may persevere in the grace of God who sanctifies and transforms hearts.

# Mary Was Conceived Without Original Sin

*The perfection of holiness that Mary enjoys from the first moment of her conception was the subject of the Holy Father's catechesis at the General Audience of Wednesday, 15 May, 1996. The Pope went on to say that the recognition of this perfect holiness "required a long process of doctrinal reflection, which finally led to the solemn proclamation of the dogma of the Immaculate Conception". Here is a translation of his talk, which was the 20th in the series on the Blessed Virgin and was given in Italian.*

1. Mary, "full of grace", has been recognized by the Church as "all holy and free from every stain of sin", "enriched from the first instant of her conception with the splendor of an entirely unique holiness" (*Lumen Gentium*, n. 56).

This recognition required a long process of doctrinal reflection, which finally led to the solemn proclamation of the dogma of the Immaculate Conception.

The title "made full of grace", addressed by the angel to Mary at the Annunciation, refers to the exceptional divine favor shown to the young woman of Nazareth in view of the motherhood which was announced, but it indicates more directly the effect of divine grace in Mary; Mary was inwardly and permanently imbued with grace and thus sanctified. The title kecharitomene has a very rich meaning and the Holy Spirit has never ceased deepening the Church's understanding of it.

## Sanctifying Grace Made Mary A New Creation

2 In the preceding catechesis I pointed out that in the angel's greeting the expression "full of grace" serves almost as a name: it is Mary's name in the eyes of God. In Semitic usage, a name expresses the reality of the persons and things to which it refers As a result, the title "full of grace" shows the deepest dimension of the young woman of Nazareth's personality: fashioned by grace and the object of divine favor to the point that she can be defined

by this special predilection.

The Council recalls that the Church Fathers alluded to this truth when they called Mary the "all-holy one", affirming at the same time that she was "fashioned as it were by the Holy Spirit and formed as a new creature" (*Lumen Gentium*, n. 56).

Grace, understood in the sense of "sanctifying grace" which produces personal holiness, brought about the new creation in Mary, making her fully conformed to God's plan.

3. Doctrinal reflection could thus attribute to Mary a perfection of holiness that, in order to be complete, had necessarily to include the beginning of her life.

Bishop Theoteknos of Livias in Palestine, who lived between 550 and 650, seems to have moved in the direction of this original purity. In presenting Mary as "holy and all-fair", "pure and stainless", he referred to her birth in these words: "She is born like the cherubim, she who is of a pure, immaculate clay" (Panegyric for the feast of the Assumption, 5-6).

This last expression, recalling the creation of the first man, fashioned of a clay not stained by sin, attributes the same characteristics to Mary's birth: the Virgin's origin was also "pure and immaculate", that is, without any sin. The comparison with the cherubim also emphasizes the outstanding holiness that characterized Mary's life from the very beginning of her existence.

Theoteknos' assertion marks a significant stage in the theological reflection on the mystery of the Lord's Mother. The Greek and Eastern Fathers had acknowledged a purification brought about by grace in Mary, either before the Incarnation (St. Gregory Nazianzen, Oratio 38, 16) or at the very moment of the Incarnation (St. Ephrem, Severian of Gabala, James of Sarug). Theoteknos of Uvias seems to have required of Mary an absolute purity from the beginning of her life. Indeed, she who was destined to become the Savior's Mother had to have had a perfectly holy, completely stainless origin.

4. In the eighth century, Andrew of Crete is the first theologian to see a new creation in Mary's birth. This is how he reasons: "Today humanity, in all the radiance of her immaculate nobility, receives its ancient beauty. The shame of sin had darkened the splendor and attraction of human nature; but when the Mother

of the Fair One par excellence is born, this nature regains in her person its ancient privileges and is fashioned according to a perfect model truly worthy of God.... The reform of our nature begins today and the aged world, subjected to a wholly divine transformation, receives the first fruits of the second creation" (Serm. I on the Birth of Mary).

Then, taking up again the image of the primordial clay, he states "The Virgin's body is ground which God has tilled, the first fruits of Adam's soil divinized by Christ, the image truly like the former beauty, the clay kneaded by the divine Artist" (Serm. I on the Dormition of Mary).

## Mary's Original Holiness Is Beginning Of Redemption

Mary's pure and immaculate conception is thus seen as the beginning of the new creation. It is a question of a personal privilege granted to the woman chosen to be Christ's Mother, who ushers in the time of abundant grace willed by God for all humanity.

This doctrine, taken up again in the eighth century by St. Germanus of Constantinople and St. John Damascene, sheds light on the value of Mary's original holiness, presented as the beginning of the world's Redemption.

In this way the Church's tradition assimilates and makes explicit the authentic meaning of the title "full of grace" given by the angel to the Blessed Virgin. Mary is full of sanctifying grace and is so from the first moment of her existence. This grace, according to the Letter to the Ephesians (1:6), is bestowed in Christ on all believers. Mary's original holiness represents the unsurpassable model of the gift and the distribution of Christ's grace in the world.

# Mary's Enmity Towards Satan Was Absolute

*The Scriptural texts on which the dogma of the Immaculate Conception is based were the subject of the Holy Father's catechesis at the General Audience of Wednesday, 29 May, 1996.*

*The images in these texts, "although not directly indicating the privilege of the Immaculate Conception, can be interpreted as an expression of the Father's loving care which surrounds Mary with the grace of Christ and the splendor of the Spirit", the Pope said. Here is a translation of his talk, which was the 21st in the series on the Blessed Virgin and was given in Italian.*

1. In the doctrinal reflection of the Eastern Church, the expression "full of grace", as we saw in the preceding catecheses, has been interpreted since the sixth century as a unique holiness which Mary enjoys throughout her existence, She thus initiates the new creation.

Along with Luke's account of the Annunciation, Tradition and the Magisterium have seen in the so-called Proto evangelium (Gn 3:15) a Scriptural source for the truth of Mary's Immaculate Conception. On the basis of the ancient Latin version: "She will crush your head", this text inspired many depictions of the Immaculata crushing the serpent under her feet.

On an early occasion we recalled that this version does not agree with the Hebrew text, in which it is not the woman but her offspring, her descendant, who will bruise the serpent's head. This text then does not attribute the victory over Satan to Mary but to her Son. Nevertheless, since the Biblical concept establishes a profound solidarity between the parent and the offspring, the depiction of the Immaculata crushing the serpent, not by her own power but through the grace of her Son, is consistent with the original meaning of the passage.

## Mary Was Granted Power To Resist The Devil

2. The same Biblical text also proclaims the enmity between the woman and her offspring on the one hand, and the serpent and his offspring on the other. This is a hostility expressly established by God, which has a unique importance, if we consider the problem of the Virgin's personal holiness. In order to be the irreconcilable enemy of the serpent and his offspring, Mary had to be free from all power of sin, and to be so from the first moment

of her existence.

In this regard, the Encyclical Fulgens corona, published by Pope Pius XII in 1953 to commemorate the centenary of the definition of the dogma of the Immaculate Conception, reasons thus: "If at a given moment the Blessed Virgin Mary had been left without divine grace, because she was defiled at her conception by the hereditary stain of sin, between her and the serpent there would no longer have been, at least during this period of time, however brief that eternal enmity spoken of in the earliest tradition up to the definition of the Immaculate Conception, but rather a certain enslavement" (AAS 45 [1953], 579).

The absolute hostility put between the woman and the devil thus demands in Mary the Immaculate Conception, that is, a total absence of sin, from the very beginning of her life. The Son of Mary won the definitive victory over Satan and enabled his Mother to receive its benefits in advance by preserving her from sin. As a result, the Son granted her the power to resist the devil, thus achieving in the mystery of the Immaculate Conception the most notable effect of his redeeming work.

3. By drawing our attention to Mary's special holiness and her complete removal from Satan's influence, the title "full of grace" and the Proto-evangelium enable us to perceive, in the unique privilege the Lord granted to Mary, the beginning of a new order which is the result of friendship with God and which, as a consequence, entails a profound enmity between the serpent and men.

The 12th chapter of Revelation, which speaks of the "woman clothed with the sun" (Rv 12:1), is often cited too as Biblical testimony on behalf of the Immaculate Conception. Current exegesis agrees in seeing in this woman the community of God's People, giving birth in pain to the risen Messiah. Along with the collective interpretation, however, the text suggests an individual one in the statement: "She brought forth a male child, one who is to rule all the nations with a rod of iron" (12:5). With this reference to childbirth, it is acknowledged that the woman clothed with the sun is in a certain sense identified with Mary, the woman who gave birth to the Messiah. The woman-community is actually described with the features of the woman-Mother of Jesus.

Identified by her motherhood, the woman a was with child and she cried out in her pangs of birth, in anguish for her delivery" (12:2). This note refers to the Mother of Jesus at the Cross (cf. Jn 19:25), where she shares in anguish for the delivery of the community of disciples with a soul pierced by the sword (cf. Lk 2:35). Despite her sufferings, she is "clothed with the sun", that is, she reflects the divine splendor and appears as a "great sign" of God's spousal relationship with his people.

These images, although not directly indicating the privilege of the Immaculate Conception, can be interpreted as an expression of the Father's loving care which surrounds Mary with the grace of Christ and the splendor of the Spirit.

Finally, Revelation invites us more particularly to recognize the ecclesial dimension of Mary's personality: the woman clothed with the sun represents the Church's holiness, which is fully realized in the Holy Virgin by virtue of a singular grace.

4. These Scriptural assertions, to which Tradition and the Magisterium refer in order to ground the doctrine of the Immaculate Conception, would seem to contradict the Biblical texts which affirm the universality of sin.

The Old Testament speaks of a sinful contamination which affects everyone "born of woman" (Ps 50 [51]:7; Jb 14:2). In the New Testament, Paul states that, as a result of Adam's sin, "all men sinned", and that "one man's trespass led to condemnation for all men" (Rom 5:12, 18). Therefore, as the Catechism of the Catholic Church recalls, original sin "affected human nature", which is thus found "in a fallen state". Sin is therefore transmitted "by propagation to all mankind, that is, by the transmission of a human nature deprived of original holiness and justice" (n. 404). Paul however admits an exception to this universal law: Christ, he "who knew no sin" (2 Cor 5:21), and was thus able, "where sin increased" (Rom 5:20), to make grace abound all the more.

## St. Irenaeus Presents Mary As The New Eve

These assertions do not necessarily lead to the conclusion that Mary was involved in spiritual humanity. The parallel, established by Paul between Adam and Christ, is completed by that between Eve and Mary: the role of woman, important in the drama of sin, is equally so in the Redemption of mankind.

St. Irenaeus presents Mary as the new Eve, who by her faith and obedience compensated for the disbelief and disobedience of Eve. Such a role in the economy of salvation requires the absence of sin. It was fitting that like Christ, the new Adam, Mary too, the new Eve, did not know sin and was thus capable of cooperating in the Redemption.

Sin, which washes over humanity like a torrent, halts before the Redeemer and his faithful Collaborator. With a substantial difference: Christ is all holy by virtue of the grace that in his humanity derives from the divine person; Mary is all holy by virtue of the grace received by the merits of the Savior.

# Christ's Grace Preserved Mary

*The explanation of how Mary's Immaculate Conception came to be accepted and explained by theologians was the topic of the Holy Father's catechesis at the General Audience of Wednesday, 5 June, 1996. "Christians look to Mary, the first to be redeemed by Christ and who had the privilege of not being subjected, even for an instant, to the power of evil and sin, as the perfect model and icon of that holiness which they are called to attain", the Pope said. Here is a translation of his catechesis, which was the 22nd in the series on the Blessed Virgin and was given in Italian.*

1. The doctrine of Mary's perfect holiness from the first moment of her conception met with a certain resistance in the West, on account of St. Paul's statements about original sin and about the universality of sin, which were taken up again and explained with particular force by St. Augustine.

This great doctor of the Church certainly realized that Mary's status as Mother of a completely holy Son required total purity and an extraordinary holiness. This is why, in the controversy with Pelagius, he stressed that Mary's holiness is an exceptional gift. of grace, and stated in this regard: "We make an exception for the Blessed Virgin Mary, whom, for the sake of the Lord's honor, I would in no way like to be mentioned in connection with sin. Do we not know why she was granted a greater grace in view of the complete victory over sin, she who merited to conceive and give birth to him who obviously had no sin?" (De natura et gratia, n. 42).

Augustine stressed Mary's perfect holiness and the absence of any personal sin in her because of her lofty dignity as Mother of the Lord. Nonetheless, he could not understand how the affirmation of a total absence of sin at the time of conception could be reconciled with the doctrine of the universality of original sin and the need of redemption for all Adam's descendants. This conclusion was later reached by an ever more penetrating understanding of the Church's faith, explaining how Mary had benefited from Christ's redemptive grace from her conception.

## Duns Scotus Overcame The Objections To The Immaculate Conception

2. In the ninth century the feast of Mary's Conception was also introduced in the West, first in southern Italy, in Naples, and then in England.

Around 1128, a monk of Canterbury, Eadmer, writing the first treatise on the Immaculate Conception, complained that its respective liturgical celebration, especially pleasing to those "in whom a pure simplicity and most humble devotion to God was found" (Tract. de conc. B.M. V, 1-2), had been set aside or suppressed. Wishing to promote the restoration of this feast, the devout monk rejected St. Augustine's objections to the privilege of the Immaculate Conception, based on the doctrine of the transmission of original sin in human generation. He fittingly employed the image of a chestnut "which is conceived, nourished and formed beneath its bur and yet is protected from being pricked by it" (Tract. 10). Even beneath the bur of an act of generation which in itself must transmit original sin, Eadmer argues, Mary was preserved from every stain by the explicit will of God who "was obviously able to do this and wanted to do so. Thus if he willed it, he did it" (ibid.).

Despite Eadmer, the great theologians of the 13th century made St. Augustine's difficulties their own, advancing this argument: the Redemption accomplished by Christ would not be universal if the condition of sin were not common to all human beings. And if Mary had not contracted original sin, she could not have been redeemed. Redemption in fact consists in freeing those who are in the state of sin.

3. Duns Scotus, following several 12th-century theologians, found the key to overcoming these objections to doctrine of Mary's Immaculate Conception. He held that Christ, the perfect mediator, exercised the highest act of mediation precisely in Mary, by preserving her from original sin.

Thus he introduced into theology the concept of Redemption by preservation, according to which Mary was redeemed in an even more wonderful way: not by being freed from sin, but by being preserved from sin.

The insight of Bl. Duns Scotus, who later become known as "the Doctor of I the Immaculata" was well received by theologians, especially Franciscans, from the very beginning of the 14th century. After Sixtus IV's approval in 1477 of the Mass of the Conception, this doctrine was increasingly accepted in the theological schools.

This providential development of liturgy and doctrine prepared for the definition of the Marian privilege by the Supreme Magisterium The latter only occurred many centuries later, and was spurred by a fundamental insight of faith: the Mother of Christ had to be perfectly holy from the very beginning of her life.

4. No one fails to see how the affirmation of the exceptional privilege granted to Mary stresses that Christ's redeeming action does not only free us from sin, but also preserves us from it. This dimension of preservation, which in Mary is total, is present in the redemptive intervention by which Christ, in freeing man from sin, also gives him the grace and strength to conquer its influence in his life.

## The Dogma Sheds Light On The Effects Of Grace

In this way the dogma of Mary's Immaculate Conception does not obscure but rather helps wonderfully to shed light on the effects in human nature of Christ's redemptive grace.

Christians look to Mary, the first to be redeemed by Christ and who had the privilege of not being subjected, even for an instant, to the power of evil and sin, as the perfect model and icon of that holiness (cf. *Lumen Gentium*, n. 65) which they are called to attain in their life with the help of the Lord's grace.

# Immaculate Conception

*At the General Audience of Wednesday, 12 June, 1996, the Holy Father continued his catechesis on the Immaculate Conception, this time discussing the dogmatic definition of the doctrine by Pope Pius IX. "We declare, pronounce and define that the doctrine which asserts that the Blessed Virgin Mary, from the first moment of her conception, by a singular grace and privilege of almighty God, and in view of the merits of Jesus Christ, Savior of the human race, was preserved free from every stain of original sin is a doctrine revealed by God and, for this reason, must be firmly and constantly believed by all the faithful, the Pope said in his Bull Ineffabilis. Here is a translation of the Holy Father's catechesis, which was the 23rd in the series on the Blessed Virgin and was given in Italian.*

1. Down the centuries, the conviction that Mary was preserved from every stain of sin from her conception, so that she is to be called all holy, gradually gained ground in the liturgy and theology. At the start of the 19th century, this development led to a petition drive for a dogmatic definition of the privilege of the Immaculate Conception.

Around the middle of the century, with the intention of accepting this request, Pope Pius IX, after consulting the theologians, questioned the Bishops about the opportuneness and the possibility of such a definition, convoking as it were a "council in writing". The result was significant: the vast majority of the 604 Bishops gave a positive response to the question.

After such an extensive consultation, which emphasized my venerable Predecessor's concern to express the Church's faith in the definition of the dogma, he set about preparing the document with equal care.

## Blessed Virgin Is Free From Every Stain Of Sin

The special commission of theologians set up by Pius IX to determine the revealed doctrine assigned the essential role to ecclesial practice. And this criterion influenced the formulation of the dogma, which preferred expressions taken from the Church's lived experience, from the faith and worship of the Christian people, to scholastic definitions.

Finally in 1854, with the Bull Ineffabilis, Pius IX solemnly proclaimed the dogma of the Immaculate Conception: "... We declare, pronounce and define that the doctrine which asserts that the Blessed Virgin Mary, from the first moment of her conception, by a singular grace and privilege of almighty God, and in view of the merits of Jesus Christ, Savior of the human race, was preserved free from every stain of original sin is a doctrine revealed by God and, for this reason, must be firmly and constantly believed by all the faithful" (DS 2803).

2. The proclamation of the dogma of the Immaculate Conception expresses the essential datum of faith. Pope Alexander VII, in the Bull Sollicitudo of 1661, spoke of the preservation of Mary's soul "in its creation and infusion into the body" (DS 2017). Pius IX's definition, however, prescinds from all explanations about how the soul is infused into the body and attributes to the person of Mary, at the first moment of her conception, the fact of her being preserved from every stain of original sin.

The freedom "from every stain of original sin" entails as a positive consequence the total freedom from all sin as well as the proclamation of Mary's perfect holiness, a doctrine to which the dogmatic definition makes a fundamental contribution. In fact, the negative formulation of the Marian privilege, which resulted from the earlier controversies about original sin that arose in the West, must always be complemented by the positive expression of Mary's holiness more explicitly stressed in the Eastern tradition.

Pius IX's definition refers only to the freedom from original sin and does not explicitly include the freedom from concupiscence. Nevertheless, Mary's complete preservation from every stain of sin also has as a consequence her freedom from concupiscence, a disordered tendency which, according to the Council of Trent, comes from sin and inclines to sin (DS 1515).

3. Granted "by a singular grace and privilege of almighty God", this preservation from original sin is an absolutely gratuitous divine favor, which Mary received at the first moment of her existence. The dogmatic definition does not say that this singular privilege is unique, but lets that be implied. The affirmation of this uniqueness, however, is explicitly stated in the Encyclical Fulgens corona of 1953, where Pope Pius XI speaks of "the very singular privilege which was never granted to another person" (AAS 45 [1953], 580), thus excluding the possibility, maintained by some but without foundation, of attributing this privilege also to St. Joseph.

The Virgin Mother received the singular grace of being immaculately conceived "in view of the merits of Jesus Christ, Savior of the human race", that is, of his universal redeeming action. The text of the dogmatic definition does not expressly declare that Mary was redeemed, but the same Bull Ineffabilis states elsewhere that "she was redeemed in the most sublime way". This is the extraordinary truth: Christ was the redeemer of his Mother and carried out his redemptive action in her "in the most perfect way" (Fulgens corona, AAS 45 [1953], 581), from the first moment of her existence. The Second Vatican Council proclaimed that the Church "admires and exalts in Mary the most excellent fruit of the Redemption" (Sacrosanctum Concilium, n. 103).

## Solemn Definition Serves The Faith Of God's People

4. This solemnly proclaimed doctrine is expressly termed a "doctrine revealed by God". Pope Pius IX adds that it must be "firmly and constantly believed by all the faithful". Consequently,

whoever does not make this doctrine his own, or maintains an opinion contrary to it, "is shipwrecked in faith" and "separates himself from Catholic unity." In proclaiming the truth of this dogma of the Immaculate Conception, my venerable Predecessor was conscious of exercising his power of infallible teaching as the universal Pastor of the Church, which several years later would be solemnly defined at the First Vatican Council. Thus he put his infallible Magisterium into action as a service to the faith of God's People; and it is significant that he did so by defining Mary's privilege.

# Mary Was Free From All Personal Sin

*The doctrine of Mary's perfect. holiness was the subject of the Holy Father's catechesis at the General Audience of Wednesday, 19 June, 1996. This truth asserts "that Mary, free from original sin, was also preserved from all actual sin and that this initial holiness was granted to her in order to fill her entire life", the Pope said. Here is a translation of his catechesis, which was the 24th in the series on the Blessed Virgin and was given in Italian.*

1. The definition of the dogma of the Immaculate Conception directly concerns only the first moment of Mary's existence, from when she was "preserved free from every stain of original sin. The papal Magisterium thus wished to define only the truth which had been the subject of controversy down the centuries: her preservation from original sin, and was not concerned with defining the lasting holiness of the Lord's Virgin Mother.

This truth already belongs to the common awareness of the Christian people. It testifies that Mary, free from original sin, was also preserved from all actual sin and that this initial holiness was granted to her in order to fill her entire life.

## No Sin Or Imperfection Can Be Attributed To Mary

2. The Church has constantly regarded Mary as holy and

free from all sin or moral imperfection. The Council of Trent expresses this conviction, affirming that no one "can avoid all sins, even venial sins, throughout his life, unless he is given a special privilege, as the Church holds with regard to the Blessed Virgin" (DS 1573). Even the Christian transformed and renewed by grace is not spared the possibility of sinning. Grace does not preserve him from all sin throughout his whole life, unless, as the Council of Trent asserts, a special privilege guarantees this immunity from sin. And this is what happened with Mary.

The Council of Trent did not wish to define this privilege but stated that the Church vigorously affirms it: "Tenet", that is, she firmly holds it. This is a decision which, far from relegating this truth to pious belief or devotional opinion, confirms its nature as a solid doctrine, quite present in the faith of the People of God. Moreover, this conviction is based on the grace attributed to Mary by the angel at the time of the Annunciation. Calling her "full of grace", kecharitomene, the angel acknowledged her as the woman endowed with a lasting perfection and a fullness of sanctity, without shadow of sin or of moral or spiritual imperfection.

3. Several early Fathers of the Church, who were not yet convinced of her perfect holiness, attributed imperfections or moral defects to Mary. Some recent authors have taken the same position. However, the Gospel texts cited to justify these opinions provide no basis at all for attributing a sin or even a moral imperfection to the Mother of the Redeemer.

Jesus' reply to his mother at the age of 12: "How is it that you sought me? Did you not know that I must be in my Father's house?" (Lk 2:49), has sometimes been interpreted as a veiled rebuke. A careful reading of the episode, however, shows that Jesus did not rebuke his mother and Joseph for seeking him, since they were responsible for looking after him.

Coming upon Jesus after an anxious search, Mary asked him only the "why" of his behavior "Son, why have you treated us so?" (Lk 2.48). And Jesus answers with another "why", refraining from any rebuke and referring to the mystery of his divine sonship.

Nor can the words he spoke at Cana: "O woman, what have you to do with me? My hour has not yet come" (Jn 2:4), be interpreted as a rebuke. Seeing the likely inconvenience which the lack of wine would have caused the bride and groom, Mary speaks to Jesus with simplicity, entrusting the problem to him. Though aware of being the Messiah bound to obey the Father's will alone, he answers the Mother's implicit request. He responds above all to the Virgin's faith and thus performs the first of his miracles, thereby manifesting his glory.

4. Later some gave a negative interpretation to the statement Jesus made when, at the beginning of his public life, Mary and his relatives asked to see him. Relating to us Jesus' reply to the one who said to him: "Your mother and your brethren are standing outside, desiring to see you", the Evangelist Luke offers us the interpretive key to the account, which must be understood on the basis of Mary's inner inclinations, which were quite different from those of his "brethren" (cf. Jn 7:5). Jesus replied: "My mother and my brethren are those who hear the word of God and do it" (Lk 8:21). In the Annunciation account, Luke in fact showed how Mary was the model of listening to the word of God and of generous docility. Interpreted in this perspective, the episode offers great praise of Mary, who perfectly fulfilled the divine plan in her own life. Although Jesus' words are opposed to the brethren's attempt, they exalt Mary's fidelity to the will of God and the greatness of her motherhood, which she lived not only physically but also spiritually.

In expressing this indirect praise, Jesus uses a particular method: he stresses the nobility of Mary's conduct in the light of more general statements, and shows more clearly the Virgin's solidarity with and closeness to humanity on the difficult way of holiness.

Lastly, the words: "Blessed rather are those who hear the word of God and keep it!" (Lk 11:28), spoken by Jesus in reply to the woman who had called his Mother blessed, far from putting into doubt Mary's personal perfection, bring out her faithful fulfillment of the word of God: so has the Church understood them, putting this sentence into the liturgical celebrations in Mary's honor.

The Gospel text actually suggests that he made this statement to reveal that the highest reason for his Mother's blessedness lies precisely in her intimate union with God and her perfect submission to the divine word.

## Mary Belonged Completely To The Lord

5. The special privilege granted by God to her who is "all holy" leads us to admire the marvels accomplished by grace in her life. It also reminds us that Mary belonged always and completely to the Lord, and that no imperfection harmed her perfect harmony with God.

Her earthly life was therefore marked by a constant, sublime growth in faith, hope and charity. For believers, Mary is thus the radiant sign of divine Mercy and the sure guide to the loftiest heights of holiness and Gospel perfection.

# Mary Freely Cooperated In God's Plan

*At the General Audience of Wednesday, 3 July, 1996, the Holy Father returned to his catechesis on the Blessed Mother. In speaking of Our Lady's response to the angel's announcement that she would be the mother of the Messiah, the Pope said: "Mary is asked to assent to a truth never expressed before. She accepts it with a simple yet daring heart. With the question: 'How can this be?', she expresses her faith in the divine power to make virginity compatible with her exceptional and unique motherhood'. Here is a translation of his catechesis, which was the 25th in the series on the Blessed Virgin and was given in Italian.*

1. In the Gospel account of the Visitation, Elizabeth, "filled with the Holy Spirit", welcomes Mary to her home and exclaims: "Blessed is she who believed that there would be a fulfillment of what was spoken to her from the Lord" (Lk 1:45). This beatitude, the first reported in Luke's Gospel, presents Mary as the one who, by her faith, precedes the Church in fulfilling the spirit of the beatitudes.

Elizabeth's praise of Mary's faith is reinforced by comparing it to the angel's announcement to Zechariah. A superficial reading of the two announcements might consider Zechariah and Mary as having given similar responses to the divine message: "How shall I know this? For I am an old man, and my wife is advanced in years", Zechariah says; and Mary: "How can this be, since I have no husband?" (Lk 1:18, 34). But the profound difference between the interior attitudes of the principals in these two episodes can be seen from the very words of the angel, who rebukes Zechariah for his disbelief, while he gives an immediate reply to Mary's question. Unlike Elizabeth's husband, Mary fully submits to the divine plan and does not condition her consent on the granting of a visible sign.

The angel, who proposed that she become a mother, is reminded by Mary of her intention to remain a virgin. Believing that the announcement could be fulfilled, she questions the divine messenger only about the manner of its accomplishment, in order better to fulfill God's will, to which she intends to submit with total readiness. "She sought the manner; she did not doubt God's omnipotence", St. Augustine remarks (Sermo 291).

## Intense Listening And Pure Faith
## Is Required Of Mary

2. The context in which the two announcements are made also helps to exalt the excellence of Mary's faith. In Luke's account, we see the more favorable situation of Zechariah and the inadequacy of his response. He receives the angel's announcement in the temple of Jerusalem, at the altar before the "Holy of Holies" (cf. Ex 30:6-8); the angel addresses him as he is offering incense, thus, as he is carrying out his priestly duties, at a significant moment in his life, the divine decision is communicated to him in a vision. These particular circumstances favor an easier understanding of the divine authenticity of the message and offer an incentive to accept it promptly.

The announcement to Mary, however, takes place in a simpler, workaday context, without the external elements of sacredness which accompanied the one made to Zechariah. Luke does not indicate the precise place where the Annunciation of the Lord's birth occurred: he reports only that Mary was in

Nazareth, a village of little importance, which did not seem predestined for the event. In addition, the Evangelist does not ascribe unusual importance to the moment when the angel appears and does not describe the historical circumstances. In meeting the heavenly messenger, one's attention is focused on the meaning of his words, which demand of Mary intense listening and a pure faith.

This last consideration allows us to appreciate the greatness of Mary's faith, especially in comparison with the tendency, then as now, to ask insistently for sensible signs in order to believe. In contrast, the Virgin's assent to the divine will is motivated only by her love of God.

3. Mary is asked to assent to a much holier truth than that announced to Zechariah. The latter was invited to believe in a wondrous birth that would take place within a sterile marital union, which God wished to make fruitful: a divine intervention similar to those benefiting several Old Testament women: Sarah (Gn 17:15-21; 18:10-14), Rachel (Gn 30:22), the mother of Samson (Jgs 13:1-7), Hanna, the mother of Samuel (1 Sm 1:11-20). In these episodes the gratuitousness of God's gift is particularly emphasized.

Mary is called to believe in a virginal motherhood, for which the Old Testament mentions no precedent. In fact, the well-known prophecy of Isaiah: "Behold, a young woman shall conceive and bear a Son, and shall call his name Emmanuel" (7:14), although not excluding such a view, was explicitly interpreted in this sense only after Christ's coming and in the light of the Gospel revelation.

Mary is asked to assent to a truth never expressed before. She accepts it with a simple yet daring heart. With the question: "How can this be?", she expresses her faith in the divine power to make virginity compatible with her exceptional and unique motherhood.

By replying: "The Holy Spirit will come upon you, and the power of the Most High will overshadow you" (Lk 1:35), the angel offers God's ineffable solution to the question Mary asked. Virginity, which seemed an obstacle, becomes the concrete context in which the Holy Spirit will accomplish in her the conception of the incarnate Son of God. The angel's response opens the way to the

Virgin's cooperation with the Holy Spirit in the begetting of Jesus.

4. The free cooperation of the human person is realized in carrying out the divine plan. By believing in the Lord's word, Mary cooperates in fulfilling the motherhood announced to her.

## Mary's Act Of Faith Recalls The Faith Of Abraham

The Fathers of the Church often stress this aspect of Jesus' virginal conception. In commenting on the Gospel of the Annunciation, St. Augustine in particular states: "The angel announces, the Virgin listens, believes and conceives" (Sermo 13 in Nat. Dom.). And again: "Christ is believed and conceived through faith. The coming of faith first occurs in the Virgin's heart and then fruitfulness comes to the Mother's womb" (Sermo 293).

Mary's act of faith recalls the faith of Abraham, who at the dawn of the Old Covenant, believed in God and thus became the father of a great posterity (cf. Gn 15:6; *Redemptoris Mater*, n. 14). At the start of the New Covenant, Mary also exerts a decisive influence with her faith on the fulfillment of the mystery of the Incarnation, the beginning and the synthesis of Jesus' entire redeeming mission.

The close relationship between faith and salvation, stressed by Jesus in his public life (cf. Mt 5:34; 10:52; etc.), helps us also to understand the fundamental role which Mary's faith exercised and continues to exercise in the salvation of the human race.

# Virginal Conception Is Biological Fact

*The virginity of Mary and Jesus' virginal conception were the subject of the Holy Father's catechesis at the General Audience of Wednesday, 10 July, 1996. This truth of faith is set forth in the Gospels and confirmed by subsequent tradition. "The uniform Gospel witness testifies how faith in the virginal conception of Jesus was firmly rooted in various milieux of the early Church", the Pope said. Here is a translation of his catechesis, which was the 26th in the series on the Blessed Virgin Mary and was given in Italian.*

1. The Church has constantly held that Mary's virginity is a truth of faith, as she has received and reflected on the witness of the Gospels of Luke, of Matthew and probably also of John.

In the episode of the Annunciation, the Evangelist Luke calls Mary a "virgin" referring both to her intention to persevere in virginity, as well as to the divine plan which reconciles this intention with her miraculous motherhood. The affirmation of the virginal conception, due to the action of the Holy Spirit, excludes every hypothesis of natural parthenogenesis and rejects the attempts to explain Luke's account as the development of a Jewish theme or as the derivation of a pagan mythological legend.

The structure of the Lucan text (cf. Lk 1:26-38; 2:19, 51) resists any reductive interpretation. Its coherence does not validly support any mutilation of the terms or expressions which affirm the virginal conception brought about by the Holy Spirit.

2. The Evangelist Matthew, reporting the angel's announcement to Joseph, affirms like Luke that the conception was "the work of the Holy Spirit" (Mt 1:20) and excluded marital relations.

Furthermore, Jesus' virginal conception is communicated to Joseph at a later time: for him it is not a question of being invited to give his assent prior to the conception of Mary's Son, the fruit of the supernatural intervention of the Holy Spirit and the cooperation of the mother alone. He is merely asked to accept freely his role as the Virgin's husband and his paternal mission with regard to the child.

Matthew presents the virginal origins of Jesus as the fulfillment of Isaiah's prophecy. "'Behold, a virgin shall conceive and bear a Son, and his name shall be called Emmanuel' (which means, God with us)" (Mt 1:23; cf. Is 7:14). In this way Matthew leads us to conclude that the virginal conception was the object of reflection in the first Christian community, which understood its conformity to the divine plan of salvation and its connection with the identity of Jesus, "God with us".

# Early Church Firmly Believed In Virginal Conception

3. Unlike Luke and Matthew, Mark's Gospel does not mention Jesus' conception and birth; nonetheless it is worth noting that Mark never mentions Joseph, Mary's husband. Jesus is called "the Son of Mary" by the people of Nazareth or in another context, "the Son of God" several times (3:11; 5:7; cf. 1:11; 9:7; 14:61-62; 15:39). These facts are in harmony with belief in the mystery of his virginal conception. This truth, according to a recent exegetical discovery, would be explicitly contained in verse 13 of the Prologue of John's Gospel, which some ancient authoritative authors (for example, Irenaeus and Tertullian) present, not in the usual plural form, but in the singular: "He, who was born, not of blood nor of the will of the flesh nor of the will of man, but of God". This version in the singular would make the Johannine Prologue one of the major attestations of Jesus' virginal conception, placed in the context of the mystery of the Incarnation.

Paul's paradoxical affirmation: "But when the time had fully come, God sent forth his Son, born of woman... so that we might receive adoption as sons" (Gal 4:4-5), paves the way to the question about this Son's personhood, and thus about his virginal birth.

The uniform Gospel witness testifies how faith in the virginal conception of Jesus was firmly rooted in various milieux of the early Church. This deprives of any foundation several recent interpretations which understand the virginal conception not in a physical or biological sense, but only as symbolic or metaphorical: it would designate Jesus as God's gift to humanity. The same can be said for the opinion advanced by others, that the account of the virginal conception would instead be a theologoumenon, that is, a way of expressing a theological doctrine, that of Jesus' divine sonship, or would be a mythological portrayal of him.

As we have seen, the Gospels contain the explicit affirmation of a virginal conception of the biological order, brought about by the Holy Spirit. The Church made this truth her own, beginning with the very first formulations of the faith (cf. Catechism of the Catholic Church, n. 496).

4. The faith expressed in the Gospels is confirmed without interruption in later tradition. The formulas of faith of the first Christian writers presuppose the assertion of the virginal birth: Aristides, Justin, Irenaeus and Tertullian are in agreement with

Ignatius of Antioch, who proclaims Jesus "truly born of a virgin" (Smyrn. 1, 2). These authors mean a real, historical virginal conception of Jesus and are far from hailing a virginity that is only moral or a vague gift of grace manifested in the child's birth.

The solemn definitions of faith by the Ecumenical Councils and the papal Magisterium, which follow the first brief formulas of faith, are in perfect harmony with this truth. The Council of Chalcedon (451), in its profession of faith, carefully phrased and with its infallibly defined content, affirms that Christ was "begotten... as to his humanity in these last days, for us and for our salvation, by the Virgin Mary, the Mother of God" (DS 301). In the same way the Third Council of Constantinople (681) proclaimed that Jesus Christ was "begotten as to his humanity, by the Holy Spirit and the Virgin Mary, she who is properly and in all truth the Mother of God" (DS 555). other Ecumenical Councils (Constantinople II, Lateran II and Lyons II) declared Mary "ever-virgin", stressing her perpetual virginity (DS 423, 801, 852). These affirmations were taken up by the Second Vatican Council, which highlighted the fact that Mary "through her faith and obedience... gave birth on earth to the very Son of the Father, not through the knowledge of man but by the overshadowing of the Holy Spirit" (*Lumen Gentium*, n. 63).

In addition to the conciliar definitions, there are the definitions of the papal Magisterium concerning the Immaculate Conception of the "Blessed Virgin Mary" (DS 2803) and the Assumption of the "Immaculate and Ever-Virgin Mother of God" (DS 3903).

## Mary's Holiness And Virginity Are Closely Linked

5. Although the definitions of the Magisterium, except for those of the Lateran Council of 649, desired by Pope Martin I, do not explain the meaning of the term "virgin", it is clear that this term is used in its customary sense: the voluntary abstention from sexual acts and the preservation of bodily integrity. However, physical integrity is considered essential to the truth of faith of Jesus virginal conception (cf. Catechism of the Catholic Church, n. 496).

The description of Mary as "Holy Ever-Virgin, Immaculate"

draws attention to the connection between holiness and virginity. Mary wanted a virginal life, because she was motivated by the desire to give her whole heart to God.

The expression used in the definition of the assumption, "the Immaculate, Ever-Virgin Mother of God" also implies the connection between Mary's virginity and her motherhood: two prerogatives miraculously combined in the conception of Jesus, true God and true man. Thus Mary's virginity is intimately linked to her divine motherhood and perfect holiness.

## Our Lady Intended To Remain A Virgin

*"The extraordinary case of the Virgin of Nazareth must not let us fall into the error of tying her inner dispositions completely to the mentality of her surroundings, thereby eliminating the uniqueness of the mystery that came to pass in her", the Holy Father said at the General Audience of Wednesday, 24 July, 1996, as he reflected on Mary's intention to remain a virgin. Here is a translation of his catechesis, which was the 27th in the series on the Blessed Mother and was given in Italian.*

1. Mary asks a question of the angel who tells her of Jesus' conception and birth: 'How can this be since I do not know man" (Lk 1:34). Such a query seems surprising, to say the least, if we call to mind the Biblical accounts that relate the announcement of an extraordinary birth to a childless woman. Those cases concerned married women who were naturally sterile, to whom God gave the gift of a child through their normal conjugal life (1 Sm 1:19-20), in response to their anguished prayers (cf. Gn 15:2; 30:22-23; 1 Sm 1:10; Lk 1:13).

Mary receives the angel's message in a different situation. She is not a married woman with problems of sterility; by a voluntary choice she intends to remain a virgin. Therefore her intention of virginity, the fruit of her love for the Lord, appears to be an obstacle to the motherhood announced to her.

At first sight, Mary's words would seem merely to express only her present state of virginity Mary would affirm that she does not 'know" man, that is, that she is a virgin Nevertheless, the context in which the question is asked "How can this be", and the affirmation that follows: 'since I do not know man", emphasize both Mary's present virginity and her intention to remain a virgin. The expression she uses, with the verb in the present tense, reveals the permanence and continuity of her state.

## Mary Cooperated Fully With God's Will

2. Mentioning this difficulty, Mary does not at all oppose the divine plan, but shows her intention to conform totally to it. Moreover, the girl from Nazareth always lived in full harmony with the divine will and had chosen a virginal life with the intention of pleasing the Lord. In fact, her intention of virginity disposed her to accept God's will "with all her human and feminine 'I', and this response of faith included both perfect cooperation with the 'grace of God that precedes and assists' and perfect openness to the action of the Holy Spirit" (*Redemptoris Mater*, n. 13).

To some, Mary's words and intentions appear improbable, since in the Jewish world virginity was considered neither a value nor an ideal to be pursued. The same Old Testament writings confirm this in several well-known episodes and expressions. In the Book of Judges, for example, Jephthah's daughter who, having to face death while still young and unmarried, bewails her virginity, that is, she laments that she has been unable to marry (Jgs 11:38). Marriage, moreover, by virtue of the divine command, "Be fruitful and multiply" (Gn 1:28), is considered woman's natural vocation which involves the joys and sufferings that go with motherhood.

3. In order better to understand the context in which Mary's decision came to maturity it is necessary to remember that in the period immediately preceding the beginning of the Christian era, a certain positive attitude to virginity began to appear in some Jewish circles. For example, the Essenes, of whom many important historical testimonies have been found at Qurnran, lived in celibacy or restricted the use of marriage because of community life and the search for greater intimacy with God.

Furthermore, in Egypt there was a community of women

who, associated with the Essene spirituality, observed continence. These women, the Therapeutae, belonging to a sect described by Philo of Alexandria (De Vita Contemplativa, 21-90), were dedicated to contemplation and sought wisdom.

It does not seem that Mary ever knew about these Jewish religious groups which practiced the ideal of celibacy and virginity. But the fact that John the Baptist probably lived a celibate life and that in the community of his disciples it was held in high esteem would support the supposition that Mary's choice of virginity belonged to this new cultural and religious context.

4. However, the extraordinary case of the Virgin of Nazareth must not lead us into the error of tying her inner dispositions completely to the mentality of her surroundings, thereby eliminating the uniqueness of the mystery that came to pass in her. In particular, we must not forget that, from the very beginning of her life, Mary received a wondrous grace, recognized by the angel at the moment of the Annunciation. "Full of grace" (Lk 1:28), Mary was enriched with a perfection of holiness that, according to the Church's interpretation, goes back to the very first moment of her existence: the unique privilege of the Immaculate Conception influenced the whole development of the young woman of Nazareth's spiritual life.

## The Lord Transforms Mary's Poverty Into Riches

Thus it should be maintained that Mary was guided to the ideal of virginity by an exceptional inspiration of that same Holy Spirit who, in the course of the Church's history, will spur many women to the way of virginal consecration.

The singular presence of grace in Mary's life leads to the conclusion that the young girl was committed to virginity. Filled with the Lord's exceptional gifts from the beginning of her life, she was oriented to a total gift of self, body and soul, to God in the offering of herself as a virgin.

In addition, her aspiration to the virginal life was in harmony with that "poverty" before God which the Old Testament holds in high esteem. Fully committing herself to this path, Mary also gives up motherhood, woman's personal treasure, so deeply appreciated in Israel. Thus she "stands out among the poor and humble of the Lord, who confidently hope for and receive salvation from him" (*Lumen Gentium*, n. 55). However, presenting herself to God as poor and aiming only at spiritual fruitfulness, the fruit of divine love, at the moment of the Annunciation, Mary discovers that the Lord has transformed her poverty into riches: she will be the Virgin Mother of the Son of the Most High. Later she will also discover that her motherhood is destined to extend to all men, whom the Son came to save (cf. Catechism of the Catholic Church, n. 501).

# Eternal Son Of God Is Also Born Of Mary

*The profound relationship between Mary's virginity and the mystery of the Incarnation was the subject of the Holy Father's catechesis at the General Audience of Wednesday, 31 July, 1996. Through the Redemption accomplished by her Son, Mary becomes the spiritual mother of all those who receive new birth to eternal life. Here is a translation of the Pope's catechesis, which was the 28th in the series on the Blessed Virgin and was given in Italian.*

1. In his saving plan, God wanted his only Son to be born of a virgin. This divine decision calls for a profound relationship between Mary's virginity and the Incarnation of the Word. "The eyes of faith can discover in the context of the whole of Revelation the mysterious reasons why God in his saving plan wanted his Son to be born of a virgin. These reasons touch both on the person of Christ and his redemptive mission, and on the welcome Mary gave that mission on behalf of all men" (Catechism of the Catholic Church, n. 502).

The virginal conception, by excluding human fatherhood, affirms that Jesus' only father is the heavenly Father and that the Son's being born in time reflects his eternal birth: the Father, who begot the Son in eternity, also begets him in time as a man.

2. The account of the Annunciation emphasizes his state as "Son of God", the result of God's intervention in his conception.

"The Holy Spirit will come upon you, and the power of the Most High will overshadow you; therefore the child to be born will be called holy, the Son of God" (Lk 1:35).

## Virginal Conception Is Result Of Mary's Cooperation

He who is born of Mary is already Son of God by virtue of his eternal birth; his virginal birth, brought about by the Most High, shows that he is Son of God even in his humanity.

The revelation of his eternal birth in his virginal birth is also suggested by the passages in the Prologue of John's Gospel which relate the manifestation of the invisible God to the work of the "the only Son, who is in the bosom of the Father" (1:18), by his coming in the flesh:

"And the Word became flesh and dwelt among us, full of grace and truth; we have beheld his glory, glory as of the only Son from the Father" (Lk 1:14).

In recounting the birth of Jesus, Luke and Matthew also speak of the role of the Holy Spirit. The latter is not the father of the Child. Jesus is the Son of the Eternal Father alone (cf. Lk 1:32-35), who through the Spirit is at work in the world and begets the Word in his human nature. Indeed, at the Annunciation the angel calls the Spirit "the power of the Most High" (Lk 1:35), in harmony with the Old Testament, which presents him as the divine energy at work in human life, making it capable of marvelous deeds. Manifesting itself to the supreme degree in the mystery of the Incarnation, this power, which in the Trinitarian life of God is Love, has the task of giving humanity the Incarnate Word.

3. The Holy Spirit, in particular, is the person who communicates divine riches to men and makes them sharers in God's life. He, who in the mystery of the Trinity is the unity of the Father and the Son, unites humanity with God by bringing about the virginal birth of Jesus.

The mystery of the Incarnation also highlights the incomparable greatness of Mary's virginal motherhood: the conception of Jesus is the fruit of her generous cooperation with the action of the Spirit of Love, the source of all fruitfulness.

In the divine plan of salvation, the virginal conception is therefore an announcement of the new creation: by the work of the Holy Spirit, he who will be the new Adam is begotten in Mary. As the Catechism of the Catholic Church states: "Jesus is conceived by the Holy Spirit in the Virgin Mary's womb because he is the New Adam who inaugurates the new creation" (n. 504).

## Believers Are Given Power
## To Become God's Children

The role of Mary's virginal motherhood shines forth in the mystery of this new creation. Calling Christ "the first-born of the Virgin" (Ad Haer., 3, 16, 4), St. Irenaeus recalls that after Jesus many others are born of the Virgin, in the sense that they receive the new life of Christ. "Jesus is Mary's only Son, but her spiritual motherhood extends to all men whom indeed he came to save: the Son whom she brought forth is he whom God placed as the first-born among many brethren, that is, the faithful in whose generation and formation she cooperates with a mother's love" (Catechism of the Catholic Church, n. 501).

4. The communication of the new life is the transmission of divine sonship. Here we can recall the perspective opened up by John in the Prologue of his Gospel: he who was begotten by God gives all believers the power to become children of God (cf. Jn 1:12-13). The virginal birth allows the extension of the divine fatherhood: men are made the adoptive children of God in him who is Son of the Virgin and of the Father.

Contemplating the mystery of the virgin birth thus enables us to realize that God chose a Virgin Mother for his Son to offer his fatherly love more generously to humanity.

# Mary's Choice Inspires Consecrated Virginity

*"Mary's virginal life inspires in the entire Christian people esteem for the gift of virginity and the desire that it should increase in the Church as a sign of God's primacy over all reality", the Holy Father said at the General Audience of Wednesday, 7 August,*

*1996, as he continued his reflection on Mary's choice of virginity, the fruit of the Holy Spirit's grace. Here is a translation of his catechesis, which was the 29th in the series on the Blessed Mother and was given in Italian.*

1. The intention to remain a virgin, apparent in Mary's words at the moment of the Annunciation, has traditionally been considered the beginning and the inspiration of Christian virginity in the Church.

St. Augustine does not see in this resolution the fulfillment of a divine precept, but a vow freely taken. In this way it was possible to present Mary as an example to "holy virgins" throughout the Church's history. Mary "dedicated her virginity to God when she did not yet know whom she would conceive, so that the imitation of heavenly life in the earthly, mortal body would come about through a vow, not a precept, through a choice of love and not through the need to serve" (De Sancta Virg., IV, PL 40 398).

The Angel does not ask Mary to remain a virgin, it is Mary who freely reveals her intention of virginity. The choice of love that leads her to consecrate herself totally to the Lord by a life of virginity is found in this commitment.

In stressing the spontaneity of Mary's decision, we must not forget that God's initiative is at the root of every vocation. By choosing the life of virginity, the young girl of Nazareth was responding to an interior call, that is, to an inspiration of the Holy Spirit that enlightened her about the meaning and value of the virginal gift of heresy. No one can accept this gilt without feeling called or without receiving from the Holy Spirit the necessary light and strength.

## Mary Made A Firm Decision For Virginity

2. Although St. Augustine uses the word "vow" to show those he calls "holy virgins" the first example of their state of life, the Gospel does not testify that Mary had expressly made a vow, which is the form of consecration and offering of one's life to God

which has been in use since the early centuries of the Church. From the Gospel we learn that Mary made a personal decision to remain a virgin, offering her heart to the Lord. She wants to be his faithful bride, fulfilling her vocation as the "daughter of Zion". By her decision however she becomes the archetype of all those in the Church who have chosen to serve the Lord with an undivided heart in virginity.

Neither the Gospels nor any other New Testament writings tell us when Mary made the decision to remain a virgin. However it is clearly apparent from her question to the angel at the time of the Annunciation that she had come to a very firm decision. Mary does not hesitate to express her desire to preserve her virginity even in view of the proposed motherhood, showing that her intention had matured over a long period.

Indeed, Mary's choice of virginity was not made in the unforeseeable prospect of becoming the Mother of God, but developed in her consciousness before the Annunciation. We can suppose that this inclination was always present in her heart: the grace which prepared her for virginal motherhood certainly influenced the whole growth of her personality, while the Holy Spirit did not fail to inspire in her, from her earliest years, the desire for total union with God.

3. The marvels God still works today in the hearts and lives of so many young people were first realized in Mary's soul. Even in our world, so distracted by the attractions of a frequently superficial and consumerist culture, many adolescents accept the invitation that comes from Mary's example and consecrate their youth to the Lord and to the service of their brothers and sisters.

This decision is the choice of greater values, rather than the renunciation of human values. In this regard, in his Apostolic Exhortation Marialis Cultus my venerable predecessor Paul VI emphasizes how anyone who looks at the witness of the Gospel with an open mind "will appreciate that Mary's choice of the state of virginity was not a rejection of any of the values of the married state but a courageous choice which she made in order to consecrate herself totally to the love of God" (n. 37).

In short, the choice of the virginal state is motivated by full adherence to Christ. This is particularly obvious in Mary. Although before the Annunciation she is not conscious of it, the Holy Spirit inspires her virginal consecration in view of Christ: she remains a virgin to welcome the Messiah and Savior with her whole being. The virginity begun in Mary thus reveals its own Christocentric dimension, essential also for virginity lived in the Church, which finds its sublime model in the Mother of Christ. If her personal virginity, linked to the divine motherhood, remains an exceptional fact, it gives light and meaning to every gift of virginity.

## Consecrated Virginity Is Source Of Spiritual Fruitfulness

4. How many young women in the Church's history, as they contemplate the nobility and beauty of the virginal heart of the Lord's Mother, have felt encouraged to respond generously to God's call by embracing the ideal of virginity! "Precisely such virginity", as I recalled in the Encyclical *Redemptoris Mater*, "after the example of the Virgin of Nazareth, is the source of a special spiritual fruitfulness: it is the source of motherhood in the Holy Spirit" (n. 43).

Mary's virginal life inspires in the entire Christian people esteem for the gift of virginity and the desire that it should increase in the Church as a sign of God's primacy over all reality and as a prophetic anticipation of the life to come. Together let us thank the Lord for those who still today generously consecrate their lives in virginity to the service of the kingdom of God. At the same time, while in various regions evangelized long ago hedonism and consumerism seem to dissuade ask God through Mary's intercession for a new flowering of religious vocations Thus the face of Christ's Mother, reflected in the many virgins who strive to follow the divine Master, will continue mercy and tenderness for humanity.

# Mary And Joseph, Lived Gift Of Virginity

*The grace to live both the charism of virginity and the gift of marriage, which was given to Mary and Joseph, was the subject of the Holy Father's catechesis at the General Audience of Wednesday, 21 August, 1996. Although Joseph did not physically generate the Lord, his was a very real fatherhood, the Pope said. Here is a translation of his catechesis, which was the 30th in the series on the Blessed Virgin and was given in Italian.*

1. In presenting Mary as a "virgin", the Gospel of Luke adds that she was "betrothed to a man whose name was Joseph, of the house of David" (Lk 1:27). These two pieces of information at first sight seem contradictory. It should be noted that the Greek word used in this passage does not indicate the situation of a woman who has contracted marriage and therefore lives in the marital state, but that of betrothal. Unlike what occurs in modern cultures, however, the ancient Jewish custom of betrothal provided for a contract and normally had definitive value: it actually introduced the betrothed to the marital state, even if the marriage was brought to full completion only when the young man took the girl to his home.

At the time of the Annunciation, Mary thus had the status of one betrothed. We can wonder why she would accept betrothal, since she had the intention of remaining a virgin forever. Luke is aware of this difficulty, but merely notes the situation without offering any explanation. The fact that the Evangelist, while stressing Mary's intention of virginity, also presents her as Joseph's spouse, is a sign of the historical reliability of the two pieces of information.

## Joseph Was Called To Cooperate In Saving Plan

2. It may be presumed that at the time of their betrothal there was an understanding between Joseph and Mary about the plan to live as a virgin. Moreover, the Holy Spirit, who had inspired Mary to choose virginity in view of the mystery of the Incarnation and who wanted the latter to come about in a family setting suited

to the Child's growth, was quite able to instill in Joseph the ideal of virginity as well.

The angel of the Lord appeared in a dream and said to him: "Joseph, Son of David, do not fear to take Mary your wife, for that which is conceived in her is of the Holy Spirit" (Mt 1:20). Thus he received confirmation that he was called to live his marriage in a completely special way. Through virginal communion with the woman chosen to give birth to Jesus, God calls him to cooperate in carving out his plan of salvation.

The type of marriage to which the Holy Spirit led Mary and Joseph can only be understood in the context of the saving plan and of a lofty spirituality. The concrete realization of the mystery of the Incarnation called for a virgin birth which would highlight the divine sonship and, at the same time, for a family that could provide for the normal development of the Child's personality.

Precisely in view of their contribution to the mystery of the Incarnation of the Word, Joseph and Mary received the grace of living both the charism of virginity and the gift of marriage. Mary and Joseph's communion of virginal love, although a special case linked with the concrete realization of the mystery of the Incarnation, was nevertheless a true marriage (cf. Apostolic Exhortation Redemptoris custos, n. 7).

The difficulty of accepting the sublime mystery of their spousal communion has led some, since the second century, to think of Joseph as advanced in age and to consider him Mary's guardian more than her husband. It is instead a case of supposing that he was not an elderly man at the time, but that his interior perfection, the fruit of grace, led him to live his spousal relationship with Mary with virginal affection.

## Leo XIII Entrusted Entire Church To Joseph's Protection

3. Joseph's cooperation in the mystery of the Incarnation also includes exercising the role of Jesus' father. The angel acknowledged this function of his when he appeared in a dream and invited him to name the Child: "She will bear a Son, and you

shall call his name Jesus, for he will save his people from their sins" (Mt 1:21).

While excluding physical generation, Joseph's fatherhood was something real, not apparent. Distinguishing between father and the one who begets, an ancient monograph on Mary's virginity the De Margarita (fourth century) states that "the commitments assumed by the Virgin and by Joseph as husband and wife made it possible for him to be called by this name (father); a father, however, who did not beget". Joseph thus carried out the role of Jesus' father, exercising an authority to which the Redeemer was freely "obedient" (Lk 2:51), contributing to his upbringing and teaching him the carpenter's trade.

Christians have always acknowledged Joseph as the one who lived in intimate communion with Mary and Jesus, concluding that also in death he enjoyed their affectionate, consoling presence. From this constant Christian tradition, in many places a special devotion has grown to the Holy Family and, in it, to St. Joseph, Guardian of the Redeemer. As everyone knows, Pope Leo XIII entrusted the entire Church to his protection.

# The Church Presents Mary As 'Ever Virgin'

*Mary's perpetual virginity was the subject of the Holy Father's catechesis at the General Audience of Wednesday, 28 August, 1996. The most ancient texts and the early Christians, the Pope said, confirm that the Church has always professed the belief that Mary never ceased to be a virgin. Here is a translation of his catechesis, which was the 31st in the series on the Blessed Virgin Mary and which was given in Italian.*

1. The Church has always professed her belief in the perpetual virginity of Mary. The most ancient texts, when referring to the conception of Jesus, call Mary simply "virgin", inferring that they considered this quality a permanent fact with regard to her whole life.

The Early Christians expressed this conviction of faith in the Greek term *aeiparthenos*, "ever virgin", created to describe Mary's person in a unique and effective manner, and to express in a single word the Church's belief in her perpetual virginity. We find it used in the second symbol of faith composed by St. Epiphanius in the year 374, in relation to the Incarnation: the Son of God "was incarnate, that is, he was generated in a perfect way by Mary, the ever blessed virgin, through the Holy Spirit" (*Ancoratus*, 119,5; DS 44).

The expression "ever virgin" was taken up by the Second Council of Constantinople (553), which affirms: the Word of God, "incarnate of the holy and glorious Mother of God and *ever virgin* Mary, was born of her" (DS 422). This doctrine is confirmed by two other Ecumenical Councils, the Fourth Lateran Council (1215) (DS 801) and the Second Council of Lyons (1274) (DS 852), and by the text of the definition of the dogma of the assumption (1950) (DS 3903) in which Mary's perpetual virginity is adopted as one of the reasons why she was taken up in body and soul to heavenly glory.

## Mary Is Virgin Before, During And After Giving Birth

2. In a brief formula, the Church traditionally presents Mary as "virgin *before, during* and *after* giving birth", affirming, by indicating these three moments, that she never ceased to be a virgin.

Of the three, the affirmation of her virginity "before giving birth" is, undoubtedly, the most important, because it refers to Jesus' conception and directly touches the very mystery of the Incarnation. From the beginning it has been constantly present in the Church's belief.

Her virginity "during and after giving birth", although implicit in the title virgin already attributed to Mary from the Church's earliest days, became the object of deep doctrinal study since some began explicitly to cast doubts on it. Pope St. Hormisdas explains that "the Son of God became Son of man, born in time in the manner of a man, opening his mother's womb to birth (cf. Lk 2:23) and, through God's power, not dissolving his mother's virginity" (DS 368). This doctrine was confirmed by the Second Vatican

Council, which states that the firstborn Son of Mary "did not diminish his Mother's virginal integrity but sanctified it" (*Lumen Gentium*, n. 57). As regards her virginity after the birth, it must first of all be pointed out that there are no reasons for thinking that the will to remain a virgin, which Mary expressed at the moment of the Annunciation (cf. Lk 1:34) was then changed. Moreover, the immediate meaning of the words: "Woman, behold, your Son!", "Behold, your mother" (Jn 19:26), which Jesus addressed to Mary and to his favorite disciple from the Cross, imply that Mary had no other children.

Those who deny her virginity after the birth thought they had found a convincing argument in the term "first-born", attributed to Jesus in the Gospel (Lk 2:7), almost as though this word implied that Mary had borne other children after Jesus. But the word "first-born" literally means "a child not preceded by another" and, in itself, makes no reference to the existence of other children. Moreover, the Evangelist stresses this characteristic of the Child, since certain obligations proper to Jewish law were linked to the birth of the firstborn Son, independently of whether the mother might have given birth to other children. Thus every only Son was subject to these prescriptions because he was "begotten first" (cf. Lk 2:23).

## Several Degrees Of Relationship Are Implied By The Term 'Brother'

3. According to some, Mary's virginity after the birth is denied by the Gospel texts which record the existence of four "brothers of Jesus": James, Joseph, Simon and Judas (Mt 13:55-56; Mk 6:3), and of several sisters.

It should be recalled that no specific term exists in Hebrew and Aramaic to express the word "cousin", and that the terms "brother" and "sister", therefore had a far broader meaning which included several degrees of relationship. In fact, the phrase "brothers of Jesus" indicates "the children" of a Mary who was a disciple of Christ (cf. Mt 27:56) and who is significantly described as "the other Mary" (Mt 28:1). "They are close relations of Jesus, according to an Old Testament expression" (Catechism of the Catholic Church, n. 500).

Mary Most Holy is thus the "ever virgin". Her prerogative is the consequence of her divine motherhood which totally consecrated her to Christ's mission of redemption.

# Mary Offers Sublime Model Of Service

*"Mary makes the Father's will the inspiring principle of her whole life, seeking in it the necessary strength to fulfill the mission entrusted to her", the Holy Father said at the General Audience of Wednesday, 4 September, 1996, as he reflected on Mary's response to the angel at the Annunciation, an act of free submission to God. Here is a translation of his catechesis, which was the 32nd in the series on the Blessed Mother and was given in Italian.*

1. Mary's words at the Annunciation "I am the handmaid of the Lord; let it be to me according to your word" (Lk 1:38), indicate an attitude characteristic of Jewish piety. At the beginning of the Old Covenant, Moses, in response to the Lord's call, proclaims himself his servant (cf. Ex 4:10; 14:31). With the coming of the New Covenant, Mary also responds to God with an act of free submission and conscious abandonment to his will, showing her complete availability to be the "handmaid of the Lord".

In the Old Testament, the qualification "servant" of God links all those who are called to exercise a mission for the sake of the Chosen People: Abraham (Gn 26:24), Isaac (Gn 24:14) Jacob (Ex 32:13; Ez 37:25), Joshua (Jos 24:29), David (2 Sam 7, 8, etc.). Prophets and priests, who have been entrusted with the task of forming the people in the faithful service of the Lord, are also servants. The Book of the Prophet Isaiah exalts, in the docility of the "suffering Servant" a model of fidelity to God in the hope of redemption for the sins of the many (cf. Is 42:53). Some women also offer examples of fidelity, such as Queen Esther who, before interceding for the salvation of the Jews, addresses a prayer to God, calling herself many times "your servant" (Est 4:17).

2. Mary, "full of grace" by proclaiming herself "handmaid of the Lord" intends to commit herself to fulfill personally and in a perfect manner the service God expects of all his people. The words: "Behold, I am the handmaid of the Lord" foretell the One who will say of himself: "The Son of man also came not to be served but to serve, and to give his life as a ransom for many" (Mk 10:45; cf. Mt 20:28). Thus the Holy Spirit brings about a harmony of intimate dispositions between the Mother and the Son, which will allow Mary to assume fully her maternal role to Jesus, as she accompanies him in his mission as Servant. In Jesus' life the will to serve is constant and surprising: as Son of God, he could rightly have demanded to be served. Attributing to himself the title "Son of Man', whom, according to the Book of Daniel, "all peoples, nations, and languages should serve' (Dn 7:14), he could have claimed mastery over others. Instead, combating the mentality of the time which was expressed in the disciples' ambition for the first places (cf. Mk 9:34) and in Peter's protest during the washing of the feet (cf. Jn 13:6), Jesus does not want to be served, but desires to serve to the point of totally giving his life in the work of redemption.

3. Furthermore, Mary, although aware of the lofty dignity conferred upon her at the angel's announcement, spontaneously declares herself "the handmaid of the Lord". In this commitment of service she also includes the intention to serve her neighbor, as the link between the episodes of the Annunciation and the Visitation show: informed by the angel of Elizabeth's pregnancy, Mary sets out "with haste" (Lk 1:39) for Judah, with total availability to help her relative prepare for the birth. She thus offers Christians of all times a sublime model of service.

The words: "let it be to me according to your word" (Lk 1:38), show in her who declared herself handmaid of the Lord, a total obedience to God's will.

The optative genoito, "let it be done" used by Luke, expresses not only acceptance but staunch assumption of the divine plan, making it her own with the involvement of all her personal resources.

## By Conforming To God's Will,
## Mary Anticipates Attitude Of Christ

4. By conforming to the divine will, Mary anticipates and makes her own the attitude of Christ who, according to the Letter to the Hebrews, coming into the world, says: "Sacrifice and offerings you did not desire, but a body you prepared for me.... Then I said "Behold, I come to do your will, O God" (Heb 10:5-7; Ps 40 [39]: 7-9).

Mary's docility likewise announces and prefigures that expressed by Jesus in the course of his public life until Calvary. Christ would say: "My food is to do the will of him who sent me, and to accomplish his work" (Jn 4:34). On these same lines, Mary makes the Father's will the inspiring principle of her whole life, seeking in it the necessary strength to fulfill the mission entrusted to her.

If at the moment of the Annunciation, Mary does not yet know of the sacrifice which will mark Christ's mission, Simeon's prophecy will enable her to glimpse her Son's tragic destiny (cf. Lk 3:34-35). The Virgin will be associated with him in intimate sharing. With her total obedience to God's will, Mary is ready to live all that divine love may plan for her life, even to the "sword" that will pierce her soul.

# Mary, The New Eve, Freely Obeyed God

*"In stating her total 'yes' to the divine plan, Mary is completely free before God. At the same time, she feels personally responsible for humanity, whose future was linked with her reply", the Holy Father said at the General Audience of Wednesday, 18 September, 1996, as he examined the significance of Mary as the New Eve. Here is a translation of the Pope's catechesis, which was given in Italian and was the 33rd in the series on the Blessed Mother.*

1. Commenting on the episode of the Annunciation, the Second Vatican Council gives special emphasis to the value of

Mary's assent to the divine messenger's words. Unlike what occurs in similar Biblical accounts, it is expressly awaited by the angel: "The Father of mercies willed that the Incarnation should be preceded by assent on the part of the predestined mother, so that just as a woman had a share in bringing about death, so also a woman should contribute to life" (*Lumen Gentium*, n. 56).

Lumen Gentium recalls the contrast between Eve's behavior and that of Mary, described by St. Irenaeus: "Just as the former that is, Eve was seduced by the words of an angel so that she turned away from God by disobeying his word, so the latter, Mary, received the good news from an angel's announcement in such a way as to give birth to God by obeying his word; and as the former was seduced so that she disobeyed God, the latter let herself be convinced to obey God, and so the Virgin Mary became the advocate of the virgin Eve. And as the human race was subjected to death by a virgin, it was liberated by a Virgin; a virgin's disobedience was thus counterbalanced by a Virgin's obedience..." (Adv. Haer., V, 19, 1).

## Mary Cooperated Through Free Faith And Obedience

2. In stating her total "yes" to the divine plan, Mary is completely free before God. At the same time, she feels personally responsible for humanity, whose future was linked with her reply.

God puts the destiny of all mankind in a young woman's hands. Mary's "yes" is the premise for fulfilling the plan which God in his love had prepared for the world's salvation.

The Catechism of the Catholic Church briefly and effectively summarizes the decisive value for all humanity of Mary's free consent to the divine plan of salvation. "The Virgin Mary cooperated through free faith and obedience in human salvation. She uttered her 'yes in the name of all human nature'. By her obedience she became the New Eve, mother of the living" (n. 511).

3. By her conduct, Mary reminds each of us of our serious responsibility to accept God's plan for our lives. In total obedience

to the saving will of God expressed in the angel's words, she becomes a model for those whom the Lord proclaims blessed, because they "hear the word of God and keep it" (Lk 11:28). Jesus, in answering the woman in the crowd who proclaimed his mother blessed, discloses the true reason for Mary's blessedness: her adherence to God's will, which led her to accept the divine motherhood.

In the Encyclical *Redemptoris Mater*, I pointed out that the new spiritual motherhood of which Jesus speaks is primarily concerned with her. Indeed, "Is not Mary the first of 'those who hear the word of God and do it'? And therefore does not the blessing uttered by Jesus in response to the woman in the crowd refer primarily to her?" (n. 20). In a certain sense therefore Mary is proclaimed the first disciple of her Son (cf. ibid.) and, by her example, invites all believers to respond generously to the Lord's grace.

4. The Second Vatican Council explains Mary's total dedication to the person and work of Christ: "She devoted herself totally, as a handmaid of the Lord, to the person and work of her Son, under and with him, serving the mystery of redemption, by the grace of almighty God" (*Lumen Gentium*, n. 56).

For Mary, dedication to the person and work of Jesus means intimate union with her Son, motherly involvement in nurturing his human growth and cooperation with his work of salvation.

## Mary Became Cause Of Salvation For All Humanity

Mary carries out this last aspect of her dedication to Jesus "under him", that is, in a condition of subordination, which is the fruit of grace. However this is true cooperation, because it is realized "with him" and, beginning with the Annunciation, it involves active participation in the work of redemption. "Rightly, therefore", the Second Vatican Council observes, "the Fathers see Mary not merely as passively engaged by God, but as freely cooperating in the work of man's salvation through faith and obedience. For, as St. Irenaeus says, she 'being obedient, became the cause of salvation for herself and for the whole human race (Adv. Haer. III,

22, 4)"' (ibid.).

Mary, associated with Christ's victory over the sin of our first parents, appears as the true "mother of the living" (ibid.). Her motherhood, freely accepted in obedience to the divine plan, becomes a source of life for all humanity.

# Visitation Is Prelude To Jesus

*At the General Audience of Wednesday, 2 October, 1996, the Holy Father returned to his series of reflections on the Blessed Virgin Mary. Speaking of the Visitation, the Pope said: "Mary's visit to Elizabeth, in fact, is a prelude to Jesus' mission and, in cooperating from the beginning of her motherhood in the Son's redeeming work, she becomes the model for those in the Church who set out to bring Christ's light and joy to the people of every time and place". Here is a translation of his catechesis, which was the 34th in the series on the Blessed Virgin and was given in Italian.*

1. In the Visitation episode, St. Luke shows how the grace of the Incarnation, after filling Mary, brings salvation and joy to Elizabeth's house. The Savior of men, carried in his Mother's womb, pours out the Holy Spirit, revealing himself from the very start of his coming into the world.

In describing Mary's departure for Judea, the Evangelist uses the verb "anistemi", which means "to arise", "to start moving". Considering that this verb is used in the Gospels to indicate Jesus' resurrection (Mk 8:31; 9:9, 31; Lk 24:7,46) or physical actions that imply a spiritual effort (Lk 5:27-28; 15:18,20), we can suppose that Luke wishes to stress with this expression the vigorous zeal which led Mary, under the inspiration of the Holy Spirit, to give the world its Savior.

## Meeting With Elizabeth Is A Joyous Saving Event

2. The Gospel text also reports that Mary made the journey "with haste" (Lk 1:39). Even the note "into the hill country" (Lk 1:39), in the Lucan context, appears to be much more than a

simple topographical indication, since it calls to mind the messenger of good news described in the Book of Isaiah: "How beautiful upon the mountains are the feet of him who brings good tidings, who publishes peace, who brings good tidings of good, who publishes salvation, who says to Zion: "Your God reigns"' (Is 52:7).

Like St. Paul, who recognizes the fulfillment of this prophetic text in the preaching of the Gospel (Rom 10:15), St. Luke also seems to invite us to see Mary as the first "evangelist", who spreads the "good news", initiating the missionary journeys of her divine Son.

Lastly, the direction of the Blessed Virgin's journey is particularly significant: it will be from Galilee to Judea, like Jesus' missionary journey (cf. 9:51).

Mary's visit to Elizabeth, in fact, is a prelude to Jesus' mission and, in cooperating from the beginning of her motherhood in the Son's redeeming work, she becomes the model for those in the Church who set out to bring Christ's light and joy to the people of every time and place.

3. The meeting with Elizabeth has the character of a joyous saving event that goes beyond the spontaneous feelings of family sentiment. Where the embarrassment of disbelief seems to be expressed in Zechariah's muteness, Mary bursts out with the joy of her quick and ready faith: "She entered the house of Zechariah and greeted Elizabeth" (Lk 1:40).

St. Luke relates that "when Elizabeth heard the greeting of Mary, the babe leaped in her womb" (Lk 1:41). Mary's greeting caused Elizabeth's Son to leap for joy: Jesus' entrance into Elizabeth's house, at Mary's doing, brought the unborn prophet that gladness which the Old Testament foretells as a sign of the Messiah's presence.

At Mary's greeting, messianic joy comes over Elizabeth too and "filled with the Holy Spirit she exclaimed with a loud cry, "Blessed are you among women, and blessed is the fruit of your womb!"' (Lk 1:41-42).

By a higher light, she understands Mary's greatness: more than Joel and Judith, who prefigured her in the Old Testament, she is blessed among women because of the fruit of her womb, Jesus, the Messiah.

4. Elizabeth's exclamation, made "with a loud cry", shows a true religious enthusiasm, which continues to be echoed on the lips of believers in the prayer "Hail Mary", as the Church's song of praise for the great works accomplished by the Most High in the Mother of his Son.

In proclaiming her 'blessed among women", Elizabeth points to Mary's faith as the reason for her blessedness: "And blessed is she who believed that there would be a fulfillment of what was spoken to her from the Lord" (Lk 1:45). Mary's greatness and joy arise from the fact the she is the one who believes.

In view of Mary's excellence, Elizabeth also understands what an honor her visit is for her: And why is this granted me, that the mother of my Lord should come to me?" (Lk 1:43). With the expression "my Lord", Elizabeth recognizes the royal, indeed messianic, dignity of Mary's Son In the Old Testament this expression was in fact used to address the king (cf. 1 Kgs 1:13,20,21 etc.) and to speak of the Messiah King (Ps 110:1). The angel had said of Jesus: The Lord God will give to him the throne of his father David" (Lk 1:32). "Filled with the Holy Spirit", Elizabeth has the same insight. Later, the paschal glorification of Christ will reveal the sense in which this title is to be understood, that is, a transcendent sense (cf. Jn 20:28; Acts 2:34-36).

## Mary Is Present In Whole Work Of Divine Salvation

With her admiring exclamation, Elizabeth invites us to appreciate all that the Virgin's presence brings as a gift to the life of every believer.

In the Visitation, the Virgin brings Christ to the Baptist's mother, the Christ who pours out the Holy Spirit. This role of mediatrix is brought out by Elizabeth's very words: "For behold, when the voice of your greeting came to my ears, the babe in my womb leaped for joy" (Lk 1:44). By the gift of the Holy Spirit, Mary's presence serves as a prelude to Pentecost, confirming a cooperation which, having begun with the Incarnation, is destined to be expressed in the whole work of divine salvation.

# Mary Sings The Praises Of God

*At the General Audience of Wednesday, 6 November, 1996, the Holy Father returned to his catechesis on the Virgin Mary with a reflection on her song known as the Magnificat. "With her wise reading of history, Mary leads us to discover the criteria of God's mysterious action. Overturning the judgments of the world, he comes to the aid of the poor and lowly", the Pope said, pointing out that it is humility of heart which the Lord finds especially attractive. Here is a translation of the Holy Father's catechesis, which was the 35th in the series on the Blessed Virgin and was given in Italian.*

1. Inspired by the Old Testament tradition, with the song of the Magnificat Mary celebrates the marvels God worked in her. This song is the Virgin's response to the mystery of the Annunciation: the angel had invited her to rejoice and Mary now expresses the exultation of her spirit in God her Savior. Her joy flows from the personal experience of God's looking with kindness upon her, a poor creature with no historical influence.

The word Magnificat, the Latin version of a Greek word with the same meaning, celebrates the greatness of God, who reveals his omnipotence through the angel's message, surpassing the expectations and hopes of the people of the Covenant, and even blest aspirations of the human soul.

## He Who Is Mighty Has Done Great Things For Me

In the presence of the powerful and merciful Lord, Mary expresses her own sense of lowliness: "My soul magnifies the Lord and my spirit rejoices in God my Savior, for he has regarded the low estate of his handmaiden" (Lk 1:47-48). The Greek word "tapeinosis" is probably borrowed from the song of Hannah, Samuel's mother. It calls attention to the "humiliation" and "misery" of a barren woman (cf. 1 Sam 1:11), who confides her pain to the

Lord. With a similar expression, Mary makes known her situation of poverty and her awareness of being little before God, who by a free decision looked on her, a humble girl from Nazareth and called her to become the Mother of the Messiah.

2. The words "henceforth all generations will call me blessed" (Lk 1:48) arise from the fact that Elizabeth was the first to proclaim Mary "blessed" (Lk 1:45). Not without daring, the song predicts that this same proclamation will be extended and increased with relentless momentum. At the same time, it testifies to the special veneration for the Mother of Jesus which has been present in the Christian community from the very first century. The Magnificat is the first fruit of the various forms of devotion, passed on from one generation to the next, in which the Church has expressed her love for the Virgin of Nazareth.

3. "For he who is mighty has done great things for me and holy is his name. And his mercy is on those who fear him from generation to generation" (Lk 1:49-50).

What are the "great things" that the Almighty accomplished in Mary? The expression recurs in the Old Testament to indicate the deliverance of the people of Israel from Egypt or Babylon. In the Magnificat, it refers to the mysterious event of Jesus' virginal conception, which occurred in Nazareth after the angel's announcement.

In the Magnificat, a truly theological song because it reveals the experience Mary had of God's looking upon her, God is not only the Almighty to whom nothing is impossible, as Gabriel had declared (cf. Lk 1:37), but also the Merciful, capable of tenderness and fidelity towards every human being.

4. "He has shown strength with his arm, he has scattered the proud in the imagination of their hearts, he has put down the mighty from their thrones, and exalted those of low degree; he has filled the hungry with good things, and the rich he has sent empty away" (Lk 1: 51-53).

With her wise reading of history, Mary' leads us to discover the criteria of God's mysterious action. Overturning the judgments of the world, he comes to the aid of the poor and lowly, to the detriment of the rich and powerful, and in a surprising way he has with good things the humble who entrust their lives to him (cf.

*Redemptoris Mater*, n. 37).

While these words of the song show us Mary' as a concrete and sublime model, they give us to understand that it is especially humility of heart which attracts God's kindness.

## God Fulfills His Promises In Mary With Abundant Generosity

5. Lastly, the song exalts the fulfillment of God's promises and his fidelity to the chosen people: "He has helped his servant Israel, in remembrance of his mercy, as he spoke to our fathers, to Abraham and to his posterity for ever" (Lk 1:54-55).

Filled with divine gifts, Mary does not limit her vision to her own personal case, but realizes how these gifts show forth God's mercy towards all his people. In her, God fulfills his promises with a superabundance of fidelity and generosity.

Inspired by the Old Testament and by the spirituality of the daughter of Zion, the Magnificat surpasses the prophetic texts on which it is based, revealing in her who is "full of grace" the beginning of a divine intervention which far exceeds Israel's messianic hopes: the holy mystery of the Incarnation of the Word.

# Nativity Shows Mary's Closeness

*At the General Audience of Wednesday, 20 November, 1996, the Holy Father returned to his catechesis on the Blessed Mother. In speaking of the Nativity, the Pope said: "Mary experiences childbirth in a condition of extreme poverty: she cannot give the Son of God even what mothers usually offer a newborn baby; instead, she has to lay him 'in a manger', an improvised cradle which contrasts with the dignity of the 'Son of the Most High ". Here is a translation of his catechesis, which was the 36th in the series on the Blessed Virgin and was given in Italian.*

1. In the story of Jesus' birth, the Evangelist Luke recounts several facts that help us better understand the meaning of the event.

He first mentions the census ordered by Caesar Augustus, which obliges Joseph, "of the house and lineage of David", and Mary his wife to go "to the city of David, which is called Bethlehem" (Lk 2:4).

In informing us about the circumstances in which the journey and birth take place, the Evangelist presents us with a situation of hardship and poverty, which lets us glimpse some basic characteristics of the messianic kingdom: a kingdom without earthly honors or powers, which belongs to him who, in his public life, will say of himself: "The Son of man has nowhere to lay his head" (Lk 9:58).

2. Luke's account contains a few seemingly unimportant notes, which are meant to arouse in the reader a better understanding of the mystery of the Nativity and the sentiments of her who gave birth to the Son of God.

The description of the birth, recounted in simple fashion, presents Mary as intensely participating in what was taking place in her: "She gave birth to her first-born Son and wrapped him in swaddling clothes, and laid him in a manger..." (Lk 2:7). The Virgin's action is the result of her complete willingness to cooperate in God's plan, already expressed at the Annunciation in her "let it be to me according to your word" (Lk 1:38).

## Mary Shares In Son's Redeeming Mission

Mary experiences childbirth in a condition of extreme poverty: she cannot give the Son of God even what mothers usually offer a newborn baby; instead, she has to lay him "in a manger", an improvised cradle which contrasts with the dignity of the "Son of the Most High".

3. The Gospel notes that "there was no place for them in the inn" (Lk 2:7). This statement, recalling the text in John's Prologue: "His own people received him not" (Jn 1:11), foretells as it were the many refusals Jesus will meet with during his earthly life. The phrase "for them" joins the Son and the Mother in this rejection, and shows how Mary is already associated with her Son's destiny of suffering and shares in his redeeming mission.

Rejected by "his own", Jesus is welcomed by the shepherds, rough men of ill repute, but chosen by God as the first to receive the good news of the Savior's birth. The message the Angel gives them is an invitation to rejoice:

"Behold, I bring you good news of a great joy which will come to all the people" (Lk 2:10), along with a request to overcome all fear: "Be not afraid".

Indeed, as it was for Mary at the time of the Annunciation, so too for them the news of Jesus' birth represents the great sign of God's goodwill towards men. In the divine Redeemer, contemplated in the poverty of a Bethlehem cave, we can see an invitation to approach with confidence the One who is the hope of humanity.

The angels' song: "Glory to God in the highest, and on earth peace among men with whom he is pleased!", which can also be translated as "men of goodwill" (Lk 2:14), reveals to the shepherds what Mary had expressed in her Magnificat Jesus' birth is the sign of God's merciful love, which is especially shown towards the poor and humble.

4. The shepherds respond enthusiastically and promptly to the angel's invitation: "Let us go over to Bethlehem and see this thing that has happened, which the Lord has made known to us" (Lk 2:15).

They did not search in vain: "And they found Mary and Joseph, and the babe" (Lk 2:16). To them, as the Council recalls, "the Mother of God joyfully showed her first-born Son" (*Lumen Gentium*, n. 57). It was the defining moment of their lives.

## Mary Pondered These Events In Her Heart

The shepherds' spontaneous desire to make known what "had been told them concerning this child" (Lk 2:17), after the wondrous experience of meeting the Mother and her Son, suggests to evangelizers in every age the importance and, even more, the necessity of a deep spiritual relationship with Mary, in order to know Jesus better and to become the joyful proclaimers of his Gospel of salvation.

With regard to these extraordinary events, Luke tells us that Mary "kept all these things, pondering them in her heart" (Lk 2:19). While the shepherds passed from fear to wonder and praise, the Virgin, because of her faith, kept alive the memory of the events involving her Son, and deepened her understanding of them by reflecting on them in her heart, that is, in the inmost core of her person. In this way she suggests that another mother, the Church, should foster the gift and task of contemplation and theological reflection, in order better to accept the mystery of salvation, to understand it more thoroughly and to proclaim it with renewed effort to the people of every age.

# Church Proclaims Mary 'Mother Of God"

*The Church "also contemplates with wonder and celebrates with veneration the immense greatness conferred on Mary by the One who wanted to be her Son," the Holy Father said at the General Audience of Wednesday, 27 November, 1996, as he discussed the Blessed Virgin's title "Mother of God." Here is a translation of his catechesis, which was the 37th in the series on the Blessed Mother and was given in Italian.*

1. Contemplation of the mystery of the Savior's birth has led Christian people not only to invoke the Blessed Virgin as the Mother of Jesus, but also to recognize her as Mother of God. This truth was already confirmed and perceived as belonging to the Church's heritage of faith from the early centuries of the Christian era, until it was solemnly proclaimed at the Council of Ephesus in 431.

In the first Christian community, as the disciples became more aware that Jesus is the Son of God, it became ever clearer that Mary is the Theotokos, the Mother of God. This is a title which does not appear explicitly in the Gospel texts, but in them the "Mother of Jesus" is mentioned and it is affirmed that Jesus is God (Jn 20:28; cf. 5:18; 10:30, 33). Mary is in any case presented as the Mother of Emmanuel, which means "God with us" (cf. Mt 1:22-23).

Already in the third century, as can be deduced from an ancient written witness, the Christians of Egypt addressed this prayer to Mary: "We fly to thy patronage, O holy Mother of God: despise not our petitions in our necessities, but deliver us from all evil, O glorious and blessed Virgin" (from the Liturgy of the Hours). The expression Theotokos appears explicitly for the first time in this ancient witness.

In pagan mythology, it often happened that a certain goddess would be presented as the mother of some god. For example, the supreme god, Zeus, had the goddess Rhea as his mother. This context perhaps helped Christians to use the title "Theotokos," "Mother of God," for the Mother of Jesus. It should nevertheless be noted that this title did not exist but was created by Christians to express a belief which had nothing to do with pagan mythology, belief in the virginal conception in Mary's womb of the One who had always been the eternal Word of God.

## Council Of Ephesus Proclaimed Mary As The Mother Of God

2. By the fourth century, the term Theotokos was frequently used in the East and West. Devotion and theology refer more and more to this term, which had by now become part of the Church's patrimony of faith.

One can therefore understand the great protest movement that arose in the fifth century when Nestorius cast doubt on the correctness of the title "Mother of God." In fact, being inclined to hold that Mary was only the mother of the man Jesus, he maintained that "Mother of Christ" was the only doctrinally correct expression. Nestorius was led to make this error by his difficulty in admitting the unity of Christ's person and by his erroneous interpretation of the distinction between the two natures, divine and human, present in him. In 431 the Council of Ephesus condemned his theses and, in affirming the subsistence of the divine and human natures in the one person of the Son, proclaimed Mary the Mother of God.

3. Now, the difficulties and objections raised by Nestorius

offer us the opportunity to make several useful reflections for correctly understanding and interpreting this title. The expression Theotokos, which literally means, "she who has begotten God," can at first sight seem surprising; in fact it raises the question as to how it is possible for a human creature to give birth to God. The answer of the Church's faith is clear. Mary's divine motherhood refers only to the human begetting of the Son of God but not, however, to his divine birth. The Son of God was eternally begotten of God the Father, and is consubstantial with him. Mary, of course, has no part in this eternal birth. However, the Son of God assumed our human nature 2,000 years ago and was conceived by and born of Mary. In proclaiming Mary "Mother of God," the Church thus intends to affirm that she is the "Mother of the Incarnate Word, who is God." Her motherhood does not, therefor, extend to all the Trinity, but only to the Second Person, the Son, who, in becoming incarnate, took his human nature from her.

Motherhood is a relationship of person to person: a mother is not only mother of the body or of the physical creature born in her womb, but of the person she begets. Thus having given birth, according to his human nature, to the person of Jesus, who is a divine person, Mary is the Mother of God.

## Blessed Virgin's Consent Precedes Incarnation

4. In proclaiming Mary "Mother of God," the Church in a single phrase professes her belief regarding the Son and the mother. This union was already seen at the council of Ephesus; in defining Mary's divine motherhood, the Fathers intended to emphasize their belief in the divinity of Christ. Despite ancient and recent objections about the appropriateness of recognizing Mary by this title. Christians of all times by correctly interpreting the meaning of motherhood, have made it a privileged expression of their faith in the divinity of Christ and their love for the Blessed virgin.

On the one hand, the Church recognizes the Theotokos as guaranteeing the reality of the Incarnation because, as St. Augustine says, "if the Mother were fictitious, the flesh would also be fictitious... and the scars of the resurrection" (Tract. In Ev. Ioannis,

8, 6-7). On the other hand, she also contemplates with wonder and celebrates with veneration the immense greatness conferred on Mary by the One who wanted to be her Son. The expression "Mother of God" refers to the word of God, who in the Incarnation assumed the lowliness of the human condition in order to raise man to divine sonship. But in the light of the sublime dignity conferred on the Virgin of Nazareth, this title also proclaims the nobility of woman and her loftiest vocation. God in fact treats Mary as a free and responsible being and does not bring about the Incarnation of his Son until after he has obtained her consent.

Following the example of the ancient Christians of Egypt, let the faithful entrust themselves to her, who, being the Mother of God, can obtain from her divine Son the grace of deliverance from evil and of eternal salvation.

## Blessed Virgin Is Model Of Perfect Love

*"Looking at the results, we can certainly conclude that Mary's teaching was deep and effective, and found very fertile soil in Jesus' human psychology", the Holy Father said at the General Audience of Wednesday, 4 December, 1996, as he focused on Mary's role in raising her Son Jesus. Here is a translation of his catechesis, which was the 38th in the series on the Blessed Virgin, and was given in Italian.*

1. Although occurring by the work of the Holy Spirit and a Virgin Mother, the birth of Jesus, like that of all human beings, went through the phases of conception, gestation and delivery. In addition, Mary's motherhood was not limited to the biological process of giving birth, but as it happens with every other mother, she also made an essential contribution to her Son's growth and development.

A mother is not only a woman who gives birth to a child, but one who brings him up and teaches him; indeed, we might well say that, according to God's plan, the educational task is the natural extension of procreation.

Mary is the Theotokos, not only because she conceived

and gave birth to the Son of God, but also because she accompanied him in his human growth.

## Mary Was Particularly Suited To Being A Teacher

2. We might think that, since Jesus possessed in himself the fullness of divinity, he had no need of teachers. But the mystery of the Incarnation reveals to us that the Son of God came into the world in a human condition similar to us in all things except sin (cf. Heb 4:15). As is the case with every human being, Jesus' growth, from infancy to adulthood (cf. Lk 2:40), also needed his parent's educational activity.

The Gospel of Luke, particularly attentive to the childhood period, says that at Nazareth Jesus was obedient to Joseph and Mary (cf. Lk 2:51). This dependence shows us that Jesus was receptive, open to the teaching of his mother and Joseph, who also carried out their task by virtue of the docility he constantly showed.

3. The special gifts which God had showered on Mary made her particularly suited to her task as mother and teacher. In the concrete circumstances of everyday life, Jesus could find in her a model to follow and imitate and an example of perfect love for God and for his brothers and sisters.

Along with Mary's motherly presence, Jesus could count on the paternal figure of Joseph, a just man (cf. Mt 1:19), who provided the necessary balance in the educational activity. Carrying out his role as father, Joseph cooperated with his wife in making the home in Nazareth an environment favorable to the growth and personal maturity of the Savior of humanity. By later introducing him to the hard work of the carpenter, Joseph enabled Jesus to be involved in the world of work and social life.

4. The few elements that the Gospel offers do not allow us to know and fully appreciate the ways in which Mary taught her divine Son. Certainly she, together with Joseph, introduced Jesus to the rites and prescriptions of Moses, to prayer to the God of the Covenant by using the Psalms, to the history of the people of Israel centered on the Exodus from Egypt. From her and Joseph Jesus learned to attend the synagogue and to make the annual

pilgrimage to Jerusalem for the Passover.

Looking at the results, we can certainly conclude that Mary's teaching was deep and effective, and found very fertile soil in Jesus' human psychology.

## Mary And Joseph Are Models For All Parents

5. Mary's educational task with regard to such a unique Son presents several special features in comparison with the role of other mothers. She only provided favorable conditions for the development of the potential and essential values for growth, already present in the Son. For example, the absence of any form of sin in Jesus demanded a constantly positive orientation from Mary, which excluded any form of corrective intervention. Furthermore, although it was his mother who introduced Jesus to the culture and traditions of the people of Israel, it was he, from the time of his finding in the temple, who would reveal his full awareness of being the Son of God, sent to spread the truth in the world and exclusively follow the Father's will. From being her Son's "teacher", Mary thus becomes the humble disciple of the divine Master to whom she had given birth.

The importance of the Virgin Mother's task remains: from his infancy to adulthood, she helped her Son Jesus to grow "in wisdom and in stature, and in favor with God and man" (Lk 2:52), and to prepare for his mission.

Mary and Joseph can therefore be seen as models for all educators. They sustain them in the great difficulties that the family encounters today, and show them the way to their children's precise and effective formation.

Their educational experience is a sure reference point for Christian parents who are called, in ever more complex and difficult conditions, to devote themselves to the service of the integral development of their children's personality, so that they will live lives worthy of man and corresponding to God's plan.

# Simeon Is Open To The Lord

*"In the episode of the Presentation we can glimpse the meeting of Israel's hope with the Messiah. We can also see in it a prophetic sign of man's encounter with Christ," the Holy Father said at the General Audience of Wednesday, 11 December, 1996, while reflecting on the mystery of Jesus' Presentation in the temple and the significance of Simeon's prophetic words. His Holiness Karekin I, Supreme Patriarch and Catholicos of All Armenians, was present at the General Audience. The Pope introduced him before delivering his catechesis, which was the 39th in the series on the Blessed Mother and was given in Italian. The Catholicos spoke after the Pope's catechesis.*

1. In the episode of the Presentation of Jesus in the temple, St. Luke emphasizes Jesus' messianic destiny. The immediate purpose of the Holy Family's journey from Bethlehem to Jerusalem according to the Lucan text was to fulfill the law: "And when the time came for their purification according to the law of Moses, they brought him up to Jerusalem to present him to the Lord (as it is written in the law of the Lord, 'Every male that opens the womb shall be called holy to the Lord'), and to offer a sacrifice according to what is said in the law of the Lord, 'a pair of turtle. doves, or two young pigeons'" (Lk 2:22 24).

With this act, Mary and Joseph show their intention of faithfully obeying God's will, rejecting every kind of privilege. Their coming to the temple in Jerusalem has the significance of a consecration to God in the place where he is present.

Obliged by her poverty to offer turtle doves or pigeons, Mary in fact gives the true Lamb who would redeem humanity, thus anticipating what was prefigured in the ritual offerings of the old law.

## Simeon Was Inspired By The Holy Spirit

2. While the law required the purification after birth of the mother alone, Luke speaks of the "time for their purification" (2:22),

intending perhaps to indicate together the prescriptions involving both the mother and the first-born Son.

The term "purification" can surprise us, because it is referred to a Mother who had been granted, by a singular grace, to be immaculate from the first moment of her existence, and to a Child who was totally holy. However, it must be remembered that it was not a question of purifying the conscience from some stain of sin, but only of reacquiring ritual purity which, according to the ideas of the time, may be harmed by the simple fact of birth without there being any form of guilt.

The Evangelist uses the occasion to stress the special link existing between Jesus, as "first-born" (Lk 2:7, 23) and God's holiness, as well as to indicate the spirit of humble offering which motivated Mary and Joseph (cf. Lk 2:24). In fact, the "two turtledoves or two young pigeons" (Lev 12:8), was the offering of the poor.

3 In the temple, Joseph and Mary meet Simeon, "righteous and devout, looking for the consolation of Israel" (Lk 2 25).

The Lucan narrative says nothing of his past or of the service he carried out in the temple; it tells of a deeply religious man who nurtures great desires in his heart and awaits the Messiah, the consolation of Israel. In fact, "the Holy Spirit was upon him" and "it had been revealed to him that he should not see death before he had seen the Lord's Christ" (Lk 2:25-26). Simeon invites us to look at the merciful action of God who pours out the Spirit on his faithful to bring to fulfillment his mysterious project of love.

Simeon, a man who is open to God's action, "inspired by the Spirit" (Lk 2:27), goes to the temple where he meets Jesus, Joseph and Mary. Taking the Child in his arms, he blesses God and says, "Lord, now let your servant depart in peace, according to your word" (Lk 2:29).

Simeon uses an Old Testament phrase to express the joy he experiences on meeting the Messiah and feels that the purpose of his life has been fulfilled; he can therefore ask the Most High to let him depart in peace to the next world.

## Joseph And Mary Present Savior Of All Mankind

In the episode of the Presentation we can glimpse the meeting of Israel's hope with the Messiah. We can also see in it a prophetic sign of man's encounter with Christ. The Holy Spirit makes it possible by awakening in the human heart the desire for this salvific meeting and by bringing it about.

Nor can we neglect the role of Mary who gives the Child to the holy old man Simeon. By divine will, it is the Mother who gives Jesus to mankind.

4. In revealing the Savior's future, Simeon refers to the prophecy of the "Servant" sent to the chosen people and to the nations. To him the Lord says, "I have taken you by the hand and kept you; I have given you as a covenant to the people, a light to the nations" (Is 42:6). And again: "It is too light a thing that you should be my servant to raise up the tribes of Jacob and to restore the preserved of Israel; I will give you as a light to the nations, that my salvation may reach to the end of the earth" (Is 49:6).

In his canticle, Simeon reverses the perspective and puts the stress on the universality of Jesus' mission: "For my eyes have seen your salvation which you have prepared in the presence of all peoples, a light for revelation to the Gentiles, and for glory for your people Israel" (Lk 2:30-32).

How can we fail to marvel at these words? "And his father and mother marveled at what was said about him" (Lk 2:33). But this experience enabled Joseph and Mary to understand more clearly the importance of their act of offering: in the temple of Jerusalem they present the One who, being the glory of his people, is also the salvation of all mankind.

## Mary Has Role In Jesus' Saving Mission

*"Beginning with Simeon's prophecy, Mary intensely and mysteriously unites her life with Christ's sorrowful mission: she was to become her Son's faithful coworker for the salvation of the human race", the Holy Father said at the General Audience of Wednesday, 18 December 1996, reflecting on the significance of*

*Simeon's predictions at the Presentation in the temple. Here is a translation of his catechesis, which was the 40th in the series on the Blessed Mother and was given in Italian.*

1. After recognizing in Jesus "a light for revelation to the Gentiles." (Lk 2:32), Simeon announces to Mary the great trial to which the Messiah is called and reveals her participation in that sorrowful destiny.

His reference to the redeeming sacrifice, absent at the Annunciation, has shown in Simeon's prophecy almost a "second Annunciation." (*Redemptoris Mater*, n. 16), which will lead the Virgin to a deeper understanding of her Son's mystery.

Simeon, who up to that moment had addressed all those present, blessing Joseph and Mary in particular, now prophesies to the Virgin alone that she will share in her Son's destiny. Inspired by the Holy Spirit, he announces to her: "Behold, this child is set for the fall and rising of many in Israel, and for a sign that is spoken against (and a sword will pierce through your own soul also), that thoughts out of many hearts may be revealed." (Lk: 2:34-35).

## Mary's Maternal Suffering Would Reach Culmination In The Passion

2. These words foretell a future of suffering for the Messiah. He is, in fact, "the sign of contradiction," destined to meet harsh opposition on the part of his contemporaries. But alongside Christ's suffering Simeon sets the vision of Mary's heart pierced by the sword, thus uniting the Mother with the sorrowful destiny of her Son.

In this way, while the venerable old man foresees the growing hostility the Messiah will face, he stresses its repercussion on the Mother's heart. This maternal suffering will culminate in the Passion, when she will unite with her Son in his redemptive sacrifice.

Following an allusion to the first songs of the Servant of the Lord (cf. Is 42:6; 49:6), cited in Luke 2:32, Simeon's words remind us of the prophecy of the Suffering Servant (Is 52:13; 53:12), who, "wounded for our transgressions" (Is 53:5), "makes himself an offering for sin." (Is 53:10) through a personal and spiritual sacrifice which far exceeds the ancient ritual sacrifices.

Here we can note how Simeon's prophecy allows us to glimpse in Mary's future suffering a unique likeness to the sorrowful future of the "Servant."

3. Mary and Joseph are astounded when Simeon proclaims Jesus as a "light for revelation to the Gentiles." (Lk 2:32). Mary, instead, with reference to the prophecy of the sword that would pierce her heart, says nothing. Together with Joseph, she accepts in silence those mysterious words which predict a deeply sorrowful trial and situate the Presentation of Jesus in the temple in its most authentic meaning.

Indeed, according to the divine plan the sacrifice offered then "according to what is said in the law of the Lord, 'a pair of turtledoves, or two young pigeons'." (Lk 2:24), prefigured the sacrifice of Jesus, "for I am gentle and lowly in heart." (Mt 11:29); in it the true "presentation" would be made (cf. Lk 2:22), which would see the Mother associated with her Son in the work of Redemption.

## Mary Was To Share In Her Son's Saving Mission

4. Simeon's prophecy is followed by the meeting with the prophetess Anna: "She gave thanks to God, and spoke of him to all who were looking for the redemption of Jerusalem." (Lk 2:38). The faith and prophetic wisdom of the old woman who nurtures the expectation of the Messiah by "worshipping with fasting and prayer night and day." (Lk 2:37), offer the Holy Family a further incentive to put their hope in the God of Israel. At this particular moment, Anna's behavior would have appeared to Mary and Joseph as a sign from the Lord, a message of enlightened faith and persevering service.

Beginning with Simeon's prophecy, Mary intensely and mysteriously unites her life with Christ's sorrowful mission: she was to become her Son's faithful co-worker for the salvation of the human race.

# Christ Calls Women To Share His Mission

*"The resurrection of many is a marvelous effect of the Redemption. This proclamation alone kindles great hope in the hearts of those to whom the fruit of the sacrifice already bears witness,"* the Holy Father said at the General Audience of Wednesday, 8 January, 1997, as he focused on the cooperation of women in the work of Redemption. Here is a translation of the Pope's catechesis, which was the 41st in the series on the Blessed Virgin and was given in Italian.

1. The words of the aged Simeon, announcing to Mary her sharing in the Messiah's saving mission, shed light on woman's role in the mystery of Redemption.

Indeed, Mary is not only an individual person, but she is also the "daughter of Zion," the new woman standing at the Redeemer's side in order to share his Passion and to give birth in the Spirit to the children of God. This reality is expressed by the popular depiction of the "seven swords" that pierce Mary's heart: this image highlights the deep link between the mother, who is identified with the daughter of Zion and with the Church, and the sorrowful destiny of the Incarnate Word.

Giving back her Son, whom she had just received from God, to consecrate him for his saving mission, Mary also gives herself to this mission. It is an act of interior sharing that is not only the fruit of natural maternal affection, but above all expresses the consent of the new woman to Christ's redemptive work.

## Mary Will Be Involved In Jesus' Suffering

2. In his words Simeon indicates the purpose of Jesus' sacrifice and Mary's suffering: these will come about so "that thoughts out of many hearts may be revealed" (Lk 2:35).

Jesus, "a sign that will be opposed" (Lk 2:34), who involves his mother in his suffering, will lead men and women to take a stand in his regard, inviting them to make a fundamental decision. In fact, he "is set for the fall and rising of many in Israel" (Lk 2:34).

Thus Mary is united to her divine Son in this "contradiction," in view of the work of salvation. Certainly there is a risk of ruin for those who reject Christ, but the resurrection of many is a marvelous effect of the Redemption. This proclamation alone kindles great hope in the hearts of those to whom the fruit of the sacrifice already bears witness. Directing the Blessed Virgin's attention to these prospects of salvation before the ritual offering, Simeon seems to suggest to Mary that she perform this act as a contribution to humanity's ransom. In fact, he does not speak to Joseph or about Joseph: his words are addressed to Mary, whom he associates with the destiny of her Son.

3. The chronological priority of Mary's action does not obscure Jesus' primacy. In describing Mary's role in the economy of salvation, the Second Vatican Council recalled that she "devoted herself totally... to the person and work of her Son, under and with him, serving the mystery of Redemption" (*Lumen Gentium*, n. 56).

At the presentation of Jesus in the temple, Mary serves the mystery of Redemption under Christ and with Christ: indeed he has the principal role in salvation and must be ransomed by a ritual offering. Mary is joined to the sacrifice of her Son by the sword that will pierce her soul.

4. The primacy of Christ does not rule out but supports and demands the proper, irreplaceable role of woman. By involving his mother in his own sacrifice, Christ wants to reveal its deep human roots and to show us an anticipation of the priestly offering of the cross.

The divine intention to call for the specific involvement of woman in the work of Redemption can be seen by the fact that Simeon's prophecy is addressed to Mary alone, although Joseph also took part in the offering rite.

The conclusion of the episode of Jesus' presentation in the temple seems to confirm the meaning and value of the feminine presence in the economy of salvation. The meeting with a woman, Anna, brings to a close these special moments when the Old Testament as it were is handed over to the New.

Like Simeon, this woman has no special status among the chosen people, but her life seems to have a lofty value in God's eyes. St. Luke calls her a "prophetess", probably because many consulted her for her gift of discernment and the holy life she led under the inspiration of the Spirit of the Lord.

Anna is advanced in age, being 84 years old, and has long been a widow. Totally consecrated to God, "she never left the temple, serving God day and night with fasting and prayer" (cf. Lk 2:37). She represents those who, having intensely lived in expectation of the Messiah, are able to accept the fulfillment of the promise with joyous exultation. The Evangelist mentions that "coming up at that very hour she gave thanks to God" (2:38).

Staying constantly in the temple, she could, perhaps more easily than Simeon, meet Jesus at the end of a life dedicated to the Lord and enriched by listening to the Word and by prayer.

At the dawn of Redemption, we can glimpse in the prophetess Anna all women who, with holiness of life and in prayerful expectation, are ready to accept Christ's presence and to praise God every day for the marvels wrought by his everlasting mercy.

## Anna Is Symbol Of Women Who Spread The Gospel

5. Chosen to meet the Child, Simeon and Anna have a deep experience of sharing the joy of Jesus' presence with Mary and Joseph and spreading it where they live. Anna in particular shows wonderful zeal in speaking about Jesus, thus witnessing to her simple and generous faith. This faith prepares others to accept the Messiah in their lives.

Luke's expression, "she... spoke of him to all who were looking for the redemption of Jerusalem" (2:38), seems to credit her as a symbol of the women who, dedicated to spreading the Gospel, will arouse and nourish the hope of salvation.

# Mary Cooperates By Personal Obedience

*"At the temple in Jerusalem, in this prelude to his saving mission, Jesus associates his Mother with himself; no longer is she merely the One who gave him birth, but the Woman who, through her own obedience to the Father's plan, can cooperate in the*

*mystery of Redemption," the Holy Father said at the General Audience of Wednesday, 15 January, 1997, as he reflected on the finding of Jesus in the temple. Here is a translation of his catechesis, which was the 42nd in the series on the Blessed Mother and was given in Italian.*

1. The Evangelist Luke describes the young Jesus' pilgrimage to the temple in Jerusalem as the last episode of the infancy narrative, before the start of John the Baptist's preaching. It is an usual occasion which sheds light on the long years of his hidden life in Nazareth.

On this occasion, with his strong personality Jesus reveals that he is aware of his mission, giving to this second "entry" into his "Father's house" the meaning of his total gift of self to God which had already marked his presentation in the temple.

This passage seems to contrast with Luke's note that Jesus was obedient to Joseph and Mary (cf. 2:51). But, if one looks closely, here he seems to put himself in a conscious and almost deliberate antithesis to his normal state as Son, unexpectedly causing a definite separation from Mary and Joseph. As his rule of conduct, Jesus states that he belongs only to the Father and does not mention the ties to his earthly family.

## Jesus' Behavior Seemed Very Unusual

2. Through this episode, Jesus prepares his Mother for the mystery of the Redemption. During those three dramatic days when the Son withdraws from them to stay in the temple, Mary and Joseph experience an anticipation of the triduum of his Passion, Death and resurrection.

Letting his Mother and Joseph depart for Galilee without telling them of his intention to stay behind in Jerusalem, Jesus brings them into the mystery of that suffering which leads to joy, anticipating what he would later accomplish with his disciples through the announcement of his Passover.

According to Luke's account, on the return journey to Nazareth Mary and Joseph, after a day's traveling, are worried and anguished over the fate of the Child Jesus. They look for him in vain among their relatives and acquaintances. Returning to Jerusalem and finding him in the temple, they are astonished to see him "sitting among the teachers, listening to them and asking them questions" (Lk 2:46). His behavior seems most unusual. Certainly for his parents, finding him on the third day means discovering another aspect of his person and his mission.

He takes the role of teacher, as he will later do in his public life, speaking words that arouse admiration: "And all who heard him were astounded at his understanding and his answers" (2:47). Revealing a wisdom that amazes his listeners, he begins to practice the art of dialogue that will be a characteristic of his saving mission.

His Mother asked Jesus: "Son, why have you treated us so? Behold, your father and I have been looking for you anxiously" (Lk 2:48). Here we can discern an echo of the "whys" asked by so many mothers about the suffering their children cause them, as well as the questions welling up in the heart of every man and woman in times of trial.

3. Jesus' reply, in the form of a question, is highly significant: "How is it that you sought me? Did you not know that I must be in my Father's house?" (Lk 2:49).

With this response, he discloses the mystery of his person to Mary and Joseph in an unexpected, unforeseen way, inviting them to go beyond appearances and unfolding before them new horizons for his future.

In his reply to his anguished Mother, the Son immediately reveals the reason for his behavior. Mary had said: "Your father," indicating Joseph; Jesus replies: "My Father," meaning the heavenly Father.

Referring to his divine origin, he does not so much want to state that the temple, his Father's house, is the natural "place" for his presence, as that he must be concerned about all that regards his Father and his plan. He means to stress that his Father's will is the only norm requiring his obedience.

This reference to his total dedication to God's plan is highlighted in the Gospel text by the words: "I must be", which will later appear in his prediction of the Passion (cf. Mk 8:31).

His parents then are asked to let him go and carry out his

mission wherever the heavenly Father will lead him.

4. The Evangelist comments: "And they did not understand the saying which he spoke to them" (Lk 2:50).

Mary and Joseph do not perceive the sense of his answer, nor the way (apparently a rejection) he reacts to their parental concern. With this attitude, Jesus intends to reveal the mysterious aspects of his intimacy with the Father, aspects which Mary intuits without knowing how to associate them with the trial she is undergoing.

## Mary Attains New Dimension In Work Of Salvation

Luke's words teach us how Mary lives this truly unusual episode in the depths of her being. She "kept all these things in her heart" (Lk 2:51). The Mother of Jesus associates these events with the mystery of her Son, revealed to her at the Annunciation, and ponders them in the silence of contemplation, offering her cooperation in the spirit of a renewed "fiat." In this way the first link is forged in a chain of events that will gradually lead Mary beyond the natural role deriving from her motherhood, to put herself at the service of her divine Son's mission. At the temple in Jerusalem, in this prelude to his saving mission, Jesus associates his Mother with himself; no longer is she merely the One who gave him birth, but the Woman who, through her own obedience to the Father's plan, can cooperate in the mystery of Redemption. Thus keeping in her heart an event so charged with meaning, Mary attains a new dimension of her cooperation in salvation.

# Mary's "Hidden Life" Is Example To Mothers

*"We can conclude that the atmosphere of tranquillity and peace in the house of Nazareth and their constant seeking to fulfill God's plan gave an extraordinary and unique depth to the union of mother and Son," the Holy Father said at the General Audience of Wednesday, 29 January, 1997, as he reflected on Mary's role in the hidden life of Christ. The Pope also referred to our lives, "hidden with Christ in God." Here is a translation of his*

*catechesis, which was the 43rd in the series on the Blessed Virgin and was given in Italian.*

1. The Gospels offer very sparse information about the years the Holy Family spent in Nazareth. St. Matthew tells of the decision taken by Joseph, after the return from Egypt, to make Nazareth the Holy Family's permanent home (cf. Mt 2:22-23), but then gives no further information except that Joseph was a carpenter (Mt 13:55). For his part, St. Luke twice mentions the Holy Family's return to Nazareth (cf. Lk 2:39,51) and gives two brief references to the years of Jesus' childhood, before and after the episode of the pilgrimage to Jerusalem: "The child grew and became strong, filled with wisdom; and the favor of God was upon him" (Lk 2:40), and "Jesus increased in wisdom, age and grace before God and men" (Lk 2:52).

## Mary Pondered These Events In Her Heart

In relating these brief remarks about Jesus' life, Luke is probably referring to Mary's memories of a period of profound intimacy with her Son. The union between Jesus and the one who was "full of grace" goes far beyond what normally exists between mother and child, because it is rooted in a particular supernatural condition and reinforced by the special conformity of both to the divine will.

Thus we can conclude that the atmosphere of tranquillity and peace in the house of Nazareth and their constant seeking to fulfill God's plan gave an extraordinary and unique depth to the union of mother and Son.

2. Mary's awareness that she was carrying out a task entrusted to her by God gave a higher meaning to her daily life. The simple, humble chores of everyday life took on special value in her eyes, since she performed them as a service to Christ's mission.

Mary's example enlightens and encourages the experience of so many women who carry out their daily tasks exclusively in the home. It is a question of a humble, hidden, repetitive effort, and is often not sufficiently appreciated. Nonetheless, the long years Mary spent in the house of Nazareth reveal the enormous potential of genuine love and thus of salvation. In fact, the simplicity of the lives of so many housewives, seen as a mission of service and love, is of extraordinary value in the Lord's eyes.

One can certainly say that for Mary life in Nazareth was not dominated by monotony. In her contact with the growing Jesus, she strove to penetrate the mystery of her Son through contemplation and adoration. St. Luke says: "Mary kept all these things, pondering them in her heart" (Lk 2:19; cf. 2:51).

"All these things": they are the events in which she was both participant and spectator, starting with the Annunciation; but above all, it is the life of her Child. Every day of intimacy with him is an invitation to know him better, to discover more deeply the meaning of his presence and the mystery of his person.

3. Someone might think that it was easy for Mary to believe, living as she did in daily contact with Jesus. In this regard, however, we must remember that the unique aspects of her Son's personality were usually hidden; even if his way of acting was exemplary, he lived a life similar to that of his peers.

During his 30 years of life in Nazareth, Jesus did not reveal his supernatural qualities and worked no miracles. At the first extraordinary manifestations of his personality, associated with the beginning of his preaching, his relatives (called "brothers" in the Gospel), assume according to one interpretation responsibility for taking him home, because they feel his behavior is not normal (cf. Mk 3:21).

In the dignified and hard-working atmosphere of Nazareth, Mary strove to understand the workings of Providence in her Son's mission. A subject of particular reflection for his Mother, in this regard, was certainly the statement Jesus made in the temple of Jerusalem when he was 12 years old: "Did you not know that I must be in my Father's house?" (Lk 2:49). Meditating on this, Mary could better understand the meaning of Jesus' divine sonship and her own motherhood, as she endeavored to discern in her Son's conduct the traits revealing his likeness to the One he called my Father."

## Our Life Is Hidden With Christ In God

4. Communion of life with Jesus in the house of Nazareth led Mary not only to advance "in her pilgrimage of faith" (*Lumen Gentium*, n. 58), but also in hope. This virtue, cultivated and sustained by her memory of the Annunciation and of Simeon's words, embraced the whole span of her earthly life, but was practiced especially during the 30 years of silence and hiddenness spent in Nazareth.

At home, the Blessed Virgin experiences hope in its highest form; she knows she will not be disappointed even if she does not know the times or the ways in which God will fulfill his promise. In the darkness of faith and in the absence of extraordinary signs announcing the beginning of her Son's messianic task, she hopes, beyond all evidence, awaiting the fulfillment of God's promise.

A setting for growth in faith and hope, the house of Nazareth becomes a place of lofty witness to charity. The love that Christ wanted to pour forth in the world is kindled and burns first of all in his Mother's heart: it is precisely in the home that the proclamation of the Gospel of divine love is prepared. Looking at Nazareth, contemplating the mystery of the hidden life of Jesus and the Blessed Virgin, we are invited to reflect on the mystery of our life which St. Paul recalls "is hidden with Christ in God" (Col 3:3). It is often a life that seems humble and obscure in the world's eyes, but which, following Mary's example, can reveal unexpected possibilities of salvation, radiating the love and peace of Christ

# Jesus Works Miracle At Mary's Request

*"Mary's request, 'Do whatever he tells you,' keeps its ever timely value for Christians of every age... It is an exhortation to trust without hesitation, especially when one does not understand the meaning or benefit of what Christ asks," the Holy Father said at the General Audience of Wednesday, 26 February, 1997, as he spoke of Mary's role at the wedding in Cana. Here is a translation of his catechesis, which was the 44th in the series on the Blessed*

*Virgin and was given in Italian.*

1. In the episode of the wedding at Cana, St. John presents Mary's first intervention in the public life of Jesus and highlights her cooperation in her Son's mission.

At the beginning of the account the Evangelist tells us that "the Mother of Jesus was there" (Jn 2:1), and, as if to suggest that her presence was the reason for the couple's invitation to Jesus and his disciples (cf. *Redemptoris Mater*, n. 21), he adds "Jesus also was invited to the marriage, with his disciples" (Jn 2:2). With these remarks, John seems to indicate that at Cana, as in the fundamental event of the Incarnation, it is Mary who introduces the Savior.

The meaning and role of the Blessed Virgin's presence become evident when the wine runs out. As a skilled and wise housewife, she immediately notices and intervenes so that no one's joy is marred and, above all, to help the newly married couple in difficulty.

Turning to Jesus with the words, "they have no wine" (Jn 2:3), Mary expresses her concern to him about this situation, expecting him to solve it. More precisely, according to some exegetes, his Mother is expecting an extraordinary sign, since Jesus had no wine at his disposal.

## Mary Strengthened The Disciples' Faith By Obtaining The Miracle

2. The choice made by Mary, who could perhaps have obtained the necessary wine elsewhere, shows the courage of her faith, since until that moment Jesus had worked no miracles, either in Nazareth or in his public life.

At Cana, the Blessed Virgin once again showed her total availability to God. At the Annunciation she had contributed to the miracle of the virginal conception by believing in Jesus before seeing him; here, her trust in Jesus' as yet unrevealed power causes him to perform his "first sign," the miraculous transformation of water into wine.

In that way she precedes in faith the disciples who, as John says, would believe after the miracle: Jesus "manifested his glory; and his disciples believed in him" (Jn 2:11). Thus, Mary strengthened their faith by obtaining this miraculous sign.

3. Jesus' answer to Mary's words, "O woman, what have you to do with me? My hour has not yet come" (Jn 2:4), appears to express a refusal, as if putting his Mother's faith to the test.

According to one interpretation, from the moment his mission begins Jesus seems to call into question the natural relationship of Son to which his mother refers. The sentence, in the local parlance, is meant to stress a distance between the persons, by excluding a communion of life. This distance does not preclude respect and esteem; the term "woman" by which he addresses his Mother is used with a nuance that will recur in the conversations with the Canaanite woman (cf. Mt 15:28), the Samaritan woman (cf. Jn 4:21), the adulteress (cf. Jn 8:10) and Mary Magdalen (cf. Jn 20:13), in contexts that show Jesus' positive relationship with his female interlocutors.

With the expression: "O woman, what have you to do with me?" Jesus intends to put Mary's cooperation on the level of salvation which, by involving her faith and hope, requires her to go beyond her natural role of mother.

4. Of much greater import is the reason Jesus gives: "My hour has not yet come" (Jn 2:4).

Some scholars who have studied this sacred text, following St. Augustine's interpretation, identify this "hour" with the Passion event. For others, instead, it refers to the first miracle in which the prophet of Nazareth's messianic power would be revealed. Yet others hold that the sentence is interrogative and an extension of the question that precedes it: "What have you to do with me? Has my hour not yet come?" Jesus gives Mary to understand that henceforth he no longer depends on her, but must take the initiative for doing his Father's work. Then Mary docilely refrains from insisting with him and instead turns to the servants, telling them to obey him.

## Miracle Shows The Power Of Mary's Prayer

In any case her trust in her Son is rewarded. Jesus, whom she has left totally free to act, works the miracle, recognizing his Mother's courage and docility: "Jesus said to them, 'Fill the jars with water.' And they filled them up to the brim" (Jn 2:7). Thus their obedience also helps to procure wine in abundance.

Mary's request: "Do whatever he tells you," keeps its ever timely value for Christians of every age and is destined to renew its marvelous effect in everyone's life. It is an exhortation to trust without hesitation, especially when one does not understand the meaning or benefit of what Christ asks.

As in the account of the Canaanite woman (Mt 15:24-26), Jesus' apparent refusal exalts the woman's faith, so that her Son's words, "My hour has not yet come," together with the working of the first miracle, demonstrate the Mother's great faith and the power of her prayer.

The episode of the wedding at Cana urges us to be courageous in faith and to experience in our lives the truth of the Gospel words: "Ask, and it will be given you" (Mt 7:7; Lk 11:9).

# Mary Is Active In Her Son's Mission

*"By emphasizing Mary's initiative in the first miracle and then recalling her presence on Calvary at the foot of the Cross, the Evangelist helps us understand how Mary's cooperation is extended to the whole of Christ's work," the Holy Father said at the General Audience of Wednesday, 5 March, 1997, as he reflected on Mary's role at Cana and her cooperation in her Son's messianic mission. Here is a translation of the Pope's catechesis, which was the 45th in the series on the Blessed Mother and was given in Italian.*

1. Describing Mary's presence in Jesus' public life, the Second Vatican Council recalls her involvement at Cana on the occasion of the first miracle: "At the marriage feast of Cana, moved with pity, she brought about by her intercession the beginning of

miracles of Jesus the Messiah (cf. Jn 2:1-11)" (*Lumen Gentium*, n. 58).

Following the Evangelist John, the Council points out the Mother's discreet and effective role, when by her words she persuades her Son to perform his "first sign." Although her influence is discreet and maternal, her presence proves decisive.

## Mary Shows What A Mother's Love Can Do

The Blessed Virgin's initiative is all the more surprising if one considers the inferior status of women in Jewish society. At Cana, in fact, Jesus does not only recognize the dignity and role of the feminine genius, but by welcoming his Mother's intervention, he gives her the opportunity to participate in his messianic work. The epithet "Woman," with which Jesus addresses Mary (cf. Jn 2:4), is not in contrast with his intention. Indeed it has no negative connotations, and Jesus will use it again when he addresses his Mother at the foot of the Cross (cf. Jn 19:26). According to some interpretations, this title "Woman" presents Mary as the New Eve, the mother in faith of all believers.

In the text cited, the Council uses the expression "moved with pity," letting it be understood that Mary was prompted by her merciful heart. Having sensed the eventual disappointment of the newly married couple and guests because of the lack of wine, the Blessed Virgin compassionately suggests to Jesus that he intervene with his messianic power.

To some, Mary's request may appear excessive, since it subordinates the beginning of the Messiah's miracles to an act of filial devotion. Jesus himself dealt with this difficulty when, by assenting to his mother's request, he shows the Lord's superabundance in responding to human expectations, manifesting also what a mother's love can do.

2. The expression "the beginning of his miracles," which the Council has taken from John's text, attracts our attention. The Greek term arche, translated as "beginning," is used by John in the Prologue of his Gospel: "In the beginning was the Word" (1:1). This significant coincidence suggests a parallel between the very

origins of Christ's glory in eternity and the first manifestation of this same glory in his earthly mission.

By emphasizing Mary's initiative in the first miracle and then recalling her presence on Calvary at the foot of the Cross, the Evangelist helps us understand how Mary's cooperation is extended to the whole of Christ's work. The Blessed Virgin's request is placed within the divine plan of salvation.

In the first "sign" performed by Jesus, the Fathers of the Church glimpsed an important symbolic dimension, seeing the transformation of the water into wine as the announcement of the passage from the Old to the New Covenant. At Cana it is precisely the water in the jars, destined for the purification of the Jews and the fulfillment of the legal prescriptions (cf. Mk 7:1-15), which becomes the new wine of the wedding feast, a symbol of the definitive union between God and humanity.

3. The context of a wedding banquet, chosen by Jesus for his first miracle, refers to the marriage symbolism used frequently in the Old Testament to indicate the Covenant between God and his People (cf. Hos 2:21; Jer 2:1-8; Ps 44; etc.), and in the New Testament to signify Christ's union with the Church (cf. Jn 3:28-30; Eph 5:25-32; Rv 21:1-2, etc.).

Jesus' presence at Cana is also a sign of God's saving plan for marriage. In this perspective, the lack of wine can be interpreted as an allusion to the lack of love that unfortunately often threatens marital unions. Mary asks Jesus to intervene on behalf of all married couples, who can only be freed from the dangers of infidelity, misunderstanding and division by a love which is based on God. The grace of the sacrament offers the couple this superior strength of love, which can reinforce their commitment to fidelity even in difficult circumstances.

## Mary Initiates The Church's Journey Of Faith

According to the interpretation of Christian authors, the miracle at Cana also has a deep Eucharistic meaning. Performing this miracle near the time of the Jewish feast Passover (cf. Jn 2:13), Jesus, as he did in multiplying the loaves.

(cf. Jn 6:4), shows his intention to prepare the true paschal banquet, the Eucharist. His desire at the wedding in Cana seems to be emphasized further by the presence of wine, which alludes to the blood of the New Covenant, and by the context of a banquet.

In this way, after being the reason for Jesus' presence at the celebration, Mary obtains the miracle of the new wine which prefigures the Eucharist, the supreme sign of the presence of her risen Son among the disciples.

4. At the end of the account of Jesus' first miracle, made possible by the firm faith of the Lord's Mother in her divine Son, the Evangelist John concludes: "and his disciples believed in him" (2:11). At Cana, Mary begins the Church's journey of faith, preceding the disciples and directing the servants' attention to Christ.

Her persevering intercession likewise encourages those who at times face the experience of "God's silence." They are asked to hope beyond all hope, always trusting in the Lord's goodness.

# Mary Had Role In Jesus' Public Ministry

*"Separation did not mean distance of heart, nor did it prevent the Mother from spiritually following her Son... as she had done during Jesus' hidden life in Nazareth. Her faith in fact enabled her to grasp the meaning of Jesus' words before and better than his disciples," the Holy Father said at the General Audience of Wednesday, 12 March, 1997, as he reflected on Mary's role in Jesus' public ministry. Here is a translation of his catechesis, which was the 46th in the series on the Blessed Mother and was given in Italian.*

1. After recalling Mary's intervention at the wedding feast of Cana, the Second Vatican Council emphasizes her participation in the public life of Jesus: "In the course of her Son's preaching she received the words whereby, in extolling a kingdom beyond the concerns and ties of flesh and blood, he declared blessed those who heard and kept the word of God (cf. Mk 3:35 par.; Lk 11:27-

28) as she was faithfully doing (cf. Lk 2:19, 51)" (*Lumen Gentium*, n. 58).

The beginning of Jesus' mission also meant separation from his Mother, who did not always follow her Son in his travels on the roads of Palestine. Jesus deliberately chose separation from his Mother and from family affection, as can be inferred from the conditions he gave his disciples for following him and for dedicating themselves to proclaiming God's kingdom.

## Mary Faithfully Put Jesus' Words Into Practice

Nevertheless, Mary sometimes heard her Son's preaching. We can assume that she was present in the synagogue of Nazareth when Jesus, after reading Isaiah's prophecy, commented on the text and applied it to himself (cf. Lk 4:18-30). How much she must have suffered on that occasion, after sharing the general amazement at "the gracious words which proceeded out of his mouth" (Lk 4:22), as she observed the harsh hostility of her fellow citizens who drove Jesus from the synagogue and even tried to kill him! The drama of that moment is evident in the words of the Evangelist Luke: "They rose up and put him out of the city, and led him to the brow of the hill on which their city was built, that they might throw him down headlong. But passing through the midst of them he went away" (4:29-30).

Realizing after this event that there would be other trials, Mary confirmed and deepened her total obedience to the Father's will, offering him her suffering as a mother and her loneliness.

2. According to the Gospels, Mary had the opportunity to hear her Son on other occasions as well. First at Capernaum, where Jesus went after the wedding feast of Cana, "with his mother and his brethren and his disciples" (Jn 2:12). For the Passover, moreover, she was probably able to follow him to the temple in Jerusalem, which Jesus called his Father's house and for which he was consumed with zeal (cf. Jn 2:16-17). Finding herself later among the crowd and not being able to approach Jesus, she hears him replying to those who had told him that she and their relatives had arrived: "My mother and my brethren are those who hear the

word of God and do it" (Lk 8:21).

With these words, Christ, although relativizing family ties, is addressing great praise to his Mother by affirming a far loftier bond with her. Indeed, in listening to her Son, Mary accepts all his words and faithfully puts them into practice.

We can imagine that, although she did not follow Jesus on his missionary journey, she was informed of her Son's apostolic activities, lovingly and anxiously receiving news of his preaching from the lips of those who had met him.

Separation did not mean distance of heart, nor did it prevent the Mother from spiritually following her Son, from keeping and meditating on his teaching as she had done during Jesus' hidden life in Nazareth. Her faith in fact enabled her to grasp the meaning of Jesus' words before and better than his disciples, who often did not understand his teaching, especially the references to his future Passion (cf. Mt 16:21-23; Mk 9:32; Lk 9:45).

3. Following the events in her Son's life, Mary shared in his drama of experiencing rejection from some of the chosen people. This rejection first appeared during his visit to Nazareth and became more and more obvious in the words and attitudes of the leaders of the people.

In this way the Blessed Virgin would often have come to know the criticism, insults and threats directed at Jesus. In Nazareth too she would have frequently been troubled by the disbelief of relatives and acquaintances who would try to use Jesus (cf. Jn 7:2-5) or to stop his mission (Mk 3:21).

Through this suffering borne with great dignity and hiddenness, Mary shares the journey of her Son "to Jerusalem" (Lk 9:51) and, more and more closely united with him in faith, hope and love, she cooperates in salvation.

## Mary Is A Model For Those Who Accept Christ's Words

4. The Blessed Virgin thus becomes a model for those who accept Christ's words. Believing in the divine message since the Annunciation and fully supporting the Person of the Son, she

teaches us to listen to the Savior with trust, to discover in him the divine Word who transforms and renews our life. Her experience also encourages us to accept the trials and suffering that come from fidelity to Christ, keeping our gaze fixed on the happiness Jesus promised those who listen to him and keep his word.

# Mary United Herself To Jesus' Suffering

*With our gaze illumined by the radiance of the resurrection, we pause to reflect on the Mother's involvement in her Son's redeeming Passion, which was completed by her sharing in his suffering," the Holy Father said at the General Audience of Wednesday, 2 April, 1997, as he reflected on Mary's participation in the mystery of Redemption and her presence at the foot of the Cross. Here is a translation of his catechesis, which was given in Italian.*

1. Regina caeli laetare, alleluia! So the Church sings in this Easter season, inviting the faithful to join in the spiritual joy of Mary, Mother of the Redeemer. The Blessed Virgin's gladness at Christ's resurrection is even greater if one considers her intimate participation in Jesus' entire life.

In accepting with complete availability the words of the Angel Gabriel, who announced to her that she would become the Mother of the Messiah, Mary began her participation in the drama of Redemption. Her involvement in her Son's sacrifice, revealed by Simeon during the presentation in the Temple, continues not only in the episode of the losing and finding of the 12 year old Jesus, but also throughout his public life.

However, the Blessed Virgin's association with Christ's mission reaches its culmination in Jerusalem, at the time of the Redeemer's Passion and Death. As the Fourth Gospel testifies, she was in the Holy City at the time, probably for the celebration of the Jewish feast of Passover.

2. The Council stresses the profound dimension of the Blessed Virgin's presence on Calvary, recalling that she "faithfully persevered in her union with her Son unto the Cross" (*Lumen*

*Gentium*, n. 58), and points out that this union "in the work of salvation is made manifest from the time of Christ's virginal conception up to his death" (ibid., a. 57).

## Mary Joins Her Suffering To Jesus' Priestly Sacrifice

With our gaze illumined by the radiance of the resurrection, we pause to reflect on the Mother's involvement in her Son's redeeming Passion, which was completed by her sharing in his suffering. let us return again, but now in the perspective of the resurrection, to the foot of the Cross where the Mother endured "with her only-begotten Son the intensity of his suffering, associated herself with his sacrifice in her mother's heart, and lovingly consented to the immolation of this victim which was born of her" (ibid., n. 58).

With these words, the Council reminds us of "Mary's compassion"; in her heart reverberates all that Jesus suffers in body and soul, emphasizing her willingness to share in her Son's redeeming sacrifice and to join her own maternal suffering to his priestly offering.

The Council text also stresses that her consent to Jesus' immolation is not passive acceptance but a genuine act of love, by which she offers her Son as a "victim" of expiation for the sins of all humanity.

Lastly, *Lumen Gentium* relates the Blessed Virgin to Christ, who has the lead role in Redemption, making it clear that in associating herself "with his sacrifice" she remains subordinate to her divine Son.

3. In the Fourth Gospel, St. John says that "standing by the Cross of Jesus were his mother, and his mother's sister, Mary the wife of Clopas, and Mary Magdalen" (19:25). By using the verb "to stand", which literally means "to be on one's feet," "to stand erect", perhaps the Evangelist intends to present the dignity and strength shown in their sorrow by Mary and the other women.

The Blessed Virgin's "standing erect" at the foot of the Cross recalls her unfailing constancy and extraordinary courage in facing suffering. In the tragic events of Calvary, Mary is sustained by faith, strengthened during the events of her life and especially during Jesus' public life. The Council recalls that "the Blessed Virgin advanced in her pilgrimage of faith and faithfully persevered in her union with her Son unto the Cross" (*Lumen Gentium*, n. 58).

Sharing his deepest feelings, she counters the arrogant insults addressed to the crucified Messiah with forbearance and pardon, associating herself with his prayer to the Father: "Forgive them, for they know not what they do" (Lk 23:34). By sharing in the feeling of abandonment to the Father's will expressed in Jesus' last words on the Cross: "Father into your hands I commend my spirit!" (ibid., 23:46), she thus offers, as the Council notes, loving consent "to the immolation of this victim which was born of her" (*Lumen Gentium*, n. 58).

## Mary's Hope Contains Light Stronger Than Darkness

4. Mary's supreme "yes" is radiant with trusting hope in the mysterious future, begun with the death of her crucified Son. The words in which Jesus taught the disciples on his way to Jerusalem "that the Son of man must suffer many things, and be rejected by the elders and the chief priests and the scribes, and be killed, and after three days rise again" echo in her heart at the dramatic hour of Calvary, awakening expectation of and yearning for the resurrection.

Mary's hope at the foot of the Cross contains a light stronger than the darkness that reigns in many hearts: in the presence of the redeeming Sacrifice, the hope of the Church and of humanity is born in Mary.

# Mary's Cooperation Is Totally Unique

*"We can... turn to the Blessed Virgin, trustfully imploring her aid in the awareness of the singular role entrusted to her by God, the role of cooperator in the Redemption, which she exercised throughout her life and in a special way at the foot of the Cross," the Holy Father said at the General Audience of Wednesday, 9 April, 1997. The Pope was continuing his catechesis*

*on the role of the Blessed Mother, calling attention to her unique cooperation in the work of salvation. Here is a translation of his reflection, which was the 48th in the series on the Blessed Virgin and was given in Italian.*

1. Down the centuries the Church has reflected on Mary's cooperation in the work of salvation, deepening the analysis of her association with Christ's redemptive sacrifice. St. Augustine already gave the Blessed Virgin the title "cooperator" in the Redemption (cf. De Sancta Virginitate, 6; PL 40, 399), a title which emphasizes Mary's joint but subordinate action with Christ the Redeemer.

Reflection has developed along these lines, particularly since the 15th century. Some feared there might be a desire to put Mary on the same level as Christ. Actually the Church's teaching makes a clear distinction between the Mother and the Son in the work of salvation, explaining the Blessed Virgin's subordination, as cooperator, to the one Redeemer.

Moreover, when the Apostle Paul says: "For we are God's fellow workers"
(1 Cor 3:9), he maintains the real possibility for man to cooperate with God. The collaboration of believers, which obviously excludes any equality with him, is expressed in the proclamation of Gospel and in their personal contribution to its taking root in human hearts.

## Mary's Cooperation Is Unique And Unrepeatable

2. However, applied to Mary, the term "cooperator" acquires a specific meaning. The collaboration of Christians in salvation takes place after the Calvary event, whose fruits they endeavor to spread by prayer and sacrifice. Mary, instead, cooperated during the event itself and in the role of mother; thus her cooperation embraces the whole of Christ's saving work. She alone was associated in this way with the redemptive sacrifice that merited the salvation of all mankind. In union with Christ and in submission to him, she collaborated in obtaining the grace of

salvation for all humanity.

The Blessed Virgin's role as cooperator has its source in her divine motherhood. By giving birth to the One who was destined to achieve man's redemption, by nourishing him, presenting him in the temple and suffering with him as he died on the Cross, "in a wholly singular way she cooperated... in the work of the Savior" (*Lumen Gentium*, n. 61). Although God's call to cooperate in the work of salvation concerns every human being, the participation of the Savior's Mother in humanity's Redemption is a unique and unrepeatable fact.

Despite the uniqueness of her condition, Mary is also the recipient of salvation. She is the first to be saved, redeemed by Christ "in the most sublime way" in her Immaculate Conception (cf. Bull Ineffabilis Deus, in Pius Ix, Acta, 1, 605) and filled with the grace of the Holy Spirit.

3. This assertion now leads to the question: what is the meaning of Mary's unique cooperation in the plan of salvation? It should be sought in God's particular intention for the Mother of the Redeemer, whom on two solemn occasions, that is, at Cana and beneath the Cross, Jesus addresses as "Woman" (cf. Jn 2:4; 19:26). Mary is associated as a woman in the work of salvation. Having created man "male and female" (cf. Gn 1:27), the Lord also wants to place the New Eve beside the New Adam in the Redemption. Our first parents had chosen the way of sin as a couple; a new pair, the Son of God with his Mother's cooperation, would reestablish the human race in its original dignity.

Mary, the New Eve, thus becomes a perfect icon of the Church. In the divine plan, at the foot of the Cross, she represents redeemed humanity which, in need of salvation, is enabled to make a contribution to the unfolding of the saving work.

## Mary Is Our Mother In The Order Of Grace

4. The Council had this doctrine in mind and made it its own, stressing the Blessed Virgin's contribution not only to the Redeemer's birth, but also to the life of his Mystical Body down the ages until the "eschaton": in the Church Mary "has cooperated"

(cf. *Lumen Gentium*, n. 63) and "cooperates" (cf. ibid., n. 53) in the work of salvation. In describing the mystery of the Annunciation, the Council states that the Virgin of Nazareth, "committing herself wholeheartedly and impeded by no sin to God's saving will, devoted herself totally, as a handmaid of the Lord, to the person and work of her Son, under and with him, serving the mystery of Redemption by the grace of Almighty God" (ibid., n. 56).

The Second Vatican Council moreover presents Mary not only as "Mother of the divine Redeemer," but also "in a singular way [as] the generous associate," who "cooperated by her obedience, faith, hope and burning charity in the work of the Savior." The Council also recalls that the sublime fruit of this cooperation is her universal motherhood: "For this reason she is a mother to us in the order of grace" (ibid., n. 61).

We can therefore turn to the Blessed Virgin, trustfully imploring her aid in the awareness of the singular role entrusted to her by God, the role of cooperator in the Redemption, which she exercised throughout her life and in a special way at the foot of the Cross.

# To The Disciple He Said, 'Behold Your Mother'

*"The universal motherhood of Mary, the 'Woman' of the wedding at Cana and of Calvary, recalls Eve, 'mother of all living' (Gn 3:20). However, while the latter helped to bring sin into the world, the new Eve, Mary, cooperates in the saving event of Redemption. Thus in the Blessed Virgin the figure of 'woman' is rehabilitated," the Holy Father said at the General Audience of Wednesday, 23 April, 1997, as he continued his catechesis on the Virgin Mary, focusing this week on her universal motherhood. Here is a translation of his reflection, which was the 49th in the series on the Blessed Mother and was given in Italian*

1. After recalling the presence of Mary and the other women at the Lord's cross, St. John relates: "When Jesus saw his mother, and the disciple whom he loved standing near, he said to his mother, 'Woman, behold, your Son!' Then he said to the disciple,

'Behold, your mother!'" (Jn 19:26-27).

These particularly moving words are a "revelation scene": they reveal the deep sentiments of the dying Christ and contain a great wealth of meaning for Christian faith and spirituality. At the end of his earthly life, as he addressed his Mother and the disciple he loved, the crucified Messiah establishes a new relationship of love between Mary and Christians.

Interpreted at times as no more than an expression of Jesus' filial piety to wards his Mother whom he entrusts for the future to his beloved disciple, these words go far beyond the contingent need to solve a family problem. In fact, attentive consideration of the text, confirmed by the interpretation of many Fathers and by common ecclesial opinion, presents us, in Jesus' twofold entrustment, with one of the most important events for understanding the Virgin's role in the economy of salvation.

## Jesus Completes His Sacrifice By Entrusting Mary To John

The words of the dying Jesus actually show that his first intention was not to entrust his Mother to John, but to entrust the disciple to Mary and to give her a new maternal role. Moreover, the epithet "woman", also used by Jesus at the wedding in Cana to lead Mary to a new dimension of her existence as Mother, shows how the Savior's words are not the fruit of a simple sentiment of filial affection but are meant to be put at a higher level.

2. Although Jesus' death causes Mary deep sorrow, it does not in itself change her normal way of life: in fact, in departing from Nazareth to start his public life, Jesus had already left his Mother alone. Moreover, the presence at the Cross of her relative, Mary of Clopas, allows us to suppose that the Blessed Virgin was on good terms with her family and relatives, by whom she could have been welcomed after her Son's death.

Instead, Jesus' words acquire their most authentic meaning in the context of his saving mission. Spoken at the moment of the redemptive sacrifice, they draw their loftiest value precisely from this sublime circumstance. In fact, after Jesus' statements to his

Mother, the Evangelist adds a significant clause: "Jesus, knowing that all was now finished..." (Jn 19:28), as if he wished to stress that he had brought his sacrifice to completion by entrusting his Mother to John, and in him to all men, whose Mother she becomes in the work of salvation.

3. The reality brought about by Jesus' words, that is, Mary's new motherhood in relation to the disciple, is a further sign of the great love that led Jesus to offer his life for all people. On Calvary this love is shown in the gift of a mother, his mother, who thus becomes our mother too.

We must remember that, according to tradition, it is John whom the Blessed Virgin in fact recognized as her Son; but this privilege has been interpreted by Christians from the beginning as the sign of a spiritual generation in relation to all humanity.

The universal motherhood of Mary, the "Woman" of the wedding at Cana and of Calvary, recalls Eve, "mother of all living" (Gn 3:20). However, while the latter helped to bring sin into the world, the new Eve, Mary, cooperates in the saving event of Redemption. Thus in the Blessed Virgin the figure of woman is rehabilitated and her motherhood takes up the task of spreading the new life in Christ among men.

In view of this mission, the Mother is asked to make the acutely painful sacrifice of accepting her only Son's death. Jesus' words: "Woman, behold your Son" enable Mary to sense the new maternal relationship which was to extend and broaden the preceding one. Her "yes" to this plan is therefore an assent to Christ's sacrifice, which she generously accepts by complying with the divine will. Even if in God's plan Mary's motherhood was destined from the start to extend to all humanity, only on Calvary, by virtue of Christ's sacrifice, is its universal dimension revealed.

## Mary Becomes The Mother Of All Disciples

Jesus' words, "Behold, your Son," effect what they express, making Mary the mother of John and of all the disciples destined to receive the gift of divine grace.

4. On the Cross Jesus did not proclaim Mary's universal motherhood formally, but established a concrete maternal

relationship between her and the beloved disciple. In the Lord's choice we can see his concern that this motherhood should not be interpreted in a vague way, but should point to Mary's intense, personal relationship with individual Christians.

May each one of us, precisely through the concrete reality of Mary's universal motherhood, fully acknowledge her as our own Mother, and trustingly commend ourselves to her maternal love.

# Devotion To Mary Is Based On Jesus' Will

*"The words, 'Behold, your mother!', express Jesus' intention to inspire in his disciples an attitude of love for and trust in Mary, leading them to recognize her as their mother, the mother of every believer," the Holy Father said at the General Audience on Wednesday, 7 May, 1997. The Pope was continuing his catechesis on the role of the Blessed Mother, focusing this time on her spiritual motherhood. Here is a translation of his reflection, which was the 50th in the series on the Blessed Virgin and was given in Italian.*

1. After entrusting John to Mary with the words "Woman, behold your Son!", Jesus, from the Cross, turns to his beloved disciple, saying to him, "Behold, your mother!" (Jn 19:26-27). With these words, he reveals to Mary the height of her motherhood: as mother of the Savior, she is also the mother of the redeemed, of all the members of the Mystical Body of her Son.

In silence the Virgin accepts the elevation to this highest degree of her motherhood of grace, having already given a response of faith with her "yes" at the Annunciation.

Jesus not only urges John to care for Mary with special love, but he entrusts her to him so that he may recognize her as his own mother.

During the Last Supper, "the disciple whom Jesus loved" listened to the Master's commandment "love one another as I have loved you" (Jn 15:12) and, leaning his head against the Lord's breast, he received from him a unique sign of love. Such experiences prepared him better to perceive in Jesus' words an invitation to accept her, who been given him as mother and to love her as Jesus did with filial affection.

May all discover in Jesus' words "Behold, your mother!" the invitation to accept Mary as mother, responding to her motherly love as true children.

## The Blessed Virgin Teaches Us To Love The Lord Deeply

2. In the light of this entrustment to his beloved disciple, one can understand the authentic meaning of Marian devotion in the ecclesial community. In fact, it places Christians in Jesus' filial relationship to his mother, putting them in a condition to grow in intimacy with both of them.

The Church's devotion to the Virgin is not only the fruit of a spontaneous response to the exceptional value of her person and the importance of her role in the work of salvation, but is based on Christ's will.

The words "Behold, your mother!", express Jesus' intention to inspire in his disciples an attitude of love for and trust in Mary, leading them to recognize her as their mother, the mother of every believer.

At the school of the Virgin, the disciples learn to know the Lord deeply, as John did, and to have an intimate and lasting relationship of love with him. They also discover the joy of entrusting themselves to the Mother's maternal love, living like affectionate and docile children.

The history of Christian piety teaches that Mary is the way which leads to Christ and that filial devotion to her takes nothing from intimacy with Jesus; indeed, it increases it and leads to the highest levels of perfection.

The countless Marian shrines throughout the world testily to the marvels wrought by grace through the intercession of Mary, Mother of the Lord and our Mother.

Turning to her, drawn by her tenderness, the men and women of our time also meet Jesus, Savior and Lord of their lives.

Above all, the poor, tried in heart, in their affections and in their material need, find refuge and peace in the Mother of God, and discover that for all people true riches consist in the grace of conversion and of following Christ.

## Every Christian Should Make Room For Mary In His Daily Life

3. According to the original Greek, the Gospel text continues: "From that hour the disciple took her among his possessions" (Jn 19:27), thus stressing John's ready and generous adherence to Jesus' words and informing us about his behavior for the whole of his life as the faithful guardian and docile Son of the Virgin.

The hour of acceptance is that of the fulfillment of the work of salvation. Mary's spiritual motherhood and the first manifestation of the new link between her and the Lord's disciples begins precisely in this context.

John took the Mother "among his possessions." These rather general words seem to highlight his Initiative, full of respect and love, not only in taking Mary to his house but also in living his spiritual life in communion with her.

In fact, a literal translation of the Greek expression "among his possessions" does not so much refer to material possessions since John as St. Augustine observes (In Ioan. Evang. tract. 119, 3) "possessed nothing of his own," but rather to the spiritual goods or gifts received from Christ: grace (Jn 1:16), the Word (Jn 12:48; 17:8), the Spirit (Jn 7:39; 14:17), the Eucharist (Jn 6:32-58). Among these gifts which come to him from the fact that he is loved by Jesus, the disciple accepts Mary as his mother, establishing a profound communion of life with her (cf. *Redemptoris Mater*, n. 45, note 130).

May every Christian, after the beloved disciple's example, "take Mary into his house" and make room for her in his own daily life, recognizing her providential role in the journey of salvation.

# Mary Was Witness To Whole Paschal Mystery

*"Lastly, the unique and special character of the Blessed Virgin's presence at Calvary and her perfect union with the Son in his suffering on the Cross seem to postulate a very particular sharing on her part in the mystery of the resurrection," the Holy Father said at the General Audience of Wednesday, 21 May, 1997, as he reflected on the question of whether the Lord appeared to Mary after his resurrection. Here is a translation of the Pope's catechesis, which was the 51st in the series on the Blessed Mother and was given in Italian.*

1. After Jesus had been laid in the tomb, Mary "alone remains to keep alive the flame of faith, preparing to receive the joyful and astonishing announcement of the resurrection" (Address at the General Audience, 3 April 1996; L'Osservatore Romano English edition, 10 April 1996, p.7). The expectation felt on Holy Saturday is one of the loftiest moments of faith for the Mother of the Lord: in the darkness that envelops the world, she entrusts herself fully to the God of life, and thinking back to the words of her Son, she hopes in the fulfillment of the divine promises.

The Gospels mention various appearances of the risen Christ, but not a meeting between Jesus and his Mother. This silence must not lead to the conclusion that after the resurrection Christ did not appear to Mary; rather it invites us to seek the reasons why the Evangelists made such a choice.

## How Could Mary Not Be Among Those Who Met The Risen Lord?

On the supposition of an "omission", this silence could be attributed to the fact that what is necessary for our saving knowledge was entrusted to the word of those "chosen by God as witnesses" (Acts 10:41), that is, the Apostles, who gave their testimony of the Lord Jesus' resurrection "with great power" (cf. Acts 4:33). Before appearing to them, the Risen One had appeared to several faithful women because of their ecclesial function: "Go and tell my brethren to go to Galilee, and there they will see me" (Mt 28:10).

If the authors of the New Testament do not speak of the Mother's encounter with her risen Son, this can perhaps be attributed to the fact that such a witness would have been considered too biased by those who denied the Lord's resurrection, and therefore not worthy of belief.

2. Furthermore, the Gospels report a small number of appearances by the risen Jesus and certainly not a complete summary of all that happened during the 40 days after Easter. St. Paul recalls that he appeared "to more than 500 brethren at one time" (1 Cor 15:6). How do we explain the fact that an exceptional event known to so many is not mentioned by the Evangelists? It is an obvious sign that other appearances of the Risen One were not recorded, although they were among the well-known events that occurred.

How could the Blessed Virgin, present in the first community of disciples (cf. Acts 1:14), be excluded from those who met her divine Son after he had risen from the dead?

3. Indeed, it is legitimate to think that the Mother was probably the first person to whom the risen Jesus appeared. Could not Mary's absence from the group of women who went to the tomb at dawn (cf. Mk 16:1; Mt 28:1) indicate that she had already met Jesus? This inference would also be confirmed by the fact that the first witnesses of the resurrection, by Jesus' will, were the women who had remained faithful at the foot of the Cross and therefore were more steadfast in faith.

Indeed, the Risen One entrusts to one of them, Mary Magdalen, the message to be passed on to the Apostles (cf. Jn 20:17-18. Perhaps this fact too allows us to think that Jesus showed himself first to his Mother, who had been the most faithful and had kept her faith intact when put to the test.

Lastly, the unique and special character of the Blessed Virgin's presence at Calvary and her perfect union with the Son in his suffering on the Cross seem to postulate a very particular sharing on her part in the mystery of the resurrection.

A fifth-century author, Sedulius, maintains that in the splendor of his risen life Christ first showed himself to his mother.

In fact, she; who at the Annunciation was the way he entered the world, was called to spread the marvelous news of the resurrection in order to become the herald of his glorious coming. Thus bathed in the glory of the Risen One, she anticipates the Church's splendor (cf. Sedulius, Paschale carmen, 5, 357-364, CSEL 10, 140f).

4. It seems reasonable to think that Mary, as the image and model of the Church which waits for the Risen One and meets him in the group of disciples during his Easter appearances, had had a personal contact with her risen Son, so that she too could delight in the fullness of paschal joy.

## Mother Of The Lord Is 'Cause Of Joy' For All People

Present at Calvary on Good Friday (cf. Jn 19:25) and in the Upper Room on Pentecost (cf. Acts 1:14), the Blessed Virgin too was probably a privileged witness of Christ's resurrection, completing in this way her participation in all the essential moments of the paschal mystery. Welcoming the risen Jesus, Mary is also a sign and an anticipation of humanity, which hopes to achieve its fulfillment through the resurrection of the dead.

In the Easter season, the Christian community addresses the Mother of the Lord and invites her to rejoice: "Regina Caeli, laetare. Allelula!". "Queen of heaven, rejoice. Alleluia!" Thus it recalls Mary's joy at Jesus' resurrection, prolonging in time the "rejoice" that the Angel addressed to her at the Annunciation, so that she might become a cause of "great joy" for all people.

# Mary Prays For Outpouring Of The Spirit

*"In contemplating Mary's powerful intercession as she waits for the Holy Spirit, Christians of every age have frequently had recourse to her intercession on the long and tiring journey to salvation, in order to receive the gifts of the Paraclete in greater abundance", the Holy Father said at the General Audience of Wednesday, 28 May, 1997, as he reflected on Mary's presence in the Upper Room at Pentecost Here is a translation of the Pope's catechesis, which was the 52nd in the series on the Blessed*

*Mother and was given in Italian.*

1. Retracing the course of the Virgin Mary's life, the Second Vatican Council recalls her presence in the community waiting for Pentecost. "But since it had pleased God not to manifest solemnly the mystery Of the salvation of the human race before he would pour forth the Spirit promised by Christ, we see the Apostles before the day of Pentecost 'persevering with one mind in prayer with the women and Mary the Mother of Jesus, and with his brethren' (Acts 1:14), and we also see Mary by her prayers imploring the gift of the Spirit, who had already overshadowed her in the Annunciation" (*Lumen Gentium*, n. 59).

## She Helped The Disciples Prepare For Spirit's Coming

The first community is the prelude to the birth of the Church; the Blessed Virgin's presence helps to sketch her definitive features, a fruit of the gift of Pentecost.

2. In the atmosphere of expectation that prevailed in the Upper Room after the ascension, what was Mary's position in relation to the descent of the Holy Spirit? The Council expressly underscores her prayerful presence while waiting for the outpouring of the Paraclete: she prays, "imploring the gift of the Spirit". This observation is particularly significant since at the Annunciation the Holy Spirit had descended upon her, "overshadowing" her and bringing about the Incarnation of the Word.

Having already had a unique experience of the effectiveness of such a gift, the Blessed Virgin was in a condition to appreciate it more than anyone; indeed, she owed her motherhood to the mysterious intervention of the Spirit, who had made her the way by which the Savior came into the world.

Unlike those in the Upper Room who were waiting in fearful expectation, she, fully aware of the importance of her Son's promise to the disciples (cf. Jn 14:16), helped the community to be well disposed to the coming of the "Paraclete".

Thus, while her unique experience made her ardently long for the Spirit's coming, it also involved her in preparing the minds and hearts of those around her.

3. During that prayer in the Upper Room, in an attitude of deep communion with the Apostles, with some women and with Jesus' "brethren", the Mother of the Lord prays for the gift of the Spirit for herself and for the community.

It was appropriate that the first outpouring of the Spirit upon her, which had happened in view of her divine motherhood, should be repeated and reinforced. Indeed, at the foot of the Cross Mary was entrusted with a new motherhood, which concerned Jesus' disciples. It was precisely this mission that demanded a renewed gift of the Spirit. The Blessed Virgin therefore wanted it for the fruitfulness of her spiritual motherhood.

While at the moment of the Incarnation the Holy Spirit had descended upon her as a person called to take part worthily in the great mystery, everything is now accomplished for the sake of the Church, whose image, model and mother Mary is called to be.

In the Church and for the Church, mindful of Jesus' promise, she waits for Pentecost and implores a multiplicity of gifts for everyone, in accordance with each one's personality and mission.

4. Mary's prayer has particular significance in the Christian community: it fosters the coming of the Spirit, imploring his action in the hearts of the disciples and in the world. Just as in the Incarnation the Spirit had formed the physical body of Christ in her virginal womb, now in the Upper Room the same Spirit comes down to give life to the Mystical Body.

Thus Pentecost is also a fruit of the Blessed Virgin's incessant prayer, which is accepted by the Paraclete with special favor because it is an expression of her motherly love for the Lord's disciples. In contemplating Mary's powerful intercession as she waits for the Holy Spirit, Christians of every age have frequently had recourse to her intercession on the long and tiring journey to salvation, in order to receive the gifts of the Paraclete in greater abundance.

## Mary Had A Deep Influence On The Early Community

5. Responding to the prayer of the Blessed Virgin and the community gathered in the Upper Room on the day of Pentecost, the Holy Spirit bestows the fullness of his gifts on the Blessed Virgin and those present, working a deep transformation in them for the sake of spreading the Good News. The Mother of Christ and his disciples are granted new strength and new apostolic energy for the Church's growth. In particular, the outpouring of the Spirit leads Mary to exercise her spiritual motherhood in an exceptional way, through her presence imbued with charity and her witness of faith.

In the nascent Church she passes on to the disciples her memories of the Incarnation, the infancy, the hidden life and the mission of her divine Son as a priceless treasure, thus helping to make him known and to strengthen the faith of believers.

We have no information about Mary's activity in the early Church, but we may suppose that after Pentecost her life would have continued to be hidden and discreet, watchful and effective. Since she was enlightened and guided by the Spirit, she exercised a deep influence on the community of the Lord's disciples.

# Mary And The Human Drama Of Death

*"The experience of death personally enriched the Blessed Virgin: by undergoing mankind's common destiny, she can more effectively exercise her spiritual motherhood towards those approaching the last moment of their life", the Holy Father said at the General Audience of Wednesday, 25 June 1997, as he reflected on the dormition of the Mother of God. Here is a translation of the Pope's catechesis, which was the 53rd in the series on the Blessed Mother and was given in Italian.*

1. Concerning the end of Mary's earthly life, the Council uses the terms of the Bull defining the dogma of the Assumption and states: "The Immaculate Virgin, preserved free from all stain of original sin, was taken up body and soul into heavenly glory, when

her earthly life was over" (*Lumen Gentium*, n. 59). With this formula, the Dogmatic Constitution *Lumen Gentium*, following my Venerable Predecessor Pius XII, made no pronouncement on the question of Mary's death. Nevertheless, Pius XII did not intend to deny the fact of her death, but merely did not judge it opportune to affirm solemnly the death of the Mother of God as a truth to be accepted by all believers.

## Christ Made Death A Means Of Salvation

Some theologians have in fact maintained that the Blessed Virgin did not die and was immediately raised from earthly life to heavenly glory. However, this opinion was unknown until the 17th century, whereas a common tradition actually exists which sees Mary's death as her entry into heavenly glory.

2. Could Mary of Nazareth have experienced the drama of death in her own flesh? Reflecting on Mary's destiny and her relationship with her divine Son, it seems legitimate to answer in the affirmative: since Christ died, it would be difficult to maintain the contrary for his Mother.

The Fathers of the Church, who had no doubts in this regard, reasoned along these lines. One need only quote St. Jacob of Sarug (1521), who wrote that when the time came for Mary "to walk on the way of all generations", the way, that is, of death, "the group of the Twelve Apostles" gathered to bury "the virginal body of the Blessed One" (Discourse on the burial of the Holy Mother of God, 87-99 in C. Vona, Lateranum 19 [1953], 188). St. Modestus of Jerusalem (‡634Y after a lengthy discussion of "the most blessed dormition of the most glorious Mother of God", ends his eulogy by exalting the miraculous intervention of Christ who "raised her from the tomb", to take her up with him in glory (Enc. in dormitionem Deiparae semperque Virginis Mariae, nn. 7 and 14: PG86 bis, 3293; 3311). St. John Damascene (1704) for his part asks: "Why is it that she who in giving birth surpassed all the limits of nature should now bend to its laws, and her immaculate body be subjected to death?". And he answers: "To be clothed in immortality, it is of course necessary that the mortal part be shed, since even the master of nature did not refuse the experience of death. Indeed, he died according to the flesh and by dying destroyed death; on corruption he bestowed incorruption and made death the source of resurrection" (Panegyric on the Dormition of the Mother of God, n. 10: SC 80, 107).

3. It is true that in Revelation death is presented as a punishment for sin. However, the fact that the Church proclaims Mary free from original sin by a unique divine privilege does not lead to the conclusion that she also received physical immortality. The Mother is not superior to the Son who underwent death, giving it a new meaning and changing it into a means of salvation.

Involved in Christ's redemptive work and associated in his saving sacrifice, Mary was able to share in his suffering and death for the sake of humanity's Redemption. What Severus of Antioch says about Christ also applies to her: "Without a preliminary death, how could the resurrection have taken place?" (Antijulianistica, Beirut 1931, 194f.). To share in Christ's resurrection, Mary had first to share in his death.

4. The New Testament provides no information on the circumstances of Mary's death. This silence leads one to suppose that it happened naturally, with no detail particularly worthy of mention. If this were not the case, how could the information about it have remained hidden from her contemporaries and not have been passed down to us in some way?

As to the cause of Mary's death, the opinions that wish to exclude her from death by natural causes seem groundless. It is more important to look for the Blessed Virgin's spiritual attitude at the moment of her departure from this world. In this regard, St. Francis de Sales maintains that Mary's death was due to a transport of love. He speaks of a dying "in love, from love and through love", going so far as to say that the Mother of God died of love for her Son Jesus (Treatise on the Love of God, bk. 7, ch. XIII-XIV).

## Mary's Death Was An Event Of Love

Whatever from the physical point of view was the organic, biological cause of the end of her bodily life, it can be said that for Mary the passage from this life to the next was the full development of grace in glory, so that no death can ever be so fittingly described as a "dormition" as hers.

5. In some of the writings of the Church Fathers we find Jesus himself described as coming to take his Mother at the time of her death to. bring her into heavenly glory. In this way they present the death of Mary as an event of love which conducted her to her divine Son to share his immortal life. At the end of her earthly life, she must have experienced, like Paul and more strongly, the desire to be freed from her body in order to be with Christ for ever (cf. Phil 1:23).

The experience of death personally enriched the Blessed Virgin: by undergoing mankind's common destiny, she can more effectively exercise her spiritual motherhood towards those approaching the last moment of their life.

## Church Believes In Mary's Assumption

*The Assumption is the culmination of the struggle which involved Mary's generous love in the redemption of humanity and is the fruit of her unique sharing in the victory of the Cross, the Holy Father said at the General Audience of Wednesday, 2 July, 1997, as he reflected on the Assumption of Mary as a truth of faith. Here is a translation of his catechesis, which was the 54th in the series on the Blessed Mother and was given in Italian.*

1. Following the Bull Munificentissimus Deus of my venerable Predecessor Pius XII, the Second Vatican Council affirms that the Immaculate Virgin was taken up body and soul into heavenly glory, when her earthly life was over" (*Lumen Gentium*, n. 59).

The Council Fathers wished to stress that Mary, unlike Christians who die in God's grace, was taken up into the glory of heaven with her body. This age-old belief is expressed in a long iconographical tradition which shows Mary "entering" heaven with her body.

The dogma of the Assumption affirms that Mary's body was glorified after her death. In fact, while for other human beings the resurrection of the body will take place at the end of the world, for Mary the glorification of her body was anticipated by a special privilege.

2. On 1 November 1950, in defining the dogma of the Assumption, Pius XII avoided using the term "resurrection" and did not take a position on the question of the Blessed Virgin's death as a truth of faith. The Bull Munificentissimus Deus limits itself to affirming the elevation of Mary's body to heavenly glory, declaring this truth a "divinely revealed dogma".

## Belief Spread Rapidly From East To West

How can we not see that the Assumption of the Blessed Virgin has always been part of the faith of the Christian people who, by affirming Mary's entrance into heavenly glory, have meant to proclaim the glorification of her body?

The first trace of belief in the Virgin's assumption can be found in the apocryphal accounts entitled Transitus Mariae, whose origin dates to the second and third centuries. These are popular and sometimes romanticized depictions, which in this case, however, pick up an intuition of faith on the part of God's People.

Later, there was a long period of growing reflection on Mary's destiny in the next world. This gradually led the faithful to believe in the glorious raising of the Mother of Jesus, in body and soul, and to the institution in the Fast of the liturgical feasts of the Dormition and Assumption of Mary.

Belief in the glorious destiny of the body and soul of the Lord's Mother after her death spread very rapidly from Fast to West, and has been widespread since the 14th century. In our century, on the eve of the definition of the dogma it was a truth almost universally accepted and professed by the Christian community in every comer of the world.

3. Therefore in May .1946, with the Encyclical Deiparae Virginsis Mariae, Pius XII called for a broad consultation, inquiring among the Bishops and, through them, among the clergy and the People of God as to the possibility and opportuneness of defining the bodily assumption of Mary as a dogma of faith. The result was

extremely positive: only six answers out of 1,181 showed any reservations about the revealed character of this truth.

Citing this fact, the Bull Munificentissimus Deus states: "Prom the universal agreement of the Church's ordinary Magisterium we have a certain and firm proof demonstrating that the Blessed Virgin Mary's bodily assumption into Heaven... is a truth revealed by God and therefore should be firmly and faithfully believed by all the children of the Church" (Apostolic Constitution Munificentissimus Deus: *AAS* 42 [1950], 757).

The definition of the dogma, in conformity with the universal faith of the People of God, definitively excludes every doubt and calls for the express assent of all Christians.

After stressing the Church's actual belief in the assumption, the Bull recalls the Scriptural basis for this truth.

Although the New Testament does not explicitly affirm Mary's assumption, it offers a basis for it because it strongly emphasized the Blessed Virgin's perfect union with Jesus' destiny. This union which is manifested, from the time of the Savior's miraculous conception, in the Mother's participation in her Son's mission and especially in her association with his redemptive sacrifice, cannot fall to require a continuation after death. Perfectly united with the life and saving work of Jesus, Mary shares his heavenly destiny in body and soul.

## Assumption Is Fruit Of Mary's Sharing In The Cross

4. The Bull Munificentissimus Deus cited above refers to the participation of the woman of the Proto-gospel in the struggle against the serpent, recognizing Mary as the New Eve, and presents the assumption as a consequence of Mary's union with Christ's saving work. In this regard it says: "Consequently, just as the glorious resurrection of Christ was an essential part and the final sign of this victory, so that struggle which was common to the Blessed Virgin and her divine Son should be brought to a close by the glorification of her virginal body" (Apostolic Constitution Munificentissimus Deus: *AAS* 42 [1950], 768).

The assumption is therefore the culmination of the struggle

which involved Mary's generous love in the redemption of humanity and is the fruit of her unique sharing in the victory of the Cross.

# Mary Is First Creature To Enjoy Eternal Life

*"Mary entered into glory because she welcomed the Son of God in her virginal womb and in her heart. By looking at her, the Christian learns to discover the value of his own body and to guard it as a temple of God, in expectation of the resurrection," the Holy Father said at the General Audience of Wednesday, 9 July, 1997, as he reflected on Mary's Assumption in the Tradition of the Church. Here is a translation of his catechesis, which was the 55th in the series on the Blessed Mother and was given in Italian.*

1. The Church's constant and unanimous Tradition shows how Mary's Assumption is part of the divine plan and is rooted in her unique sharing in the mission of her Son. In the first millennium sacred authors had already spoken in this way.

Testimonies, not yet fully developed, can be found in St. Ambrose, St. Epiphanius and Timothy of Jerusalem. St. Germanus I of Constantinople (1730) puts these words on Jesus' lips as he prepares to take his Mother to heaven: "You must be where I am, Mother inseparable from your Son..." (Hom. 3 in Dormitionem, PG 98, 360).

In addition, the same ecclesial Tradition sees the fundamental reason for the assumption in the divine motherhood.

We find an interesting trace of this conviction in a fifth century apocryphal account attributed to Pseudo-Melito. The author imagines Christ questioning Peter and the Apostles on the destiny Mary deserved, and this is the reply he received: "Lord, you chose this handmaid of yours to become an immaculate dwelling place for you.... Thus it seemed right to us, your servants, that just as you reign in glory after conquering death, so you should raise your Mother's body and take her rejoicing with you to heaven" (Transitus Mariae, 16, PG 5, 1238). It can therefore be said that the divine motherhood, which made Mary's body the immaculate dwelling place of the Lord, was the basis of her glorious destiny.

## Absence Of Original Sin Calls For Her Full Glorification

2. St. Germanus maintains in a richly poetic text that it is Jesus' affection for his Mother which requires Mary to be united with her divine Son in heaven: "Just as a child seeks and desires its mother's presence and a mother delights in her child's company, it was fitting that you, whose motherly love for your Son and God leaves no room for doubt, should return to him. And was it not right, in any case, that this God who had a truly filial love for you, should take you into his company?" (Hom. 1 in Dormitionem, PG 98, 347). In another text, the venerable author combines the private aspect of the relationship between Christ and Mary with the saving dimension of her motherhood, maintaining that "the mother of Life should share the dwelling place of Life" (ibid., PG 98, 348).

3. According to some of the Church Fathers, another argument for the privilege of the assumption is taken from Mary's sharing in the work of Redemption. St. John Damascene underscores the relationship between her participation in the Passion and her glorious destiny: "It was right that she who had seen her Son on the Cross and received the sword of sorrow in the depths of her heart... should behold this Son seated at the right hand of the Father" (Hom. 2, PG 96, 741). In the light of the paschal mystery, it appears particularly clear that the Mother should also be glorified with her Son after death.

The Second Vatican Council, recalling the mystery of the assumption in the Dogmatic Constitution on the Church, draws attention to the privilege of the Immaculate Conception: precisely because she was "preserved free from all stain of original sin" (*Lumen Gentium*, n. 59), Mary could not remain like other human beings in the state of death until the end of the world. The absence of original sin and her perfect holiness from the very first moment of her existence required the full glorification of the body and soul of the Mother of God.

4. Looking at the mystery of the Blessed Virgin's assumption, we can understand the plan of divine Providence plan for humanity: after Christ, the Incarnate Word, Mary is the first human being to achieve the eschatological ideal, anticipating the fullness of happiness promised to the elect through the resurrection of the body.

In the assumption of the Blessed Virgin we can also see the divine will to advance woman.

In a way analogous to what happened at the beginning of the human race and of salvation history, in God's plan the eschatological ideal was not to be revealed in an individual, but in a couple. Thus in heavenly glory, beside the risen Christ there is a woman who has been raised up, Mary: the new Adam and the new Eve, the first fruits of the general resurrection of the bodies of all humanity.

The eschatological conditions of Christ and Mary should not, of course, be put on the same level. Mary, the new Eve, received from Christ, the new Adam, the fullness of grace and heavenly glory, having been raised through the Holy Spirit by the sovereign power of the Son.

## The Assumption Shows The Value Of The Human Body

5. Despite their brevity, these notes enable us to show clearly that Mary's assumption reveals the nobility and dignity of the human body.

In the face of the profanation and debasement to which modern society frequently subjects the female body, the mystery of the assumption proclaims the supernatural destiny and dignity of every human body, called by the Lord to become an instrument of holiness and to share in his glory.

Mary entered into glory because she welcomed the Son of God in her virginal womb and in her heart. By looking at her, the Christian learns to discover the value of his own body and to guard it as a temple of God, in expectation of the resurrection.

The assumption, a privilege granted to the Mother of God, thus has immense value for the life and destiny of humanity.

# Christians Look To Mary Queen

*"Mary is Queen not only because she is Mother of God, but also because, associated as the new Eve with the new Adam, she cooperated in the work of the redemption of the human race", the Holy Father said at the General Audience of Wednesday, 23 July, 1997, as he reflected on Mary's universal queenship. Here is a translation of his catechesis, which was the 56th in the series on the Blessed Mother and was given in Italian.*

1. Popular devotion invokes Mary as Queen. The Council, after recalling the assumption of the Blessed Virgin in "'body and soul into heavenly glory'", explains that she was "exalted by the Lord as Queen over all things, that she might be the more fully conformed to her Son, the Lord of Lords (cf. Rv 19:16) and conqueror of sin and death" (*Lumen Gentium*, n. 59).

In fact, starting from the fifth century, almost in the same period in which the Council of Ephesus proclaims her "Mother of God") the title of Queen begins to be attributed to her. With this her recognition of her sublime dignity, the Christian people want to place her above all creatures, exalting her role and importance in the life of every person and of the whole world.

But already a fragment of a homily, attributed to Origen, contains this comment on the words Elizabeth spoke at the Visitation "It is I who should have come to visit you, because you are blessed above all women, you are the Mother of my Lord, you are my Lady" (Fragment, PG 13, 1902 D). The text passes spontaneously from the expression the "the Mother of my Lord" to the title, "my Lady", anticipating what St. John Damascene was later to say, attributing to Mary the title of "Sovereign": "When she became Mother of the Creator, she truly became queen of all creatures" (De fide orthodoxa, 4, 14, PG 94, 1157).

# Mary's Queenship Does Not
# Replace Her Maternal Role

2. My venerable Predecessor Pius XII, in his Encyclical Ad coeli Reginam to which the text of the Constitution *Lumen Gentium* refers, indicates as the basis for Mary's queenship in addition to her motherhood, her cooperation in the work of the Redemption. The Encyclical recalls the liturgical text: "There was St. Mary, Queen of heaven and Sovereign of the world, sorrowing near the Cross of our Lord Jesus Christ" (*AAS* 46 [1954] 634). It then establishes an analogy between Mary and Christ, which helps us understand the significance of the Blessed Virgin's royal status. Christ is King not only because he is Son of God, but also because he is the Redeemer; Mary is Queen not only because she is Mother of God, but also because, associated as the new Eve with the new Adam, she cooperated in the work of the redemption of the human race (*AAS* 46 [1954] 635).

In Mark's Gospel, we read that on the day of the ascension the Lord Jesus "was taken up into heaven, and sat down at the right hand of God" (16:19). In Biblical language "to sit at the right hand of God" means sharing his sovereign power. Sitting "at the right hand of the Father", he establishes his kingdom, God's kingdom. Taken up into heaven, Mary is associated with the power of her Son and is dedicated to the extension of the Kingdom, sharing in the diffusion of divine grace in the world.

In looking at the analogy between Christ's ascension and Mary's assumption, we can conclude that Mary, in dependence on Christ, is the Queen who possesses and exercises over the universe a sovereignty granted to her by her Son.

3. The tide of Queen does not of course replace that of Mother: her queenship remains a corollary of her particular maternal mission and simply expresses the power conferred on her to carry out that mission.

Citing Pius IX's Bull Ineffabilis Deus, the Supreme Pontiff highlights this maternal dimension of the Blessed Virgin's queenship: "Having a motherly affection for us and being concerned for our Salvation, she extends her care to the whole human race. Appointed by the Lord as Queen of heaven and earth, raised above all the choirs of angels and the whole celestial hierarchy of saints, sitting at the right hand of her only Son, our Lord Jesus Christ, she obtains with great certainty what she asks with her motherly prayers; she obtains what she seeks and it cannot be denied her" (cf. *AAS*. 46 [1954] 636-637).

## Mary Is A Queen Who Gives All She Possesses

4. Therefore Christians look with trust to Mary Queen and this not only does not diminish but indeed exalts their filial abandonment to her, who is mother in the order Of grace.

Indeed, the concern Mary Queen has for mankind can be fully effective precisely by virtue of her glorious state which derives from the assumption. St. Germanus I of Constantinople, highlights this very well. He holds that this state guarantees Mary's intimate relationship with her Son and enables her to intercede in our favor. Addressing Mary he says: Christ wanted "to have, so to speak, the closeness of your lips and your heart; thus he assents to all the desires you express to him, when you suffer for your children, with his divine power he does all that you ask of him" (Hom. 1 PG 98, 348).

5. One can conclude that the assumption favors Mary's full communion not only with Christ; but with each one of us: she is beside us, because her glorious state enables her to follow us in our daily earthly journey. As we read again in St. Cermanus: "You dwell spiritually with us and the greatness of your vigilance over us makes your communion of life with us stand out" (Hom. 1, PG 98, 344).

Thus far from creating distance between her and us, Mary's glorious state brings about a continuous and caring closeness. She knows everything that happens in our life and supports us with maternal love in life's trials.

Taken up into heavenly dedicates herself totally to the work of salvation in order to communicate to every living person the happiness granted to her. She is a Queen who gives all that she possesses, participating above all in the life and love of Christ.

# Mary Is Pre-eminent Member Of The Church

*"Mother of the only begotten Son of God, Mary is Mother of the community which constitutes Christ's mystical Body and guides its first steps. In accepting this mission, she is committed to encouraging ecclesial life with her maternal and exemplary presence,"* the Holy Father said at the General Audience of Wednesday, 30 July, 1997, reflecting on Mary as a pre-eminent member of the Church since her origins. Here is a translation of his catechesis, which was the 57th in the series on the Blessed Mother and was given in Italian.

1. Mary's exceptional role in the work of salvation invites us to deepen the relationship that exists between her and the Church.

According to some people Mary cannot be considered a member of the Church, since the privileges conferred on her, the Immaculate Conception, her divine motherhood and her unique cooperation in the work of salvation, place her in a condition of superiority with respect to the community of believers.

The Second Vatican Council, however, does not hesitate to present Mary as a member of the Church, nevertheless specifying that she is "pre-eminent and wholly unique" (*Lumen Gentium*, n. 53): Mary is the type of the Church, her model and mother. Differing from all the other faithful, because of the exceptional gifts she received from the Lord, the Blessed Virgin nonetheless belongs to the Church and is fully entitled to be a member.

## Mary Lives In Communion With Her Son, Present In The Eucharist

2. Conciliar teaching finds a significant basis in Sacred Scripture. The Acts of the Apostles show Mary present from the beginning of the primitive community (cf. Acts 1:14), while she shares with the disciples and some women believers the prayerful expectation of the Holy Spirit, who will descend on them.

After Pentecost, the Blessed Virgin continues to live in fraternal communion with the community and takes part in the prayers, in listening to the Apostles teaching, and in the "breaking of bread", that is, in the Eucharistic celebration (cf. Acts 2:42).

She who had lived in close union with Jesus in the house of Nazareth, now lives in the Church in intimate communion with her Son, present in the Eucharist.

3. Mother of the only begotten Son of God's, Mary is Mother of the community which constitutes Christ's mystical Body and guides its first steps.

In accepting this mission, she is committed to encouraging ecclesial life with her maternal and exemplary presence. This solidarity derives from her belonging to the community of the redeemed. In fact, unlike her Son, she had need of redemption since "being of the race of Adam, she is at the same time also united to all those who are to be saved (*Lumen Gentium*, n. 53). The privilege of the Immaculate Conception preserved her from the stain of sin, because of the Redeemer's special saving influence.

As "preeminent and as a wholly unique member of the Church", Mary uses the gifts God's has granted her to achieve fuller solidarity with the brothers and sisters of her Son, now her children too.

## Mary Shares With Believers Filial Obedience And Heartfelt Gratitude

4. As a member of the Church, Mary places her personal holiness, the fruit of God's grace and of her faithful collaboration, at the service of her brothers and sisters. The Immaculate Virgin is an unfailing support for all Christians in their fight against sin and a constant encouragement to live as those redeemed by Christ, sanctified by the Spirit, and children of the Father.

As a member of the first community, "Mary the Mother of Jesus" (Acts 1:14) is respected and venerated by all. Each one understands the preeminence of her who brought forth the Son of God's, the one universal Savior. Furthermore, the virginal character of her motherhood allows her to witness to the extraordinary contribution to the Church's good offered by the one who, giving up human fruitfulness through docility to the Holy Spirit, puts herself completely at the service of God's kingdom.

Called to collaborate intimately in her Son's sacrifice and the gift of the divine life to humanity, Mary continues her motherly work after Pentecost. The mystery of love contained in the Cross inspires her apostolic zeal and commits her, as a member of the Church, to spreading the Good News.

The words of the crucified Christ on Golgotha: "Woman, behold, your Son" (Jn 19:26), with which her role as the universal mother of believers is recognized, unfold before her motherhood with new and limitless horizons. The gift of the Holy Spirit, received at Pentecost through the exercise of this mission, induces her to offer the help of her motherly heart to all who are on their way towards the total fulfillment of God's kingdom.

5. A pre-eminent member of the Church, Mary lives a unique relationship with the divine persons of the Most Holy Trinity: with the Father, the Son and the Holy Spirit. The Council, in calling her "Mother of the Son of God's", and therefore "beloved daughter of the Father and the temple of the Holy Spirit" (*Lumen Gentium*, n. 53), recalls the primary effect of the Father's love which is the divine motherhood.

Aware of the gift she has received, Mary shares with believers the attitudes of filial obedience and heartfelt gratitude, encouraging each one to recognize the signs of divine benevolence in his own life.

The Council uses the expression "temple" (sacrarium) of the Holy Spirit, intending to emphasize the link of presence, love and collaboration that exists between the Blessed Virgin and the Holy Spirit. The Blessed Virgin, who is already invoked by Francis of Assisi as the "Bride of the Holy Spirit" (Antiphon "Santa Maria Vergine" in: Fonti Francescane, 281), by her example encourages the other members of the Church to entrust themselves generously to the mysterious action of the Paraclete, and to live with him in constant communion of love.

# Mary Is Outstanding Figure Of Church

*The plan of salvation which orders the prefigurations of the Old Testament to fulfillment in the New Covenant likewise determines that Mary would live in a perfect way what was later to be fulfilled in the Church", the Holy Father said at the General Audience of Wednesday, 6 August, 1997, as he reflected on Mary as "the Church's type and outstanding model in faith and charity". Here is a translation of his catechesis, which was the 58th in the series on the Blessed Mother and was given in Italian.*

1. The Dogmatic Constitution *Lumen Gentium* of the Second Vatican Council, after presenting Mary as "pre-eminent and as a wholly unique member of the Church", declares her to be the Church's "type and outstanding model in. faith and charity." (*Lumen Gentium*, n. 53).

The Council Fathers attribute to Mary the function of "type", that is, figure, "of the Church", borrowing the term from St. Ambrose who expresses himself thus in his commentary on the Annunciation: "Yes, she [Mary] is betrothed, but she is a virgin because she is a type of the Church which is immaculate but a bride: a virgin, she conceived us by the Spirit; a virgin, she gave birth to us without pain" (In Ev. sec. Luc., II, 7, CCL, 14, 33, 102-106). Thus Mary is a type of the Church because of her immaculate holiness, her virginity, her betrothal and her motherhood.

St. Paul uses the word "type", to give tangible form to a spiritual reality. In fact he sees in the crossing of the Red Sea by the People of Israel a "type" or image of Christian Baptism, and in the manna and in the water which gushed from the rock, a "type" or image of the Eucharistic food and drink (cf. 1 Cor 10:1-11).

By defining Mary as a type of the Church, the Council invites us to see in her the visible figure of the Church's spiritual reality, and in her spotless motherhood, the announcement of the Church's virginal motherhood.

# In Mary The Spiritual Reality Proclaimed Is Completely Fulfilled

2. It is necessary to explain that, unlike the Old Testament images or types, which are only prefigurations of future realities, in Mary the spiritual reality signified is already eminently present.

The Red Sea crossing described in the Book of Exodus is a saving event of liberation, but it was certainly not a baptism capable of remitting sins and giving new life. Likewise, the manna, a precious gift from Yahweh to his people wandering in the desert, contained nothing of the future reality of the Eucharist, the Body of the Lord, nor did the water which gushed from the rock already contain Christ's Blood, shed for the multitude.

The Exodus is the great work accomplished by Yahweh for his people, but it does not constitute the definitive spiritual redemption which Christ would achieve in the paschal mystery.

Moreover, referring to Jewish practices, Paul recalls: "These are only a shadow of what is to come; but the substance belongs to Christ" (Col 2:17). This is echoed in the letter to the Hebrews which, systematically developing this interpretation, presents the worship of the Old Covenant as "a copy and shadow of the heavenly sanctuary" (Heb 8:5).

3. However, in affirming that Mary is a type of the Church, the Council does not intend to equate her with the figures or types of the Old Testament, but instead to affirm that in her the spiritual reality proclaimed and represented is completely fulfilled.

In fact, the Blessed Virgin is a type of the Church, not as an imperfect prefiguration, but as the spiritual fullness which will be found in various ways in the Church's life. The particular relationship that exists here between the image and the reality represented is based on the divine plan, which establishes a close bond between Mary and the Church. The plan of salvation which orders the prefigurations of the Old Testament to fulfillment in the New Covenant likewise determines that Mary would live in a perfect way what was later to be fulfilled in the Church.

The perfection God conferred upon Mary, therefore, acquires its most authentic meaning if it is interpreted as a prelude to divine life in the Church.

## Mary's Perfection Surpasses That Of All Other Church Members

4. After saying that Mary is a "type of the Church", the Council adds that she is her "outstanding model", an example of perfection to be followed and imitated. Indeed, Mary is an "outstanding model" because her perfection surpasses that of all the other members of the Church.

Significantly, the Council adds that she carries out this role "in faith and in charity". Without forgetting that Christ is the first model, the Council suggests In this way that there are interior dispositions proper to the model realized in Mary, which help the Christian to establish an authentic relationship with Christ. In fact, by looking at Mary, the believer learns to live in deeper communion with Christ, to adhere to him with a living faith and to place his trust and his hope in him, loving him with his whole being.

The functions of "type and model of the Church" refer in particular to Mary's virginal motherhood and shed light on her particular place in the work of salvation. This basic structure of Mary's being is reflected in the motherhood and virginity of the Church.

# Mary Is Model For Church's Motherhood

'In contemplating Mary, the Church imitates her charity, her faithful acceptance of the Word of God and her docility in fulfilling the Father's will By following the Blessed Virgin's example, she achieves a fruitful spiritual motherhood", the Holy Father said at the General Audience of Wednesday, 13 August, 1997, as he reflected on Mary's motherhood as a model for the Church. Here is a translation of his catechesis, which was the 59th in the series on the Blessed Mother and was given in Italian.

1. It is precisely in the divine motherhood that the Council perceives the basis of the special relationship between Mary and the Church. We read in the Dogmatic Constitution *Lumen Gentium*: "By reason of the gift and role of her divine motherhood, by which she is united with her Son, the Redeemer, and with her unique graces and functions, the Blessed Virgin is also intimately united to the Church" (n. 63). The Dogmatic Constitution on the Church constantly refers to this same presupposition to illustrate the prerogatives of "type" and "model" which the Blessed Virgin enjoys in relation to the Mystical Body of Christ: "In the mystery of the Church, which Is herself rightly called mother and virgin, the Blessed Virgin stands out in eminent and singular fashion as exemplar both of virgin and mother" (ibid.).

Mary's motherhood is defined as "eminent and singular", since it represents a unique and unrepeatable fact: Mary, before carrying out her motherly role for humanity, is the Mother of the only begotten Son of God made man. On the other hand, the Church is a mother because she gives spiritual birth to Christ in the faithful, thus carrying out her maternal role for the members of the Mystical Body.

In this way the Blessed Virgin is a superior model for the Church, precisely because of the uniqueness of her prerogative as Mother of God.

## Mary's Virtues Are For The Church To Imitate

2. *Lumen Gentium*, in reflecting on Mary's motherhood, recalls that it is also expressed in the eminent dispositions of her soul: "Through her faith and obedience she gave birth on earth to the very Son of the Father, not through the knowledge of man but by the overshadowing of the Holy Spirit, in the manner of a new Eve who placed her faith not in the serpent of old, but in God's messenger without wavering in doubt" (*Lumen Gentium*, n. 63).

From these words it can be clearly seen that Mary's faith and obedience at the Annunciation are virtues for the Church to imitate and, in a certain sense, they begin her motherly journey in service to men called to salvation.

The divine motherhood cannot be isolated from the universal dimension given to it in God's saving plan, which the Council does not hesitate to recognize: "The Son whom she brought forth is he whom God placed as the first-born among many brethren (Rom 8:29), that is, the faithful, in whose generation and formation she cooperates with a mother's love" (ibid.).

3. The Church becomes a mother, taking Mary as her model. In this regard the Council says: "The Church indeed, contemplating her hidden sanctity, imitating her charity and faithfully fulfilling the Father's will, by receiving the Word of God in faith becomes herself a mother. By preaching and Baptism she brings forth sons, who are conceived of the Holy Spirit and born of God, to a new and immortal life" (ibid. n. 64).

Analyzing this description of the Church's maternal work, we can note how the Christian's birth is linked here in a certain way to the birth of Jesus, as though a reflection of it: Christians are "conceived by the Holy Spirit", and therefore their birth, the fruit of preaching and Baptism, resembles the Savior 's.

Moreover, in contemplating Mary, the docility in fulfilling the Father's will. By following the Blessed Virgin's example, she achieves a fruitful spiritual motherhood.

4. But the Church's motherhood does not make Mary's superfluous: continuing to exercise her influence on the life of Christians, Mary helps to give the Church a maternal face. In the light of Mary the motherhood of the ecclesial community, which might seem somewhat general, is called to be expressed in a more concrete and personal way t wards every person redeemed by Christ.

By showing herself to be the Mother of all believers, Mary fosters in them relations of authentic spiritual brotherhood and constant dialogue.

## Both Mothers Are Essential To Christian Life

The daily experience of faith, in every age and place, highlights the need many feel to entrust their daily necessities to Mary and they trustfully open their hearts to implore her motherly intercession and obtain her reassuring protection.

The prayers addressed to Mary by people in every age, the many forms and expressions of Marian devotion, the pilgrimages to shrines and places which commemorate the miracles worked by God the Father through the Mother of his Son show Man's extraordinary influence on the Church's life. The love of the People of God for the Blessed Virgin points to the need for close personal relations with their heavenly Mother. At the same time Mary's spiritual motherhood supports and increases the Church's concrete practice of her own motherhood.

5. The two mothers, the Church and Mary, are both essential to Christian life. It could be said that the one is a more objective motherhood and the other more interior.

The Church becomes a mother in preaching God's Word and administering the sacraments, particularly Baptism, in celebrating the Eucharist and in forgiving sins.
Mary's motherhood is expressed in all the areas where grace is distributed, particularly within the framework of personal relations.

They are two inseparable forms of motherhood: indeed both enable us to recognize the same divine love which seeks to share itself with mankind.

# Mary Fully Adhered To Revealed Truth

*"Having fully adhered to the Word of the Lord, Mary represents for the Church an unsurpassable model of 'virginally integral' faith, for with docility and perseverance she accepts the revealed Truth whole and entire", the Holy Father said at the General Audience of Wednesday, 20 August, 1997, as he reflected on Mary's virginity as a model for the Church. Here is a translation of his catechesis, which was the 60th in the series on the Blessed Mother and was given in Italian.*

1. The Church is a mother and virgin. After affirming that she is a mother, modeled on Mary, the Council gives her the title of virgin, explaining its significance: "She herself is a virgin, who keeps in its entirety and purity the faith she pledged to her spouse. Imitating the Mother of her Lord, and by the power of the Holy

Spirit, she preserves with virginal purity an integral faith, firm hope and sincere charity" (*Lumen Gentium*, n. 64).

Thus Mary is also a model of the Church's virginity. In this regard, it is necessary to explain that virginity does not belong to the Church in the strict
sense, since it does not represent the state of life of the vast majority of the faithful. Indeed, by virtue of God's providential plan, marriage is the most widespread and, we could say, common state for those called to the faith. The gift of virginity is reserved to a limited number of the faithful, who are called to a particular mission within the ecclesial community.

## Mary's Virginity Has Beneficial Influence On The Church

Nevertheless, in mentioning St. Augustine's teaching, the Council maintains that the Church is virginal in the spiritual sense of integrity in faith, hope and charity. Therefore, the Church is not a virgin in the body of all her members, but possesses a virginity of the spirit (virginitas mentis), that is, "integral faith, firm hope and sincere charity" (In Io. Tr., 13, 12; PL 35, 1499).

2. The Constitution *Lumen Gentium* therefore takes pains to recall that Mary's virginity, a model for that of the Church, also includes the physical dimension, by which she virginally conceived Jesus by the power of the Holy Spirit without man's intervention.

Mary is a virgin in body and a virgin in heart, as appears from her intention to live in deep intimacy with the Lord, decisively manifested at the time of the Annunciation. Thus she who is invoked as "Virgin of virgins" is without doubt for everyone a very lofty example of purity and of total self-giving to the Lord. But she is a special source of inspiration for Christian virgins and for those who are radically and exclusively dedicated to the Lord in the various forms of consecrated life.

Thus after its important role in the work of salvation, Mary's virginity continues to have a beneficial influence on the Church's life.

3. let us not forget that Christ is certainly the first and highest example for every chaste life. However Mary is a special model of chastity lived for love of the Lord Jesus.

She encourages all Christians to live chastity with particular commitment according to their own state, and to entrust themselves to the Lord in the different circumstances of life. She who is the sanctuary of the Holy Spirit par excellence helps believers rediscover their own body as the temple of God (cf. 1 Cor 6:19) and to respect its nobility and holiness.

Young people seeking genuine love look to the Blessed Virgin and invoke her motherly help to persevere in purity.

Mary reminds married couples of the fundamental values of marriage by helping them overcome the temptation to discouragement and to subdue the passions that try to sway their hearts. Her total dedication to God is a strong encouragement to them to live in mutual fidelity, so that they will never give in to the difficulties that beset conjugal communion.

4. The Council urges the faithful to look to Mary so that they may Imitate her "virginally integral" faith, hope and charity.

## Mary Accepted Revealed Truth With Docility

To preserve the integrity of the faith is a demanding task for the Church, which is called to constant vigilance even at the cost of sacrifice and struggle. In fact, the Church's faith is not only threatened by those who reject the Gospel message, but especially by those who, in accepting only part of the revealed truth, refuse to share fully in the entire patrimony of the faith of Christ's Bride.

Unfortunately, this temptation, which we find from the Church's very beginning, continues to be present in her life, urging her to accept Revelation only in part, or to give the Word of God a limited, personal interpretation in conformity with the prevailing mentality and individual desires. Having fully adhered to the Word of the Lord, Mary represents for the Church an unsurpassable model of "virginally integral" faith, for with docility and perseverance she accepts the revealed Truth whole and entire. And by her constant intercession, she obtains for the Church the light of hope and the flame of charity, virtues of which, in her earthly life, she was an incomparable example for everyone.

# Mary: Model Of Faith, Hope And Charity

*Mary as the Church's model of faith, hope and charity was the subject of the Holy Father's weekly catechesis at the General Audience of Wednesday, 3 September, 1997. Taking his theme from the Second Vatican Council's statement that "in the most Blessed Virgin the Church has already reached perfection" Lumen Gentium, n. 65), the Pope said that on their way to holiness the faithful are encouraged by the example of their Mother who is the "model of virtues". Here is a translation of his catechesis, which was the 61st in the series on the Blessed Virgin and was given in Italian.*

1. In the Letter to the Ephesians St. Paul explains the spousal relationship between Christ and the Church in the following words: "Christ loved the Church and gave himself up for her, that he might sanctify her, having cleansed her by the washing of water with the word, that he might present the Church to himself in splendor, without spot or wrinkle or any such thing, that she might be holy and without blemish" (Eph 5:25-27).

The Second Vatican Council takes up the Apostle's assertions and recalls that "in the most Blessed Virgin the Church has already reached perfection", while "the faithful still strive to conquer sin and increase in holiness" (*Lumen Gentium*, n. 65).

In this way the difference between Mary and the faithful is emphasized, although both belong to the holy Church which Christ made "without spot or wrinkle". In fact, while the faithful receive holiness through Baptism, Mary was preserved from all stain of original sin and was redeemed antecedently by Christ. Furthermore, although the faithful have been freed "from the law of sin" (cf. Rom 8:2), they can still give in to temptation, and human frailty continues to manifest itself in their lives. "We all make many mistakes", says the Letter of James (3:2). For this reason the Council of Trent teaches: "No one can avoid all sins, even venial sins, throughout his life" (DS 1573). By divine privilege, however, the Immaculate Virgin is an exception to this rule, as the Council of Trent itself recalls (ibid.).

## Mary Is The Perfect Expression Of Faith

2. Despite the sins of her members, the Church is first and foremost the community of those who are called to holiness and strive each day to achieve it.

In this arduous path to perfection they feel encouraged by her who is the "model of virtues". The Council notes: "Devoutly meditating on her and contemplating her in the light of the Word made man, the Church reverently penetrates more deeply into the great mystery of the Incarnation and becomes more and more like her Spouse" (*Lumen Gentium*, n. 65).

So the Church looks to Mary. She not only contemplates the wondrous gift of her fullness of grace, but strives to imitate the perfection which in her is the fruit of her full compliance with Christ's command: "You, therefore, must be perfect as your heavenly Father is perfect" (Mt 5:48). Mary is all-holy. For the community of believers she represents the paradigm of the authentic holiness that is achieved in union with Christ. The earthly life of the Mother of God is characterized by perfect harmony with the person of her Son and by her total dedication to the redeeming work he accomplished.

The Church turns her gaze to the maternal intimacy that grew in silence during life in Nazareth and reached perfection at the moment of sacrifice, and she strives to imitate it in her daily journey. In this way, she is increasingly conformed to her Spouse. United like Mary with the Redeemer's Cross, the Church, amid the difficulties, contradictions and persecutions that renew in her life the mystery of her Lord's Passion, constantly seeks to be fully configured to him.

3. The Church lives by faith, seeing in her "who believed that there would be a fulfillment of what was spoken to her from the Lord" (Lk 1:45), the first and perfect expression of her faith. On this journey of trusting abandonment to the Lord, the Virgin goes

before the disciples, adhering to the divine Word with an increasing intensity that embraces all the stages of her life and spreads to the very mission of the Church.

Her example encourages the People of God to practice their faith and to study and develop its content, by keeping in their heart and meditating on the events of salvation.

Mary also becomes a model of hope for the Church. In listening to the angel's message, the Virgin first directs her hope to the kingdom without end, which Jesus had been sent to establish.

She stands firm near the cross of her Son, waiting for the divine promise to be fulfilled. After Pentecost, the Mother of Jesus sustains the Church's hope despite the threat of persecution. She is thus the Mother of hope for the community of believers and for individual Christians, and she encourages and guides her children as they await the kingdom, supporting them in their daily trials and throughout the events of history, however tragic.

## Mary Continues To Support The Christian Community

Lastly, the Church sees in Mary the model of her charity. By looking at the situation of the first Christian community, we discover that the unanimity of their hearts, which was shown as they awaited Pentecost, is associated with the presence of the Holy Virgin (cf. Acts 1:14). And precisely because of Mary's radiant charity, ft is possible to maintain harmony and fraternal love at all times within the Church.

4. The Council expressly underscores Mary's exemplary role for the Church's apostolic mission, with the following observation: "The Church, therefore, in her apostolic work too, rightly looks to her who gave birth to Christ, who was thus conceived of the Holy Spirit and born of the Virgin, in order that through the Church he could be born and increase in the hearts of the faithful. In her life the Virgin has been a model of that motherly love with which all who join in the Church's apostolic mission for the regeneration of mankind should be animated" (*Lumen Gentium*, n. 65).

After having cooperated in the work of salvation by her motherhood, her association with Christ's sacrifice and her motherly aid to the newborn Church, Mary continues to support the Christian community and all believers in their generous commitment to proclaiming the Gospel.

# Mary: Model Of The Church At Prayer

*Mary's role as a model of the Church at worship was the subject of the Holy Father's catechesis at the General Audience of Wednesday, 10 September, 1997. Quoting the Servant of God Paul VI, the Pope said: "That the Blessed Virgin is an exemplar in this field derives from the fact that she is recognized as a most excellent exemplar of the Church in the order of faith, charity and perfect union with Christ" (Marialis Cultus, n. 16). Her example encourages Christians to "offer spiritual sacrifices acceptable to God through Jesus Christ" (1 Pt 2:5), the Holy Father added. Here is a translation of his catechesis, which was the 62nd in the series on the Blessed Virgin and was given in Italian.*

1. In the Apostolic Exhortation Marialis Cultus the Servant of God Paul VI, of venerable memory, presents the Blessed Virgin as a model of the Church at worship. This assertion is a corollary as it were to the truth that points to Mary as a paradigm for the People of God on the way to holiness: "That the Blessed Virgin is an exemplar in this field derives from the fact that she is recognized as a most excellent exemplar of the Church in the order of faith, charity and perfect union with Christ, that is, of that interior disposition with which the Church, the beloved spouse, closely associated with her Lord, invokes Christ and through him worships the eternal Father" (n. 16).

2. She who at the Annunciation showed total availability for the divine plan represents for all believers a sublime model of attentiveness and docility to the Word of God.

In replying to the angel: "Let it be to me according to your word" (Lk 1:38) and in stating her readiness to fulfill perfectly the Lord's will, Mary rightly shares in the beatitude proclaimed by

Jesus: "Blessed are those who hear the Word of God and keep it!" (Lk 11:28).

## Mary Grasped Deep Meaning Of The Saving Events

With this attitude, which encompasses her entire life, the Blessed Virgin indicates the high road of listening to the Word of the Lord, an essential element of worship, which has become typical of the Christian liturgy. Her example shows us that worship does not primarily consist in expressing human thoughts and feelings, but in listening to the divine Word in order to know it, assimilate it and put it into practice in daily life.

3. Every liturgical celebration is a memorial of the mystery of Christ in his salvific action for all humanity and is meant to promote the personal participation of the faithful in the paschal mystery re-expressed and made present in the gestures and words of the rite.

Mary was a witness to the historical unfolding of the saving events, which culminated in the Redeemer's Death and resurrection, and she kept "all these things, pondering them in her heart" (Lk 2:19)

She was not merely present at the individual events, but sought to grasp their deep meaning, adhering with all her soul to what was being mysteriously accomplished in them.

Mary appears therefore as the supreme model of personal participation in the divine mysteries. She guides the Church in meditating on the mystery celebrated and in participating in the saving event, by encouraging the faithful to desire an intimate, personal relationship with Christ in order to cooperate with the gift of their own life in the salvation of all.

4. Mary also represents the model of the Church at prayer. In all probability Mary was absorbed in prayer when the angel Gabriel came to her house in Nazareth and greeted her. This prayerful setting certainly supported the Blessed Virgin in her. reply to the angel and in her generous assent to the mystery of the Incarnation.

In the Annunciation scene, artists have almost always depicted Mary in a prayerful attitude. Of them all we recall Fra

Angelico. This shows to the Church and every believer the atmosphere that should prevail during worship.

We could add that for the People of God Mary represents the model of every expression of their prayer life. In particular, she teaches Christians how to turn to God to ask for his help and support in the various circumstances of life.

## Christians Are Encouraged To Offer Spiritual Sacrifices

Her motherly intercession at the wedding in Cana and her presence in the Upper Room at the Apostles' side as they prayed in expectation of Pentecost suggest that the prayer of petition is an essential form of cooperation in furthering the work of salvation in the world. By following her model, the Church learns to be bold in her asking, to persevere in her intercessions and, above all, to implore the gift of the Holy Spirit (cf. Lk 11:13).

5. The Blessed Virgin also represents the Church's model for generously participating in sacrifice.

In presenting Jesus in the temple and, especially, at the foot of the Cross, Mary completes the gift of herself which associates her as Mother with the suffering and trials of her Son. Thus in daily life as in the Eucharistic celebration, the "Virgin presenting offerings" (Marialis Cultus, n. 20) encourages Christians to "offer spiritual sacrifices acceptable to God through Jesus Christ" (1 Pt 2:5).

# Blessed Virgin Is Mother Of The Church

*Mary as Mother of the Church was the topic of the Holy Father's catechesis at the General Audience of Wednesday, 17 September, 1997. "The title 'Mother of the Church' reflects the deep conviction of the Christian faithful, who see in Mary not only the mother of the person of Christ, but also of the faithful She who is recognized as mother of salvation, life and grace, mother of the saved and mother of the living, is rightly proclaimed Mother of the Church", the Pope said. Here is a translation of his catechesis, which was the 63rd in the series on the Blessed Virgin and was given in Italian.*

1. After proclaiming Mary a "pre-eminent member", the "type" and "model" of the Church, the Second Vatican Council says: "The Catholic Church, taught by the Holy Spirit, honors her with filial affection and devotion as a most beloved mother" (*Lumen Gentium*, n. 53).

To tell the truth, the conciliar text does not explicitly attribute the title "Mother of the Church" to the Blessed Virgin, but it unmistakably expresses its content by repeating a statement made in 1748, more than two centuries ago, by Pope Benedict XIV (Bullarium Romanum, series 2, t. 2, n. 61, p.428).

In this document my venerable Predecessor, in describing the filial sentiments of the Church, which recognizes Mary as her most beloved mother, indirectly proclaims her Mother of the Church.

## Title Expresses Mary's Maternal Relationship With The Church

2. This title was rather rarely used in the past, but has recently become more common in the pronouncements of the Church's Magisterium and in the devotion of the Christian people. The faithful first called upon Mary with the title "Mother of God", "Mother of the faithful" or "our Mother", to emphasize her personal relationship with each of her children.

Later, because of the greater attention paid to the mystery of the Church and to Mary's relationship to her, the Blessed Virgin began more frequently to be invoked as "Mother of the Church".

Before the Second Vatican Council, this expression was found in Pope Leo XIII' s Magisterium, in which it is affirmed that Mary is "in all truth mother of the Church" (Acta Leonis XII, 15, 302). The title was later used many times in the teachings of John XXIII and Paul VI.

3. Although the title "Mother of the Church" was only recently attributed to Mary, it expresses the Blessed Virgin's maternal

relationship with the Church as shown already in several New Testament texts.

Since the Annunciation, Mary was called to give her consent to the coming of the messianic kingdom, which would take place with the formation of the Church.

When at Cana Mary asked the Son to exercise his messianic power, she made a fundamental contribution to implanting the faith in the first community of disciples, and she cooperated in Initiating God's kingdom, which has its "seed" and "beginning" in the Church (cf. *Lumen Gentium*, n. 5).

On Calvary, Mary united herself to the sacrifice of her Son and made her own maternal contribution to the work of salvation, which took the form of gather into one the children of God who are scattered abroad" (Jn 11:52), indicates the Church's birth as the fruit of the redemptive sacrifice with which Mary is maternally associated.

The Evangelist St. Luke mentions the presence of Jesus' Mother in the first community of Jerusalem (Acts 1:14). In this way he stresses Mary's maternal
hood in the work of Christ and therefore in that of the Church, although in terms which are not always explicit.

According to St. Irenaeus, Mary "became a cause of salvation for the whole human race" (Haer. 3, 22, 4; PG 7, 959), and the pure womb of the Virgin regenerates men in God" (Haer. 4, 33, 11; PG 7, 1080). This is re-echoed by St. Ambrose, who says: "A Virgin has begotten the salvation of the world, a Virgin has given life to all things" (Ep. 63, 33; PL 16, 1198), and by other Fathers who call Mary "Mother of salvation" (Severian of Gabala, Or. 6 in mundi creationem, 10, PG 54; 4; Faustus of Riez, Max. Bibl. Patrum, VI, 620-621).

In the Middle Ages, St. Anselm addressed Mary in this way: "You are the mother of justification and of the justified, the Mother of reconciliation and of the reconciled, the mother of salvation and of the saved" (Or. 52, 8; PL 158, 957), while other authors attribute to her the tides "Mother of grace" and "Mother of life".

## Pope Paul VI Proclaimed Mary
## "Mother Of The Church"

5. The tide "Mother of the Church" thus reflects the deep conviction of the Christian faithful, who see in Mary not only the mother of the person of Christ, but also of the faithful. She who is recognized as mother of salvation, life and grace, mother of the saved and mother of the living, is rightly proclaimed Mother of the Church.

Pope Paul VI would have liked the Second Vatican Council itself to have proclaimed "Mary Mother of the Church, that is, of the whole People of God, of the faithful and their Pastors". He did so himself in his speech at the end of the Council's third session (21 November 1964), also asking that "henceforth the Blessed Virgin be honored and invoked with this tide by all the Christian people" (*AAS* 1964, 37).

In this way, my venerable Predecessor explicitly enunciated the doctrine contained in chapter eight of *Lumen Gentium*, hoping that the tide of Mary, Mother of the Church, would have an ever more important place in the liturgy and piety of the Christian people.

# Mary Has Universal Spiritual Motherhood

*The Blessed Virgin, "having entered the Father's eternal kingdom, closer to her divine Son and thus closer to us all, can more effectively exercise in the Spirit the role of maternal intercession entrusted to her by divine Providence", the Holy Father said at the General Audience of Wednesday, 24 September, 1997, as he discussed Mary's motherhood in the order of grace. He went on to explain the meaning of the Marian titles of Advocate, Helper, Benefactress and Mediatrix. Here is a translation of the Pope's catechesis, which was the 64th in the series on the Blessed Virgin and was given in Italian.*

1. Mary is mother of humanity in the order of grace. The Second Vatican Council highlights this role of Mary, linking it to

her cooperation in Christ's Redemption.

"In the designs of divine Providence, she was the gracious mother of the divine Redeemer here on earth, and above all others and in a singular way the generous associate and humble handmaid of the Lord" (*Lumen Gentium*, n. 61). With these statements, the Constitution *Lumen Gentium* wishes to give proper emphasis to the fact that the Blessed Virgin was intimately associated with Christ's redemptive work, becoming the Savior's "generous associate", "in a singular way". With the actions of any mother, from the most ordinary to the most demanding, Mary freely cooperated in the work of humanity's salvation in pro and constant harmony with her divine Son.

## Our Lady's Motherhood Has Universal Scope

2. The Council also points out that Mary's cooperation was inspired by the Gospel virtues of obedience, faith, hope and charity, and was accomplished under the influence of the Holy Spirit. It also recalls that the gift of her universal spiritual motherhood stems precisely from this cooperation: associated with Christ in the work of Redemption, which includes the spiritual regeneration of humanity, she becomes mother of those reborn to new life.

In saying that Mary is "a mother to us in the order of grace" (cf. ibid.), the Council stresses that her spiritual motherhood is not limited to the disciples alone, as though the words spoken by Jesus on Calvary: "Woman, behold your Son (Jn 19:26), required a restrictive interpretation. Indeed, with these words the Crucified One established an intimate relationship between Mary and his beloved disciple, a typological figure of universal scope, intending to offer his Mother as Mother to all mankind.

On the other hand, the universal efficacy of the redeeming sacrifice and Mary's conscious cooperation with Christ's sacrificial offering does not allow any limitation of her motherly love. Mary's universal mission is exercised in the context of her unique relationship with the Church. With her concern for every Christian, and indeed for every human creature, she guides the faith of the Church towards an ever deeper acceptance of God's Word, sustains her hope, enlivens her charity and fraternal communion and encourages her apostolic dynamism.

3. During her earthly life, Mary showed her spiritual motherhood to the Church for a very short time. Nonetheless, the full value of her role appeared after the assumption and is destined to extend down the centuries to the end of the world. The Council expressly states: "This motherhood of Mary in the order of grace continues uninterruptedly from the consent which she gave in faith at the Annunciation and which she sustained without wavering beneath the Cross, until the eternal fulfillment of all the elect" (*Lumen Gentium*, n. 62).

Having entered the Father's eternal kingdom, closer to her divine Son and thus closer to us all, she can more effectively exercise in the Spirit the role of maternal intercession entrusted to her I by divine Providence.

4. The heavenly Father wanted to place Mary close to Christ and in communion with him who can "save those who draw near to God through him, since he always lives to make intercession for them" (Heb 7:25): he wanted to unite to the Redeemer's intercession as a priest that of the Blessed Virgin as a mother. It is a role she carries out for the sake of those who are in danger and who need temporal favors and, especially, eternal salvation: "By her maternal charity, she cares for the brethren of her Son, who still journey on earth surrounded by dangers and difficulties, t until they are led into their blessed home. Therefore the Blessed Virgin is invoked in the Church under the titles of Advocate, Helper, Benefactress and Mediatrix" (*Lumen Gentium*, n. 62). These titles, suggested by the faith of the Christian people, help us better to understand the nature of the Mother of the Lord's intervention in the life of the Church and of the individual believer.

5. The title "Advocate" goes back to St. Irenaeus. With regard to Eve's disobedience and Mary's obedience, he says that at the moment of the Annunciation "the Virgin Mary became the Advocate" of Eve (Haer. 5, 19, 1; PG 7, 1175-1176). In fact, with her "yes" she defended our first mother and freed her from the consequences of her disobedience, becoming the cause of salvation for her and the whole human race.

Mary exercises her role as "Advocate by cooperating both with the Spirit the Paraclete and with the One who interceded on the Cross for his persecutors (cf. Lk 23:34), whom John calls our "advocate with the Father" (1 Jn 2:1). As a mother, she defends her children and protects them from the harm caused by their own sins.

## Mary Is Close To Those Suffering Or In danger

Christians call upon Mary as "Helper", recognizing her motherly love which sees her children's needs and is .Ready to come to their aid, especially when their eternal salvation is at stake. The conviction that Mary is close to those who are suffering or in situations of serious danger has prompted the faithful to invoke her as "Benefactress". The same trusting certainty is expressed in the most ancient Marian prayer with the words: "We fly to thy patronage, O holy Mother of God; despise not our petitions in our necessities but deliver us always from all dangers, O glorious and blessed Virgin" (from the Roman Breviary).

As maternal Mediatrix, Mary presents our desires and petitions to Christ, and transmits the divine gifts to us, interceding continually on our behalf.

# Mary's Mediation Derives From Christ's

*"Far from being an obstacle to the exercise of Christ's unique mediation, Mary instead highlights its fruitfulness and efficacy", the Holy Father said at the General Audience of Wednesday, 1 October, 1997 In his talk, the Pope focused on Mary's role as "Mediatrix", which derives from Christ's and in no way overshadows it. Here is a translation of his catechesis, which was the 65th in the series on the Blessed Mother and was given in Italian.*

1. Among the titles attributed to Mary in the Church's devotion, chapter eight of *Lumen Gentium* recalls that of "Mediatrix". Although some Council Fathers did not fully agree

with this choice of title (cf. Acta Synodalia III, 8, 163-164), it was nevertheless inserted into the Dogmatic Constitution on the Church as confirmation of the value of the truth it expresses. Care was therefore taken not to associate it with any particular theology of mediation, but merely to list it among Mary's other recognized titles.

Moreover the conciliar text had already described the meaning of the title "Mediatrix" when it said that Mary "by her manifold intercession continues to bring us the gifts of eternal salvation "(Lumen Gentium, n. 62).

As I recalled in my Encyclical Redemptoris Mater: "Mary's mediation is intimately linked with her motherhood. It possesses a specifically maternal character, which distinguishes it from the mediation of the other creatures" (n. 38).

From this point of view it is unique in its kind and singularly effective.

## Mediation Of Christ Is Not Obscured By Mary's

2. With regard to the objections made by some of the Council Fathers concerning the term "Mediatrix", the Council itself provided an answer by saying that Mary is "a mother to us in the order grace of (Lumen Gentium, n. 61). We recall that Mary's mediation is essentially defined by her divine motherhood. Recognition of her role as mediatrix is moreover implicit in the expression "our Mother", which presents the doctrine of Marian mediation by putting the accent on her motherhood. Lastly, the title "Mother in the order of grace" explains that the Blessed Virgin cooperates with Christ in humanity's spiritual rebirth.

3. Mary's maternal mediation does not obscure the unique and perfect mediation of Christ. Indeed, after calling Mary "Mediatrix", the Council is careful to explain that this "neither takes away anything from nor adds anything to the dignity and efficacy of Christ the one Mediator" (Lumen Gentium, n. 62). And on this subject ft quotes the famous text from the First Letter to Timothy: "For there is one God and there is one mediator between God and men, the man Christ Jesus, who gave himself as a ransom for all" (2:5-6).

In addition, the Council states that "Mary's function as mother of men in no way obscures or diminishes this unique mediation of Christ, but rather shows its power (*Lumen Gentium*, n. 60).

Therefore, far from being an obstacle to the exercise of Christ's unique mediation, Mary instead highlights its fruitfulness and efficacy. "The Blessed Virgin's salutary influence on men originates not in any inner necessity but in the disposition of God. It flows forth from the superabundance of the merits of Christ, rests on his mediation, depends entirely on it and draws all its power from it (*Lumen Gentium*, n. 60).

4. The value of Mary's mediation derives from Christ and thus the salutary influence of the Blessed Virgin "does not hinder in any way the immediate union of the faithful with Christ but on the contrary fosters it" (ibid.).

The intrinsic orientation to Christ of the "Mediatrix's" work spurred the Council to recommend that the faithful turn to Mary "so that, encouraged by this maternal help they may the more closely adhere to the Mediator and Redeemer" (*Lumen Gentium*, n. 62).

In proclaiming Christ the one mediator (cf. 1 Tm 2:5-6), the text of St. Paul's Letter to Timothy excludes any other parallel mediation, but not subordinate mediation. In fact, before emphasizing the one exclusive mediation of Christ, the author urges "that supplications prayers, intercessions and thanksgivings be made for all men" (2:1). Are not prayers a form of mediation? Indeed, according to St. Paul, the unique mediation of Christ is meant to encourage other dependent, ministerial forms of mediation. By proclaiming the uniqueness of Christ's mediation, the Apostle intends only to exclude any autonomous or rival mediation, and not other forms compatible with the infinite value of the Savior's work.

5. It is possible to participate in Christ's mediation in various areas of the work of salvation. After stressing that "no creature could ever be counted along with the Incarnate Word and Redeemer" (n. 62), *Lumen Gentium* describes how it is possible or captures to exercise certain forms of mediation which are dependent on Christ. In fact, "just as the priesthood of Christ is

shared in various ways both by his ministers and the faithful, and as the one goodness of God is radiated in different ways among his creatures, so also the unique mediation of the Redeemer does not exclude but rather gives rise to a manifold cooperation which is but a sharing in this one source" (*Lumen Gentium*, n. 62).

## Mary's Maternal Role
## Depends On Christ's Mediation

This desire to bring about various participations in the one mediation of Christ reveals the gratuitous love of God who wants to share what he possesses.

6. In truth, what is Mary's maternal mediation if not the Father's gift to humanity? This is why the Council concludes: "The Church does not hesitate to profess this subordinate role of Mary, which it constantly experiences and recommends to the heartfelt attention of the faithful" (ibid.).

Mary carries out her maternal role in constant dependence on the mediation of Christ and from him receives all that his heart wishes to give mankind.

On her earthly pilgrimage the Church "continuously" experiences the effective action of her "Mother in the order of grace."

# Mary Has Always Been Specially Venerated

*"The Second Vatican Council, in stressing the particular character of Marian devotion, says: 'Mary has by grace been exalted above all angels and men to a place second only to her Son, as the most holy Mother of God who was involved in the mysteries of Christ: she is rightly honored by a special cult in the Church' (Lumen Gentium, n. 66)", the Holy Father said at the General Audience of Wednesday, 15 October, 1997, as he reflected on the development of Marian devotion in the history of the Church. Here is a translation of his catechesis, which was the 66th in the series on the Blessed Mother and was given in Italian.*

1. "When the time had fully come, God sent forth his Son, born of woman" (Gal 4:4). Marian devotion is based on the wondrous divine decision, as the Apostle Paul recalls, to link forever the Son of God's human identity with a woman, Mary of Nazareth.

The mystery of the divine motherhood and of Mary's cooperation in the work of Redemption has filled believers in every age with an attitude of praise, both for the Savior and for her who gave birth to him in time, thus cooperating in Redemption.

A further reason for grateful love for the Blessed Virgin is offered by her universal motherhood. By choosing her as Mother of all humanity, the heavenly Father has wished to reveal the motherly dimension, so to speak, of his divine tenderness and concern for all people in every era.

On Calvary, with the words: "Behold, your Son!", "Behold, your mother!" (Jn 19:26-27), Jesus gave Mary in advance to all who would receive the Good News of salvation, and was thus laying the foundation of their filial affection for her. Following John, the faithful would prolong Christ's love for his Mother with their own devotion, by accepting her into their own lives.

## Devotion To Blessed Virgin
## Dates From Church's Origins

2. The Gospel texts attest to the presence of Marian devotion from the Church's origins.

The first two chapters of St. Luke's Gospel seem to relate the particular attention to Jesus' Mother on the part of Jewish Christians, who expressed their appreciation of her and jealously guarded their memories of her.

Moreover, in the infancy narratives we can discern the initial expressions of and reasons for Marian devotion, summarized in Elizabeth's exclamations: "Blessed are you among women.... And blessed is she who believed that there would be a fulfillment of what was spoken to her from the Lord" (Lk 1:42, 45).

Traces of a veneration already widespread among the first Christian community are present in the Magnificat canticle: "An generations will call me blessed" (Lk 1:48). By putting these words on Mary's lips, Christians recognized her unique greatness, which would be proclaimed until the end of time.

In addition, the Gospel accounts (cf. Lk 1:24-35; Mt 1:23 and Jn 1:13), the first formulas of faith and a passage by St. Ignatius of Antioch (cf. Smyrn. 1, 2: SC 10, 155) attest to the first communities' special admiration for Mary's virginity, closely linked to the mystery of the Incarnation.

John's Gospel, by noting Mary's presence at the beginning and at the end of her Son's public life, suggests that the first Christians were keenly aware of Mary's role in the work of Redemption, in full loving dependence on Christ.

3. The Second Vatican Council in stressing the particular character of Marian devotion, says: "Mary has by grace been exalted above all angels and men to a place second only to her Son, as the most holy Mother of God and who was involved in the mysteries of Christ: she is rightly honored by a special cult in the Church" (*Lumen Gentium*, n. 66).

Then, alluding to the third century Marian prayer, "Sub tuum praesidium", "We fly to thy patronage", it adds that this characteristic emerges from the very beginning: "From the earliest times the Blessed Virgin is honored under the title of Mother of God in whose protection the faithful take refuge together in prayer in all their perils and needs" (ibid.).

4. This assertion has been confirmed in iconography and in the teaching of the Fathers of the Church since the second century.

In Rome, in the catacombs of Priscilla, it is possible to admire the first depiction of the Madonna and Child, while at the same time, St. Justin and St. Irenaeus speak of Mary as the new Eve who by her faith and obedience makes amends for the disbelief and disobedience of the first woman. According to the Bishop of Lyons, it was not enough for Adam to be redeemed in Christ, but "it was right and necessary that Eve be restored in Mary" (Demonstratio apostolica, 33). In this way he stresses the importance of woman in the work of salvation and lays the foundation for the inseparability of Marian devotion from that shown to Jesus, which will endure down the Christian centuries.

## Marian Devotion Is Firmly Rooted In Christian Faith

5. Marian devotion is first expressed in the invocation of Mary as "Theotokos", a title which was authoritatively confirmed, after the Nestorian crisis, by the Council of Ephesus in 431.

The same popular reaction to the ambiguous and wavering position of Nestrius, who went so far as to deny Mary's divine motherhood, and the subsequent joyful acceptance of the Ephesian Synod's decisions, confirm how deeply rooted among Christians was devotion to the Blessed Virgin. However "following the Council of Ephesus, there was a remarkable growth in the devotion of the People of God towards Mary, in veneration and love, in invocation and imitation" (*Lumen Gentium*, n. 66). It was expressed especially in the liturgical feasts, among which, from the beginning of the fifth century, "the day of Mary Theotokos" acquired particular importance. It was celebrated on 15 August in Jerusalem and later became the feast of the Dormition or the Assumption.

Under the influence of the "Proto-Evangelium of James", the feasts of the Nativity, the Conception and the Presentation were also introduced, and notably contributed to highlighting some important aspects of the mystery of Mary.

6. We can certainly say that Marian devotion has developed down to our day in wonderful continuity, alternating between flourishing periods and critical ones that, nonetheless, often had the merit of fostering its renewal even more.

Since the Second Vatican Council, Marian devotion seems destined to develop in harmony with a deeper understanding of the mystery of the Church and in dialogue with contemporary cultures, to be ever more firmly rooted in the faith and life of God's pilgrim people on earth.

# Faithful Have Filial Devotion To Mary

*"When the faithful call upon Mary as 'Mother of God' and contemplate in her the highest dignity conferred upon a creature, they are still not off a veneration equal to that of the divine Persons.*

*There is an infinite distance between Marian veneration and worship of the Trinity and the Incarnate Word",* the Holy Father said at the General Audience of Wednesday, 22 October, 1997, as he spoke about the nature of the Church's devotion to Mary. Here is a translation of his catechesis, which was the 67th in the series on the Blessed Mother and was given in Italian.

1. The Second Vatican Council states that devotion to the Blessed Virgin, "as it has always existed in the Church, for all its uniqueness, differs essentially from the cult of adoration, which is offered equally to the Incarnate Word and to the Father and the Holy Spirit, and it is most favorable to it" (*Lumen Gentium*, n. 66).

With these words the Constitution *Lumen Gentium* stresses the characteristics of Marian devotion. Although the veneration of the faithful for Mary is superior to their devotion to the other saints, it is nevertheless inferior to the cult of adoration reserved to God, from which it essentially differs. The term "adoration" indicates the form of worship that man offers to God, acknowledging him as Creator and Lord of the universe. Enlightened by divine Revelation, the Christian adores the Father "in spirit and truth" (Jn 4:23). With the Father, he adores Christ, the Incarnate Word, exclaiming with the Apostle Thomas: "My Lord and my God! (Jn 20:28). Lastly, in this same act of adoration he includes the Holy Spirit, who "with the Father and the Son is worshipped and glorified" (DS 150), as the Nicene-Constantinopolitan Creed recalls.

## Veneration Of Mary Leads To Adoration Of The Trinity

When the faithful call upon Mary as "Mother of God" and contemplate in her the highest dignity conferred upon a creature, they are still not offering her a veneration equal to that of the divine Persons. There is an infinite distance between Marian veneration and worship of the Trinity and the Incarnate Word.

As a consequence, although the Christian community addresses the Blessed Virgin in language that sometimes recalls the terms used in the worship of God, it has a completely different meaning and value. Thus the love of the faithful for Mary differs from what they owe God: while the Lord must be loved above everything with all one's heart, with all one's soul and with all one's mind (cf. Mt 22:37), the sentiment joining Christians to the Blessed Virgin suggests, at a spiritual level, the affection of children for their mother.

2. Nevertheless there is a continuity between Marian devotion and the worship given to God: indeed, the honor paid to Mary is ordered and leads to adoration of the Blessed Trinity.

The Council recalls that Christian veneration of the Blessed Virgin "is most favorable to" the worship of the Incarnate Word, the Father and the Holy Spirit. It then adds from a Christological viewpoint that "the various forms of piety towards the Mother of God, which the Church has approved within the limits of sound and orthodox doctrine, according to the dispositions and understanding of the faithful, ensure that while the Mother is honored, the Son through whom all things have their being (cf. Col 1:15-16) and in whom it has pleased the Father that all fullness should dwell (cf. Col 1:19) is rightly known, loved and glorified and his commandments are observed" (*Lumen Gentium*, n. 66).

Since the Church's earliest days, Marian devotion has been meant to foster faithful adherence to Christ. To venerate the Mother of God is to affirm the divinity of Christ. In fact, the Fathers of the Council of Ephesus, in proclaiming Mary Theotokos, "Mother of God", intended to confirm the belief in Christ, true God.

The conclusion of the account of Jesus' first miracle, obtained at Cana by Mary's intercession, shows how her action was directed to the glorification of her Son. In fact the Evangelist says: "This, the first of his signs, Jesus did at Cana in Galilee, and manifested his glory; and his disciples believed in him" (Jn 2:11).

3. Marian devotion also encourages adoration of the Father and the Holy Spirit in those who practice it according to the Church's spirit. In fact, by recognizing the value of Mary's motherhood, believers discover in it a special manifestation of God the Father's tenderness.

The mystery of the Virgin Mother highlights the action of the Holy Spirit, who brought about the conception of the child in her womb and continually guided her life.

The titles of Comforter, Advocate, Helper attributed to Mary by popular Christian piety do not overshadow but exalt the action of the Spirit, the Comforter, and dispose believers to benefit from his gifts.

## Gifts Conferred On Mary Are Exceptional

4. Lastly, the Council recalls the "uniqueness" of Marian devotion and stresses the difference between adoration of God and veneration of the saints.

This devotion is unrepeatable because it is directed to a person whose personal perfection and mission are unique.

Indeed, the gifts conferred upon Mary by divine love, such as her immaculate holiness, her divine motherhood, her association with the work of Redemption and above all the sacrifice of the Cross, are absolutely exceptional. Devotion to Mary expresses the Church's praise and recognition of these extraordinary gifts. To her, ho is Mother of the Church and Mother of humanity, the Christian people turn, encouraged by filial trust, to request her motherly intercession and to obtain the necessary goods for earthly life in view of eternal happiness.

# Church Urges Faithful To Venerate Mary

*The Second Vatican Council exhorted the Church's members to promote the various forms of Marian piety, especially liturgical devotion to Our Lady. The veneration of the Virgin Mary was the subject of the Holy Father's catechesis at the General Audience of Wednesday, 29 October, 1997. Quoting the Second Vatican Council, the Pope urged that "the cult, especially the liturgical cult, of the Blessed Virgin, be generously fostered, and that the practices and exercises of devotion towards her, recommended by the teaching authority of the Church in the course of centuries, be highly esteemed". Here is a translation of his catechesis, which was the 68th in the series on the Blessed Mother and was given in Italian.*

1. After giving doctrinal justification to veneration of the Blessed Virgin, the Second Vatican Council exhorts all the faithful to promote it: "The Sacred Synod teaches this Catholic doctrine advisedly and at the same time admonishes all the sons of the Church that the cult, especially the liturgical cult, of the Blessed Virgin, be generously fostered, and that the practice and exercise of devotion towards her, recommended by the teaching authority of the Church in the course of centuries, be highly esteemed" (*Lumen Gentium*, n. 67). With this last statement the Council Fathers, without going into particulars, intended to reaffirm the validity of certain prayers such as the Rosary and the Angelus, dear to the tradition of the Christian people and frequently encouraged by the Supreme Pontiffs as an effective means of nourishing the life of faith and devotion to the Blessed Virgin.

## Nicaea II Affirmed The Veneration Of Sacred Images

2. The conciliar text goes on to ask believers "that those decrees, which were given in the early days regarding the veneration of images of Christ, the Blessed Virgin and the saints, be religiously observed" (*Lumen Gentium*, n. 67). Thus it reproposes the decisions of the Second Council of Nicaea, held in 787, which confirmed the legitimacy of the veneration of sacred images in opposition to those who wished to destroy them, since they considered them inadequate for representing the divinity (cf. *Redemptoris Mater*, n. 33).

"We define", said the Fathers of that Council, "with full precision and care that, like the representation of the precious life-giving Cross, so the venerated and holy images either painted or mosaic or made of any other suitable material, should be exposed in holy churches of God on sacred furnishings and vestments, on wails and panels in homes and streets, be they images of the Lord God and our Savior Jesus Christ, or of our immaculate lady, the Holy Mother of God, of the holy angels, or of all the saints and the just" (DS 600).

By recalling this definition, *Lumen Gentium* intended to stress the legitimacy and validity of sacred images, in contrast to certain tendencies to remove them from churches and shrines in order to focus full attention on Christ.

3. The Second Council of Nicaea does not only affirm the legitimacy of images, but seeks to describe their usefulness for Christian piety: "Indeed, the more often these images are contemplated, the more those who look at them are brought to remember and desire the original models and, in kissing them, to show them respect and veneration" (DS 601).

These directives apply in a particular way to the veneration of the Blessed Virgin. Images, icons and statues of Our Lady, present in houses, public places and countless churches and chapels, help the faithful to invoke her constant presence and her merciful patronage in the various circumstances of life. By making the Blessed Virgin's motherly tenderness concrete and almost visible, they invite us to turn to her, to pray to her trustfully and to imitate her in generously accepting the divine will. None of the known images is an authentic reproduction of Mary's face, as St. Augustine had already acknowledged (De Trinitate, 8, 7); however they help us establish a more living relationship with her. Therefore the practice of exposing images of Mary in places of worship and in other buildings should be encouraged, in order to be aware of her help in moments of difficulty and as a reminder to lead a life that is ever more holy and faithful to God.

4. To encourage the proper use of sacred images, the Council of Nicaea recalls that "the honor paid to the image is really paid to the person it represents, and those who venerate the image are venerating the reality of the person it represents" (DS 601). Hence in adoring the Person of the Incarnate Word in the image of Christ the faithful are making a genuine act of worship, which has nothing in common with idolatry. Similarly, when he venerates images of Mary, the believer's act is ultimately intended as a tribute to the person of the Mother of Jesus.

5. Therefore, the Second Vatican minimizing the special dignity of the Mother of God. It adds: "Following the study of Sacred Scripture, the Fathers, the doctors and liturgy of the Church, and under the guidance of the Church's Magisterium, let them rightly illustrate the duties and privileges of the Blessed Virgin, which always refer to Christ, the source of all truth, sanctity and devotion"

(*Lumen Gentium*, n. 67).

## Marian Devotion Stems From Faith And Filial Love

Authentic Marian doctrine is ensured by fidelity to Scripture and Tradition, as well as to the liturgical texts and the Magisterium. Its indispensable characteristic is the reference to Christ: everything in Mary derives from Christ and is directed to him.

6. Lastly, the Council offers believers several criteria for authentically living their filial relationship with Mary: "Let the faithful remember moreover that true devotion consists neither in sterile nor transitory affection, nor in a certain vain credulity, but proceeds from true faith, by which we are led to recognize the excellence of the Mother of God, and we are moved to a filial love towards our Mother and to the imitation of her virtues" (*Lumen Gentium*, n. 67). With these words, the Council Fathers put people on guard against "vain credulity" and the predominance of sentiment. They aim above all at reaffirming authentic Marian devotion, which proceeds from faith and the loving recognition of Mary's dignity, fosters filial affection for her and inspires the firm resolution to imitate her virtues.

# We Can Count On Mary's Intercession

*The faithful have always recognized the value of the Blessed Virgin's maternal presence and have had recourse to her for every kind of grace. By highlighting the human dimension of the Incarnation, devotion to Mary helps the faithful ""to discern the face of a God who shares the joys and sufferings of humanity", the Holy Father said at the General Audience of Wednesday, 5 November, 1997. The Pope spoke of various Marian prayers, particularly the Hail Mary, the Angelus and the Rosary. Here is a translation of his catechesis, which was the 69th in the series on the Blessed Mother and was given in Italian.*

1. Down the centuries Marian devotion has enjoyed an interrupted development. In addition to the traditional liturgical

feasts dedicated to the Lord's Mother, there has been a flowering of countless expressions of piety, often approved and encouraged by the Church's Magisterium.

Many Marian devotions and prayers are an extension of the liturgy itself and have sometimes contributed to its overall enrichment, as is the case with the Office in honor of the Blessed Virgin and other pious compositions which have become part of the Breviary.

The first known Marian invocation goes back to the third century and begins with the words: "We fly to thy patronage (Sub tuum praesidium), O holy Mother of God...." However, since the 14th century the most common prayer among Christians has been the "Hail Mary".

By repeating the first words the angel addressed to Mary, it leads the faithful to contemplate the mystery of the Incarnation. The Latin word "Ave" translates the Greek word "Chaire": it is an invitation to joy and could be translated "Rejoice". The Eastern hymn "Akathistos" repeatedly stresses this "rejoice". In the "Hail Mary" the Blessed Virgin is called "full of grace" and is thus recognized for the perfection and beauty of her soul.

## Rosary Has Important Place In Marian Devotion

The phrase "The Lord is with thee" reveals God's special personal relationship with Mary, which fits into the great plan for his covenant with all humanity. Next, the statement "Blessed art thou among women and blessed is the fruit of thy womb, Jesus" expresses the fulfillment of the divine plan in the Daughter of Zion's virginal body.

Calling upon "Holy Mary, Mother of God", Christians ask the one who was the immaculate Mother of the Lord by a unique privilege: "Pray for us sinners", and entrust themselves to her at the present moment and at the ultimate moment of death.

2. The traditional prayer of the "Angelus" also invites Christians to meditate on the mystery of the Incarnation, urging them to take Mary as their point of reference at different times of their day in order to imitate her willingness to fulfill the divine

plan of salvation. This prayer makes us relive in a way that great event in human history, the Incarnation, to which every "Hail Mary" refers. Here we find the value and attraction of the "Angelus", expressed so many times not only by theologians and pastors but also by poets and painters.

In Marian devotion the Rosary has taken on an important role. By repeating the "Hall Mary", it leads us to contemplate the mysteries of faith. In nourishing the Christian people's love for the Mother of God, this simple prayer also orients Marian prayer in a clearer way to its goal: the glorification of Christ.

Pope Paul VI, like his Predecessors, especially Leo XIII, Pius MI and John XXIII, held the recitation of the Rosary in great esteem and wished it to be widely spread among families. Moreover, in the Apostolic Exhortation Marialis Cultus, he explained its doctrine by recalling that it is a "Gospel prayer, centered on the mystery of the redemptive Incarnation", and stressing its "clearly Christological orientation" (n. 46%).

Popular piety frequently adds a litany to the Rosary. The best known is the one used at the Shrine of Loreto and is therefore called the "Litany of Loreto".

With very simple invocations it helps us concentrate on Mary's person, in order to grasp the spiritual riches which the Father's love poured out in her.

3. As the liturgy and Christian piety demonstrate, the Church has always held devotion to Mary in high esteem, considering it inseparably linked to belief in Christ. It is in fact based on the Father's plan, the Savior's will and the Paraclete's inspiration.

Having received salvation and grace from Christ, the Blessed Virgin is called to play an important role in humanity's redemption. Through Marian devotion Christians acknowledge the value of Mary's presence on their journey to salvation, having recourse to her for every kind of grace. They especially know that they can count on her motherly intercession to receive from the Lord everything necessary for growing in the divine life and for attaining eternal salvation.

As the many titles attributed to the Blessed Virgin and the continual pilgrimages to Marian shrines attest, the trust of the faithful in Jesus' Mother spurs them to call upon her for their dally needs.

## Mary Is Not Indifferent To Her Children's Needs

They are certain that her maternal heart cannot remain indifferent to the material and spiritual distress of her children.

By encouraging the confidence and spontaneity of the faithful, devotion to the Mother of God thus helps to brighten their spiritual life and enables them to make progress on the demanding path of the Beatitudes.

4. Lastly, we would like to recall that devotion to Mary, by highlighting the human dimension of the Incarnation, helps us better to discern the face of a God who shares the joys and sufferings of humanity, the "God with us" whom she conceived as man in her most pure womb, gave birth to, cared for and followed with unspeakable love from his days in Nazareth and Bethlehem to those of the Cross and resurrection.

# Separated Brethren Also Honor Mary

*Today many Anglican and Protestant Christians venerate Mary, and the Orthodox have always loved and revered her with ardent devotion. It is a source of great joy "that among the separated brethren too there are those who give due honor to the Mother of our Lord and Savior", the Holy Father said at the General Audience of Wednesday, 12 November, 1997, as he continued his catechesis on Our Lady. In the present talk the Pope discussed the honor paid to Mary by various Protestant and Orthodox Christians. Here is a translation of his catechesis, which was the 70th in the series on the Blessed Virgin and was given in Italian.*

1. After explaining the relationship between Mary and the Church, the Second Vatican Council rejoices in observing that the Blessed Virgin is also honored by Christians who do not belong to the Catholic community: "It gives great joy and comfort to this sacred Synod that among the separated brethren too there are

those who give due honor to the Mother of our Lord and Savior..."
(*Lumen Gentium*, n. 69; cf. *Redemptoris Mater*, nn. 29-34). In
view of this fact, we can say that Mary's universal motherhood,
even if it makes the divisions among Christians seem all the sadder,
represents a great sign of hope for the ecumenical journey.

Many Protestant communities, because of a particular
conception of grace and ecclesiology, are opposed to Marian
doctrine and devotion, maintaining that Mary's cooperation in
the work of salvation prejudices Christ's unique mediation. In this
view, devotion to Mary would compete in a way with the honor
owed the Son.

## Eastern Christians Have Particular Devotion To Mary

The study of Luther and Calvin's thought, as well as the
analysis of some texts of Evangelical Christians, have contributed
to a renewed attention by some Protestants and Anglicans to
various themes of Mariological doctrine.

Some have even arrived at positions very close to those of
Catholics regarding the fundamental points of Marian doctrine,
such as her divine motherhood, virginity, holiness and spiritual
motherhood.

The concern for stressing the presence of women in the
Church encourages the effort to recognize Mary's role in salvation
history.

All these facts are so many reasons to have hope for the
ecumenical journey. Catholics have a deep desire to be able to
share with all their brothers and sisters in Christ the joy that comes
from Mary's presence in life according to the Spirit.

3. Among the brethren who "give due honor to the Mother
of our Lord and Savior", the Council mentions Eastern Christians,
"who with devout mind and fervent impulse give honor to the
Mother of God, Ever-Virgin" (*Lumen Gentium*, n. 69).

As we can see from their many expressions of devotion,
veneration for Mary represents a significant element of communion
between Catholics and Orthodox. However, there remain some
disagreements regarding the dogmas of the Immaculate
Conception and the Assumption, even if these truths were first

expounded by certain Eastern theologians, one need only recall great writers like Gregory Palamas (†1359), Nicholas Cabasilas († after 1369) and George Scholarios († after 1472).

These disagreements, however, are perhaps more a question of formulation than of content and must never make us forget our common belief in Mary's divine motherhood, her perpetual virginity, her perfect holiness and her maternal intercession with her Son. As the Second Vatican Council recalled, this "fervent impulse" and "devout mind" unite Catholics and Orthodox in devotion to the Mother of God.

4. At the end of *Lumen Gentium* the Council invites us to entrust the unity of Christians to Mary: The entire body of the faithful pours forth urgent supplications to the Mother of God and of men that she, who aided the beginnings of the Church by her prayers, may now, exalted as she is above all the angels and saints, intercede before her Son in the fellowship of all the saints" (ibid.).

Just as Mary's presence in the early community fostered oneness of heart, which prayer strengthened and made visible (cf. Acts 1:14), 50 the most intense communion with her whom Augustine called the "Mother of unity" (Sermo 192, 2; PL 38, 1013) will be able to bring Christians to the point of enjoying the long-awaited gift of ecumenical unity.

## Through Mary We Pray For Unity And Harmony

We ceaselessly pray to the Blessed Virgin so that, just as at the beginning she supported the journey of the Christian community's oneness in prayer and the proclamation of the Gospel, so today she may obtain through her intercession reconciliation and full communion among all believers in Christ.

Mother of men, Mary knows well the needs and aspirations of humanity. The Council particularly asks her to intercede so that "all families of people, whether they are honored with the title of Christian or whether they still do not know the Savior, may be happily gathered together in peace and harmony into one People of God, for the glory of the Most Holy and Undivided Trinity" (*Lumen Gentium*, n. 69).

The peace, harmony and unity for which the Church and humanity hope still seem far away. Nevertheless, they are a gift of the Spirit to be constantly sought, as we learn from Mary and trust in her intercession.

5. With this petition Christians share the expectation of her who, filled with the virtue of hope, sustains the Church on her journey to the future with God. Having personally achieved happiness because she "believed that there would be a fulfillment of what was spoken to her from the Lord" (Lk 1:45), the Blessed Virgin accompanies believers, and the whole Church, so that in the world, amid the joys and sufferings of this life, they may be true prophets of the hope that never disappoints.

# -Chapter 8-

# Other Teachings Of John Paul II On Mary

## History Of Salvation Begins
## With The Virgin Mary's "Fiat"
### Angelus: 22 October, 1978

It was about 13:20 on Sunday 22 October. The celebration of the Mass for the beginning of John Paul II's ministry as Supreme Pastor had just ended. The echo of the last impressive burst of applause had not yet faded. The most painstaking reporters counted forty seven of them in the course of the celebration. The people in the Square begin to disperse slowly. Others, and so many had been here for over four hours, showed no sign of wanting to go away. It was a magic moment, almost mysterious, during which they observed the strictest silence, breaking it only to pray. They were still waiting for something. They wanted to see the Pope again for a moment. At 13.25 the window of the Holy Father's private study opened. John Paul II appeared at the window, smiling. It was an unusual hour for the recitation of the "Angelus", but John Paul II wished to follow faith fully the lines laid down by his predecessors. So here he was to recite the "Angelus Domini" with the faithful at 13.30. Before the prayer the Holy Father delivered the following address.

I wish to resume the magnificent habit of my Predecessors and recite the "Angelus" together with you, dear Brothers and Sisters.

The solemn Mass for the inauguration of my ministry as Peter's Successor has just ended. To live intensely this historic moment, we had to make the profession of faith in common, which we recite every day in the Apostles' Creed: "I believe in the

Holy Catholic Church", and in the Nicene-Constantinople Creed: "I believe the Church to be one, holy, catholic and apostolic."

All together we became aware of this marvelous truth about the Church, which the Second Vatican Council explained in two documents: in the dogmatic Constitution *Lumen Gentium* and in the pastoral Constitution Gaudium et Spes, on the Church in the modern world.

Now, we must go even deeper. We must arrive at this moment in the history of the world, when the Word becomes flesh: when the Son of God becomes Man. The history of salvation reaches its climax and, at the same time, begins again in its definitive form when the Virgin of Nazareth accepts the announcement of the Angel and utters the words: "fiat mihi secundum verbum tuum (Let it be to me according to your word) (Lk 1:38).

The Church is, as it were, conceived at that moment. So let us go back to the beginning of the mystery. And in it let us embrace once more the whole content of today's solemnity. In it let us embrace the whole past of Christianity and of the Church, which has found her center here, in Rome. In it let us try to embrace the whole future of the pontificate, of the People of God and of the whole human family, because the family begins with the Father's will, but is always conceived under the Mother's heart.

With this faith and with this hope let us pray.

After the recitation of the prayer in Latin, with an expression in Polish slipped in, John Paul II, before leaving the window, wished to address another word to the large numbers of young people who, after having been present at the ceremony, were still in the Square, acclaiming the Pope.

"You are", John Paul II says, "the future of the world, the hope of the Church. You are my hope." It was then 13.40. John Paul II was reluctant to turn away from the magnificent image that the Square still offered. But it was getting late and he added: "We must close now, for it is time for lunch: for you and for the Pope." And then a final word in Polish to the thousands of Poles present: "Czas no obiad" (It is time for lunch).

# Pope Lauds Rosary: So Rich, So Simple
## Angelus: 29 October, 1978

On Sunday 29 October, before the recitation of the "Angelus" in St. Peter's Square, the Holy Father delivered the following address.

Dear Brothers and Sisters,

Here we are again? meeting as we did a week ago to recite the "Angelus" together. This week has passed quickly, rich in important meetings and visits.

Today, the last Sunday of October I wish to draw your attention to the Rosary. In fact, throughout the whole Church, October is the month dedicated to the Rosary.

The Rosary is my favorite prayer. A marvelous prayer! Marvelous in its simplicity and in its depth. In this prayer we repeat many times the words that the Virgin Mary heard from the Archangel, and from her kinswoman Elizabeth. The whole Church joins in these words. It can be said that the Rosary is, in a certain way, a prayer commentary on the last chapter of the Constitution "*Lumen Gentium*" of Vatican II, a chapter which deals with the wonderful presence of the Mother of God in the mystery of Christ and the Church.

In fact, against the background of the words "Ave Maria" there pass before the eyes of the soul the main episodes in the life of Jesus Christ. They are composed altogether of the joyful, sorrowful and glorious mysteries, and they put us in living communion with Jesus through, we could say, his Mother's heart.

At the same time our heart can enclose in these decades of the Rosary all the facts that make up the life of the individual, the family, the nation, the Church and mankind. Personal matters and those of one's neighbor, and particularly of those who are closest to us? who are dearest to us. Thus the simple prayer of the Rosary beats the rhythm of human life.

During the last few weeks I have had the opportunity to meet many persons, representatives of various nations and of different environments, as well as of various Christian Churches and communities. I wish to assure you that I have not failed to translate these relations into the language of the Rosary prayer, in order that everyone might find himself at the heart of the prayer which gives a full dimension to everything. In these last weeks both I and the Holy See have had numerous proofs of goodwill from people in the whole world. I wish to translate my gratitude into decades of the Rosary in order to express it in prayer? as well as in the human manner; in this prayer so simple and so rich.

Yesterday afternoon I went down to the crypt of the Vatican Basilica to celebrate Mass for the month's mind of my predecessor, Pope John Paul I; and yesterday, as you well know, there occurred also the twentieth anniversary of the election of Pope John XXIII, whose paternal figure is ever alive in the hearts of the faithful. John XXIII was a Pope who loved much and who was intensely loved. Let us remember him in prayer, and above all, let us seek to put into practice the precious legacy of the teachings he left us with his word? with his commitment of fidelity to tradition and of "aggiornamento", with his life, and with his holy death.

## The Doctrine Of The Church On The Immaculate Conception

### Angelus: 8 December, 1978

The feast of the Immaculate Conception, 8 December, was celebrated by the Romans with the customary solemnity. At midday about 50,000 people had assembled in St. Peter's Square to recite the "Angelus" with John Paul II and to receive his blessing. The Holy Father delivered the following address.

1. We will shortly recite the "Angelus". In this prayer we will recall the event that took place in a town of Galilee called Nazareth. The event awaited by the whole world, immersed in the darkness of advent, of expectation. "Hail, full of grace, the Lord is with you!" (Lk 1 :28).

These are the words of God that the Angel addresses to a poor girl of Nazareth, by name Miriam (Mary), whose parents, according to tradition, were Joachim and Anne, and who from her earliest childhood wished to belong unreservedly, completely, to the Lord, as is testified by the commemoration of the Presentation, which is recalled every year on 21 November.

2. Hail, full of grace. What do these words mean? The Evangelist Luke writes that Mary (Miriam), at these words spoken by the Angel, "was greatly troubled..., and considered in her mind what sort of greeting this might be" (Lk 1 :29).

These words express a singular election. Grace means a particular fullness of creation through which the being, who resembles God, participates in God's own interior life. Grace means love and the gift of God himself, the completely free gift ("given gratuitously",) in which God entrusts to man his Mystery, giving him, at the same time, the capacity of being able to bear witness to the Mystery, of filling with it his human being, his life, his thoughts, his will and his heart.

The fullness of grace is constituted by Christ himself. Mary of Nazareth receives Christ, and together with Christ and through Christ she receives the fullest participation in the eternal Mystery, in the interior life of God: of the Father the Son and the Holy Spirit. This participation is the fullest of the whole of creation, it surpasses everything that separates man from God. It even excludes original sin: the inheritance of Adam. Christ, who is the author of divine life, that is, of grace, in every man, by means of the Redemption effected by him, must be particularly generous with his Mother. He must redeem her in an especially superabundant way from sin ("copiosa apud eum redemptio" - with him is plenteous redemption: Psalm 130:7). This generosity of the Son towards his Mother goes back to the first moment of her existence. It is called the Immaculate Conception

3. One hundred years ago there died a great Pope, the Servant of God Pius IX. Let us recall today the words in which he expressed the doctrine of the Church on the Immaculate Conception:

By the authority of Our Lord Jesus Christ, by the authority of the Blessed Apostles Peter and Paul, and by Our own authority, We declare, pronounce and define: the doctrine that maintains that the Blessed Virgin Mary in the first instant of her conception, by a unique grace and privilege granted to her by Almighty God, in consideration of the merits of Jesus Christ the Savior of mankind, was preserved free from all stain of original sin is a doctrine revealed by God and therefore must be firmly and constantly believed by all the faithful." (Bull Ineffabilis Deus).

Keeping all that in our minds, let us recite the "Angelus" with special fervor today.

With this greeting of the Angel, Rome, the whole Church and the world prays.

# In The Light Of The Virgin Mary
## Angelus: 1 January, 1979

The Holy Father was acclaimed by over sixty thousand people when he came to the window of his study to recite the "Angelus" with them on 1 January. Pope John Paul spoke as follows:

At the beginning of a new year, with what other words could I address you dear friends, than words of good wishes? "Happy New Year", therefore, to you, my brothers and sisters! To you who have come to this square to bear witness with your presence to the affection you cherish for the Pope; and "Happy New Year" to all those who are present here in spirit. The Pope would like to be able to cross the threshold of all houses, especially those in which poverty, illness, and loneliness make their weight felt, including hospitals and prisons, and bring everywhere a word of comfort, encouragement and hope.

"Happy New Year" to everyone, in the light that shines forth from the sweet face of the Virgin Mary, whom the Liturgy invites us to venerate, today, in the mystery of her divine motherhood! "Concepit de Spiritu Sancto", she conceived through the Holy Spirit, we will shortly say in the "Angelus" and our mind will be invited to reflect on the decisive moment of the incarnation of the Word of God. That solemn moment, even if so humble and hidden, puts us in an attitude of thoughtful admiration and instinctive respect before the initial moment of the earthly existence of every human being.

On the first day of this new year, I wish to address a special greeting to all those who will be born in the course of the next months, to those who will receive the gift of life in the year of the Lord 1979. May they find the affectionate warmth of hearts that wait for them and are able to rejoice in the marvelous miracle of a new life.

Today the World Day of Peace is celebrated. This subject of peace, if it is near to the heart of every responsible and generous human being, arouses a particular very deep concern in the Pope, who knows that he has been placed by Christ as pastor of the whole of mankind. In this connection, I wish to recommend to your prayer today two delicate situations, for which the Holy See has considered it its duty to start specific initiatives. I am referring to the tormented vicissitudes of Lebanon, in which so much blood, too much blood, has already been shed, and to the more recent controversy that has broken out between Argentina and Chile over the Beagle Canal Islands. The missions sent by the Holy See have been given, in both cases, a cordial reception both by the Authorities and by the population. It is now necessary that the prayer of everyone should obtain from God abundant gifts of farsightedness, balance, and courage, in order that the ways of peace may be followed and the goal of a just and honorable solution be reached as soon as possible.

In this day, too, a day that should be one of joy for everyone, my thought goes to the victims of kidnapping, who are still kept with unjust violence far from their families. I am saddened in particular by the situation of those who, still in childhood, are more exposed to the psychological traumas of such a dramatic experience. Let all of us, gathered here, raise our prayer to God for them, trusting that the characteristic atmosphere with which these days are suffused, may reawaken in the hearts of their oppressors sentiments of a rightful change of heart and of renewed humanity.

# Hope Through The Virgin Mary

Angelus: 15 August, 1979

On Wednesday, 15 August, Feast of the Assumption of the Blessed Virgin, John Paul II delivered the following address to the faithful who had come to his summer residence for the recitation of the Angelus.

Today, I wish to recite the Angelus with all of you: this prayer of Nazareth. the prayer of the Annunciation.

We recite it on the feast of the As. gumption of Mary into heaven. The Annunciation resounds today in this prayer in a final accord. It is an accord of glorification, which is added to all the mysteries of the earthly life of the Mother of God: joyful and sorrowful mysteries. This same assumption of Mary into heaven completes the glorious mysteries of her Son: the resurrection and the ascension into heaven. Following in the footsteps of him who is risen and has ascended into heaven, Mary, his mother, is assumed into heaven and crowned with that glory which belongs to the Mother of God.

## Protection of Mary

I also wish, today here at Castel Gandolfo, to turn my glance, together with you, towards her whom the great Paul VI indicated as the "great sign" and whom he, with prophetic spirit, called: "the beginning of a better world".

However much the world may weigh upon us, whatever evil, whatever sin, whatever suffering the world may include within itself, the glance of faith, focused on the Mother of God, will always rediscover in it the "beginning of a better world". This is the particular fruit of the feast of the assumption of Mary into heaven.

As you know, in the last days of September and in the early days of October, I will travel to Ireland and then to the Headquarters of the United Nations Organization, and to the United States of America. These are new stages of my apostolic program which I have taken upon myself as Supreme Pastor of the Holy Church. I wish, right from this moment, to place this journey under the protection of Mary, Assumed into heaven, Mother of the Church, so that, with her maternal protection, it may produce joyful and lasting steps along the way of charity, of justice and of peace.

I extend my thoughts and good wishes to all who are passing, in well merited relaxation, this traditional holiday period of these days of August, called in fact "ferragosto". From my heart I wish that this vacation from the daily burden some worries of work will be a particularly propitious occasion to be in even greater contact with nature, shrine of the ineffable beauties of God the creator, and the generous dispenser, whether at the sea or in the mountains of renewed physical well-being. But above all, I would like to foresee that, to the renewed energies of the body there should be linked very closely the enrichment of the spirit, which, from the contemplation of so many wonders, may more easily unite itself to him who is their source and their uncreated principle.

Nor can I forget those whom the lack of material goods does not permit a well-deserved holiday away from their own home, even if, perhaps even more than others, they are in need of help and attention.

My particular word of comfort and fatherly understanding goes out to these brothers and sisters: may their humble acceptance of discomfort be converted into a spiritual increase for themselves and for the good of the whole Church.

May Our Lady of the Assumption assist everyone with that ineffable generosity of which only the Mother of God is capable.

## Look Up Towards The Virgin

Angelus: 26 August, 1979

The meeting of the Pope with the mountaineers on the Marmolada for the recitation of the Angelus and the blessing of the statue "Queen of the Dolomites" was one of the highlights of the Holy Father's pilgrimage to the land of his predecessor, Pope Luciani. On the top of Punta Rocca, covered with snow which continued to fall during the time of the Pope's stay, there were gathered about 300 of the faithful. The Pope arrived by cable car about 12:30. Before the recitation of the Angelus and the blessing of the statue, Pope John Paul delivered the following address.

1. "I lift up my eyes to the mountains..." (Ps 120 [121]:1). These words of the Psalmist come spontaneously to my mind on the occasion of reciting the Angelus together with those gathered here to share in this Sunday prayer and in union with those participating in it through radio and television throughout the land of Italy and in other countries.

We have all been brought together here by the memory of Pope John Paul 1, the first to take, after being elected to the See of Saint Peter, the names of both his Predecessors. We have been led here by the memory of the day of his election, for it was exactly 8 year ago, on 26 August, at about six o'clock in the evening, that Cardinal Ah bino Luciani, Patriarch of Venice, was asked by the Cardinal Camerlengo, after the conclusion of the voting, whether he accepted the election, and he repined in a gentle voice: "I do." I remember that, while giving his reply, he smiled in his habitual manner. And the Church, which had been an orphan since the death of Paul VI, again had a Pope.

It was a particular need of my heart to come here on this very day, the first anniversary of the election of John Paul 1, to his birthplace amid these mountains from which the Lord sent his servant to Rome.

These mountains, where he was born, remind me also of my own native mountains. And they remind me of Jasna Góra (the Bright Mountain), where on this very day the Feast of Our Lady of Jasna Góra is being solemnly celebrated.

But they remind me above all of John Paul I at the moment when the Lord's will was manifested through the votes of the cardinals in conclave and he lifted up the eyes of his soul and found the answer to the question that the Church had asked him: "Do you accept?"

"I lift up my eyes to the mountains.
From where shall come my help?

2. Much has been spoken and much written about this conclave that was convened after the fifteen years of Paul VI's pontificate to elect his successor. The College of Cardinals was

more numerous than ever before. Paul VI had definitively achieved its internationalization. It was therefore very different from the preceding conclaves. Many thought that this would make the con crave more difficult and longer. Instead, on the evening of the first day, on the fourth vote, the new Pope was elected.

That showed that human forecasts and all the objective circumstances that I seemed difficult, humanly speaking, to overcome were surpassed by the working from on high of Light and Power, by the working of the Holy Spirit, to whom the electors wished to be absolutely obedient. The whole Church saw in the election of John Paul I a sign of this divine working and rejoiced at the presence of the Holy Spirit who comes 'from on high" to blow where he wills (cf. Jn 3:8) in order that the whole Church should continue to have certainty about his activity and readiness to submit to his holy gifts.

3. "I lift up my eyes to the mountains."

Coming today to this magnificent peak of the Dolomites as part of my pilgrimage to the place of the birth and the youth of John Paul I, whom the heavenly Father called to himself after thirty three days of pastoral ministry on the chair of Saint Peter, I wish to lift up my eyes, with the whole Church, to her whose image stands from today as a resplendent crown above the heights of the Dolomites.

May all the Churches, all lands and all people raise to her a look full of love and hope.

Thus it is that my native land of Poland looks on her as it celebrates the Solemnity of Our Lady of Jasna Góra.

Thus also it is that the whole of the land of Italy, from south to north, turns its gaze on Mary, towards these mountains. For it is twenty years since the solemn consecration to the Mother of God in September 1959 after the triumphal progress through the cities of Italy of the pilgrim statue of Our Lady brought from Fatima.

May the statue of the Mother of Christ on the peak of the Dolomites recall that consecration, renew it and give it life.

Modern man must lift up his gaze, turn it upwards. He feels more and more insistently the danger of exclusive attachment to the earth. And it is all the more easy to turn our gaze upwards when our eyes meet that sweet Mother who is all simplicity and love, the lowly handmaid of the Lord.

And so, in memory of the first anniversary of the extraordinary election of Pope John Paul I to the See of Saint Peter, we leave on the land that gave him birth this sign of her maternal presence. We leave this sign, this statue of the Mother of God, here on this circle of mountains, in order that from here she may gaze on the whole of Italy, and that she may look into the hearts of all throughout this land who lift their eyes to her.

May all who wish to walk the paths of faith, hope and charity, all who hold dear the mystery of Christ in the history of mankind, which is bound up with the spiritual heritage of the See of Saint Peter, find in today a day of blessing and of grace.

# "I Entrust To Mary My Pilgrimage Of Peace!"

### Angelus: 23 September, 1979

At the usual meeting with the faithful for the recitation of the Angelus on Sunday, 23 September, the Holy Father delivered the following address.

1. On Friday next, 28 September, there occurs the first anniversary of the death of John Paul 1, which we will commemorate with a solemn Eucharistic Liturgy in St. Peter's Basilica and with a visit to the tomb of that Pope, to whom Providence entrusted for only thirty three days the exercise of the supreme service in the Church.

On the day immediately following, Saturday 29 September, I will go on a journey to Ireland, from where I will continue to the United States of America on I October. As I have already mentioned previously, the first incentive for this journey was the invitation of the Secretary General of the U.N., Dr. Kurt Waldheim. It was addressed to me by this illustrious statesman shortly after the beginning of the Pontificate, and was then renewed at the meeting in May of this year. I attach great importance to the task that my presence before the Assembly of the United Nations imposes on me, and today, once more, I ask everyone for the spiritual aid of prayer.

2. At the same time my heart turns, today already, to Ireland this country which, throughout the trials of its whole history, has bound itself so deeply to' the Catholic Church. In this year the Church in Ireland celebrates the centenary of the sanctuary of the Blessed Virgin, at Knock. This solemnity was for the Irish Episcopate and then for the President of that Republic the immediate occasion for the invitation extended to the Pope. I go to Ireland, therefore, as a pilgrim, just as I did first in Mexico and then in Poland, my native land. Today already I express my joy at being able, by means of this pilgrimage, to; find myself in those ways along which, the whole People of God of the Emerald Isle has walked towards the Lord, for centuries. I wish my presence to become for all the sons and daughters of Ireland a strengthening of their faithfulness and dedication to Christ in his Church; to become an eloquent sign of how the Apostolic See and the whole Church is with them and how it shares their merits, but also their sufferings and trials. Before the Mother of the Church, to whom I entrust this pilgrimage, I express the unshakable confidence that it will serve the great cause of peace and reconciliation, for which the whole Irish nation longs so much.

3. It is a good thing that our way to New York, to the session of U.N.O. should pass through Ireland, so as to become, in this way, a new pilgrimage along the paths of papal service of the Church. It is a good thing that this pilgrimage should be continued in the United States, as a visit to that Church and that society. I am grateful for the invitation of the Episcopal Conference of the USA, as well as for the invitation that Mr. Jimmy Carter, President of the United States of America, addressed to me at the same time. Planning to stay in America till Sunday 7 October (I cannot stay any longer, since my duties call me to Rome), I am not able to respond to all the individual invitations which have reached the Secretariat of State in large numbers, in the last few weeks. Today, on the other hand, I wish to express my heartfelt thanks for these invitations and for the many proofs of goodwill.

Traveling along the ways chosen by the pilgrimage, I will try to meet the appeal which, from so many communities and so many hearts, reaches the unworthy Successor of St. Peter in Rome. I ask them all for a prayer, in order that I may carry out this service of mine in the land of Washington, for the glory of God and for the good of men, my beloved brothers and sisters.

I express once more my deep grief at the terrible calamity that has stricken the populations of central Italy and, in particular, those of Force and Cascia, as a result of the earthquake in the last few days, which has caused five deaths and a number of wounded, as well as very serious destruction in that smiling region.

While I renew prayers for the souls of the victims of S. Marco and Chiavano that the Lord may receive them in the light and peace of Heaven, I assure all those who are now suffering as a result of the consequences of the earth quake, of my fatherly and practical solidarity.

I invoke the provident divine assistance on everyone.

After reciting the Marian prayer and imparting the Blessing, John Paul II greeted the members of the Union of master bellringers of Bologna and Romagna. They had erected a small belfry of four bells in the Square, and entertained the Holy Father with a concert of bellringing. He thanked them as follows:

The members of the Union of Bell ringers, of Bologna and Romagna who have let us hear melodious chimes, are present in St. Peter's Square. On behalf of all those present, I express to you, beloved brothers, my grateful pleasure in this harmonious homage of yours and hope that the sound of bells, which calls to elevation of the soul, fervent prayer and feelings of mutual love and universal peace, will always be welcomed.

# Look At Mary! Love Mary! Imitate Mary!

### Angelus: 21 October, 1979

On Sunday 21 October, the Holy Father went by helicopter to Pompeii and Naples. An account of his visit and the text of his discourses there, will be published in a future issue.

After celebrating Mass at an altar erected in the Square outside the Sanctuary of Our Lady of the Rosary of Pompeii, the Holy Father reentered the Basilica and later appeared on the loggia of the Basilica for the recitation of the Angelus with the faithful. In so doing he fulfilled a prophecy uttered by ven. Bartolo Longo, who had been responsible for the erection of the Marian Sanctuary at Pompeii. On 5 May 1901 he foretold: "One day we shall see on that loggia the white-clad figure of the representative of Christ blessing the people gathered in the Square below applauding universal peace."

Before the recitation of the Angelus Pope John Paul II gave the following brief address.

Today I feel great joy because I can recite the Angelus prayer, together with you, here, in the Sanctuary dedicated to Our Lady of the Rosary of Pompeii.

1. There is a very close link between the Angelus and the Rosary, both eminently Christological prayers and, at the same time, Marian. They make us, in fact, contemplate and study the mysteries of the History of Salvation, in which Mary is closely united with her Son Jesus. And this Sanctuary resounds perennially with the Rosary, the simple humble Marian prayer, but not for that reason less rich in Biblical and theological content, so dear, in its long history, to the faithful of all classes and from all walks of life, united in the profession of faith in Christ, who died and rose again for our salvation.

This place sacred to prayer had its origin in the mind and heart of a great layman, Venerable Bartolo Longo, who lived between the last century and ours, and so is a contemporary of our own. It was his wish to erect a temple, where the glories of the Mother of God would be proclaimed and where man could find refuge, comfort, hope and certainty.

In a few moments we will recite the Angelus together, which reminds us of the joyful announcement of the mystery of the Incarnation of the Son of God. We will recite it with special intensity and devotion, because we would like to proclaim together our Christian faith, and, likewise, to thank God for the wonders that he has carried out and continues to carry out through the intercession of the Blessed Virgin, to whom we will express all our filial veneration.

2. To this proclamation of faith, to this profession of veneration for the Blessed Virgin, I wish to invite particularly, at this moment and on this occasion, the thousands of young people

present in this square, especially those belonging to Italian Catholic Action of the Campania region.

Beloved young people! Your presence, so numerous, and your irrepressible enthusiasm are the confirmation that Christ's message is not a message of death, but of life; not of old things, but of new ones; not of sadness, but of joy! Tell all this to those of your own age, to all men, with your songs, with your ideals, but especially with your lives! "The wilderness becomes a fruitful field", the prophet Isaiah had said, speaking of Messianic (Is 32:15).

If we glance at this area, we find the impressive remains of the ancient city of Roman times, reduced to a "dead" city, a city 'of death", by the terrible eruption in the year 79 A.D. But where death seemed to dominate, after about 1.800 years there began to flourish, like a spiritual garden, this Sanctuary, a center of Eucharistic and Marian life, a prophetic sign of that fullness which Jesus. came to bring to us and to communicate to us.

Beloved young people! Look at Mary! Love Mary! Imitate Mary! Imitate her complete openness to God, whose willing and obedient "servant" she professes to be; her silent, generous and active openness to brothers and sisters, in need of help, assistance and comfort; her continual, persevering "following" of her Son Jesus from the manger in Bethlehem to the cross on Calvary.

May the Virgin smile on you and protect you always!

# A Peerless Beauty Called Mary

## Homily: 8 December, 1979

The Holy Father delivered the following address to the thousands of faithful who gathered in St. Peter's Square at noon on Saturday 8 December to recite with the Pope the Angelus on the Solemnity of the Immaculate Conception.

1. "Tote pulchra es, Maria!...."

Today the whole of Rome wishes to manifest its veneration and love for that peerless Beauty called Mary.

This afternoon we will go to Piazza di Spagna, to the column on the top of which there is the statue of Mary Immaculate. We will go to speak to her, as is done every year, with the language of this particular Roman tradition.

Then we will gather at St. Mary Major's the principal Marian Basilica of Rome, to celebrate the solemn liturgy, to offer the Sacrifice of her Son in thanksgiving to the Holy Trinity for the gift of the Immaculate Conception.

We will give thanks for this gift against the background of advent in the Church and in mankind, advent which is renewed every year, in the liturgy and remains incessantly in the history of man.

Just as, against the background of that advent which preceded the first coming of Christ, God, by means of the mystery of the Immaculate Conception, of her whom he chose as his Mother, lit the hidden light of the Spirit, so too the same Light, revealed to the Church, act companies us in our progress through the time of the second advent.

Man's hope, the ways of which of ten lead through darkness, accompanies us and illuminates us.

2. Today, to speak of Mary, of that Beauty which is fully known only, by God, but which, at the same time, appeals so much to man, we wish to use the words of two of the greatest Fathers and writers of the Church of the East and of the West.

Commenting on a verse of Psalm 86, St. Germanus of Constantinople writes as follows: "Glorious things are spoken of you, O city of God", holy David sings to us, inspired by the Spirit. Naming very clearly the city of the great King, of which glorious things are spoken he is certainly speaking of her who was really elect and who is raised above everyone, not because of higher houses not because of lofty hills, but because she excels by far through the splendor of magnificent divine virtues, through extraordinary purity; (he speaks) of Mary the pure and immaculate Mother of God in whom there dwelt the One who is really King of Kings and Lord of lords, or rather, the one in whom the fullness of divinity inhabited bodily" (Om 9; PG 98; 372).

And here is how the great Bishop of Milan, St. Ambrose, presents Mary to us as the one "pre-redeemed" by Christ, her Son: "(Mary was) really Blessed, because she was superior to the priest (Zechariah). While the latter had yet fused to believe, the Virgin corrected his error. It is not surprising that the Lord, having to redeem the world, should have begun his work with Mary if salvation for all men was being prepared through her, she should be the first to obtain the fruit of salvation from her Son" (Exposit. Evangelii sec. Lucam, 11, 17: PL 15, 1559).

I wished particularly to link these two voices together so that both traditions may speak in them: that of the East and that of the West, united in veneration of that Beauty, which God himself pre pared at the beginning of the mystery of Incarnation.

We will shortly repeat the words with which the Archangel Gabriel greeted Mary at the moment of the Annunciation: "Hail, full of grace" (Lk 1:28). Man is sensitive to visible beauty, which is perceived by the sense, but also to the beauty of the spirit.

In the words of the Archangel, uttered during the Annunciation, the greatest spiritual beauty, which has its beginning in God himself, is called by name. And above all he himself finds pleasure in it.

Let us pray that this beauty, the beauty of Cod's grace, will never cease: to attract human hearts.

# "I Entrust To God's Mother This City And This Church"
### Angelus: 13 April, 1980

At the conclusion of the Mass celebrated by John Paul II outside the Duomo of Turin during his pastoral visit to that city on 13 April, he gave the following address before reciting with the faithful the Paschal antiphon "Regina Caeli."

1. The prayer of the antiphon "Regina Caeli," which at Easter time replaces the Angelus, is raised today, Sunday "in albis," not, as usual, under the sky of Rome, but under that of Turin, of his "august" city, which finds in the Marian sanctuaries of the Consolata, Our Lady Help of Christians, and of the Great Mother of God, the ideal points of its devotion to the Blessed Virgin. Marian piety, in fact, has deeply marked the spiritual life of the people of

Turin throughout the centuries. It finds a typical expression in the best known saints of this city, as in all these persons who lived and worked in the light and under the motherly patronage of her who is called the Mother of the Saints and then the Mother of the Church, as she was proclaimed by my venerated predecessor, Paul VI, at the end of the Second Vatican Council. Mary, who in the mystery of Redemption became the Mother of all men, cannot but be, indeed, the Mother of the Church. So to her, to the Mother of all men, and in particular to the Mother of the Church, I come today together with you, who make up the Holy Church of Turin, I Pope John Paul II who have arrived here as a pilgrim, and I say to her: Regina caeli, laetare!

2. Today, ending the octave of Easter which is, in a certain sense, the single paschal day of the resurrection ("haec est dies!") we have still vivid in our memory the Passion and the Cross of Christ. Our hearts do not forget that she was standing by the cross of Jesus (cf. Jn 19:25): stabat Mater dolorosa. Nor can we forget that, from the Cross, Jesus looked at his mother and John, the disciple whom he loved, and, as to a special witness, indicated to the disciple Mary, as Mother, and entrusted the disciple to his Mother: "Behold, your mother"! "Woman, behold your Son" (Jn 19:27, 26)! We believe that in this one man, precisely in John, Jesus indicated Mary as Mother of every man, he entrusted everyone to her, as if every man were her child, her Son or her daughter.

From this fact is derived the particular necessity that we, obedient to these words of Christ's testament, should entrust ourselves and everything that belongs to us, to Mary.

3. Letting myself be guided by this faith and at the same time by this hope, today I wish to renew what is part of Christ's paschal testament and entrust to the Mother of God this city and this Church which welcomes me as a pilgrim today. May she be the good star and the wise guide of alt those who are concerned about its true welfare "ad its true social and spiritual progress. May she shed her light on this large family and make known to everyone the urgency of a new way of being and acting. May she inspire the young to attain the great, peaceful ideals of Christian faith and social justice; because the Christian faith is never contrary to social

justice. And if they tell you that in the name of social justice, you must abandon the faith, do not believe it. May she cause concord and the 'mile of children to blossom in every family. May she enlighten men of culture and of science in the search for truth, in order to understand it more deeply and transmit it to others. May she make the workers feel how precious their work is and how much the Church loves them and appreciates them. May she be the hope and help of those who are unemployed or feel excluded from society; the consolation and the comfort of the sick, of those who mourn and of those are persecuted for righteousness' sake. May she be a Mother for everyone! Let us pray to her to grant everyone faith, strength, goodness and grace, and to cause the redeeming light of the Risen Christ, "the blessed fruit of her womb", to shine forth on the face of every man and every woman.

4. Regina caeli, laetare...

All those whom we entrust to you today, Mary, Consolata, Our Lady Help of Christians, Great Mother of God, have their part in the modern stage of the history of the world, of the Church, and of Italy. The mysterious current of the history of man's salvation, which corresponds to the eternal intentions of the Father's Love, passes through the hearts of everyone. At the same time there continues in these same hearts, on this earth, the struggle between good and evil, in which man has participated since original sin.

The Eternal Father resolved and chose you, Mary Immaculate, as the Mother of the Word Incarnate. At the beginning of this struggle between good and evil he established you, as the Woman who bruises the serpent's heel (cf. Gn 3:15). In this way he marked your humble maternity as the sign of hope for all those who, in this battle, in this struggle, wish to persevere with your Son and overcome evil with good.

We men who are approaching the end of the second millennium, feel these struggles deeply. The events in which we are involved show us continually how threatening the forces of sin, hate, ferocity and death are, in us and around us. So let us turn our eyes again to the Mother of the Redeemer of the world to the Woman of John's Revelation, to the "woman clothed with the sun" (12:1), in whom we see you, full of gushing light that illuminates the dark and dangerous stages of human lives on earth.

O Mother, may this prayer and this abandonment, which we renew once more, tell you everything about us. May it again bring us nearer to you, the Mother of God and of men, Consolata, Our Lady help of Christians, Great Mother of God and ours, and may it again bring you closer to us. Do not let the brothers of your Son perish. Bestow on our hearts the power of truth. Bestow peace and order on our existence.

Show that you are our Mother!

Regina caeli, laetare!

# Inviting Mary To Visit Family Homes And Prosper Work Of Synod Of Bishops

## Angelus: 15 August, 1980

The short catechesis of the Holy Father which preceded the Angelus prayer on the feast of the Assumption of Our Lady was centered on the coming Synod of Bishops. The Pope spoke as follows:

1. Today we wish to fill our common prayer of the Angelus with the sentiment of a particular veneration and love for Mary. It is, in fact, the feast of her Assumption into Heaven. She who conceived in her virginal womb and gave birth to the Son of God, the Eternal Word, experiences today the glorification of soul and body in the heart of the Holy Trinity. And our hearts as always, today too, but today more than ever, turn to her with all the simplicity and faith of children. We are happy for the eternal glory of the Mother of Christ and our Mother!

2. In the Gospel of today's solemnity we see Mary when, after the annunciation, full of the Holy Spirit and of the Mystery conceived in her womb by this same Spirit, she enters the house of Zechariah. She crosses the threshold of a house in which there lives a family so close to her in spirit and kinship. And right on the threshold she is greeted by Elizabeth who extols her faith: "Blessed are you who have believed" (Luke 1:45). And she greets Mary with the same words with which we all constantly greet her when we recite the "Hail Mary."

3. Mary crosses the threshold of a house and enters into a family circle. How that event associates us with the one for which the Episcopate of the entire world is preparing in regard to this year's Synod of Bishops! The Synod's theme, "The Duties of the Christian Family Today," turns our attention towards all the families who live in today's world, towards the families to whom the Church is sent, and through whom it wishes to fulfill a mission. We think of the great family tasks, bound to the transmission of life and to the enormous task of educating the new man. We think of the joys, but also of the difficulties, of this love on which the life of a married couple and of a family is built. We think also of the sufferings, the crises, and the tragedies which sometimes accompany family life. Through the work of the Synod of Bishops we wish to enter into the sphere of all this, with full respect, but also with the faith and love with which the Church surrounds the Christian family, built on the foundation of the sacrament of marriage.

And therefore we ask Mary to cross the threshold of all family homes, just as she once did at the home of Zechariah. We pray to her to bring everyone the same message of maternal faith and love. We ask her also to visit the works of the Synod now in preparation, and whose members, with their eyes fixed on her as Elisabeth did a long time ago, wish to repeat: Blessed are you who have believed. The Synod, on its part, following the example of this Mother, wishes to let itself be guided by the faith and the love towards all families to whom its particular service will soon be directed.

# -Chapter 9-

# The Five "M's" Of Mary

In addition to these four official teachings about Mary that all Catholics are bound to believe as articles of faith, there are many other aspects of Catholic belief about Mary that are helpful in understanding her role in God's plan and in approaching her in prayer. One way of remembering some important truths about Mary is to think of five of her attributes that begin with the letter "M": member, model, mother, mediatrix and messenger. The first three of these "M's" are mentioned in one paragraph of the chapter on Mary in the Dogmatic Constitution on the Church of the Second Vatican Council:

> ... Therefore, she is also hailed as a pre-eminent and altogether singular member of the Church, and as the Church's model and excellent exemplar in faith and charity. Taught by the Holy Spirit, the Catholic Church honors her with filial affection and piety as the most beloved mother..." (*Lumen Gentium*, no. 53).

## 1. Mary as a Member of the Church

The Second Vatican Council included its discussion of Mary in the last chapter of the Dogmatic Constitution on the Church in order to emphasize that Mary is a member, albeit "a pre-eminent and altogether singular member," of the Church. This attribute of Mary is a reminder that however much we might rightfully honor and exalt Mary for her response to God and for her role in God's saving plan, she remains fully human and is not be adored by Christians. Mary is not a goddess, but a fully human servant of God whom he has highly favored through his mercy and grace. This fact can enable Catholics to identify ore fully with Mary and to realize that the holiness and full consecration to God that she exhibited is something which is possible for every Christian. It is, in fact, the goal of the Christian life.

## 2. Mary as Model

The last statement above implies that Mary provides an ideal model for each individual Christian of a life of discipleship, consecration, and holiness. God calls each person to make the unconditional "yes" to him and to his will that Mary expressed at the Annunciation and proceeded to live out until the end of her life. Catholics honor Mary because she is the model disciple, the perfect, most faithful follower of her Son, Jesus Christ. Thus, she is a model of true discipleship for each Christian.

Mary is not only a model for individual Christians but she is a model for the Church as a whole. The Church is called to be God's presence in the world through its faithfulness to the gospel and to following Jesus as he guides the Church through the Holy Spirit. Mary manifested God's presence most perfectly by pondering the events and words that constituted her call and experience and by carrying out faithfully everything God told her. Because the Church has not attained the perfection of discipleship tat Mary attained, we continue to look to her as the best example of what we, as the Church, are called by God to be and to do.

As the Second Vatican Council's Dogmatic Constitution on the Church notes:

As St. Ambrose taught, the Mother of God is a model of the Church in the matter of faith, charity and perfect union with Christ... The followers of Christ still strive to increase in holiness by conquering sin. And so they raise their eyes to Mary who shines forth to the whole community of the elect as a model of the virtues... (*Lumen Gentium*, nos. 63, 65).

## 3. Mary as Mother

Mary is not only a model, she is much more. She is our Mother. Mary is the Mother of God, but also by God's grace and call she is the spiritual mother of the Church and of each Christian. The basis of this is found in the Gospel of John, chapter 19. As his last act before his death, Jesus told the beloved disciple, who represents all of Jesus' disciples, "Behold, your mother" (Jn 19:27). Christian tradition from the earliest times confirms that Mary is, indeed, the mother in the order of grace of the Church and of each Christian.

## 4. Mary as Mediatrix

Because Mary is our mother, she is committed to pray and intercede for each of her children and for the Church as a whole. Catholic tradition has ascribed a number of different titles to Mary to describe her role of intercession. As the Second Vatican Council explains:

> By her maternal charity, Mary cares for the brethren of her Son who still journey on earth surrounded by dangers and difficulties, until they are led to their happy fatherland. Therefore the Blessed Virgin is involved by the Church under the titles of Advocate, Auxiliatrix, Adjutrix, and Mediatrix. There, however, are to be so understood that they neither take away from nor add anything to the dignity and efficacy of Christ the one Mediator. For no creature could ever be classed with the Incarnate Word and Redeemer... (*Lumen Gentium*, No. 62).

The Dogmatic Constitution on the Church goes on to explain that just as Jesus' priesthood is shared in various ways by members of the Church, he also gives us a share in his unique role as Mediator (1 Tm 2:5-6), one who prays or intercedes on behalf of others before the Father. The Catholic Church has long held that because of her sinlessness and close union with her Son, Mary has been given a role of mediation of intercession before God above any other human being. In that role, Catholics speak of Mary as Mediatrix.

Is it not appropriate that God should have given a special role of mediation or intercession to the mother of the Church? Who on earth pleads for a person as effectively and fervently as that person's mother? The Church, as God's family, has been blessed by God with Mary as a mother to mediate and intercede for all Christians in order to lead them to her divine Son, Jesus Christ. The Second Vatican Council's concluding statement on Mary as Mediatrix affirms:

> The Church does not hesitate to profess this subordinate role of Mary. She experiences it continuously and commends it to the hearts of the faithful, so that encouraged by this maternal help they may more closely adhere to the Mediator and Redeemer [Jesus Christ] (*Lumen Gentium*, no. 62).

## 5. Mary as Messenger

Mary's role as messenger has become more prominent in recent times. This refers to the appearances, or apparitions, of Mary that have been reported by Catholics at various times throughout the Church's history, and notably more often in the past 150 years. In these appearances, Mary usually presents a prophetic message. The message is sometimes directed toward an individual or local Church, but sometimes Mary's words are intended for the whole Church or for a large segment of the Church.

How does the Catholic Church view these apparitions of Mary and their accompanying messages? The Church does not require its members to believe in the authenticity of any apparitions or particular messages, since these are private revelation. As Pope John Paul II explained in an address at Fatima on May 13, 1982:

> The Church has always taught and continues to proclaim that God's revelation was brought to completion in Jesus Christ, who is the fullness of that revelation, and that "no new public revelation is to be expected before the glorious manifestation of the Lord" (*Lumen Gentium*, no. 4). The Church evaluates and judges private revelations by the criterion of conformity with that single public revelation.

Therefore, private revelations such as appearances of Mary must conform fully to the standard of public revelation that comes from Jesus Christ if they are to be accepted and heeded.

It is noteworthy that recent popes have visited and preached at some sites of Mary's reported appearances, such as Lourdes, France and Fatima, Portugal and that the messages of Mary presented at these and other sites have been judged by the Catholic Church to be in full conformity with Biblical teaching and authentic Catholic tradition. Numerous miracles have also been confirmed at some of these sites, such as a multitude of medically verified physical healings at Lourdes. Just as God sent angels as messengers of his work in the Old Testament, it appears that he has chosen in this age to speak particular words of encouragement, instruction and warning through Mary.

Most of the reported appearances of Mary in recent times have followed the same, Biblically based pattern. Mary appears to simple, humble, and usually poor people. The appearances are accompanied by an outpouring of the Holy Spirit, manifesting itself by the good fruit of joy, thanksgiving, worship and praise of God, and deepened trust in the Lord even in the midst of persecution or oppression. Often healings and other miracles accompany such apparitions.

The effects of such apparitions of Mary and her messages have been profound. Mary's appearance to a poor Mexican peasant, Juan Diego, in 1531, as Our Lady of Guadalupe, led to the conversion to Christianity of an estimated eight million native people within seven years. Thousands of people who have visited Lourdes since her appearance there in 1858 to Bernadette Soubirous have been healed and turned to Jesus Christ. In 1917, Mary appeared to three children (ages seven to ten) at Fatima, Portugal, and called for prayer, especially the rosary, and consecration of Russia to her immaculate heart. She warned, "if my requests are heard, Russia will be converted and there will be peace. If not, she will spread her errors throughout the entire world, provoking wars and persecution of the Church..." At that time, Russia was a poor country torn by civil war, and this prediction seemed almost laughable. But history has proven it true. Mary's appearance at Fatima reminds Christians that the things we do now and our prayers and faith have consequences for our own salvation and for that of the world. as Pope John Paul II stated in his homily at Fatima on May 13, 1982:

> If the Church has accepted the message of Fatima, it is above all because that message contains a truth and a call whose basic content is the truth and call of the gospel itself. "Repent, and believe in the Gospel!" (Mk 1:15): these are the first words that the Messiah addressed to humanity. the message of Fatima is, in its basic nucleus, a call to conversion and repentance, as in the Gospel...

At Fatima, Mary promised a sign of the validity and truth of her appearances there. It is estimated that about one hundred thousand people witnessed this sign: the sun dancing in the sky at mid-day. Many secular observers witnessed this sign, and have not been able to explain it. It has often been ignored, but never effectively denied.

There are many more reported appearances of Mary. The Catholic Church has always been wary about placing undue emphasis on these private revelations, but many of them have been accepted as legitimate by the local bishops, whose role it is to discern their validity. In the most widely accepted apparitions, Mary has consistently called Christians to prayer, repentance and conversion to God. Sometimes she has warned of serious consequences for the world if this message remains unheeded. Mary always has presented herself in authentic apparitions as a messenger or servant of God. Although she has affirmed traditional Catholic titles for herself and encourages the use of Marian prayers, such as the rosary, her focus is always unmistakably centered on Jesus Christ. The most recent reported appearances of Mary in Medjugorge, Yugoslavia, repeat many of the themes of the message of Mary at Fatima and affirm the basic truths of the gospel and Catholic Christian teaching.

## Conclusion

Catholics are encouraged to foster a proper devotion to Mary, the Mother of God. we honor her, as God honors her, for her special role in his plan of salvation. We imitate her faithfulness as the model disciple of Jesus Christ. We approach her as the spiritual mother that Jesus has given to each Christian and to his Church, and we continually ask her, as our mother, to pray and intercede for us before the throne of God. We also must carefully weigh the meaning of the many urgent prophetic words that have come to the Church in our time through her reported appearances.

Mary should have a special place in the life of each Christian. Although the form of our relationship with Mary may differ somewhat from person to person, the Catholic Church recommends certain forms of honor and devotion, especially the rosary, prayed either individually or in families and groups; and the observance of the feasts of Mary that occur throughout the Church year, such as the feast of the Annunciation (March 25); the Assumption (August 15); the Immaculate Conception (December 8); and the Mother of God (January 1). Through a proper relationship and devotion to Mary, Catholics grow ever deeper in their love of God and their following of her Son, Jesus Christ.

# Appendix 1

## Mary:
### Coredemptrix    Mediatrix    Advocate[1]

W e know that the Marian Mystery in God's plan of salva tion does not end with the Earthly life of the Virgin of Nazareth and her departure. The Second Vatican Coun-cil reminds us, "Taken up in Heaven she did not lay aside this saving office, but by her manifold intercession continues to bring us the gifts of eternal salvation."[2]

The Council goes on to say, "Therefore the Blessed Virgin is invoked in the Church under the titles of Advocate, Helper, Benefactress, and Mediatrix."[3] These titles of Mary, such as Mediatrix and Advocate, refer to roles given to Mary by the heav-enly Father and sustained by the Holy Spirit because of her inti-mate sharing in the redemptive work of Jesus Christ.

To understand, therefore, the roles of Mary as Mediatrix and Advocate, which she now exercises with the aid of the Holy Spirit from her rightful place in Heaven, we must examine the meritorious foundation for these God-given roles during her earthly life as the "handmaid of the Lord" (Lk 1:38).

"Thus the daughter of Adam, Mary, consenting to the word of God, became the Mother of Jesus. Committing herself whole-heartedly and impeded by no sin to God's saving will, she de-voted herself totally, as a handmaid of the Lord, to the person and work of her Son, under and with him, serving the work of redemp-tion...."[4] Mary's intimate cooperation *with the Redeemer* began at the Annunciation, where she freely participated in the work of Man's salvation through faith and obedience (cf. Lk 1:28).

But the cooperation of the Mother of the Redeemer in the work of redemption did not cease with her *fiat* to the angel. "The Blessed Virgin advanced in her pilgrimage of faith and faithfully persevered in her union with her Son unto the cross, where she stood, in keeping with the divine plan, enduring with her only begotten Son the intensity of his suffering, associated herself with his sacrifice in her mother's heart, and lovingly consenting to the immolation of this victim which was born of her."[5] These profound words of the Second Vatican Council describe the spiritual sufferings and intimate cooperation Mary experienced *with the Redeemer* at the foot of the cross (cf. Jn 19:26) in perfect maternal obedience to God's plan of salvation.

It is in light of Mary's unique and intimate cooperation with the Redeemer, both at the Incarnation (cf. Lk 1:28) and at the work of Redemption at Calvary (cf. Jn 19:26), that the Church has invoked Mary under the title, "Coredemptrix."[6]

The prefix "co" does not mean equal, but comes from the Latin word, *"cum"*, which means "with". The title of Coredemptrix applied to the Mother of Jesus *never places Mary on a level of equality with Jesus Christ, the divine Lord of all, in the saving process of humanity's redemption*. Rather, it denotes Mary's singular and unique *sharing with her Son* in the saving work of redemption for the human family. The Mother of Jesus *participates* in the redemptive work of her *Savior Son, who alone could reconcile humanity with the Father in his glorious divinity and humanity*. Jesus Christ, true God and true man, redeems the human family, *as the God-man*. Mary, who is *completely subordinate and dependent* to her redeeming Son even for her own human redemption,[7] *participates* in the redemptive acts of her Son *as his exalted human mother*.

Because of her intimate and unparalleled sharing in the mysterious *work with the divine Redeemer*, Mary, human Mother of the Redeemer, has merited the Church title, "Coredemptrix" which literally means, *"with the Redeemer."*

Mary's other roles in the Church as Mediatrix[8] and Advocate[9] are in fact a flowing over of her role as Coredemptrix. Pope John Paul II tells us, "Mary's role as Coredemptrix did not cease with the glorification of her Son."[10]

There remains one final doctrinal pillar of the Marian mystery revealed by God that seems to call for the proclamation of clarity and truth that only the Church can provide in its crucial task of "giving an authentic interpretation of the Word of God."[11] It is the Christian revelation of Mary as *Coredemptrix with the Redeemer*, as well as the resulting roles of *Mediatrix and Advocate for the People of God*. For the People of God, as the Council tells, us, "still journey on earth surrounded by dangers and difficulties, until they are led into their blessed home."[12]

Let us proceed to examine these Marian roles of Coredemptrix, Mediatrix, and Advocate, as they manifest themselves in the rich revelation of the Word of God entrusted to the Church.[13] Let us in a special way invoke the guidance of the Holy Spirit, the Spirit of Truth, for "the Holy Spirit, through whom the living voice of the Gospel rings out in the Church – and through her to the world – leads believers to the full truth, and makes the Word of Christ dwell in them in all its richness" (cf. Col 3:16).[14] Hence the Christian faithful will be able to listen attentively to what "the Spirit" is "saying to the Churches" today about the "Handmaid of the Lord" (cf. Rv 2:7,11,17; Lk 1:38).[15]

\* \* \* \* \* \* \* \* \*

## Endnotes

[1]     Extract from the Introduction to "Mary: Coredemptrix    Mediatrix Advocate" by Mark I. Miravalle, S.T.D., p. xiv-xvi.

[2]     Vatican Council II, *Lumen Gentium*, n. 62.

[3]     Vatican Council II, *Lumen Gentium*, n. 62.

[4]     Vatican Council II, *Lumen Gentium*, n. 56.

[5]     Vatican Council II, *Lumen Gentium*, n. 58.

[6]     For example, see Pope Pius XI, Radio message to Lourdes, 28 April 1935, *L'Osservatore Romano*: "O Mother of piety and mercy, who as *Coredemptrix* stood by your most sweet Son suffering with him when he consummated the redemption of the human race on the altar of the cross...(emphasis added)." For other appearances of the Marian title "Coredemptrix" in official Church documents, see Sacred Congregation of Rites, 13 May 1908, *Acta Apostolicae Sedis* (in later references *"AAS"*) 41, 1908, p. 408; Holy Office, Decree of 26 June 1913, *AAS*, 5, 1913, p. 364;

Holy Office, Decree of 22 January 1914, *AAS*, 6, 1914, p. 1108; Pope Pius XI, *L'Osservatore Romano*, 1 December 1933, *L'Osservatore Romano*, 25 March 1934. Cf. P. Gabriele M. Roschine O.S.M., *Maria Santissima Nella Storia Della Salvezza*, Isola de Liri, Italy, Editrice m. Pisani, 1969, p. 126.

[7]  Mary herself is redeemed by the saving merits of Jesus Christ at Calvary through an application of the graces of redemption at the moment of her conception by God who is out of time, cf. Pope Pius IX, *Ineffabilis Deus*, 1854.

[8]  Vatican Council II, *Lumen Gentium*, n. 62.

[9]  Vatican Council II, *Lumen Gentium*, n. 62.

[10]  Pope John Paul II, Papal Address at the Sanctuary of Our Lady of Alborada in Guayaquil, 31 January 1985, *L'Osservatore Romano*, 11 March 1985.

[11]  Vatican Council II, *Dei Verbum* (Dogmatic Constitution of Divine Revelation), n. 10.

[12]  Vatican Council II, *Lumen Gentium*, n. 62.

[13]  Cf. Vatican Council II, *Dei Verbum*, n. 10.

[14]  Vatican Council II, *Dei Verbum*, n. 8.

[15]  Cf. Pope John Paul II, Encyclical Letter, *Redemptoris Mater*, n. 30.

# Appendix 2

# Mary And Ecumenism[1]

N ear to the center of the mystery of salvation by her maternal relation to the Word incarnate, Mary is in close relation with the mystery of the Church and its unity. In the conflicts that have divided and continue to divide Christians, cultic and doctrinal expressions of this relation between the Church and Mary play an important role. If at times this role appears to be negative, a factor of oppositions, fundamentally it cannot but serve a positive end, lighting the way that is leading Christians unceasingly to unity in Jesus Christ.

## 1. "Mary, Mother of God" at the Council of Ephesus

One of the first great disputes that has divided Christians since the 5th century has to do with Christological doctrine, the nature and person of Christ. Antiocheans emphasized the distinction between the Humanity and the Divinity in Jesus Christ. Nestorius went so far as to assert an absolute separation between the two "natures" of Christ, denting in effect the real union between them. In contrast, Alexandrians stressed the fact that there was no common measure between the Humanity and the Divinity and tended toward absorption of Christ's Humanity by his Divinity ("One only nature of the incarnate Son of God" – Cyril of Alexandria), a tendency which led logically to the heresy of Monophysitism.

In proclaiming Mary "Theotokos," Mother of God, the Council of Ephesus restored and expressed the unity of the Church regarding its belief in the Word incarnate. This Marian teaching – that Mary is the Mother of God – became a touchstone of orthodoxy and unity.

## 2. Mary in the Western Controversy between Catholics and Protestants

To the extent that Western Christianity was organized around the Church of Rome not only art but spiritual doctrine and in time theology itself sought to express the privileges of Mary and her role in the economy of salvation. In addition, her place in the Church's worship and belief was extolled and made secure.

Yet it was not this place of Mary in worship and belief that played a determining role in the first disputes of the 16th-century Reformation. We can cite passages and prayers of Luther, of Zwingli, and of Anglican theologians which show a high regard for and a fervent attitude toward Mary as the woman whom *"all ages to come shall call blessed."* But in spite of this, and rather soon, there arose points of controversy between the Reformers and Catholics on the subject of Mary. Among these points were: the veneration of Mary, the prayers addressed to her, the prominence given to her active participation in the redemption, and beliefs relating to Mary's conception and bodily assumption, which were challenged as non-Scriptural. It can be said that today still the basic contentions of the Reformation find application in Mary:

· *"Soli Deo Gloria"* ("to God alone the glory") – hence the veneration accorded to Mary runs the risk of becoming idolatry.
· *"Jesus Christ as only Mediator between God and human beings"* – hence what place is there for a Marian mediation, for the intercession sought in prayer addressed to her...
· *"Sola fide, sola gratia"* (by faith alone, by grace alone) – the fundamental principle of justification by faith alone, to the exclusion of works, calls into question Mary's active participation in the work of our salvation.
· *"Scriptura sola"* (Scripture only) – which is to say,, only what is found in Scripture can be made a belief for Christians. The appeal to Tradition as in some way additional to Scripture is declared unacceptable. But the Church believes a number of things about Mary which are not explicitly taught in the New Testament.

The impassioned character of the controversies in regard to Mary made dialogue rather difficult. This was especially true with Protestant fundamentalists and Evangelical conservatives. On the other hand where currents of High Church and Low Church coexisted within the same communion, it was possible to see fruitful dialogue taking place.

Such was (and is) the case with the Anglican Church, in which since the Reformation "Catholics" and "Evangelicals" have been in constant interrelation and have maintained unity as to Sacraments and Liturgy.

Not only are there in the Anglican Liturgy Marian expressions, Marian feasts, and Marian names of churches (Church of St. Mary the Virgin, Feast of the Purification of Mary the Blessed Virgin, etc.). There have been as well in every period of the Anglican church theological currents in favor of Marian devotion and traditional Marian belief (Carolinian Fathers of the 17th century; Oxford Movement of the 19th; contemporary Anglo-Catholics). And as for theologians of Evangelical bent, today we see many of them in renewed study of Mary's place in the New Testament and substantiating the inseparable link between Mariology and Christology (cf. John de Satgé, *Mary and the Christian Gospel*, London, 1976).

Dialogue along this line between Roman Catholics and representative non-Catholic groups has now been created. In the more friendly and trustful contemporary climate there is reason to hope for positive results in regard to Marian doctrine and prayer. On the Catholic side, it can be said that there has been a return to the Scriptural supports, owing to a greater interest in Biblical theology. This in turn has led to a recentering of Marian doctrine on Christ. Chapter 8 of the *Constitution on the Church (Lumen Gentium)* is typical of this orientation. In a related development, a growing number of Protestants have begun to take a closer look at the Scriptural evidence concerning Mary and are finding in Jesus Christ the key to a truly spiritual understanding of the mystery of Mary.

## 3. Mary in Eastern Christianity

If it were possible for such a dialogue to be created in the West, the reason in large part was that Orthodox (Eastern) Christians had entered into ecumenical dialogue as early as 1920. In the view of the Orthodox, the Marian teaching transmitted by the Tradition of the Church belongs to the very essence of the faith. A Christianity deprived of the Blessed Virgin would be a mutilated Christianity with a nature different from that of established teaching.

This insistence of the Eastern Church is maintained in dialogue, and its Liturgy leaves a marked place for the Mother of God in the celebration of every mystery of Christ. Hence, contact with the liturgical prayer of Eastern Christians offers the possibility of seeing more clearly what is the place of Mary in relation to her Son and the Holy Spirit, as well as her place in the domain of faith, prayer, and the communal life of the Church.

Dialogue with the Eastern Church on the subject of Mary may also show Catholics the way to a better balance, through Christ and the Holy Spirit, between various levels of life in the Church – personal, local, and universal.

## 4. Toward a Conciliar Community

The way to Christian unity seems today to lie in the pursuit of a "conciliar" community embracing various Christian Churches. We have seen that while Mary may have been a sign of discord, dialogue concerning her has now made possible a growth of this conciliar community. Mary is at the heart of the living memory of the Church, which receives the present gift of the Holy Spirit. By this gift the Church continuously imparts renewed being to the Body of Christ in the present world and directs the hope of all believers toward the Lord who is coming: *"Do whatever he tells you"* (Jn 2:5).

\* \* \* \* \* \* \* \* \*

### Endnotes

[1]    Dictionary of Mary – "Behold Your Mother", © 1985 by Catholic Book Publishing Co., NY.

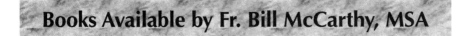

# Books Available by Fr. Bill McCarthy, MSA

## THE OUR FATHER
### Four Commentaries on the Lord's Prayer
**by FR. BILL McCARTHY, MSA**

Compling four of the most inspiring treatments on the 'Lord's Prayer,' the four commentaries found in this book are taken from St. Cyprian in the 3rd Century, St. Thomas Acquinas in the 13th Century, the new Catechism of the Catholic Church, and Fr. Bill McCarthy's five "P's".

Unlock the secrets hidden in this timeless and powerful prayer!

**Only $8.95**

**Listening to God Ways of Hearing God's Voice**

This beautifully illustrated prayer book outlines several sure fire methods for listening to the many ways God speaks to His people. Offering several principles for discerning God's voice both internally and externally, the practical suggestions in this book will teach readers how to enter into God's Will more deeply. 64 pages **Only $3.00**

**The Joy of Being Catholic**

Containing over 45 color illustrations and paintings, this wonderful prayer book tells of the countless joys of being Catholic. Covering the joy of the sacraments, the joy of a personal relationship with Jesus Christ, the joy of of Mary our mother, and the joy of being part of the Church founded by Jesus Christ, these beautiful writings and prayers will be sure to inspire all who read. 48 pages **Only $3.00**

| | |
|---|---|
| **A Personal Relationship with Jesus** | $6.00 |
| **A Walk through the New Catechism** | $3.00 |

**To Order call:** *My Father's House*: (860) 873-1581 or fax: (860) 873-2357

# About this Painting

## MARY, MOTHER OF THE CHURCH
by ANNA MAY McCALLUM

This painting on the cover is an original done precisely for this book. Mary is pictured being crowned as Queen and Mother by the Spirit (her spouse), by Jesus (blood red), and by the Father (divine blue). She is holding St. Peter's Church (Rome), symbol for the one, holy, Catholic Church, founded by her son upon Peter, as a rock (cf. Mt. 16:18 ff). Mary is the mother of Jesus in His Resurrected Body, in His Eucharistic Body and His Mystical Body - the Church. She ever intercedes that Christ be fully formed in us, her children. (cf. Rev. 12:17).

Anna May, one of the foremost religious artists of our day, is wife and mother of twelve, including a priest and a daughter who is a consecrated member of Regnum Christi. Anyone interested in this painting or any of her artwork can contact her at:

**Anna May T. McCallum**
**1706 Lake Drive**
**Braham, MN 55006**

Phone:   (320) 396-3764
Fax:       (320) 396-3629

11 x 14 $8.00 plus shipping plus $3.20 shipping
 8 x 10 $6.00 plus shipping plus $3.20 shipping
 4 x  6 $4.00 plus shipping plus $1.00 shipping

Color print may also be signed at your request.

---

**Toll-Free (888) 654-6279 or (412) 787-9735 www.SaintAndrew.com**

475

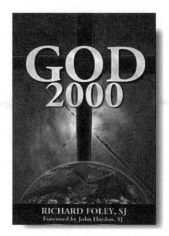

476

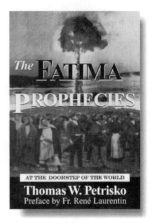